Osipow

D1488565

HEALTH AND BEHAVIOR
Frontiers of Research
in the Biobehavioral Sciences

Edited by
David A. Hamburg, Glen R. Elliott,
and Delores L. Parron

Division of Mental Health and
Behavioral Medicine

INSTITUTE OF MEDICINE

NATIONAL ACADEMY PRESS
Washington, D.C.   1982

This study was supported by the Alcohol, Drug Abuse, and Mental Health Administration and the National Institutes of Health, U.S. Public Health Service, Department of Health and Human Services, Contract No. 282-78-0163-EJM.

IOM Publication 82-010

Library of Congress Catalog Card Number 82-81830

International Standard Book Number 0-309-03279-2

Available from

NATIONAL ACADEMY PRESS
2101 Constitution Avenue, N.W.
Washington, D.C. 20418

Printed in the United States of America

Health and Behavior:
A Research Agenda

Steering Committee

Chair

DAVID A. HAMBURG, M.D., Director, Division of Health Policy Research and Education, Harvard University, Cambridge, Massachusetts

Members

JACK D. BARCHAS, M.D., Nancy Friend Pritzker Professor, Department of Psychiatry and Behavioral Sciences, Stanford University School of Medicine, Stanford, California

MILDRED MITCHELL-BATEMAN, M.D., Professor and Chair, Department of Psychiatry, Marshall University School of Medicine, Huntington, West Virginia

PETER B. DEWS, M.B., Ch.B., Ph.D, Stanley Cobb Professor of Psychiatry and Psychobiology, Lab of Psychobiology, Harvard Medical School, Boston, Massachusetts

CARL EISDORFER, Ph.D, M.D., President, Montefiore Hospital and Medical Center, and Professor of Psychiatry and Neurosciences, Albert Einstein College of Medicine, New York, New York

LEON EISENBERG, M.D., Presley Professor of Social Medicine and Health Policy and Chairman, Department of Social Medicine and Health Policy, Harvard Medical School, Boston, Massachusetts

RUTH T. GROSS, M.D., Katharine Dexter and Stanley McCormick Professor of Pediatrics, Stanford University School of Medicine, Stanford, California

SAMUEL B. GUZE, M.D., Spencer T. Olin Professor and Head, Department of Psychiatry, and President of the Medical Center, Washington University School of Medicine, St. Louis, Missouri

ROBERT J. HAGGERTY, M.D., President, W. T. Grant Foundation, New York, New York

JULES HIRSCH, M.D., Professor and Senior Physician, Laboratory of Human Behavior and Metabolism, The Rockefeller University, New York, New York

IRVING JANIS, Ph.D, Professor, Department of Psychology, Yale University, New Haven, Connecticut

iii

The committee is especially grateful to the John D. and Catherine T. MacArthur Foundation for support to the Division of Health Policy Research and Education, Harvard University, which made possible formation of the *Task Force on the Health and Behavior Monograph*. The following individuals were members of this task force and contributed substantially to drafts of this report:

GLEN R. ELLIOTT, Ph.D, M.D., Executive Officer of the Task Force
DELORES L. PARRON, Ph.D, Health and Behavior Study Director

KATY BENJAMIN
CHARLES CZEISLER, Ph.D., M.D.
BARBARA FILNER, Ph.D. (Institute of Medicine staff)
LYNN GORDON, Ph.D.
LYNDA MCGINNIS, Ph.D.
ANN MORAN, Dr.P.H.

Institute of Medicine

President

FREDERICK C. ROBBINS, M.D.

Study Staff, Division of Mental Health and Behavioral Medicine

DELORES L. PARRON, Ph.D., Study Director and Associate Division
   Director
FREDRIC SOLOMON, M.D., Division Director
GLEN R. ELLIOTT, Ph.D., M.D., Josiah Macy Fellow
JANE S. TAKEUCHI, Ph.D., Staff Officer
JOHN C. CARL, Research Assistant
PAULINE SOBEL, Research Assistant
CARRIE SIMPSON, Administrative Secretary

Acknowledgments

Through their active assistance and collaboration, numerous individuals greatly enriched this study. They provided helpful suggestions, timely observations, and data bearing on the complex scientific, clinical, and societal issues that were being explored by the committee, staff, and Task Force on the Health and Behavior Monograph. We especially wish to express our gratitude for contributions made by:

SARAH SPAGHT BROWN, Institute of Medicine
THOMAS DELBANCO, M.D., Harvard Medical School
JOEL DIMSDALE, M.D., Harvard Medical School
HARRIET DUSTAN, M.D., University of Alabama Medical School
BEATRIX A. HAMBURG, M.D., Harvard Medical School
ROBERT L. KAHN, Ph.D., University of Michigan
JOYCE LASHOF, M.D., University of California (Berkeley)
ELENA NIGHTINGALE, M.D., Ph.D., Institute of Medicine
ROBERT STRAUS, Ph.D., University of Kentucky Medical School
DONALD WARE, M.D., Harvard University
TERRIE WETLE, Ph.D., Harvard University
THE INTERAGENCY COMMITTEE FOR THE HEALTH AND BEHAVIOR STUDY
    PETER KRAMER, M.D., Alcohol, Drug Abuse, and Mental Health Administration, and Co-chairman of the Interagency Committee
    MATILDA WHITE RILEY, D.Sc., National Institute on Aging and Co-chairman of the Interagency Committee
    JOSEPH PERPICH, M.D., J.D., National Institutes of Health

THE INSTITUTE OF MEDICINE COUNCIL REPORT REVIEW PANEL
  CLAIRE FAGIN, Ph.D., University of Pennsylvania School of Nursing
    (Chair)
  H. KEITH BRODIE, M.D., Duke University Medical Center
  ROBERT LAWRENCE, M.D., Cambridge Hospital and Harvard Medical
    School
  ALEXANDER LEAF, M.D., Harvard Medical School
  HENRY SILVER, M.D., University of Colorado Medical School

The study *Health and Behavior: A Research Agenda* grew out of many discussions during 1978, initially between then Assistant Secretary for Health/ Surgeon General Julius B. Richmond and Institute of Medicine President David A. Hamburg and later with Donald Fredrickson, Director, National Institutes of Health, and Gerald Klerman, Administrator, Alcohol, Drug Abuse, and Mental Health Administration. We are most grateful to them for encouraging and supporting this initiative from its inception to its completion.

Finally, we wish to thank the many individuals, listed in Appendix B of this report, who participated in the series of Institute of Medicine conferences on the linkage of behavior and health. These leaders in the biomedical and behavioral sciences were extraordinarily generous with their time and thoughtful in sharing their perspectives on the diverse problems under consideration.

Contents

HEALTH AND BEHAVIOR

Frontiers of Research
in the Biobehavioral Sciences

I
SUMMARY
AND
INTRODUCTION

Summary

This report assembles the informed assessments of more than 400 leaders in the biomedical and behavioral sciences on problems of great importance to the health of people everywhere. These scientists participated in a series of novel studies and conferences convened by the Institute of Medicine over the past few years to consider thoroughly the linkages between health and behavior. They examined the extent of behavior-related disease and disability and evaluated scientific approaches to understanding, treating, and preventing such illnesses. Each chapter of this report highlights especially promising lines of inquiry. These research directions, selected from the large array of possibilities considered, have great potentiality for future progress and deserve vigorous pursuit.

Nature and Scope of the Problem

The heaviest burdens of illness in the United States today are related to aspects of individual behavior, especially long-term patterns of behavior often referred to as "lifestyle." As much as 50 percent of mortality from the 10 leading causes of death in the United States can be traced to lifestyle. Known behavioral risk factors include cigarette smoking, excessive consumption of alcoholic beverages, use of illicit drugs, certain dietary habits, reckless driving, nonadherence to effective medication regimens, and maladaptive responses to social pressures.

One important advance of the twentieth century is recognition that it is possible to employ scientific methods to gain a better understanding of

3

human behavior. The task is difficult and complex, but human behavior can be observed systematically, reliably, and reproducibly. As knowledge progresses, observations can become increasingly quantitative and have considerable predictive power. Human behavior is sufficiently regular to permit dependable, specific propositions about patterns and themes. Underlying causes will be identified with more certainty when the intimate interplay between genetic and environmental factors and the rich variability of individuals and societies are taken into account.

The Health and Behavior Project

Over the past few years, the Institute of Medicine, National Academy of Sciences, has been responding to the heightened awareness of behavioral factors in health in a variety of ways. This study, *Health and Behavior: A Research Agenda*, was a natural extension of such interests. The Assistant Secretary for Health of the Department of Health, Education, and Welfare asked the Institute of Medicine to collaborate with the National Institutes of Health and the Alcohol, Drug Abuse, and Mental Health Administration to (1) clarify the behavioral aspects of selected major public health problems; (2) delineate the biobehavioral sciences' contributions to and future prospects for improving the diagnosis, treatment, and prevention of serious and widespread illnesses; and (3) facilitate strengthening of the biomedical and biobehavioral sciences in these areas.

The two and one-half year project had two components, both conducted by a broadly interdisciplinary steering committee. The first part of the study consisted of six invitational conferences. At each, a small group of scientists and health practitioners from a range of relevant disciplines considered biobehavioral research issues relating to a major health problem. Summaries of highlights and promising lines of inquiry for each conference were published (Appendix A).

This volume constitutes the second part of the Health and Behavior project. Drawing on conference summaries, related Institute of Medicine reports, and other recent major studies, the committee has attempted to integrate available information into a perspective of the frontiers of the biobehavioral sciences, of their relevance for public health, and of implications for science policy. Coverage is broad but not exhaustive. Rather, this monograph describes briefly many promising research directions at the interface of health and behavior. Still, we have tried to include representative samples of the many components of the biobehavioral sciences that can contribute to efforts to improve the health of people in the United States and throughout the world.

Scope of the Biobehavioral Sciences

The term *biobehavioral sciences* is used in this volume to refer to the panoply of basic, applied, and clinical sciences that contribute to an understanding of behavior. Thus, the term includes not only the behavioral sciences that conduct experimental analyses of animal and human behavior but also such basic sciences as neuroanatomy, neurology, neurochemistry, endocrinology, as well as the fields of psychology, psychiatry, ethology, sociology, and anthropology. Broadly inclusive, this term transcends the many changes in specialties and subspecialties that currently characterize the area. Fields of overlapping interests are emerging constantly, with such names as behavioral genetics, psychoneuroimmunology, immunohistochemistry, physiological sociology, or behavioral medicine. All are part of the biobehavioral sciences.

The Contribution of Behavior to the Burden of Illness

Many measures have been employed to assess the societal and personal impact of disease, including disease prevalence, death rates, economic costs, drain on health care resources, and activity restrictions such as lost work. Regardless of the measure used, diseases in which behavior may play a significant role constitute a major component of the current burden of illness in the United States and other developed countries (Table 1).

Research has confirmed that some behaviors are major risk factors of disease. For example, people who smoke cigarettes expose themselves to risk as surely as does someone who ventures unprotected into a swamp known to harbor malarial mosquitoes. To be termed a risk factor, the behavior must be present before the disease begins, rather than constituting an early disease symptom, for example, as coughing is an early indication of lung disease. However, a risk factor need not cause the disorder. It may be closely associated with some underlying process that eventually produces the disease state. Once a behavior is identified as a risk factor, additional studies are needed to determine whether changing the behavior is of any value in preventing or treating the disease.

Mortality and Morbidity

Almost two million deaths each year in the United States are caused by cardiovascular diseases, cancers, accidents, violence (including homicide and suicide), diabetes mellitus, cirrhosis of the liver, and respiratory diseases. "Premature mortality"—death before the usual life expectancy—is an important aspect of the burden of illness. To assess the relative impact of different disease categories, potential years of life lost can be calculated

TABLE 1 Burden of Illness in the United States in 1974

Measure	Total (millions)	Accidents, Poisoning, Violence	Cancer	Cardio-vascular Diseases	Mental Disorders	Other
		Percent of the Total				
Deaths	2	8	19	53	1	19
Potential years of life lost	33	17	18	37	1	27
Short-stay hospital days	255	11	10	19	6	54
Long-term care days	616	3	1	27	40	29
Physician office visits[b]	521	9	2	11	6	72
Work loss days	461[a]	18	2	8	3	69
Bed days	1,783[a]	9	4	13	3	71
Social Security Disability benefit days	561	7	9	27	20	37
Causes of major activity limitations	34[a]	4	2	23	4	67
Direct cost dollars[c]	99,000	7	5	16	10	62

[a] More than one condition may cause a work loss day, a bed day, or a limitation in major activity. Days or limitations thus may be counted more than once. For the 22 million persons reporting major activity limitations, there were an average of 1.5 chronic conditions per person. There were an estimated 1,392 million bed days; each bed day was counted about 1.3 times. There were 414 million work loss days; each loss day was counted an average of 1.1 times.

[b] For the year 1973.

[c] For the year 1975.

SOURCE: See Chapter 2, Table 2.1.

either as total number of years of life lost for the entire population or as average number of years lost by each person who dies. Cardiovascular disease, which kills the largest number of people each year, ranks at the top in the first measure; infant mortality—death in the first year of life—ranks at the top in the second. In 1974, more than a third of the 33 million potential years of life lost were attributed to hypertension, atherosclerosis, heart disease, and stroke. Almost 12 years of life were lost for each death by cardiovascular disease; almost 27 years, for each by cancer; and almost 36 years, for each by accident, poisoning, or violence.

Many of the leading causes of death are chronic and progressively disabling diseases, which means that years of limitation in function and associated health care costs may precede death. Therefore, a full accounting of the associated burden requires consideration of morbidity measures such as prevalence, use of health care resources, functional limitations, and economic costs. Prevalence data provide a relatively simple way to quantitate health problems. Among the 220 million Americans in 1978, 36 million had cardiovascular disease and 3 million had cancer. Each year, about 60 to 70 million persons are injured by accidents, poisoning, or violence serious enough to require medical attention or to restrict activity for at least one day. Also, each year, as much as 15 percent of the population (33 million people) experiences a mental disorder.

Diseases for which lifestyle factors are especially significant have a dominant position in causes of mortality and morbidity. In 1977, when the overall age adjusted death rate was 612 per 100,000 population, fully three quarters of the deaths were caused by three disease categories: (1) heart disease and stroke, 42 percent; (2) cancer, 22 percent; and (3) accidents and violence, 11 percent. In 1976, of the 7.5 million Americans prevented by poor health from pursuing their major activity, 37 percent attributed their disability to heart conditions, hypertension, and diabetes. The chronic nature of many mental disorders leads to a relatively large demand on the health care system; for instance, patients with schizophrenia occupy about 25 percent of *all* hospital beds in the United States.

Indirect costs, such as the value of lost productivity or years of life, also constitute a portion of the burden of illness. By one conservative analysis, indirect costs of the burden of illness in 1975 were $146 billion. Of this total, cardiovascular diseases accounted for 24 percent; accidents, poisoning, and violence, for 20 percent; cancer, for 12 percent; and mental disorders, for 7 percent.

Behavioral Risks to Health

The impact of behavior on the burden of illness is reflected in the fact that alcohol abuse, cigarette smoking, nonadherence to proven medical regi-

mens, and overeating to obesity are present disproportionately among patients with high hospitalization costs. In a recent hospital survey, from 31
to 69 percent of the high-cost patients had at least one of these habits,
compared with 20 to 45 percent of lower-cost patients.

A variety of specific behaviors have been implicated as risk factors of
certain major physical and mental disorders. Behavioral factors identify
high-risk populations that might benefit especially from early disease detection and intervention efforts. For diseases in which behavior has a causative role, interventions may be appropriate. However, it has become clear
that individuals often find it very difficult to change their lifestyles, even
in the face of known risks to health. Thus, research on prevention must
determine not only which behavioral changes are potentially beneficial but
also how such changes can be adopted and maintained.

Cigarette Smoking   In the United States in 1979, one third of people over
19 years of age were current smokers—25 million men and 23 million
women; 3 to 4 million teenagers (about 12 percent of that age group) also
were current smokers. In a 12-year follow-up of one million men and
women in the United States, mortality rates were greater for smokers than
for nonsmokers regardless of age or sex. Risk consistently increased for
both men and women with increasing daily doses of cigarettes. Mortality
from respiratory tract cancers, emphysema, and cardiovascular disease is
especially prevalent among cigarette smokers. About 320,000 deaths annually probably are linked to cigarette smoking. General morbidity measures also are considerably higher for smokers than for nonsmokers. For
example, in 1974 smoking resulted in 81 million excess workdays lost and
145 million excess days of bed disability.

Trends in the pattern of cigarette use by women of childbearing age are
of special concern. Since 1965, current smokers among women 20 to 44
years of age decreased from about 43 percent to 34 percent, but the proportion of heavy smokers increased. Cigarette smoking during pregnancy
doubles the risk of having a low birth weight infant; about one third of the
incidence of low birth weight is attributable to cigarette smoking. Death in
the first year of life is 20 times more likely for low birth weight infants
than for heavier infants. There also is suggestive evidence of lower scores
on tests of intellectual function and higher frequencies of minimal cerebral
dysfunction, neurological abnormalities, and behavior problems among children of mothers who had smoked during pregnancy.

Excessive Alcohol Consumption   In 1979, 10 million adult men and women
in the United States were heavy drinkers, consuming an average of four

drinks per day; another 3.5 million teenagers were heavy drinkers, consuming five or more drinks per drinking occasion. Overall mortality rates are higher for heavy drinkers than for lighter drinkers or nondrinkers. In a study in the United States, mortality was 2.5 times greater than expected, with the greatest increase among younger alcoholics. Cirrhosis of the liver accounts for 60 to 80 percent of alcohol-related deaths. Alcohol use also contributes to many accidents, suicides, and homicides. In 1975, the direct and indirect cost of alcoholism was estimated to be about $43 billion.

Pregnant women are at special risk of problems from alcoholism. Heavy drinkers are more likely to deliver babies who have the fetal alcohol syndrome, characterized by certain physical abnormalities and often associated with mental retardation. Possible adverse effects even of moderate drinking during pregnancy are being studied. There are reports of lowered viability at birth, poor sucking ability, heart rate abnormalities, and various other behaviors associated with poor functioning of the central nervous system.

Unhealthful Dietary Habits Major dietary inadequacies can seriously impair health. Much current research focuses on adverse consequences of excess consumption, for example, of calories and fats. Several studies have shown a higher mortality rate for those markedly above average weight. For people who are 20 to 30 percent overweight, mortality is 20 to 40 percent greater than for people of average weight; for those 50 to 60 percent overweight, it is 150 to 250 percent greater. Obesity increases the risk of hypertension, diabetes, and hyperlipidemia—each a risk factor for heart disease. Also, obesity may be an independent risk factor of cardiovascular disease. In addition, there is strong epidemiological evidence that high blood levels of cholesterol are associated with increased rates of cardiovascular disease and death; in part, this may be reflective of dietary intake of cholesterol and saturated fats.

Scientific Opportunities: Major Disorders and Conditions

Certain behavior patterns such as cigarette smoking and excessive use of alcohol contribute greatly to many components of the current burden of illness. For that reason, it is useful to focus directly on ways of helping people not to engage in health-risky behaviors. For several important diseases, including cardiovascular disease and some mental disorders, behavior-related factors appear to be closely associated with the production of the disease or play a major role in aspects of preventing or treating it. This section examines issues about such behaviors and diseases that the biobehavioral sciences can usefully address.

Stress, Coping, and Health

Stress research may be the earliest forum in which scientists studied effects of behavior on health. An impressive body of knowledge has been assembled, much of it relevant to other interests in the biobehavioral sciences. The information can be divided broadly into research on physiological systems through which stress affects bodily function and studies of how individuals cope with stress.

Major advances are being made in understanding the nervous system, with recognition and detailed study of a rapidly expanding number of neuroregulators, the chemicals that control communication among nerve cells. Increasingly sophisticated research is examining coordinated responses of the nervous and endocrine systems to stressors. Genetic and environmental factors pertinent to individual responses are being specified. Such research offers the promise of establishing the steps between being exposed to a stressor and developing a disease consequence. That knowledge is directly relevant to devising better ways to treat and to prevent health-damaging physical and emotional stress responses.

Much has been learned about successful and unsuccessful coping patterns, and there have been efforts to apply existing concepts to prevention of disease and promotion of health. One direction of inquiry involves early adolescence—a major but neglected phase of human development that lends itself to analysis of developmental tasks and coping strategies. Also important is research on health-related decisions. For example, studies have shown that a sense of personal control helps people cope with stressful experiences and affects their commitment to health-enhancing behavior patterns. In addition, there is great interest in learning why some individuals cope better than others and in discovering ways to help people improve their coping strategies. Further applications of such basic learning principles as operant conditioning, social learning, and cognitive problem solving merit pursuit in the years to come.

Alcoholism, Alcohol Abuse, and Health

Alcohol abuse and related problems have biological, psychological, and social dimensions. Prominent among important issues in research are efforts to understand how extrinsic influences interact with factors unique to a person in the etiology of problem drinking and associated adverse health effects. An individual's physiological predispositions are shaped by genetic endowment and affected by family, school, work place, and other social influences.

It still is unclear exactly which of alcohol's many effects are most relevant to alcoholism. Among promising lines of research are studies of acute and chronic effects of alcohol and its metabolites on cell membrane fluidity and neuroregulator function. Animal and human evidence of a genetic contribution affirms the value of a continued search for specific genes that place an individual at higher risk for alcoholism. In conjunction with psychological and social approaches, basic physiological research may suggest ways to identify people at high risk for becoming alcoholics.

Relationships among the stress of life events, social supports, and various styles of coping are a rich area of research opportunity. Young adolescents are a high-risk group deserving special attention. Interest in research on alcohol-related problems among the elderly also is growing. Another important research focus is social influences such as work settings. Factors affecting remission of alcoholism merit more attention; new research should provide a better understanding of how to design effective and appropriately targeted prevention and therapy programs.

Smoking and Health

Most cigarette smokers begin the habit as adolescents or young adults. Because smoking is so difficult to give up, we should learn why young people start smoking and what methods are most effective in helping them not to do so. Successful prevention programs have in common the active involvement of young people in developing strategies to avoid pressures to smoke from peers, media, and adults.

Of everyone in the United States who regularly smokes, about 60 percent have tried to quit, and another 30 percent want to quit. A combination of biobehavioral science disciplines is needed to explore pharmacological, physiological, neurochemical, behavioral, psychological, and social factors that contribute to this powerful addiction. Nicotine may be a major pharmacological reinforcer for cigarette use, but behavioral factors appear to be crucial in initiation of the smoking habit and in day-to-day fluctuations in smoking.

A key research issue about quitting is better understanding of why some can stop smoking on their own; belief in self-efficacy may predict success. Methods are needed to help large portions of the population to quit smoking if they wish to do so. For those wanting to use formal programs, more effective and safer techniques are needed, as are ways to match interventions to the person. Studies of factors that predispose to relapse and of ways to maintain abstinence also are important.

Sleep, Biological Clocks, and Behavior

Currently, about 27 percent of U.S. employees have work schedules that shift regularly from day to evening or night. Also, several hundred million times each year people fly across time zones to an environment to which their internal biological clocks are not adjusted. The best documented health consequences of shift work are disorders of sleep and digestion. There are also potential hazards in operating complex equipment, monitoring safety indicators, or making important decisions while affected by a disrupted routine. People differ greatly in their ability to tolerate working or sleeping on abnormal schedules. One frontier area of biobehavioral research attempts to clarify the nature and extent of such changes and factors that influence them.

Over the past decade, investigators have made considerable gains in understanding the physiological and behavioral processes that affect the sleep-wake cycle and its relation to the day-night cycle. Basic research is beginning to define both the characteristics of biological clocks and some of the neural systems that regulate them. A specific area of the brain hypothalamus now is known to be the central pacemaker for many circadian rhythms. Further research on pacemakers and control systems is highly appropriate.

Cardiovascular Disease and Behavior

Among established risk factors for cardiovascular disease are hypercholesterolemia, hypertension, cigarette smoking, advanced age, being a male, diabetes, and marked obesity. Several of these have clear behavioral aspects. Thus, strong evidence of an association between atherosclerosis and elevated blood cholesterol has led to studies to find if reducing cholesterol concentrations by various means will alter cardiovascular disease rates. Similarly, an association between cardiovascular disease and Type A behavior has created interest in helping people to change that type of behavior, characterized as harsh competitiveness, unusual aggressiveness, intense work orientation, and a persistent time urgency. Behavioral aspects of smoking were discussed earlier; those of diabetes are discussed later.

Sudden cardiac death is of special interest to the biobehavioral sciences. Although the heart is almost invariably diseased in such deaths, the type of disease typically is compatible with many years of active and satisfactory life. Identification of factors that lead to sudden cardiac death may be useful in designing programs to reduce its incidence. Areas that must be explored in order to better understand neural controls of the heart relating to sudden cardiac death include describing the neural pathways involved, delineating the influences of internal and external stimuli, and finding ways to prevent or reverse pathological responses to psychosocial stressors.

Diabetes and Behavior

Diabetes results from a variety of causes of abnormal glucose utilization. Recent research has revealed multifactorial regulation of glucose utilization; many of the regulators are responsive to stress. In diabetes, emotional stress and other psychosocial influences affect disease complications and treatment adherence. Only recently have systematic, interdisciplinary studies begun to address those issues.

The treatment of diabetes typically entails diet modification, insulin replacement, and adherence to a demanding medical regimen. Techniques are needed to identify individuals and families who are unlikely to meet such demands. It still is unclear how handling of early episodes affects a patient's ability to accept diabetes as a tolerable routine of daily life. How best to help patients and families cope with the complications of diabetes is another key area for study. Also, innovations in self-care, medical service delivery, and use of community resources may lead to better metabolic control, decreased hospitalization, and substantial cost savings.

About 90 percent of diabetics are overweight. Some effects of excessive caloric intake are beginning to be understood, as are ways to help patients lose weight. One successful approach to weight loss uses an interdisciplinary team to evaluate and educate patients and provide continuous follow-up care. Continuity of care is critically important, as is a stepped-care approach that is responsive to the needs of individual patients. Much more remains to be learned about helping people lose weight and maintain the weight loss.

Major Mental Disorders and Behavior

The population in psychiatric hospitals increased for many years and then peaked in 1955. Since then it has declined steadily, coinciding with increased use of drug therapies and improved psychosocial treatments. Despite great progress, mental disorders continue to impose major burdens on individuals, their families, and society. The biobehavioral sciences still have much to offer in the search for a permanent solution to these illnesses.

In the 1950s, investigators discovered effective drug treatments for major depression, mania, and schizophrenia, as well as antianxiety agents used for a variety of physical and mental problems. Research into the actions of such drugs has greatly enriched concepts about brain function, leading in turn to biochemical hypotheses about major mental disorders that have influenced clinical research and practice. The surge of knowledge within the neurosciences has been fostered by many technological innovations. With one new technique, investigators can study in normal human beings the localized changes in brain activity that accompany performance of specific behaviors.

Psychological and social sciences have helped both to clarify the effect of environmental factors on the onset and course of mental disorders and to create psychosocial treatments either as an alternative to drugs or in combination with them. There are indications that biologically and psychosocially oriented investigators and clinicians now are willing to explore the junction of their fields in research on mental illness. Such collaborative efforts add to other forms of progress being made in the treatment and eventual prevention of mental disorders.

Scientific Opportunities: Special Life Circumstances

Another of the health and behavior interfaces is that of specific settings in which interactive forces may be especially relevant. Examples of such special life circumstances are the work place, the aged population, and social disadvantage. At times, research on such subgroups has been especially innovative, focusing on environmental influences or behavior patterns long accepted as unremarkable and demonstrating their broad effects on health. Such research holds the promise of suggesting interventions that may be applicable to broad segments of society. Some other special life circumstances are explored in the next section, with respect to prevention efforts.

Work and Health

Much remains to be learned about the effect on employee health of the many administrative, psychological, and physical characteristics that define an organization. A factory or industry may provide a "natural experiment" for researchers to study the effects of change in a reasonably controlled and well-defined setting. Examples of such potential experiments include introduction of automation into a plant or layoffs because of company decline or general economic recession. It is becoming clear that factors such as lines of authority and social interactions may be as important to health as are physical safety factors.

Contributions of the individual to work stress also need to be explored. Studies should look for interactions between work demands and resources on the one hand and worker needs and abilities on the other. In that regard, looking at the effect of schools on subsequent functioning in work settings may offer a useful life course perspective. Little attention has been given to similarities and differences of school for children and work for adults. A better appreciation of the ways in which individual characteristics affect responses to specific settings may suggest better ways to identify and prevent undesirable conditions.

Of continuing interest is the potential role of the work place for prevention and treatment. Programs such as alcohol abuse detection, hypertension detection and treatment, and smoking cessation already have been introduced in many settings with great success. Other programs also might be valuable, for instance, courses for people about to retire. However, the actual efficacy of such efforts, as well as potential undesirable side effects such as invasion of privacy, have yet to be evaluated adequately.

Aging and Health

The rising numbers and special problems of the elderly present challenges to basic sciences, clinical investigation, service delivery, and social organization. Studies of health and behavior in the elderly must consider not only environmental and social factors but also age-related physical and psychological changes that can affect disease presentation, response, and complications. For example, studies have shown that even relatively simple steps that promote independence among older people in rest homes can result in better health, including improved family relationships, treatment responses, and quality of life. Long-term follow-up is essential to clarify the effects and mechanisms of action of such interventions.

Research is needed to specify the effects on the health of the elderly of historical events and of biological and psychosocial processes. A growing number of longitudinal studies are becoming available for such research. But current systems are not designed to foster integration of biomedical and psychosocial disciplines; computerized inventories and bibliographies of research on aging, health, and behavior are needed. Also, it is important to recognize the heterogeneity of the elderly population in designing studies. A full range of ages among the elderly should be studied, as should both people who are relatively resistant to the vulnerabilities of advancing age and those who are much less resistant.

Social Disadvantage and Health

The burden of illness rests disproportionately on the socially disadvantaged. A growing body of research goes beyond documenting disease among the poor and looks at the effects of such factors as differential exposure to and treatment by health care professionals. Studies of the cumulative effects of psychosocial and economic stress show promise of identifying mechanisms by which the environment can influence the health of the disadvantaged. Even though physiological mechanisms that translate environmental factors into illness are not well understood, the influence of social disadvantage on the development of disease, on recovery opportunities, and on survival is becoming increasingly clear.

There are many opportunities for research on the effects of social disadvantage and of targeted intervention programs. Biobehavioral research should focus on identifying preventable causal factors and effective interventions. In basic research, challenging research issues cut across all social and ethnic groups. Studies of connections between illness and social isolation, bereavement, and cumulative life stress are especially relevant. Clinicians need dependable information about effects of racial and social factors on diagnosis and treatment. Available research suggests that specially targeted interventions such as detection and treatment of hypertension in designated subpopulations can be highly effective. Such studies should include measures of the type, features, and mixture of health care personnel, their attitudes toward patients, and the effects of staff class on management of minorities and the poor.

Crosscutting Themes: Prevention and Treatment

Regardless of the health-risky behavior or the disease, treatment and prevention should be major research issues for the biobehavioral sciences. Attention is being given to methods of altering the burden of illness by changing behavior. This requires first that changes in behavior can be shown to result in improved health and second that effective methods be found to help large numbers of people to make such changes. Much remains to be learned, but the existing research base provides strong evidence that the biobehavioral sciences can make substantial and unique contributions to dealing with much of the disease that now constitutes the main burden of illness in this country.

Prevention Efforts in Early Life

Early life provides a wealth of openings for useful preventive interventions, many of which may have lifelong benefits. With the control of infectious disease, behavior-related disorders have taken a more dominant role in the burden of illness in early life. Recognition of this shift has provided impetus recently for a number of detailed assessments of child health care needs. Interventions take several forms. Some, including neonatal metabolic screens, help to identify problems before they do permanent damage; others such as immunizations forestall some future risk; still others, for example, good dental hygiene, provide the child with a more general orientation toward prevention. All require active collaboration among parents, schools, other community organizations, and health professions.

Research is needed in all of these types of prevention. Efforts continue to develop techniques for earlier, safer, and more reliable detection of abnormalities and new vaccines against dangerous infections. In addition, there is strong interest in finding ways to make early interventions that will diminish risks associated with low birth weight and prematurity. Attention also must be given to ways of engaging parents in disease prevention and health promotion for their children.

Research is needed into developmental problems of early childhood, including mental retardation and clinically apparent emotional disturbance. Additional research on infants and families with multiple sources of high risk for developmental dysfunction is likely to enhance both basic understanding and provision of care. Sound intervention programs already have shown the interdependence of research and practice, of evaluation and treatment, and of assessment and counseling in the service of children in the first months of life. Progress in this area holds promise of yielding substantial gains, both in decreasing the burden of illness and in increasing the quality of life.

Prevention Efforts in Adolescence

In recent years, greater attention has been given to adolescence as an important, lengthy, and developmentally complex part of the life course. One feature of adolescence is behavioral experimentation, some of it damaging to health. Some behaviors affect health immediately, as in contracting venereal disease or having a severe accident related to alcohol use. Others produce deleterious effects only later in life, as seen with lifelong habits that can contribute to adult cardiovascular disease. Naturally, adolescence also is a time for adopting healthful habits, with correspondingly good short- and long-range effects.

The need for more adolescent-oriented research on prevention and on behavioral issues pertinent to health and disease recently has become widely recognized, and many issues have been identified. Studies of the antecedents of adult disease, particularly such chronic ones as cancer and cardiovascular disease, would be directly relevant to prevention. Also needed are better strategies to promote health-enchancing behaviors in adolescents and to prevent adoption of such habits as cigarette smoking and drug use. A special area of concern is teenage pregnancy. The complexity of that issue creates a formidable research agenda, including evaluation of current and preferred roles of such institutions as schools and hospitals in adolescent pregnancy and creation of new programs to help lower the incidence of adolescent pregnancies or provide ways of improving the lives of teenage mothers and their infants.

Prevention Efforts in Adult Life: Cardiovascular Risk Factors

For most diseases considered in this volume, interventions constitute preventing or altering such behaviors as smoking or unhealthful dietary habits. Common experience makes it clear that many individuals are unable to change these habits readily. Yet change is possible. In the past decade, real shifts have occurred in the lifestyles of many people in the United States, arguing against the pessimism that often clouds prevention efforts. The evidence demonstrates that, at least for cardiovascular disease, effective large-scale interventions are feasible. Encouraging results of smoking prevention and cessation programs have positive implications for prevention of some prevalent types of cancer, chronic lung diseases, and cardiovascular diseases.

Much remains to be learned about the most cost-effective methods of conducting prevention efforts. For example, studies are needed about selecting the best communication medium for specific kinds of health messages. Much is known already about the learning process, but it needs to be applied systematically in prevention programs. Some prevention efforts—particularly those that can be expressed in simple, short, and clear messages—may be especially suitable for the mass media. Others such as helping people to stop smoking may require more individualized and small-group attention. But the task now seems to be determining how to do it best, rather than whether it can be done at all.

The Interface of Drug and Psychosocial Treatments

For many chronic diseases, drugs alone are not enough. Social and psychological influences also affect the disease course and prognosis. Broadly speaking, psychosocial interventions involve either clinical management or specific therapies. Clinical management refers to issues that arise during the course of treatment of any type, for example, explaining a diagnosis or warning about side effects. Specific psychotherapies are designed to relieve the symptoms of disease. Thus, relaxation techniques might be used to reduce mild hypertension, or cognitive therapy could be used to treat depression. Psychotherapy need not be a competitor of drug treatments. At times, it may be more effective than drug treatments, or it may be a useful adjunct, so that patients receiving both types of therapy do much better than those who receive only one of them. Thus, counseling often is essential for achieving long-term adherence to a treatment regimen in diseases such as hypertension and diabetes.

Needed studies at this interface are beginning to emerge. An understanding of the psychological and social factors that influence attitudes about illness, seeking help, and deciding whether medical advice is reliable would be of value for individualizing treatment regimens. Also, comparative data are needed to enable physicians and patients to select rationally between drug and psychotherapeutic treatments of the same illness or to choose efficacious combinations of them. In some cases, psychosocial interventions require skills for which health practitioners lack training, time, or interest. Incorporation of such treatments into health care may necessitate innovations in the delivery system.

Mental Health Care in General Health Care Systems

The primary care sector has a major role in caring for 60 percent of the adults and a large proportion of the children who have a discernible mental disorder. A concerted effort is needed to overcome serious deficiencies in communication between mental health and general health services. Beneficial health results can be achieved from increased primary care commitment to identification of mental disorders in the patient population, more effective counseling, improved drug-prescribing regimens, and better referral mechanisms to mental health care professionals. Primary care practitioners must be able to convey to patients an interest in health-related behavioral issues as a vital link in prevention or recovery processes.

Research could facilitate collaboration between primary care and mental health services in several ways. For example, primary health care providers need simple and precise methods for identifying mental disorders, determining whether or not to refer a patient, selecting the best treatment for patients not referred, and monitoring side effects. Also needed are tests of alternative ways of providing well-integrated mental health care in primary health care settings. Such studies should include assessments of the effectiveness of various types of manpower in dealing with carefully differentiated problems in various treatment settings.

Changes in Human Societies, Families, Social Supports, and Health

The human species is intensely social. This fact is so much a part of daily life that it is easy to overlook its significance in human adaptation. People everywhere are organized in societies and therefore are inevitably torn between serving individual interests and those of the group. Modern industrial societies have made rapid and drastic changes in social relations.

The pace of change has accelerated in the twentieth century, and social complexity is at an all-time high. We are still learning to cope with the changes, and the effects on health remain to be assessed adequately.

Many research opportunities exist for probing relationships among stress, illness, social support, and utilization of medical services. For example, it should be possible to examine ways in which support systems can buffer or mediate effects on health, either through physiological effects or by reducing health-damaging behaviors. Also of interest is whether some kinds of social support protect against specific types of stressors. It will be important to examine the relative merits of various levels of intervention, including removing or moderating stressors, teaching coping skills to indiviudals, and strengthening social supports. With respect to social supports, studies are needed of ways to foster attachment behavior and stimulate development of support networks where they are inadequate. As such experimental networks are formed, their effects on health should be compared with those of naturally occurring networks.

Health Science Policy Considerations

In recent years, several Institute of Medicine study groups have examined the entire gamut of science policy pertinent to health. Basic points germane to the present report emerged with a high degree of consensus from a range of biomedical and other scientists participating in that analysis. Those points are summarized in Table 2. The present report is replete with specific suggestions about scientific and institutional opportunities, but the steering committee explicitly decided not to undertake detailed prescriptions. Rather, policy makers in different settings may flexibly consider how best to proceed in light of the framework and suggestions provided.

Role of Basic Research Relating to Health and Behavior

Examination of this nation's burden of illness helps to point up the importance of behavioral factors for health. As noted throughout this report, cardiovascular disease, cancer, lung disease, accidents, and homicide and other violence constitute major drains on life and health. Such disorders have substantial behavioral components, so approaches to preventing or managing them must include a strong biobehavioral perspective. As the burden of illness changes, the sciences needed to lessen it also change. Increasingly, it will be in the public's interest to foster progress in the full range of health sciences. Discovering how best to achieve this goal will require cooperation and innovation within and among the scientific com-

TABLE 2   Basic Concepts of Research in Health and Behavior

The burden of illness has shifted from acute infectious diseases to chronic diseases with multiple interacting risk factors, which prominently include such behavioral elements as smoking, alcohol, exercise, diet, and response to stress.

The definition of health sciences must be expanded beyond biomedical fields to include the biobehavioral sciences.

The biobehavioral sciences have a major role to play in elucidating and alleviating many components of the current burden of illness.

Biobehavioral sciences already have made significant contributions to improved health and hold great promise for further progress.

The science base in the biobehavioral sciences should be strengthened, and adequate support should be provided for such research.

Multidisciplinary, collaborative programs are a valuable and needed component of some types of health research.

SOURCES:
Brown, S. S. *Policy Issues in the Health Sciences* Washington, D.C.: National Academy of Sciences, 1977.
Institute of Medicine *DHEW's Research Planning Principles: A Review* Washington, D.C.: National Academy of Sciences, 1979.
Institute of Medicine *DHEW Health Research Planning, Phase II* Washington, D.C.: National Academy of Sciences, 1980.

munity; the health professions; and policy makers in government, philanthropies, industry, and academic institutions.

The biobehavioral and other health-related sciences share several fundamental needs: (1) greater interdisciplinary collaboration within the scientific community and more communication between it and clinical practitioners, medical educators, public and private policy makers, and the general public; (2) productive allocation of resources in an era of economic constraints; (3) better understanding of the impact of research discoveries and science policy decisions on individuals and society, and concomitant ethical dilemmas; (4) strengthened data collection, epidemiology, and other supporting sciences to improve disease prevention and health promotion efforts; and (5) improved research methods.

Interdisciplinary Cooperation and Collaboration

Interdisciplinary collaboration is not an end in itself but rather a means to a higher goal—solving a problem. Collaboration is achieved only when the task demands it. Still, there are several key determinants to the ease and productivity of cooperation among disciplines. This report suggests ways in which factors such as communication, institutional structure, and study review committees can be influenced constructively.

In a substantial number of major research awards, funding agencies should acknowledge explicitly the role of biobehavioral factors in disease. In the areas considered in this report, agencies should review the nature and extent of their support for research on biobehavioral factors in pathogenesis, clinical care and rehabilitation, and primary and secondary prevention. Consideration should include ways to foster interdisciplinary activities between the neural and behavioral sciences and the biomedical disciplines.

Universities or medical centers with appropriate capabilities may find it useful to establish centers in which goals of funded research can be met only through sustained collaboration across disciplines. A focus for such a center could be the study of biobehavioral factors in disease. Academic medical centers could encourage active involvement of departments of medicine, family medicine, geriatrics, pediatrics, and psychiatry. Similar links to basic science departments of genetics, biochemistry, pharmacology, and neurobiology also can be helpful. Such cooperative ventures could be fostered by joint grants, given only for research requiring cooperative links between biobehavioral and biomedical disciplines.

Strengthening Research Capabilities in Health and Behavior

The dynamic interplay of clinical and basic research can be profoundly beneficial over time, in this field as in others. The fruits of basic research can grow into valuable applications, and the stimulus of clinical observations can lead to basic discoveries. This circumstance poses important questions for agencies that sponsor research and for institutions that engage in it. How can programs be formulated, applications reviewed, grants made, and research organized in ways that foster the interplay of basic and clinical research? What institutional arrangements are most conducive to such linkage? Such basic policy questions deserve sustained attention from government, industry, philanthropies, and research institutions.

Essential to the success of the mission described in this report is attraction of talented and dedicated young people to health and behavior research. The first step is wider recognition of the importance of these problems, the burden of illness they impose, their human impact, and the urgency of progress. The second is awareness that scientific opportunities exist for grappling with the problems.

Interdisciplinary research depends first on training young investigators to expand the scope of inquiry beyond their primary discipline. Professional development and training also can be enhanced by interdisciplinary workshops, conferences, and symposia. A vigorous, systematic interdisciplinary research training effort in this area is essential to bring young investigators into the field and provide settings in which they can make significant contributions. Several requirements of research training must be met:

1. *M.D.-Ph.D. training programs in biobehavioral sciences* This approach has been highly successful in biological sciences and urgently needs to be broadened now to include such fields as psychology and sociology.

2. *Appropriate research training stipends* It must be feasible for young scientists to learn their craft well, and this takes considerable time.

3. *Targeted funding to institutions supporting postdoctoral training programs on the design and conduct of biobehavioral research* Such training should be available to both physicians and nonphysicians. Programs for the former could emphasize basic science, and those for the latter, pathology and aspects of clinical medicine, helping to build bridges between the laboratory and clinic.

4. *Stipends for students to do biobehavioral research* Such projects could spark interest at a crucially formative stage of career development; stipends for appropriate medical students or graduate students in biological and biobehavioral sciences could be a valuable asset for developing the essential scientific cadre.

When young people have completed research training in health and behavioral sciences, they must be able to find acceptable career pathways, if their skills are not to be wasted. Relevant agencies and institutions must consider long-term career pathways through which the problems delineated in this report can be addressed effectively. In the decade ahead, the time will be ripe for appointing more behavioral scientists to medical school faculties. One encouraging prospect is the emergence of departments of behavior in schools of medicine that emphasize research. Such departments provide a fundamental resource for many fields of medicine and a powerful stimulus for research advances in health and behavior.

Allocation of Resources for Research on Health and Behavior

Available figures indicate that research into health and behavior is not funded at a level commensurate with the costs that behavior-related illness and disability impose on society. Federal funding of research on alcoholism and mental illness is modest indeed compared with funding for cancer and heart disease. Yet the burden of illness in terms of human suffering and economic costs is heavy in all these cases. By the same token, the behavioral components of cardiovascular disease and cancer have constituted a very small portion of the research effort in these fields.

Philanthropic foundations can play a path-breaking role, but they cannot take primary responsibility for progress in this sphere. Similarly, contributions from industry, except for drug development, are modest and are unlikely to increase greatly in the near future, except where applications of biotechnology are foreseeable. Altogether, there is a remarkable discrepancy between unprecedented scientific opportunities on the one hand and diminishing support for research on the other.

Concluding Perspective

Given deep national concern and strong data on the contribution of behavioral factors to the national burden of illness, do scientific opportunities exist to form the basis of a logical response to this great challenge? The bulk of this report examines various lines of potential scientific inquiry. Many substantial opportunities for research do in fact exist. They offer the promise of revealing the linkages of behavior to health and the potential of suggesting more effective therapeutic and preventive interventions in the future. This being the case, the present low level of funding for research in this sphere deserves serious reexamination. It would be tragic to allow a prolonged decline in support at a time of expanding scientific opportunity. A principal opportunity for health science policy today is to find ways to bring support of the promising lines of research described in this report into more rational alignment with costs to society of the heavy burden of behavior-related illnesses.

1
Nature and Scope of This Inquiry

At the Institute of Medicine annual meeting in 1976, a memorable presentation summed up the total burden of illness in the United States (Rice et al., 1977). It reported such dimensions as potential years of life lost compared with an appropriate population measure of life expectancy, inpatient days, work loss days, limitations on major activities, and economic costs. The results resembled those of a major Canadian report (Lalonde, 1974).

Both works document a burden of illness that is characteristic of industrialized, affluent nations. In the Canadian analysis, motor vehicle accidents accounted for about 13 percent of years of life lost from an average life expectancy of age 70. Their effect is especially heavy in such an analysis because so many of them occur early in life, usually in adolescence and young adulthood. Cardiovascular diseases accounted for 12 percent of the years of life lost; other accidents apart from motor vehicles accounted for 11 percent; respiratory diseases, particularly lung cancer, accounted for 8 percent; and suicide, for 4 percent.

As detailed in the paper by Rice et al. (1977), behavioral factors contribute to much of our burden of illness, early death, and related long-term disability in the United States and other industrial, affluent countries. Moreover, poor and socially disadvantaged people tend not to benefit adequately from biomedical advances, for example, the preventive measures of early prenatal and perinatal care. Both access to such care and regard for its advice are behaviorally influenced.

In the past few years, there has emerged a heightened awareness of the importance of behavioral factors in effective therapeutic and preventive interventions across a wide range of diseases and disabilities (U.S. Department of Health, Education, and Welfare, 1979). That awareness has been accompanied by a striking expansion in the scientific study of such factors. This report assembles the informed assessments of more than 400 leaders in the biomedical and behavioral sciences on problems of great importance to the health of people everywhere. These distinguished scientists participated in a series of novel studies and conferences convened by the Institute of Medicine, National Academy of Sciences, over the past few years to consider thoroughly the linkages between health and behavior. Each chapter of this report highlights especially promising lines of scientific inquiry to understanding, treating, and preventing behavior-related components of the burden of illness. The materials presented reflect the consensus of those who participated that these research directions, selected from the large array of possibilities considered, have much potentiality for future progress and deserve vigorous pursuit in the years ahead.

A Health Role for the Biobehavioral Sciences

One of the significant changes of the twentieth century is the growing recognition that the methods of science can be employed in understanding human behavior, even though the task is difficult and complex. Human behavior can be systematically observed. Such observations can be made in a reliable and reproducible way, and as knowledge progresses they can be increasingly quantitative and have useful predictive power. Human behavior is sufficiently regular to enable the construction of dependable, specific propositions about patterns and themes.

Individuals who smoke cigarettes expose themselves to risk as surely as does someone who ventures without protection into a swamp known to harbor malarial mosquitoes. Behavioral factors can be as directly and concretely causative of disease as can physical or microbial factors. As pathogenic lifestyle patterns are identified, it seems likely that some will be relatively discrete and alterable and will not require a major reorganization of society. The sheer magnitude of such problems as hypertension, stroke, and coronary disease ensures that some significant progress may be made, even if only a fraction of affected individuals can be persuaded to alter their health-damaging behaviors.

The Health and Behavior Theme in the Work of the Institute of Medicine

Over the past several years, the Institute of Medicine has been responding in a variety of ways to the heightened awareness of behavioral factors in health. The effort has engaged several of the Institute's operating divisions, including Mental Health and Behavioral Medicine, Science Policy, and Health Promotion and Disease Prevention. A number of the Institute's publications have addressed some aspect of the role of the biobehavioral sciences in health:

- *Policy Issues in the Health Sciences*, 1977
- *The Current Burden of Illness in the United States*, 1977
- *Conference on Health Promotion and Disease Prevention*, 1978
- *DHEW's Research Planning Principles: A Review*, 1979
- *Mental Health Services in General Health Care*, 1979
- *Healthy People: The Surgeon General's Report on Health Promotion and Disease Prevention/Background Papers*, 1979
- *Sleeping Pills, Insomnia, and Medical Practice*, 1979
- *DHEW Health Research Planning, Phase II*, 1980
- *Alcoholism, Alcohol Abuse, and Related Problems: Opportunities for Research*, 1980
- *Research on Stress in Human Health*, 1981
- *The Revson Conferences: Critical Issues in Medical Sciences and Health*, 1981

The Health and Behavior Study

Health and Behavior: A Research Agenda was an outgrowth of these interests. The Assistant Secretary for Health of the Department of Health, Education, and Welfare asked the Institute of Medicine to collaborate with the Alcohol, Drug Abuse, and Mental Health Administration and the National Institutes of Health to: (1) clarify behavioral aspects of selected major public health problems; (2) delineate the biobehavioral sciences' present contributions to and future prospects for improving the diagnosis, treatment, and prevention of serious and widespread illnesses; and (3) facilitate the strengthening of biomedical and biobehavioral sciences in such areas.

The two and one-half year project had two parts, both conducted by an interdisciplinary steering committee. The first part of the study consisted of six invitational conferences. At each conference, a small group of scientists and health practitioners from a range of relevant disciplines was asked to focus on research issues in the biobehavioral sciences relating to a specific major health problem. The topics and dates of those conferences were:

Smoking and Behavior   September 27–28, 1979

Combining Psychosocial and Drug Therapy: Hypertension, Depression, and Diabetes	May 28–29, 1980
Biobehavioral Factors in Sudden Cardiac Death	August 5–6, 1980
Infants at Risk for Developmental Dysfunction	August 28–29, 1980
Health, Behavior, and Aging	January 26–27, 1981
Behavior, Health Risks, and Social Disadvantage	May 7–8, 1981

Each conference has a published summary of highlights and promising lines of inquiry for that particular health problem (Appendix A).

This volume constitutes the second part of the Health and Behavior project. Drawing on conference summaries, related Institute of Medicine reports, and other recent major studies, the committee has attempted to integrate available information into a perspective of the frontiers of the biobehavioral sciences, their relevance for public health, and implications for science policy. Coverage is broad but not exhaustive. Rather, this monograph provides a brief sampling of a large number of promising research directions into the effects of behavior on health. We have attempted to include a representative selection of the many components of the biobehavioral sciences that can contribute to efforts to improve health.

Scope of the Biobehavioral Sciences

The term *biobehavioral sciences* is used in this volume to refer to the panoply of basic, applied, and clinical sciences that contribute to an understanding of behavior. It naturally includes the behavioral sciences that conduct experimental analyses of animal and human conduct. It also includes such basic sciences as neurology, neurochemistry, endocrinology, and neuroantatomy as well as the fields of psychology, ethology, sociology, and anthropology. One merit of a broadly inclusive terminology is that it encompasses the many changes in specialties and subspecialties that currently characterize the area. As overlapping areas of interest emerge, they often are labeled with compound names, such as behavioral genetics, physiological sociology, psychoneuroimmunology, immunohistochemistry, or behavioral medicine. All are part of the biobehavioral sciences.

One powerful stimulus to the biobehavioral sciences has been the remarkable progress of neurobiology pertinent to behavior, recognized, for instance, in the Nobel prizes in medical/physiology of 1977 and 1981. This area of research has been singled out for special attention in a broad, authoritative survey of scientific progress (National Academy of Sciences, 1979). An unprecedented array of molecules, cells, circuits, systems, techniques, and concepts now are available for research on problems of central interest to behavior and health. Neurobehavioral science has far-reaching ramifications as basic science and is likely to have many clinical implications in the 1980s.

The recently discovered opioid peptides provide a clear example of the exciting developments in the neurobehavioral sciences. In the early 1970s, a number of investigators demonstrated that opiates related to heroin and morphine would bind to specific sites, called receptors, in the brain (Snyder and Pert, 1975). Maps of these opiate binding sites showed that the receptors were most common in areas of the brain associated with pain transmission. The presence of specific receptors suggested the existence of natural substances in the brain with opiatelike properties. Some very clever analytic work with peptides revealed a whole family of such substances, now called endorphins (Hughes et al., 1975; Barchas et al., 1977). They have been found in many parts of the body, often associated with systems that are responsive to stress (cf. Chapter 3). They appear to have a role in pain transmission, they may have a regulatory function in stress response, and they probably are involved in drug addiction (Barchas et al., 1977). Also, there are suggestions that they may be involved in some major mental disorders, including schizophrenia and depression. Studies of these peptides have required major innovations in analytic techniques; these innovations have, in turn, led to the identification of a growing number of previously unsuspected peptides that also may have important functions in regulating behavior.

Especially encouraging are recent explicit efforts to explore the role of the biobehavioral sciences in specific aspects of health. For example, there recently have been such conferences as *Behavioral and Psychosocial Issues in Diabetes* (Hamburg et al., 1980) and *Perspectives on Behavioral Medicine* (Weiss et al., 1981). Other recent texts that address issues in health and behavior are *Medical Psychology: Contributions to Behavioral Medicine* (Prokop and Bradley, 1981), *Pediatric Behavioral Medicine* (Williams et al., 1981), and *Health Psychology—A Handbook* (Stone et al., 1979). These and others attest to a rich and growing body of knowledge.

Some Obstacles to Research in the Biobehavioral Sciences

As repeatedly illustrated throughout this volume, developments in many fields in the biobehavioral sciences have great potential for alleviating major components of the burden of illness. However, the scientific study of human behavior continues to face both new and traditional obstacles.

The newness of scientific tradition in this sphere is important. Although there were early pioneers, it is only in the second half of the twentieth century that a fairly large group of well-trained scientists have entered the arena of biobehavioral sciences. They often have faced old prescientific uneasiness about applying the tools of science to the most intimate matters of human experience. Moreover, there is a long and powerful tradition of conventional wisdom about human behavior: any person may feel expert in the subject.

The architectural complexity of the brain is intimidating—more so if one includes its manifestations in behavior and the complexity of social environments around the world and through time. Yet this complexity could yield more readily to scientific analysis were it not for the urgent necessity of exercising strict restraints on experiments. Ethical constraints in human experimentation are essential in this field; many promisingly informative experiments simply cannot be done. Nevertheless, some useful human studies can be done, and the appropriate restraints can stimulate efforts to garner information from quasi-experimental observations, experiments in nature, and unobtrusive methods (Webb et al., 1966). Also, animal models are helpful for some purposes.

Learning is a cardinal feature of the human species. Human beings have made major behavioral changes as they adapted to new circumstances over the centuries. Many unhealthful practices are of relatively recent origin. For example, cigarette smoking has been a widespread behavior only in this past century. As information about health-damaging behavior accumulates, new adaptive patterns are likely to emerge.

Changes of behavioral or social factors that damage health need not require intrusive compulsions that threaten our freedom (Wikler, 1978). Changes in and by a society to improve the health and well-being of its members may be indirect and may have other benefits. For example, a social decision to combat malaria by draining a swamp may not only improve health but also may benefit society by adding to the land available for food growing and recreation.

Even when social actions to improve health entail changing the behavior of members of the society, they need not be coercive or threaten liberty. For instance, suppose riding a bicycle to work were shown to be more healthful than driving. Society initially might offer some incentives to encourage people to ride bicycles; but, if people enjoyed it, the practice might spread voluntarily. Consequent environmental improvements such as cleaner air and less noise could provide additional obvious benefits, including saving money, which would encourage still greater participation in the activity. No coercion need be involved. Action of society to improve its health may well reduce, rather than add to, the immense costs of modern health care (Scheffler, 1979).

Conclusions

The scientific study of behavior is flourishing as never before, even though the task is difficult and complex. Nowhere is that study more needed than at the conjunction of the biomedical and biobehavioral sciences, where lie many possibilities for future interventions to prevent and treat disease. The Health and Behavior project was designed to foster collaboration among biobehavioral and biomedical scientists in tackling problems of great significance for health and to identify important questions, promising lines of inquiry, and questions of basic science underlying public health problems. This quest goes beyond current applications to include exploration of research needs over the next decade or more. Not all plausible lines of inquiry will yield useful applications. Still, basic inquiry should be fostered in its own right, for its intrinsic worth and for its potential applications to these problems.

Investigators need to be drawn into the domain of health and behavior from both the biobehavioral and the biomedical sciences. In the case of the biobehavioral sciences, many excellent researchers have had little or no occasion to explore health questions. With respect to the biomedical sciences, there historically has been little interest in behavioral questions; but interest is now on the rise. This and similar projects may help to attract the interest of some biomedical scientists who have been concerned with health issues but who have not previously studied behavioral linkages. Similarly, some behavioral scientists who have previously ignored health questions now may find them of increasing interest. The shift of attention of even a few outstanding scientists can make a great difference in the progress of research. The remainder of this volume attests to the need for and the potential benefits of such a reordering of research interests.

References

Barchas, J. D., Berger, P. A., Ciaranello, R. D., and Elliott, G. R. (Eds.) *Psychopharmacology: From Theory to Practice* New York: Oxford University Press, 1977.

Hamburg, B. A., Lipsett, L. F., Inoff, G. E., and Drash, A. L. (Eds.) *Behavioral and Psychosocial Issues in Diabetes* Washington, D.C.: U.S. Government Printing Office, 1980, Publ. No. (NIH) 80–1993.

Hughes, J., Smith, T. W., Kosterlitz, H. W., Fothergill, L. A.,Morgan, B. A., and Morris, H. R. Identification of two related pentapeptides from the brain with potent opiate agonist activity. *Nature* 258:577–579, 1975.

Lalonde, M. *A New Perspective on the Health of Canadians. A Working Document* Ottawa: Government of Canada, 1974.

National Academy of Sciences *Science and Technology: A Five-Year Outlook* San Francisco: Freeman, 1979.

Prokop, C. K., and Bradley, L. A. *Medical Psychology: Contributions to Behavioral Medicine* New York: Academic Press, 1981.

Rice, D., Feldman, J., and White, K. *The Current Burden of Illness in the United States* Washington, D.C.: National Academy of Sciences, 1977.

Scheffler, R. M. The economic evidence on prevention. IN: *Healthy People. Background Papers* (United States Department of Health, Education, and Welfare) Washington, D.C.: U.S. Government Printing Office, 1979, DHEW Publ. No. (PHS) 79–55071A, pp. 439–455.

Snyder, S. H., and Pert, C. B. Membrane receptors. IN: *Opiate Receptor Mechanisms* (Snyder, S. H., and Matthysse, S., eds.) Cambridge: MIT Press, 1975, pp. 26–34.

Stone, G. C., Cohen, F., and Adler, N. E. (Eds.) *Health Psychology—A Handbook* San Francisco: Jossey-Bass, 1979.

United States Department of Health, Education, and Welfare *Healthy People* Washington, D.C.: U.S. Government Printing Office, 1979, DHEW Publ. No. (PHS) 79–55071.

Webb, E. J., Campbell, D. T., Schwartz, R. D., and Sechrest, L. *Unobtrusive Measures: Nonreactive Research in the Social Sciences* Chicago: Rand McNally, 1966.

Weiss, S. M., Herd, J. A., and Fox, B. H. *Perspectives on Behavioral Medicine* New York: Academic Press, 1981.

Wikler, D. I. *Ethical Issues in Governmental Efforts to Promote Health* Washington, D.C.: National Academy of Sciences, 1978.

Williams, B. J., Foreyt, J. P., and Goodrick, G. K. (Eds.) *Pediatric Behavioral Medicine* New York: Praeger, 1981.

2

The Contribution of Behavior to the Burden of Illness

The heaviest burdens of illness in the United States today are related to aspects of individual behavior, especially long-term patterns of behavior often referred to as "lifestyle" (Lalonde, 1974; U.S. Department of Health, Education, and Welfare, 1979b; U.S. Department of Health and Human Services, 1980c). The Centers for Disease Control (1980) of the United States Public Health Service have estimated that 50 percent of mortality from the 10 leading causes of death in the United States can be traced to lifestyle.

Research has confirmed that some behaviors are risk factors of disease. That means that people who engage in such behaviors are more likely to develop certain types of illnesses than are people who do not. Perhaps the most widely known association of this type is that of cigarette smoking as a risk factor of lung cancer. To be a risk factor, the behavior must be present before the disease begins; it cannot be an early symptom of the disease, as coughing, for example, is an early indication of lung disease. However, a risk factor need not cause the disorder. It may merely be closely associated with some underlying process that eventually produces the disease state. As a result, once a type of behavior is identified as a risk factor, additional studies are needed to determine whether changes in behavior are of value in preventing or treating the disease. Known behavioral risk factors include cigarette smoking, excessive consumption of alcoholic beverages, use of illicit drugs, certain dietary habits, insufficient exercise, reckless driving, nonadherence with sound medication regimens, and maladaptive responses to social pressures.

This chapter provides a brief summary of the current burden of illness in the United States and of the significance of lifestyle to that burden of illness. It primarily provides a perspective of the overall magnitude of the contribution behavioral factors make to the current burden of illness. Specific kinds of behavior and disease states are examined in Section II of this report. This chapter does not explicitly examine the effects of broad social influences on the burden of illness; behavioral issues relating to health and work, aging, and social disadvantage are discussed in Section III.

The Current Burden of Illness

A number of measures of the societal and personal impact of disease have been used as indices of the burden of illness, including the number of people directly afflicted by a condition (prevalence), mortality (rates of death per unit population), direct economic costs (costs of care and treatment), indirect economic costs (loss of wages or premature death of a wage earner), use of health care resources (hospital inpatient days), and functional restrictions imposed by disease (lost work or school days) (U.S. Department of Health and Human Services, 1980c). No single measure is fully satisfactory; even the aggregate of many measures does not convey the full burden of illness, because the emotional and interpersonal toll of these illnesses has yet to be quantified.

Mortality

The major causes of the almost two million deaths each year in the United States are cardiovascular diseases, including heart disease, stroke, hypertension, and the various manifestations of atherosclerosis; cancers; accidents; violence, including homicide and suicide; diabetes mellitus; cirrhosis of the liver; and lung disease (U.S. Department of Health, Education, and Welfare, 1979b).

The leading causes of death vary with age. Low birth weight, birth-associated conditions, and congenital defects are the major conditions associated with infant mortality. Accidents and violence are the leading causes of death for those age 1–24 years, with cancer and heart disease also prevalent. Accidents continue to rank first for the age group 25–44. Above age 44, cardiovascular disease and cancer are the leading causes of death, but accidents and violence continue to be important. Cirrhosis of the liver, diabetes mellitus, and respiratory disease, especially for those over age 65 in the latter case, also are major contributors to adult mortality (U.S. Department of Health, Education, and Welfare, 1979b; National Center for

Health Statistics, 1981). Although accidents and violence contribute to mortality for several age groups, the type of accident or violence is age-dependent. For very young children, injury typically is due to behavior of others; for older children, fatal injuries are more likely to result from their own behavior.

"Premature mortality" is an important aspect of the burden of illness. The term refers to deaths that occur prior to the age of average longevity. To assess the relative impact of different disease categories, "potential years of life lost" can be calculated from mortality data. Comparisons are made of (1) total number of years of life lost for the entire population and (2) average number of years lost by each person who dies. Cardiovascular disease, which kills the largest number of people each year, ranks at the top in the first measure. Infant mortality, that is death in the first year of life, necessarily ranks at the top in the second.

In 1974, one third of the 33 million potential years of life lost could be attributed to cardiovascular disease, including heart disease, hypertension, atherosclerosis, and stroke (Rice et al., 1977). Almost 12 years of life were lost for each cardiovascular disease death. For each cancer death, almost 27 years of life were lost, and for each accident/poisoning/violent death, almost 36 years of life were lost (Rice et al., 1977). As noted above, the latter conditions dominate the mortality of younger age groups.

Morbidity

Mortality data demonstrate the preeminence of conditions for which aspects of lifestyle constitute risk factors, but the data do not fully elucidate the importance of these conditions in the burden of illness. Many of the leading causes of death are chronic and progressively disabling diseases; years of limitation in function and associated health care costs may precede death. For a full accounting of the magnitude of the associated burden, morbidity measures such as prevalence, functional limitations, use of health care resources, and economic costs associated with illness must be taken into account.

Prevalence data provide a relatively simple estimate of the extent of health problems. Among the 220 million Americans in 1978, there were 3 million cases of cancer* (American Cancer Society, 1979). For hypertension, from 23 to 60 million people are affected, depending on the definition of high

---

* The cancer figure includes those with a history of cancer as well as current cases; the cardiovascular disease figure includes double counting of those with more than one condition.

TABLE 2.1 Burden of Illness in the United States in 1974

Measure	Total (millions)	Percent of the Total				
		Accidents, Poisoning, Violence	Cancer	Cardio-vascular Diseases	Mental Disorders	Other
Deaths	2	8	19	53	1	19
Potential years of life lost	33	17	18	37	1	27
Short-stay hospital days	255	11	10	19	6	54
Long-term care days	616	3	1	27	40	29
Physician office visits[b]	521	9	2	11	6	72
Work loss days	461[a]	18	2	8	3	69
Bed days	1,783[a]	9	4	13	3	71
Social Security Disability benefit days	561	7	9	27	20	37
Causes of major activity limitations	34[a]	4	2	23	4	67
Direct cost dollars[c]	99,000	7	5	16	10	62

[a] More than one condition may cause a work loss day, a bed day, or a limitation in major activity. Days or limitations thus may be counted more than once. For the 22 million persons reporting major activity limitations, an average of 1.5 chronic conditions per person were responsible. There were an estimated 1,392 million bed days; each bed day was counted about 1.3 times. There were 414 million work loss days; each loss day was counted an average of 1.1 times.

[b] For the year 1973.

[c] For the year 1975.

SOURCE: Tables 1, 2, 4, 5, 6, 7, 8, and 11 of Rice et al., 1977.

blood pressure used* (National Institutes of Health, 1979). Each year, about 30 percent of the population (60 to 70 million persons) suffer injuries from accidents, poisoning, or violence serious enough to require medical attention or to restrict activity for at least one day (U.S. Department of Health, Education, and Welfare, 1978). Also, each year, about 15 percent (33 million persons) experience some form of mental disorder (President's Commission on Mental Health, 1978; Regier et al., 1978).

More sensitive measures of the relative burden imposed by the several categories of disease include days in short-stay hospitals or long-term care facilities, number of visits to physicians, days of restricted activity, direct costs of treatment, and indirect costs such as work days lost. Table 2.1 summarizes 1974 estimates for several of these measures. Contributions of the categories of accidents/poisoning/violence, cancer, cardiovascular disease, and mental illness are listed specifically, because of the major behavioral factors in their etiology.

Cardiovascular diseases dominate the burden of illness: they account for more than half of the deaths; about one third of the potential years of life lost; almost one quarter of long-term care days, major activity limitations, and Social Security Disability benefit days; and about one fifth of the short-stay hospital days each year (Rice et al., 1977). For seven of eight indicators of the burden of illness analyzed in a comprehensive survey, the category of cardiovascular disease ranked first or second (Rice et al., 1977).

The chronicity of many mental disorders leads to a relatively large share of long-term care days for this category of illness. It ranks first for inpatient days and third for Social Security Disability benefit days (Rice et al., 1977). Relatively few deaths are attributed to mental disorders, but a considerable share of deaths attributed to the accident/poisoning/violence category probably are associated with mental disorders.

Accidents, poisoning, and violence—all especially a problem for younger persons—contributed a large share to potential years of life lost and to work days lost. This category ranked second, third, or fourth in six of eight indicators (Rice et al., 1977). Cancer caused a large share both of total deaths and of potential years of life lost, by virtue of its impact on relatively young persons; it ranked second in premature mortality and fourth in Social Security Disability benefit days and economic costs (Rice et al., 1977).

Indirect costs, for example, the value of lost productivity or years of life, also constitute a portion of the burden of illness. It is difficult to calculate

---

* Over 60 million people have had one or more blood pressure measurements of 140/90 or greater. Of these, about 35 million have definite hypertension (blood pressure of 160/95 or greater) and 25 million have borderline hypertension (blood pressure of 140/90 to 159/94). In aggregate, this accounts for nearly one fourth of the entire U.S. population.

values based in the future; researchers have used several models employing different assumptions (Institute of Medicine, 1981b). In one analysis, using a discount rate of 4 percent, indirect costs of the burden of illness were calculated to be $146 billion in 1975. Of this total, 24 percent was derived from cardiovascular disease; 20 percent, from accidents, poisoning, and violence; 12 percent, from cancer; and 7 percent, from mental disorders (Rice et al., 1977).

More recent data continue to indicate the dominant position of diseases for which lifestyle factors are especially significant. In 1977, when the overall age-adjusted death rate was 612 per 100,000 population, fully three quarters of the deaths were caused by three disease categories (U.S. Department of Health and Human Services, 1980c): (1) heart disease and stroke, 42 percent; (2) cancer, 22 percent; and (3) accidents and violence, 11 percent. Hypertension, heart conditions, and diabetes were among the five most often cited causes of health-related restrictions of activity in 1976. Of the 7.5 million Americans prevented by poor health from pursuing their major activity, 37 percent (over 2.5 million) attributed their disability to those three conditions (Colvez and Blanchet, 1981).

The impact of behavior on the burden of illness also is reflected in the recent observation that alcohol abuse, cigarette smoking, and obesity are disproportionately present among the 20 percent of patients with highest hospitalization costs. In a survey of six hospitals, each with a distinct patient population, from 31 to 69 percent of the high-cost patients, but only 20 to 45 percent of the lower-cost patients, had at least one unhealthful habit (alcohol or drug abuse, cigarette smoking, obesity, noncompliance with medical advice) (Zook and Moore, 1980). There also are reports that treatments for alcoholism and mental disorders reduce the subsequent use of medical care resources (Jones and Vischi, 1979).

Behavioral Risks to Health

Many types of behavior have been implicated as risk factors of certain major physical and mental disorders. As indicated earlier, such evidence does not mean that such behaviors cause disease. In some cases, behavior may only provide useful indicators of people who are especially in danger of developing a health problem and might especially benefit from early disease detection and intervention efforts.

For diseases in which behavior is found to play an etiological role, interventions may be appropriate. However, it has become clear that many people find it extremely difficult to change their lifestyles, even in the face of clear risks to health. Thus, research on prevention must determine not only which behavioral changes are potentially beneficial but also how such changes can be adopted and maintained by the affected individuals.

Consideration of some kinds of behavior that have been identified as risk factors for major disorders helps to highlight the variety of ways in which behavior can affect health. As mentioned earlier, such research is discussed in more detail in the next two sections of this report.

Cigarette Smoking

In the United States in 1979, one third of the population over 19 years of age were current smokers—25 million men and 23 million women (U.S. Department of Health and Human Services, 1980c); 3 to 4 million teenagers (about 12 percent of that age group) also were current smokers (National Institute of Education, 1979).

The Surgeon General, in the report *Smoking and Health*, identified cigarette smoking as "the single most important environmental factor contributing to premature mortality in the United States" (U.S. Department of Health, Education, and Welfare, 1979a). In a 12-year follow-up of one million men and women in the United States, mortality rates were greater for smokers than for nonsmokers regardless of age or sex (Hammond, 1966). In the age group 45–54, for example, men and women who smoked between one and two packs of cigarettes a day were respectively 1.5 and 2.4 times more likely to die in the 12-year study period than were comparable nonsmokers. Risk consistently increased for both men and women as the daily dose of cigarettes increased (Table 2.2) (Hammond, 1966; U.S. Department of Health, Education, and Welfare, 1979a; U.S. Department of Health and Human Services, 1980b).

TABLE 2.2   Mortality Ratios for Cigarette Smokers Age 45–54

Number of Cigarettes (per day)	Mortality Ratio	
	Men	Women
Nonsmokers	1.0	1.0
1–9	1.8	0.9
10–19	2.3	1.2
20–39	2.4	1.5
40+	2.8	2.0
All smokers	2.2	1.3

SOURCE: Table 2, U.S. Department of Health and Human Services (1980b), and Table 6, U.S. Department of Health, Education, and Welfare (1979a).

Mortality attributed to respiratory tract cancers, emphysema, cardiovascular disease, and a number of other disorders appears to be especially significant in relation to cigarette smoking (Table 2.3) (U.S. Department of Health, Education, and Welfare, 1979a). The greatest relative risk is posed by lung and bronchial cancer, with a tenfold increase in mortality for cigarette smokers. A relatively modest twofold increase in cardiovascular mortality risk belies a great public health impact: the baseline rate of cardiovascular disease mortality is so high that even a doubling represents many thousands of additional deaths. A total of 320,000 deaths annually probably are linked to cigarette smoking (U.S. Department of Health and Human Services, 1980a).

General morbidity measures also are considerably higher for smokers than for nonsmokers. Compared with people who never smoked, current and exsmokers reported a 35 to 45 percent excess of work days lost in 1974. This represents 81 million excess work days lost that year attributable to cigarette smoking. Similarly, there were 145 million excess days of bed disability (U.S. Department of Health, Education, and Welfare, 1979a).

There are several lines of evidence that cigarette smoking actually has a causal role in heart disease, cancer (lung, larynx, esophagus, and oral cavity), and respiratory disease (chronic obstructive lung disease, bronchitis, and emphysema) (U.S. Department of Health, Education, and Welfare, 1979a; Wynder and Hoffman, 1979). For example, the effect depends on the dose: greater morbidity and mortality occur with more cigarettes smoked, higher tar and nicotine content, greater inhalation of cigarette smoke, and earlier

TABLE 2.3   Causes of Excess Death Among Cigarette Smokers

Cause of Death	Mortality Ratio[a]	
	Median	Range
All causes	1.5	1.2– 1.9
Lung and bronchial cancer	10.7	3.6–15.9
Coronary heart disease	1.7	1.3– 2.0
Hypertension	1.4	1.0– 2.5
Arteriosclerosis	2.0	1.4– 3.3
Emphysema/bronchitis	6.6	1.6–24.7
Influenza/pneumonia	1.9	1.4– 2.6
Cirrhosis	2.3	0.8– 4.0
Stomach or duodenal ulcer	2.9	0.5– 6.9

[a] Data from eight prospective epidemiological studies.
SOURCE: Table 41, U.S. Department of Health, Education, and Welfare (1979a).

TABLE 2.4   Risk of Oral Cavity Cancer in White Men
40–65 Years Old

Daily Dose		Relative Risk
Alcohol	Cigarettes	
0	0	1.0
7 oz +	0	2.5
0	one pack +	10.0
7 oz +	one pack +	24.0

SOURCE: McCoy and Wynder, 1979.

age of smoking initiation. Multivariate analyses of epidemiologic data reveal that cigarette smoking contributes to disease risk independently of other known risk factors. Risk is reduced with quitting, although it may take many years to return to the risk levels of individuals who never have smoked. Furthermore, cigarette smoke and its constituents are carcinogenic at several sites (lung, larynx, esophagus, and oral cavity) in several different animals (U.S. Department of Health, Education, and Welfare, 1979a; Wynder and Hoffman, 1979).

In addition to the direct role played by cigarette smoking, a growing body of evidence indicates that smoking exacerbates risks from other factors. Sometimes the effect can be synergistic, creating a greater risk than expected from the additive risk of each factor alone. Smoking and alcohol are synergistic risk factors of oral cavity cancer (McCoy and Wynder, 1979), and smoking and oral contraceptives are synergistic for risk of stroke (subarachnoid hemorrhage) (Petitti et al., 1979) (see Tables 2.4 and 2.5). The synergy of asbestos exposure and cigarette smoking in risk of lung cancer also is well documented (Hammond et al., 1979).

TABLE 2.5   Subarachnoid Hemorrhage in Women
Under 45 Years Old

Oral Contraceptive Use	Cigarette Use	Hemorrhage Rate (per 100,000/year)
No	No	8.3
Yes	No	26.6
No	Yes	33.7
Yes	Yes	127.0

SOURCE: Petitti et al., 1979.

Trends in cigarette use by women of child-bearing age are of special concern, because of the known adverse fetal effects of maternal smoking during pregnancy. Between 1965 and 1980, the portion of current smokers among women age 20–44 decreased from about 43 percent to 34 percent, but a greater proportion of those who still smoke now are heavy smokers (U.S. Department of Health and Human Services, 1980c). Among women smokers, the number who smoke more than one pack a day increased from 16 percent to 25 percent; the percentage of all women age 20–44 who smoke more than one pack daily has not declined since 1965 (U.S. Department of Health and Human Services, 1980c). Furthermore, the percentage of current smokers among women age 17–19 increased from about 19 percent to about 30 percent (U.S. Department of Health and Human Services, 1980b). On the more positive side, there is a recent decline among younger teenage girls (age 12–16) in the percentage who smoke; as these cohorts reach their late teens, the current trend of increased smoking among 17- to 19-year olds may be reversed.

On average, infants of women who smoked during pregnancy weigh 200 grams less at birth than do infants born to nonsmokers (U.S. Department of Health and Human Services, 1980b). An association between smoking and reduced birth weight has been confirmed by more than 45 studies covering a total of half a million births (U.S. Department of Health, Education, and Welfare, 1979a). The reduced birth weight is independent of such other factors as gestational age of the infant and nutritional status of the mother (U.S. Department of Health and Human Services, 1980b).

About 7 percent of infants born in the United States each year are of low birth weight (2,500 grams or less) (U.S. Department of Health and Human Services, 1980c). Death in the first year of life is 20 times more likely for low birth weight infants than for heavier infants, and almost two thirds of infants who die are of low birth weight (Shapiro et al., 1968). Cigarette smoking during pregnancy doubles the risk of having a low birth weight infant, and about one third of low birth weight babies are attributable to maternal cigarette smoking (Meyer et al., 1976; U.S. Department of Health and Human Services, 1980b). Women who smoke during pregnancy also are at greater risk of spontaneous abortion, fetal death, premature delivery, and such complications as placenta previa (U.S. Department of Health and Human Services, 1980b).

There also is evidence suggesting long-term consequences to children of mothers who smoked during pregnancy. For example, in the large British Perinatal Mortality Study, 11-year-old children of women who had smoked after the fourth month of pregnancy had lower scores on tests of reading comprehension and mathematics ability than did comparable children of women who had been nonsmokers during pregnancy (U.S. Department of

Health and Human Services, 1980b). Other studies have reported trends of lower scores on tests of intellectual function and of higher frequency of minimal cerebral dysfunction, neurological abnormalities, and behavior problems among children of mothers who had smoked during pregnancy, although the differences did not always reach statistical significance (U.S. Department of Health and Human Services, 1980b). More research is needed on possible confounding factors and to confirm and explore reasons for detrimental effects of maternal prenatal smoking on the physical, intellectual, and emotional development of the offspring.

Excessive Consumption of Alcohol

In the United States, about 56 million adult men (age 18 and over) and 50 million adult women drink alcoholic beverages (National Institute on Alcoholism and Alcohol Abuse, 1981). Another 16.5 million teens age 12–17 have had alcohol at least once; 8.5 million of them are "current drinkers," i.e., they had alcohol during the month previous to the survey (Fishburne et al., 1980).

Alcoholism, alcohol abuse, problem drinking, and heavy drinking are variably defined and partly overlapping terms for degrees of alcohol consumption and associated problems. Criteria typically use some combination of number and frequency of drinks, indicators of alcohol dependence such as drinking in the morning or having had delerium tremors, extent of social disruption or personal or family concern, and medical complications such as liver cirrhosis.

In 1979, 10 million adult men and women in the United States were heavy drinkers, consuming an average of four drinks per day (National Institute on Alcoholism and Alcohol Abuse, 1981). Perhaps another 3.5 million teenagers are heavy drinkers, consuming five or more drinks per drinking occasion. Heavy alcohol consumption does not invariably lead to problems, but even light drinking can create difficulties for some people. These two potential sources of error tend to negate each other, so that estimates of problem drinkers in the United States (10 million adults and 3 million teens) are about the same as those for heavy drinkers (Eckardt et al., 1981; National Institute on Alcoholism and Alcohol Abuse, 1981).

The burden of illness associated with alcohol derives from several major adverse health consequences of chronic excessive consumption of alcohol and from the additional morbidity and mortality associated with occasional social drinking. In 1975, direct and indirect costs of alcoholism were estimated at about $43 billion (Berry et al., 1977; Institute of Medicine, 1980).

Overall mortality rates are higher for heavy drinkers than for moderate, light, or nondrinkers (Klatsky et al., 1981). Among 6,000 Swedish men age 48 or 49, for example, 55 percent of those dying during a four-year study period had a history of heavy drinking; one third of the 63 deaths were judged likely to be related to alcohol (Peterson et al., 1980). Among a cohort of alcoholics in the United States, mortality within four years of admission to a treatment program was 2.5 times that expected for persons of their age, with the greatest relative mortality increase among younger alcoholics; 57 percent of the deaths were deemed likely to be related to alcohol (National Institute on Alcoholism and Alcohol Abuse, 1981).

In 1977, 5,100 death certificates in the United States listed alcoholism as the principal cause of death; 318 additional deaths were attributed to alcoholic psychoses; and 30,848, to cirrhosis of the liver (National Center for Health Statistics, 1981). Various studies indicate that 22 to 95 percent of liver cirrhosis deaths are associated with alcohol; most estimates fall between 60 and 80 percent (National Institute on Alcoholism and Alcohol Abuse, 1979). Alcohol probably was a contributory factor in another 40,000 to 60,000 deaths from accidents, suicides, and homicides (National Institute on Alcoholism and Alcohol Abuse, 1979). Cancers of the oral cavity and esophagus also are linked to heavy consumption of alcohol; as mentioned earlier, this effect is independent of but synergistic with cigarette smoking, which often is associated with heavy drinking (National Institute on Alcoholism and Alcohol Abuse, 1981). Heavy alcohol consumption also is a risk factor for primary liver cancer, probably because of liver cirrhosis (Eckardt et al., 1981). In addition, both retrospective and prospective studies have suggested that spontaneous abortion is doubled among pregnant women who drink heavily (Harlap and Shiono, 1980; Kline et al., 1980). The abortion risk associated with moderate drinking by pregnant women needs further study (Sokol, 1980).

There have been considerable publicity and debate about possible "harmful" effects of *not* drinking alcohol (Gonzalez, 1979). Some epidemiological studies can be interpreted to suggest that moderate drinkers are at less risk of coronary death than are abstainers (Hennekens et al., 1979; Marmot et al., 1981). Observed positive correlations between alcohol consumption and HDL-cholesterol level (Castelli et al., 1977) also are consistent with this hypothesis, as discussed later in this chapter. However, there are inconsistencies and conflicts among the studies. For example, moderate drinkers have been reported as having lower mortality rates than abstainers (Marmot et al., 1981) but higher rates than those who drink less than once a month (Kozararevic et al., 1980). For coronary death, it still is unclear whether any type of alcoholic drink (Kozararevic et al., 1980) or only wine (St. Leger et al., 1979) reduces risk. Additional questions have been raised about the reliability of data on consumption and the role of confounding variables (Wigfield and Hill, 1981). For the present, it is generally agreed that heavy drinkers have high risk of early death; it is unresolved whether abstention may entail a health risk.

Pregnant women who drink heavily are at risk of delivering a baby who has the fetal alcohol syndrome—characterized by certain morphological abnormalities and frequently associated with mental retardation. Prospective studies of alcoholic women who did or did not limit their drinking during pregnancy (Rosett et al., 1978) and studies of laboratory animals (Streissguth et al., 1980; Eckardt et al., 1981) both suggest that alcohol is the agent responsible. There is some evidence of significantly decreased birth weight among children of women who report consumption of two drinks daily and reports of increases in spontaneous abortion rates at consumption levels as low as two drinks twice a week. Given the current state of uncertainty about the amount of alcohol consumption that can be dangerous for the fetus, the Surgeon General (1981) recently issued an Advisory on Alcohol and Pregnancy that cautioned pregnant women not to drink alcoholic beverages.

The possible adverse effects even of moderate drinking during pregnancy are a continuing subject of research. Suggestions of lowered viability at birth, heart rate abnormalities, poor sucking ability, and a variety of behaviors associated with poor functioning of the central nervous system need to be explored. Such studies must give careful attention to obtaining reliable consumption data and accurate and complete information on potential confounding variables such as cigarette smoking (Streissguth et al., 1980).

In addition to alcohol-related physiological changes leading to clinical problems, alcohol plays a role in numerous accidents and incidents of violence. Multiple interacting factors contribute to accidents and violence, so it is difficult to assign a precise share of the burden of illness from such events to alcohol. Nonetheless, there are suggestions that alcohol is involved, including evidence that between 35 and 64 percent of drivers in fatal motor vehicle accidents drank prior to the accident and laboratory demonstrations of detrimental effects of even moderate amounts of alcohol on psychomotor performance (National Institute on Alcoholism and Alcohol Abuse, 1981).

Unhealthful Dietary Habits

Major inadequacies of diet can be devastating to health: there are well-known adverse effects of insufficient calories, vitamins, and protein. Much current research attention in the United States is focused on the consequences of excess consumption, for example, of calories, fats, and salt. There also are possible detrimental effects of certain food additives such as artificial sweeteners, artificial coloring agents, and nitrites; but evidence in this area is not as clearcut (Institute of Medicine, 1979). This review of the health impact of diet will be limited to the health risks of overeating (obesity) and diets rich in certain fats and in salt.

Obesity   Definitions of obesity vary but generally specify a degree of overweight or excess fat substantially above a "desirable" value, for example, a weight 20 percent or more above average for a given age, height, and gender group (Van Itallie, 1979). Desirable weight may reflect averages of samples from the general population or life insurance data on weights that correlate with longevity. In the United States, about 15 percent of men and 25 percent of women age 20–74 are 20 percent or more overweight (Abraham and Johnson, 1980).

Several studies have shown a higher mortality rate for those markedly above average weight. Within the obese group, the greater the weight excess, the greater the additional risk (Van Itallie, 1979). Thus, men and women 20 to 30 percent overweight have a mortality 20 to 40 percent greater than that of average-weight persons; men and women 50 to 60 percent overweight have a mortality 150 to 250 percent greater. Heart disease and stroke mortality rates are 1.5- to 2-fold greater in men 40 percent above average weight, and diabetes mortality is 3- to 5-fold greater for these men.

In the Framingham study—a longitudinal study of risk factors for cardiovascular disease—investigators concluded that, aside from not smoking, "reduction of overweight is probably the most important hygienic measure . . . available for the control of cardiovascular disease" (Kannel and Gordon, 1979). Obesity increases the risk of hypertension, diabetes, and hyperlipidemia, each of which is itself a risk factor for heart disease (Kannel and Gordon, 1979; National Heart, Lung, and Blood Institute, 1981). On average, systolic blood pressure increases 6.5 mm of mercury, fasting blood sugar increases 2 mg/dl, and plasma cholesterol increases 12 mg/dl for each 10 percent rise in relative weight (Kannel and Gordon, 1979). In addition to its effects through these mechanisms, obesity may be an independent risk factor of cardiovascular disease. Such an independent effect has not been shown in studies with follow-up periods of up to five years; but a 16-year follow-up study of one population is consistent with an elevated risk among those who were obese as young adults (when 20–40 years old), even controlling for obvious possible confounding factors (Rabkin et al., 1977).

Despite popular belief, simple overconsumption of sugars does not increase rates of diabetes mellitus (Bierman, 1979). However, obesity—which results from overconsumption of calories relative to their expenditure as energy—does appear to be a major risk factor of adult-onset diabetes (Rabkin et al., 1977; Van Itallie, 1979). A prospective study revealed a 30-fold increase in risk of developing diabetes among those 45 percent overweight (Van Itallie, 1979). Part of the association between obesity and diabetes may result from metabolic changes associated with the early stages of the disease process. Such interactive effects have not yet been elucidated.

Other morbidity associated with obesity includes increased rates of gallstones and possibly increased rates of complications from falls or from surgery, as well as increased psychosocial disability. Such psychosocial disability may manifest itself as feelings of inferiority, psychoneuroses, and employee absenteeism.

Lipids Epidemiological studies since the 1950s indicate that a high level of cholesterol in the blood is a risk factor of mortality and morbidity from cardiovascular disease (National Heart, Lung, and Blood Institute, 1981). Men age 40–49 with blood cholesterol levels of 240 mg/dl or greater are twice as likely to develop heart disease as are men of the same age with levels below 220 mg/dl, the national average; blood cholesterol of 270 mg/dl carries a threefold greater risk (National Heart, Lung, and Blood Institute, 1981).

In blood, cholesterol is part of lipoprotein complexes that can be distinguished on the basis of their density: high-density lipoprotein (HDL), low-density lipoprotein (LDL), and very low density lipoprotein (VLDL). Each of these substances is chemically distinct and has a unique role in the uptake and deposition of cholesterol throughout the body. More detailed analyses of the relation of blood cholesterol to risk for cardiovascular disease suggest that risk is directly related to total cholesterol and cholesterol as LDL and inversely related to HDL. Thus, a high total cholesterol or a high proportion of cholesterol as LDL is a risk factor of atherosclerotic heart disease; HDL-cholesterol appears to be "protective" (National Heart, Lung, and Blood Institute, 1981).

Blood cholesterol is derived only in part from dietary intake of cholesterol; there also is important endogenous synthesis. Still, controlled experiments carried out in metabolic wards and recent epidemiological studies with a 20-year follow-up period indicate that the amount of dietary intake of cholesterol correlates directly with blood cholesterol levels (McGill, 1979; National Heart, Lung, and Blood Institute, 1981). Cross-sectional data from epidemiological studies done in the United States and in Israel have not, however, confirmed this association. In laboratory studies, serum cholesterol increases have been reported in the range of 3 to 12 mg/dl per 100 mg cholesterol consumed per 1,000 kcal of food, up to a total intake of 600 mg of cholesterol daily (McGill, 1979). No additional effect is seen at higher intake levels.

Consumption of saturated and polyunsaturated fatty acids also appears to influence the amount of cholesterol present in blood and its distribution among HDL and LDL fractions (Glueck, 1979; Shekelle et al., 1981), with saturated fatty acids such as those found in dairy and meat products being a greater health risk. However, dietary factors interact with individual physiological and genetic traits and, perhaps, exercise habits and other behaviors in determining blood cholesterol levels (Glueck, 1979; National Heart, Lung, and Blood Institute, 1981). There is considerable evidence that certain types of behavioral challenge raise blood cholesterol levels (Jenkins et al., 1969; Rahe et al., 1972).

Low blood cholesterol and a high proportion of cholesterol as HDL-cholesterol may be associated with lower risk of cardiovascular disease. However, there is a possibility that such lipid profiles are risk factors for other disorders such as cancer. Epidemiological data and studies of animals yield contradictory findings with regard to diet, lipids, and mortality from noncardiovascular causes such as cancer (National Heart, Lung, and Blood Institute, 1980; U.S. Congress, 1981). The *American Journal of Epidemiology* presented in its July 1981 issue reports from four major long-term prospective studies in Framingham, Massachusetts; Honolulu, Hawaii; Puerto Rico; and Yugoslavia. All four showed a significant inverse correlation between serum cholesterol levels and cancer mortality in men, even after adjustments were made to eliminate the effect of persons who may have had undiscovered disease at intake. However, cancer death rates overall are considerably lower than cardiovascular death rates, leading Keys et al. (1981) to conclude that the prospective Seven Countries Study (in which more than 12,500 men were followed for 10 years) provided "no support for the suggestion that the advantage for coronary disease of a diet restricted in saturated fats may be offset by increased non-coronary mortality."

Resolution of some apparent contradictions probably will entail careful epidemiological analyses and a search for mechanisms. Studies need to address the relationship of dietary lipids to cholesterol metabolism, membrane cholesterol, bile acid turnover, and the metabolism and pharmacokinetics of carcinogens and possible anticarcinogens such as vitamin A (Leveille and Rodgers, 1981).

Salt   Studies of both animals and human beings indicate that high salt intake can lead to hypertension under some circumstances (Tobian, 1979). In international comparisons, hypertension and age-related increases in blood pressure are absent among populations consuming less than 30 mEq of sodium daily; migrations leading to increased salt consumption correlate with appearance of hypertension (Tobian, 1979). High-salt diets of over 800 mEq per day lead to modest rises of blood pressure in normotensive volunteers but rarely to hypertensive levels (Murray et al., 1978); restriction of salt intake, either alone or in conjunction with diuretic therapy, lowers blood pressure for some hypertensives (Parijs et al., 1973).

There are strains of rats that are genetically either resistant or sensitive to developing hypertension when fed high salt diets but are normotensive on low salt diets (Dahl et al., 1962). Investigators have postulated that 10 to 20 percent of people in the United States may be genetically susceptible to developing hypertension by middle age. According to this hypothesis, lifelong daily consumption of the 100 to 200 mEq of sodium typical of American diets can induce hypertension in those so genetically predisposed; a restriction in dietary salt to under 60 mEq daily probably would be sufficient to prevent development of that hypertension (Tobian, 1979). Once hypertension has developed, more stringent salt limitations, down to 20 mEq per day, might be necessary to reduce blood pressure to normal values. At present, this remains a hypothesis; there are no tests to identify those people who may be predisposed to high blood pressure induced by high salt intake (Skrabal et al., 1981).

Exercise

Many people who participate in a regular program of vigorous physical exercise report feelings of psychological well-being that they find rewarding. In addition, there are reports of reduced risk of atherosclerotic coronary heart disease (Paffenbarger et al., 1978; Morris et al., 1980). Cross-sectional studies have revealed large differences in HDL-cholesterol between people active in sports such as running and tennis and those who are not (Wood et al., 1977; Vodak et al., 1980). Observed changes in lipoprotein profile would be consistent with reduced risk of coronary heart disease. Some longitudinal studies that have monitored changes in lipoproteins following inception of a period of increased exercise reveal marked changes (Huttunen et al., 1979; Kiens et al., 1980); others do not (Lipson et al., 1980). Most research to date suggests that vigorous exercise is needed for significant elevation of the fraction of cholesterol as HDL, but there also are reports that brisk walking and calisthenics will reduce LDL-cholesterol levels (Weltman et al., 1980; Nye, 1981). Possible explanations for the differing results include small sample size, inadequate monitoring of diet, and short training periods (only two to four months) in some studies.

Psychosocial Stressors

The burden of illnesses and disabilities in the United States and the world is closely related to social, psychological, and behavioral aspects of the way of life of the population. This principle applies to communicable and non-communicable diseases, to mental illnesses, to accidents, and to medically unnecessary disabilities. There are at least four channels by which mode of living, "stress," and other psychosocial factors affect the health of individuals and groups:

1. use of health information;
2. health-related behaviors, both those that damage health and those that are protective;
3. effects on "biological" risk factors and physiological functioning, through perception, cognition, and reactivity of the central nervous system and through the endocrine and autonomic nervous systems; and
4. influences on interpersonal relationships and social supports that affect lifestyle, use of health services, morbidity, and even survival (Berkman and Syme, 1979).

There is persuasive evidence that stressful events can be risk factors of physical and mental disorders (Institute of Medicine, 1981a). Studies have shown that natural disasters arouse both emotional consequences such as anxiety and nightmares and physical consequences such as acute elevations of blood pressure. More common events, for example, death of a loved one, divorce, or loss of a job, also have been associated with adverse health changes. Major stressors typically are sudden and adverse and demand a change in behavior or attitude. Such life events have been identified as risk factors for a variety of physical disorders, including peptic ulcer disease (Wolf et al., 1979) and sudden cardiac death (Talbott et al., 1977; Rissanen et al., 1978). Evidence regarding the relation of life crises to myocardial infarction is mixed, with positive findings coming from retrospective studies but not from prospective studies (Jenkins, 1976).

Any comprehensive search for psychosocial factors that may influence a given illness or disability state should include the following categories of exploration: socioeconomic deprivation, social mobility, anxiety, depression and other sustained painful emotions, life dissatisfactions, stress and life change, and predisposing personality traits. Specific variables within all of these categories have been found to be associated with risk of coronary heart disease in numerous studies (Jenkins, 1976).

A particularly well-documented risk factor of coronary heart disease is the Type A behavior pattern. This is not a form of stress but rather a behavioral predisposition to being harshly competitive, strongly aggressive, driven to achievement, hurried, impatient, and abrupt in language and gesture (Friedman and Rosenman, 1974). The Type A behavior pattern is a risk factor of coronary heart disease (myocardial infarction and angina pectoris) both retrospectively and prospectively in scores of studies in several parts of the world. An expert task force on coronary-prone behavior and coronary heart disease convened by the National Heart, Lung, and Blood Institute has concluded that the Type A pattern is a valid risk factor for coronary disease and that further investigations are needed both of pathophysiological mechanisms and of possible intervention programs (Review Panel on Coronary-Prone Behavior and Coronary Heart Disease, 1981).

Life events also have been implicated in raising the risk of psychiatric problems both in general (Theorell et al., 1975) and for specific types of disorder, including depression (Brown and Harris, 1978), schizophrenia (Jacobs and Meyers, 1976), and alcoholism and drug abuse (Robins, 1978).

Modifying Behavior to Alter Risk

The last two decades have witnessed increasing attention to health promotion and disease prevention (Lalonde, 1974; Nightingale et al., 1978; U.S. Department of Health, Education, and Welfare, 1979a,b; U.S. Department of Health and Human Services, 1980a,b,c). Research has identified behavior that constitutes a risk to health, and the American people generally have adopted a more healthful lifestyle over the past few decades: they exercise more (Paffenbarger, 1979; U.S. Department of Health and Human Services, 1980a); have lower blood cholesterol levels (Beaglehole et al., 1979; National Heart, Lung, and Blood Institute, 1981); and are less likely to smoke cigarettes (U.S. Department of Health, Education, and Welfare, 1979a; U.S. Department of Health and Human Services, 1980c). Still, Americans weigh more than they used to (Abraham and Carroll, 1979), and adults who smoke typically smoke more (Kleinman et al., 1979; U.S. Department of Health and Human Services, 1980c).

Proof that a certain behavior is a risk factor of a given disease does not necessarily mean that changing that behavior will alter subsequent risk of disease. In some instances, the risk factor may have no causal role; in others, irreversible pathological changes already may have occurred. Fortunately, evidence is accumulating that "healthful" changes can reduce subsequent risk. The 20 percent decline in coronary heart disease mortality during the 1970s probably is linked to changes in smoking habits, diet, and hypertension control, although changes in these risk factors do not fully explain the observed decline in mortality. Of particular interest are the discrepancies in the temporal sequence of changes in behavior observed at the population level and changes observed in mortality statistics (Havlik and Feinleib, 1979).

Representative reports of the health-promoting benefits of certain changes in behavior will be summarized here. Included are losing weight to control blood pressure, quitting cigarette smoking to reduce risk of lung cancer and heart disease, and modifying diet to decrease serum cholesterol and produce favorable changes in the distribution of cholesterol between HDL and LDL fractions.

Weight Reduction

Weight reduction is especially beneficial for hypertensives and adult-onset diabetics (Van Itallie, 1979); reduction in the number of acute gout attacks also has been reported (Hall et al., 1967). Large-scale epidemiological studies such as the Framingham study have shown that weight reduction correlates with healthful changes in blood pressure, plasma lipids, glucose tolerance, and plasma uric acid content (Tobian, 1978; Kannel and Gordon, 1979).

Although quantitative relationships between weight loss and blood pressure reduction vary among studies (Tobian, 1978), small controlled studies have confirmed epidemiological evidence that weight loss lowers blood pressure—whether for normotensive or hypertensive subjects or for normal-weight or obese subjects (Fletcher, 1954; Reissen et al., 1978). In one group of overweight hypertensives, 75 percent achieved normal blood pressure with weight loss alone, without either antihypertensive medication or salt restriction (Reissen et al., 1978). Also of interest is the finding that 61 percent of the overweight hypertensives not able to obtain adequate control with medication achieved normal blood pressure following weight loss (in conjunction with continued antihypertensive medication); another 28 percent reduced their blood pressure, although not to within normal limits (Reissen et al., 1978).

Smoking Cessation

Overall mortality rates for men who quit smoking are lower than rates for those who continue to smoke (Hammond and Horn, 1958; Rogot, 1974). Within 10 to 15 years of quitting, risk of death for exsmokers of less than one pack per day is equivalent to that of men who never smoked (Hammond and Horn, 1958; Rogot, 1974). There is a comparable decline in risk over 10 to 15 years for those who smoked more than one pack a day, but a residual excess risk remains even after 15 years. Surprisingly, the mortality rates for current smokers are lower than are those for exsmokers the first year after quitting—possibly because ill health stimulated the cessation of smoking for some of these people (U.S. Department of Health, Education, and Welfare, 1979a) (Table 2.6).

TABLE 2.6   Mortality Ratios of Smokers and Exsmokers

	Mortality Ratio				
	All Causes[a]			Coronary Heart Disease[c]	
Smoking Status	1^d	$1+^d$	Lung Cancer[b]	1^d	$1+^d$
Nonsmoker	1.0	1.0	1.0	1.0	1.0
Current smoker	1.6	2.0	15.8	1.9	2.6
Exsmoker					
Less than 1 year	2.0	2.7	16.0	1.6	1.6
5–9 years	1.3	1.8	5.9	1.2	1.2
More than 15 years	1.1	1.5	2.0	1.0	1.2

[a] Four-year follow-up period.
[b] Twenty-year follow-up period.
[c] Six-year follow-up period.
[d] Cigarette packs/day.
SOURCE: Tables 2–29, 4–4 and 5–15, U.S. Department of Health, Education, and Welfare, 1979a.

A similar pattern of gradual decline in mortality with years of smoking cessation is seen for lung cancer and coronary heart disease (U.S. Department of Health, Education, and Welfare, 1979a). There are no lung cancer mortality decreases the first few years after cessation, but a marked decline occurs by five years (Doll and Peto, 1976). Coronary heart disease mortality relative to that for nonsmokers declines immediately with cessation of smoking; within 10 to 20 years, there is no excess mortality attributable to the smoking history (Public Health Service, 1976) (Table 2.6).

Additional benefits of smoking cessation include those to infants: if a woman gives up cigarette smoking during pregnancy, her risk of delivering a low birth weight infant resembles that of a nonsmoker (U.S. Department of Health, Education, and Welfare, 1979a). For infants born to women who smoked during pregnancy, the average birth weight rises as the number of cigarettes being smoked decreases (U.S. Department of Health, Education, and Welfare, 1979a), suggesting some benefit even from a reduction in the number of cigarettes smoked. However, simple reduction might not be enough, if it is offset by compensating changes in smoking patterns, for example, rate of puffing or extent of inhaling.

Modification of Diet: Cholesterol and Fatty Acids

Epidemiological studies, metabolic ward studies of human beings, and laboratory studies of animal models provide evidence of a link between heart disease and dietary cholesterol and saturated fatty acids, probably through blood lipoprotein-cholesterol. Typically, study committees worldwide have cautiously recommended decreased intake of total fat and a shift from saturated to polyunsaturated fat (National Heart, Lung, and Blood Institute, 1981). One source of controversy has been the distinction between data on changes in whole populations and data on changes in individuals. Recently, however, the 19-year follow-up data of the Western Electric Study of almost 2,000 men who were middle-aged in 1957 have provided evidence that the lipid composition of an individual's diet does affect the serum cholesterol level (Shekelle et al., 1981).

It also has been problematic to demonstrate that a shift in diet protects against heart disease. The Western Electric Study showed a positive association of coronary mortality with a composite score monitoring intake of saturated fat, polyunsaturated fat, and cholesterol. No association of heart disease was demonstrated for saturated fat intake alone (Shekelle et al., 1981)—a finding not in accord with some other large studies (Gordon et al., 1977; National Heart, Lung, and Blood Institute, 1980). Continued research is needed to provide definitive evidence on this important question; nevertheless, the Western Electric results have reassured many who have been recommending a coronary "protective" diet.

Conclusions

Even a brief survey of the major components of the current burden of illness in the United States and other affluent, developed countries highlights the importance of behavioral factors. Some common lifestyle patterns are risk factors for a number of the most prevalent components of that burden. It seems likely that basic research aimed at discovering how behavior can affect such disorders would yield valuable insights into possible interventions. But even before that is completed, it is appropriate to conduct clinical field trials to ascertain the degree of protection that can be obtained by preventing or reducing the psychosocial risk factor.

Available evidence suggests that the biobehavioral sciences must continue to seek more effective ways of helping people to change unhealthful habits. In many cases, simple awareness of the benefits of changing a behavior is insufficient to produce lasting adoption of a new lifestyle. The biobehavioral sciences have made considerable theoretical and practical progress in identifying the motivation and behavior management approaches to modifying lifestyle (Jenkins, 1980). In some instances, this entails helping people develop new perspectives about their lives, so that prevention becomes sufficiently valued to serve as a motivation for change.

For many, the magnitude of behaviorally related diseases may seem overwhelming. Indeed, many complex problems remain to be solved, but remaining sections of this monograph amply illustrate the many aspects of those problems in which research opportunities await innovative investigators.

References

Abraham, S., and Carrol, M. D. Food consumption patterns in the United States and their potential impact on the decline in coronary heart disease mortality. IN: *Proceedings of the Conference on the Decline in Coronary Heart Disease Mortality* (Havlik, R. J., and Feinleib, M., eds.) Washington, D.C.: U.S. Government Printing Office, 1979, DHEW Publ. No. (NIH) 79–1610, pp. 253–281.

Abraham, S., and Johnson, C. L. Prevalence of severe obesity in adults in the United States. *Am. J. Clin. Nutr. 33*:364–369, 1980.

American Cancer Society *Cancer Facts and Figures, 1980* New York: American Cancer Society, 1979.

Beaglehole, R., La Rosa, J. C., Heiss, G. E., Davis, C. E., Rifkind, B. M., Muesing, R. M., and Williams, O. D. Secular changes in blood cholesterol and their contribution to the decline in coronary mortality. IN: *Proceedings of the Conference on the Decline in Coronary Heart Disease Mortality* (Havlik, R. J., and Feinleib, M., eds.) Washington, D.C.: U.S. Government Printing Office, 1979, DHEW Publ. No. (NIH) 79–1610, pp. 282–295.

Berkman, L. F., and Syme, S. L. Social networks, host resistance and mortality: A nine-year follow-up study of Alameda County residents. *Am. J. Epidemiol. 198*:186–204, 1979.

Berry, R. E., Boland, J. P., Smart, C. N., and Kanak, J. R. *The Economic Cost of Alcohol Abuse, 1975. Final Report* Bethesda, Md.: National Institute on Alcohol Abuse and Alcoholism, 1977, Contract No. ADM 281–76–0016.

Bierman, E. L. Carbohydrates, sucrose, and human disease. *Am. J. Clin. Nutr. 32*:2712–2722, 1979.

Brown, G. W., and Harris, T. *Social Origins of Depression: A Study of Psychiatric Disorder in Women* London: Tavistock, 1978.

Castelli, W. P., Doyle, J. T., Gordon, T., Hanes, C. G., Ajortland, M. C., Hulley, S. B., Kagan, A., and Zukel, W. J. Alcohol and blood lipids: The cooperative lipoprotein phenotyping study. *Lancet 2*:153–155, 1977.

Center for Disease Control *Ten Leading Causes of Death in the United States, 1977* Washington, D.C.: U.S. Government Printing Office, 1980.

Colvez, A., and Blanchet, M. Disability trends in the United States population, 1966–1976: Analysis of reported causes. *Am. J. Publ. Health 71*:464–471, 1981.

Dahl, L. K., Heine, M., and Tassinari, L. Effects of chronic salt ingestion. Evidence that genetic factors play an important role in susceptibility to experimental hypertension. *J. Exp. Med. 115*:1173–1190, 1962.

Doll, R., and Peto, R. Mortality in relation to smoking: 20 years' observation on male British doctors. *Br. Med. J. 2*:1525–1536, 1976.

Eckardt, M. J., Harford, T. C., Kaelber, C. T., Parker, E. S., Rosenthal, L. S., Ryback, R. S., Salmoiraghi, G. C., Vanderveen, E., and Warren, K. R. Health hazards associated with alcohol consumption. *J. Am. Med. Assoc. 246*:648–666, 1981.

Fishburne, P. M., Abelson, H. I., and Cisin, I. *National Survey on Drug Abuse: Main*

Findings, 1979 Bethesda, Md.: National Institute on Drug Abuse, 1980, DHEW Publ. No. (ADAMHA) 017–024–01008–1.

Fletcher, A. P. The effect of weight reduction upon the blood pressure of obese hypertensive women. *Q. J. Med.* 23:331–345, 1954.

Friedman, M., and Rosenman, R. H. *Type A: Your Behavior and Your Heart* New York: Knopf, 1974.

Glueck, C. J. Dietary fat and atherosclerosis. *Am. J. Clin. Nutr.* 32:2703–2711, 1979.

Gonzalez, E. R. Unresolved issue: Do drinkers have less coronary heart disease? *J. Am. Med. Assoc.* 242:2745–2747, 1979.

Gordon, T., Castelli, N. P. Hjortland, M. C., Kannel, W. B., and Dawber, T. R. Predicting coronary heart disease in middle-aged and older persons. *J. Am. Med. Assoc.* 238:497–499, 1977.

Hall, A. P., Barry, P. E., Dawber, T. R., and McNamara, P. M. Epidemiology of gout and hyperuricemia. A long-term population study. *Am. J. Med.* 42:27–37, 1967.

Hammond, E. C. Smoking in relation to the death rates of one million men and women. IN: *Epidemiologic Approaches to the Study of Cancer and Other Chronic Diseases* (Haenszel, W., ed.) Bethesda, Md.: National Cancer Institute, 1966, pp. 127–204.

Hammond, E. C., and Horn, D. Smoking and death rates. Report on forty-four months of follow-up on 187,783 men. I. Total mortality. *J. Am. Med. Assoc.* 166:1159–1172, 1958.

Hammond, E. C., Selikoff, I. J., and Seidman, H. Asbestos exposure, cigarette smoking, and death rates. *Ann. N.Y. Acad. Sci.* 330:473–490, 1979.

Harlap, S., and Shiono, P. H. Alcohol, smoking and incidence of spontaneous abortions in the first and second trimester. *Lancet* 2:173–176, 1980

Havlik, R. J., and Feinleib, M. Summary of the conference. IN: *Proceedings of the Conference on the Decline in Coronary Heart Disease Mortality* (Havlik, R. J., and Feinleib, M., eds.) Washington, D.C.: U.S. Government Printing Office, 1979, DHEW Publ. No. (NIH) 79–1610, pp. xxiii–xxvii.

Hennekens, C. H., Willett, W., Rosner, B., Cole, D. S., and Mayrent, S. L. Effects of beer, wine and liquor in coronary deaths. *J. Am. Med. Assoc.* 242:1973–1974, 1979.

Huttunen, J. K., Lansimies, E., Voutilainen, E., Ehnholm, C., Heitanen, E., Penttila, I., Shtonen, O., and Rauramaa, R. Effect of moderate physical exercise on serum lipoproteins: A controlled clinical trial with special reference to serum high density lipoproteins. *Circulation* 60:1220–1229, 1979.

Institute of Medicine *Food Safety Policy: Scientific and Societal Considerations* Washington, D.C.: National Academy of Sciences, 1979.

Institute of Medicine *Alcoholism, Alcohol Abuse, and Related Problems: Opportunities for Research* Washington, D.C.: National Academy of Sciences, 1980.

Institute of Medicine *Research on Stress and Human Health* Washington, D.C.: National Academy Press, 1981a.

Institute of Medicine *Costs of Environment-Related Health Effects: A Plan for Continuing Study* Washington, D.C.: National Academy Press, 1981b.

Jacobs, S., and Myers, J. Recent life events and acute schizophrenic psychosis: A controlled study. *J. Nerv. Ment. Dis.* 162:75–87, 1976.

Jenkins, C. D. Recent evidence supporting psychological and social risk factors for coronary disease. *N. Engl. J. Med.* 294:987–994 and 1033–1038, 1976.

Jenkins, C. D. Diagnosis and treatment of behavioral barriers to good health. IN: *Public Health and Preventive Medicine* (J. M. Last, ed.) New York: Appleton-Century-Crofts, 1980.

Jenkins, C. D., Hames, D. G., Zyzanski, S. J., Rosenman, R. H., and Friedman, M. Psychological traits and serum lipids. *Psychosom. Med. 31*:115–128, 1969.

Jones, K. R., and Vischi, T. R. Impact of alcohol, drug abuse and mental health treatment on medical care utilization. A review of the research literature. *Med. Care 17 (Suppl. 12)*:1–82, 1979.

Kannel, W. B., and Gordon, T. Physiological and medical concomitants of obesity: The Framingham Study. IN: *Obesity in America* (Bray, G. A., ed.) Washington, D.C.: U.S. Government Printing Office, 1979, DHEW Publ. No. (NIH) 79–359, pp. 125–163.

Keys, A., Aravanis, C., Van Buchen, F. S. P., et al. The diet and all causes death rate in the Seven Countries Study. *Lancet 2*:58–61, 1981.

Kiens, B., Jorgensen, I., Lewis, S., Jenson, G., Lithell, H., Vessby, B., Hoe, S., and Schnohr, P. Increased plasma HDL-cholesterol and apo-A-1 in sedentary middle-aged men after physical conditioning. *Eur. J. Clin. Invest. 10*:203–209, 1980.

Klatsky, A. L., Friedman, G. D., and Siegelaub, A. B. Alcohol and mortality. A ten-year Kaiser-Permanente experience. *Ann. Intern. Med. 95*:139–145, 1981.

Kleinman, J. C., Feldman, J. J., and Monk, M. A. Trends in smoking and ischemic heart disease. IN: *Proceedings of the Conference on the Decline in Coronary Heart Disease Mortality* (Havlik, R. J., and Feinleib, M., eds.) Washington, D.C.: U.S. Government Printing Office, 1979, DHEW Publ. No. (NIH) 79–1610, pp. 195–209.

Kline, J., Shrout, P., Stein, Z., Susser, M., and Warburton, D. Drinking during pregnancy and spontaneous abortion. *Lancet 2*:176–180, 1980.

Kozararevic, D., McGee, D., Vojvodic, N., Dawber, T., McGee, D., Racic, Z., Gordon, T., and Zukel, W. Frequency of alcohol consumption and morbidity and mortality: The Yugoslovia Cardiovascular Disease Study. *Lancet 1*:613–616, 1980.

Lalonde, M. *A New Perspective on the Health of Canadians. A Working Document* Ottawa: Information Canada, 1974.

Leveille, G. A., and Rogers, A. E. Summary of proceedings. Working group II. Fatty acids, steroids, and cancer. *Cancer Res. 41*:3752–3754, 1981.

Lipson, L. C., Bonow, R. O., Schaefer, E. J., et al. Effect of exercise conditioning on plasma high density lipoproteins and other lipoproteins. *Atherosclerosis 37*:529–538, 1980.

McCoy, G. D., and Wynder, E. L. Etiological and preventive implications in alcohol carcinogenesis. *Cancer Res. 39*:2844–2850, 1979.

McGill, H. C. The relationship of dietary cholesterol to serum cholesterol concentration and to atherosclerosis in man. *Am. J. Clin. Nutr. 32*:2664–2702, 1979.

Marmot, M. G., Rose, G., Shipley, M. J., and Thomas, B. J. Alcohol and mortality: A U-shaped curve. *Lancet 1*:580–583, 1981.

Meyer, M. B., Jonas, B. S., and Tonascia, J. A. Perinatal events associated with maternal smoking during pregnancy. *Am. J. Epidemiol. 103*:464–476, 1976.

Morris, J. N., Everitt, M. G., Pollard, R., and Chave, S. P. W. Vigorous exercise in leisure-time: Protection against coronary heart disease. *Lancet 2*:1207–1210, 1980.

Murray, R. H., Luft, F. C., Block, R., and Weyman, A. E. Blood pressure responses to extremes of sodium intake in normal man. *Proc. Soc. Exp. Biol. Med. 159*:432–436, 1978.

National Center for Health Statistics *Health United States, 1981* Washington, D.C.: U.S. Government Printing Office, 1981.

National Heart, Lung, and Blood Institute, Division of Heart and Vascular Diseases *Summary Report of the NHLBI Cholesterol Workshop* Washington, D.C.: National Heart, Lung, and Blood Institute, 1980.

National Heart, Lung, and Blood Institute *Arteriosclerosis, 1981. Report of the Working Group. Summary, Conclusions and Recommendations* Washington, D.C.: U.S. Government Printing Office, 1981, DHHS Publ. No. (NIH) 81–2034.

National Institute of Education *Teenage Smoking: Immediate and Long-Term Patterns* Washington, D.C.: U.S. Government Printing Office, 1979.

National Institute on Alcohol Abuse and Alcoholism *Third Special Report to the U.S. Congress on Alcohol and Health. Technical Support Document* Washington, D.C.: U.S. Government Printing Office, 1979, DHEW Publ. No. (ADM) 79–832.

National Institute on Alcohol Abuse and Alcoholism *Fourth Special Report to the U.S. Congress on Alcohol and Health* Washington, D.C.: U.S. Government Printing Office, 1981, DHHS Publ. No. (ADM) 81–1080.

National Institutes of Health *Report of the Hypertension Task Force, Volume Two: Scientific Summary and Recommendations* Washington, D.C.: U.S. Government Printing Office, 1979, DHEW Publ. No. (NIH) 79–1624.

Nightingale, E. O., Cureton, M., Kalmar, V., and Trudeau, M. B. *Perspectives on Health Promotion and Disease Prevention in the United States* Washington, D.C.: National Academy of Sciences, 1978.

Nye, E. R., Carlson, K., Kirstein, P., and Rossner, S. Changes in high density lipoprotein subfractions and other lipoproteins induced by exercise. *Clin. Chem. Acta 113*:51–57, 1981.

Paffenbarger, R. S. Countercurrents of physical activity and heart attack trends. IN: *Proceedings of the Conference on the Decline in Coronary Heart Disease Mortality* (Havlik, R. J., and Feinleib, M., eds.) Washington, D.C.: U.S. Government Printing Office, 1979, National Institutes of Health Publ. No. 79–1610, pp. 298–309.

Paffenbarger, R. S., Wing, A. L., and Hyde, R. T. Physical activity as an index of heart attack risk in college alumni. *Am. J. Epidemiol. 108*:161–175, 1978.

Parijs, J., Joossens, J. V., Linden, L. V., Verstreken, G., and Amery, A. K. P. C. Moderate sodium restriction and diuretics in the treatment of hypertension. *Am. Heart J. 85*:22–34, 1973.

Peterson, B., Kristenson, H., Sternby, N. A., Trell, E., Fex, G., and Hood, B. Alcohol consumption and premature death in middle-aged men. *Br. Med. J. 280*:1403–1406, 1980.

Petitti, D. B., Wingerd, J., Pellegrin, F., and Ramcharan, S. Risk of vascular disease in women. Smoking, oral contraceptives, noncontraceptive estrogens, and other factors. *J. Am. Med. Assoc. 242*:1150–1154, 1979.

President's Commission on Mental Health *Report to the President, Vol. I* Washington, D.C.: U. S. Government Printing Office, 1978.

Public Health Service *The Health Consequences of Smoking. A Reference Edition: 1976* Washington, D.C.: U.S. Government Printing Office, 1976, DHEW Publ. No. (CDC) 78–8357.

Rabkin, S. W., Mathewson, F. A. L., and Hsu, P. H. Relation of body weight to development of ischemic heart disease in a cohort of young North American men after a 26-year observation period. The Manitoba Study. *Am. J. Cardiol.* 39:452–458, 1977.

Rahe, R. H., Rubin, R. T., Gunderson, E. K. E. Measures of subjects' motivation and affect correlated with their serum uric acid, cholesterol and cortisol. *Arch. Gen. Psychiatry* 26:357–359, 1972.

Regier, D. A., Goldberg, I. D., and Taube, C. A. The defacto mental health services system. *Arch. Gen. Psychiatry* 35:685–693, 1978.

Reissen, E., Abel, R., Modan, M., Silverberg, D. S., Eliahou, H., and Modan, B. Effect of weight loss without salt restriction on the reduction of blood pressure in overweight hypertensive patients. *N. Engl. J. Med.* 298:1–6, 1978.

Review Panel on Coronary-Prone Behavior and Coronary Heart Disease. Coronary-prone behavior and coronary heart disease: A critical review. *Circulation* 63:1199–1215, 1981.

Rice, D. P., Feldman, J. J., and White, K. L. *The Current Burden of Illness in the United States* Washington, D.C.: National Academy of Sciences, 1977.

Rissanen, V., Romo, M., and Siltanen, P. Pre-hospital sudden death from ischemic heart disease. A post-mortem study. *Br. Heart J.* 40:1025–1033, 1978.

Robins, L. Interaction of setting and predisposition in explaining new behavior: Drug initiation behavior before, in, and after Vietnam. IN: *Longitudinal Research in Drug Use: Important Findings and Methodologies* (Kandel, D., ed.) Washington, D.C.: Hemisphere, 1978.

Rogot, E. Smoking and mortality among U.S. veterans. *J. Chronic Dis.* 27:189–203, 1974.

Rosett, H. L., Oulette, E. M., Weiner, L., et al. Therapy of heavy drinking during pregnancy. *J. Obstet. Gynecol.* 51:41–46, 1978.

Shapiro, S., Schlesinger, E. R., and Nesbitt, R. E. L. *Infant, Perinatal, Maternal and Childhood Mortality in the United States* Cambridge, Mass.: Harvard University Press, 1968.

Shekelle, R. B., Shryock, A. M., Paul, O., Lepper, M. Stamler, J., Liu, S., and Raynor, W. J. Diet, serum cholesterol, and death from coronary heart disease. The Western Electric Study. *N. Engl. J. Med.* 304:65–70, 1981.

Skrabal, F., Aubock, J., and Hortnagl, H. Low sodium/high potassium diet for prevention of hypertension: Probable mechanisms of action. *Lancet* 2:895–900, 1981.

Sokol, R. J. Alcohol and spontaneous abortion. *Lancet* 2:1079, 1980.

St. Leger, A. S., Cochrane, A. L., and Moore, F. Factors associated with cardiac mortality in developed countries with particular reference to the consumption of wine. *Lancet* 1:1017–1020, 1979.

Streissguth, A. P., Landesman-Dwyer, S., Martin, J. C., and Smith, D. W. Teratogenic effects of alcohol in humans and laboratory animals. *Science* 209:353–361, 1980.

Surgeon General Advisory on alcohol and pregnancy. *FDA Drug Bull.* 11:9–10, 1981.

Talbott, E., Kuller, L. H., Detre, K., and Perper, J. Biologic and psychosocial risk factors of sudden death from coronary disease in white women. *Am. J. Cardiol.* 39:858–864, 1977.

Theorell, T., Lind, E., Floderus, B. The relationship of disturbing life changes and emotions to the early development of myocardial infarction and other serious illnesses. *Int. J. Epidemiol.* 4:281–293, 1975.

Tobian, L. Hypertension and obesity. *N. Engl. J. Med.* 298:46–48, 1978.

Tobian, L. The relationship of salt to hypertension. *Am. J. Clin. Nutr.* 32:2739–2748, 1979.

United States Congress, Office of Technology Assessment *Assessment of Technologies for Determining Cancer Risks from the Environment* Washington, D.C.: U.S. Government Printing Office, 1981.

United States Department of Health, Education, and Welfare *Health United States, 1978* Washington, D.C.: U.S. Government Printing Office, 1978, DHEW Publ. No. (PHS) 78–1232.

United States Department of Health, Education, and Welfare *Smoking and Health* Washington, D.C.: U.S. Government Printing Office, 1979a, DHEW Publ. No. (PHS) 79–50066.

United States Department of Health, Education, and Welfare *Healthy People* Washington, D.C.: U.S. Government Printing Office, 1979b, DHEW Publ. No. (PHS) 79–55071.

United States Department of Health and Human Services *Promoting Health, Preventing Disease. Objectives for the Nation* Washington, D.C.: U.S. Government Printing Office, 1980a.

United States Department of Health and Human Services *The Health Consequences of Smoking for Women* Washington, D.C.: U.S. Government Printing Office, 1980b.

United States Department of Health and Human Services *Health United States, 1980, With Prevention Profile* Washington, D.C.: U.S. Government Printing Office, 1980c, DHHS Publ. No. (PHS) 81–1232.

Van Itallie, T. B. Obesity: Adverse effects on health and longevity. *Am. J. Clin. Nutr.* 32:2723–2733, 1979.

Vodak, P. A., Wood, P. D., Haskell, W. L., and Williams, P. T. HDL-cholesterol and other plasma lipid and lipoprotein concentrations in middle-aged male and female tennis players. *Metabolism* 29:745–752, 1980.

Weltman, A., Matter, S., and Stamford, B. A. Caloric restriction and/or mild exercise: Effects on serum lipids and body composition. *Am. J. Clin. Nutr.* 33:1002–1009, 1980.

Wigfield, W. J., and Hill, W. J. Alcohol and mortality. *Lancet* 1:1052, 1981.

Wolf, S., Almy, T. P., Bachrach, W. H., Spiro, H. M., Sturdevant, R. A. L., and Weiner, H. The role of stress in peptic ulcer disease. *J. Hum. Stress* 5:27–37, 1979.

Wood, P. D., Haskell, W. L., Stern, M. P., et al. Plasma lipoprotein distributions in male and female runners. *Ann. N.Y. Acad. Sci.* 301:748–762, 1977.

Wynder, E. L., and Hoffman, D. Tobacco and health. A societal challenge. *N. Engl. J. Med.* 300:894–903, 1979.

Zook, C. J., and Moore, F. D. High-cost users of medical care. *N. Engl. J. Med.* 302:996–1002, 1980.

II

SCIENTIFIC OPPORTUNITIES: MAJOR DISORDERS AND CONDITIONS

3
Stress, Coping, and Health

Begun early in this century, stress research may have been the earliest scientific examination of the effects of behavior on health. As investigators began to learn how the brain monitors and controls the rest of the body, they raised questions about how such mechanisms might affect disease processes. Scientists such as Walter Cannon and Hans Selye demonstrated that exposure to severe physical or psychological conditions produced profound hormonal and other physiological responses, some of which could result in permanent physical injury or death. Such clinical investigators as Franz Alexander, Arthur Mirsky, Roy Grinker, and Stewart Wolf demonstrated associations in human beings between some diseases and certain persistently disruptive situations.

The Institute of Medicine (1981; Elliott and Eisdorfer, 1982) conducted recently a study reported as *Research on Stress and Human Health*. An interdisciplinary group of scientists and clinicians assessed the current state of research on stress and sought promising areas of inquiry that might advance the field. They concluded that a large body of knowledge already has been assembled, much of it directly relevant to the biobehavioral sciences. In addition, they identified a number of directions for future research at biological, psychological, social, and clinical levels.

Psychobiology of Stress Responses

Do some types of experience increase the likelihood of illness, at least for some people? For example, can bereavement make people more vulnerable? Are some more vulnerable than others? How could a stressful experience make someone ill? What are the biological mechanisms of stress responses? How can they precipitate illness, or perhaps promote health? Is it possible to protect against harmful stressful experiences, possibly through specific protective coping strategies? What contribution is made by social support networks, mutual aid relationships, and self-help groups? Could discovery of biological mechanisms lead to specific preventive or therapeutic interventions, or to self-help for people at high risk? These are all subjects for study not only to satisfy long-standing human curiosity but also for the future relief of much human suffering.

Biological research has helped to explain the ways in which human beings have adapted, although much more remains to be learned (Luria et al., 1981). Adaptation occurs on all organizational levels. For example, exposure to a very cold environment produces changes at the level of molecules within the cell, of whole cells, of organs, of functional systems, and of the whole organism—what is usually called behavior. Biological sciences typically have focused on the lower levels, the component parts of the organism; behavioral sciences mainly have studied whole organisms or aggregates of them. An adequate understanding of human adaptation will require both biological and behavioral perspectives.

In biological research, behavior is viewed in a framework of adaptation. How does behavior meet adaptive requirements to survive and reproduce? Sometimes adaptation is easy and unremarkable; other times it is difficult, even alarming. These latter instances are called stressful. Fundamental motivations incline everyone to do what is necessary to ensure survival and reproduction (Hamburg, 1963). Throughout history, survival criteria in most societies have been extended into a set of basic values for a person of worth. If basic values—however defined in a particular group—are threatened, an experience becomes stressful. Such a drastic environmental condition produces a flow of adaptive changes that affects the organism at all levels of biological organization.

Neuroregulatory Systems Involved in Stress

The interests of the biomedical and biobehavioral sciences come together in considering pathways through which the brain controls the endocrine and autonomic nervous systems (Krieger and Hughes, 1980). Over the past three decades, much has been learned about these systems and their roles in mediating human responses to changing conditions.

Major advances are being made in understanding biochemical, anatomical, physiological, pharmacological, pathological, and behavioral aspects of the nervous system (Hubel, 1979). For example, less than 30 years ago many students of the brain believed that communication among brain nerve cells had to be electrical; only in the 1950s did the overwhelming importance of chemical communication become clear. Ten years ago, fewer than a dozen chemicals had been identified as probable neuroregulators in the brain. In the past few years, many more have been found, precise maps of brain distribution have been made for several neuroregulators, and good progress has been made in clarifying the function of some of them in normal and abnormal behavior (Barchas et al., 1978). Many neuroregulator systems are involved in stress reactions. The catecholamines—compounds of the adrenalin family (epinephrine, norepinephrine) found both in the adrenal gland and in several parts of the brain—have long been linked to stress. Another relevant class of substances is the endorphins, recently discovered morphinelike peptides in the brain, pituitary gland, and adrenals that are involved in perception of and response to pain. Pain is closely related to other stress responses.

In the past few years, neuroscientists have discovered and begun to study dozens of neuroactive substances whose presence was previously unsuspected (Snyder, 1980; Bloom, 1981; Krieger and Martin, 1981). Much of this research is possible because of new techniques—fluorimetric, enzymatic, gas chromatographic, mass spectrometric, and radioimmunologic— for detecting and measuring these neuroactive compounds, their precursors, and their metabolic products. In addition, researchers are beginning to find ways to investigate in living animals and human beings the basic regulatory mechanisms that control neuroregulator functions such as synthesis, storage, release, receptor interaction, and metabolism.

Advances in sample collection now enable monitoring of nearly all parts of the body, including the brain, while the subject moves about freely or undergoes controlled exposure to stressors or other behavioral circumstances. Scientists have long associated blood catecholamine concentrations with stress responses, but only in the past few years have they been able to take small blood samples from freely moving human subjects and measure how these substances change during exposure to a stressor (Dimsdale and Moss, 1980). In combination, animal and human studies should provide a wealth of new information about the effects of stress.

A change in personal circumstances stimulates an appraisal of the change, usually automatically, but sometimes with conscious deliberation. Such appraisals may be freely translated into a set of questions of direct relevance to adaptation. What is it? What does it mean? What responses are possible? Is action required? If so, what action would be effective in meeting the challenge? Such questions, even if vaguely formulated, are answered in ways that produce coordinated metabolic and cardiovascular alterations that prepare the organism for action. The course of action is guided by the brain as reappraisal proceeds in light of continuing feedback. Recent research has done much to clarify brain circuits that mediate these integrative processes (Nauta and Feritag, 1979).

Early stress researchers looked primarily at biological stress responses, especially in the form of changes in hormones of the adrenal gland—catecholamines made by the adrenal medulla and corticosteroids made by the adrenal cortex (Selye, 1950). Many other hormones have since been found to be responsive to stress. Among these are prolactin, growth hormone, insulin, testosterone, and luteinizing hormone (Rose, 1980). A growing body of evidence indicates that hormonal responses to stress are quite variable among individuals and from circumstance to circumstance. They can be affected by many biological and psychosocial mediators.

Stressors activate both the adrenal cortex and the adrenal medulla, but the two parts work in different ways. For both, the major control related to the response to stress is through the brain; the brain controls all of the hormonal responses to stress. For the adrenal cortex, messages from areas of the brain are sent to the pituitary gland, sometimes referred to as the "master gland"; the pituitary secretes a polypeptide messenger, adrenocorticotropic hormone (ACTH), which goes via the bloodstream to the adrenal cortex, where it stimulates corticosteroid synthesis. For the adrenal medulla, a message is sent directly from the brain through nerve cells; those impulses stimulate the release of the adrenal medullary hormones, particularly epinephrine. Curiosity about stress has done much to clarify the structure and function of brain-adrenal relations and the effects of adrenal secretions on most other parts of the body.

In general, the adrenals are activated by situations that elicit a sense of threat, alarm, or distress (Levine and Ursin, 1980). But it is interesting to note that adrenal activation is not limited to such circumstances. For example, unpredictability can be a fairly potent stimulus for this system in human beings and other animals. If a strange situation is encountered or established and predictable events are altered so that expectations are no longer met, adrenal activation is likely to occur.

Elevated corticosteroid levels are often observed under stressful conditions. For a particular person, the more distressing the experience, the greater the hormone elevation (Hamburg, 1962). Such elevations in adrenal hormone levels may be sustained or recurrent for weeks or even months, if the stress persists; but adaptation usually occurs rather quickly. The extent of hormone elevation is related to the degree of distress and to the effectiveness of coping behavior. Corticosteroids and their metabolites can affect brain function and behavior. Variations in metabolism of these hormones may have a bearing on a person's response to major stresses such as the loss of a close human relationship (cf. Chapter 9).

The past few decades have seen the rise of research on the coordinated functioning of nervous and endocrine systems in the adaptation of the whole organism to environmental conditions. Until recently, the brain and the endocrine glands were viewed largely as separate entities mediating quite different functions. The brain was thought mainly to mediate the organism's relation to the environment through behavior—oriented to the external environment. The endocrine system was regarded mainly as regulating reproduction, growth, and metabolism—oriented to the internal environment.

A major reason for believing that behavior and the endocrine system must be independent involved the apparent physical isolation of the two systems. Several decades ago, it was known that there were no connecting nerves between the anterior pituitary and the rest of the brain. An important advance came with discovery of a "portal system," a distinctively rich network of blood vessels that link the hypothalamus at the base of the brain with the pituitary gland located immediately beneath it. These blood vessels could, in principle, carry chemical messengers from brain to pituitary and thence to adrenals, gonads, thyroid, and elsewhere, thus influencing every tissue in the body.

Geoffrey Harris (1955) showed that these vessels did indeed transmit brain substances that had potent effects on the pituitary, but the amounts were minute and their chemical compositions were unknown. To isolate, purify, and characterize each of these substances seemed almost impossible. In Hans Selye's pioneering stress research laboratory in Montreal, Roger Guillemin and Andrew Schally began a major effort to meet this challenge. Later, they continued their work in separate laboratories elsewhere. With imaginative, painstaking, and extensive work, they discovered and precisely characterized several hypothalamic hormones that are produced in the brain and pass through the portal system to regulate the anterior pituitary. For this achievement, they shared a Nobel prize in 1977 (Guillemin, 1978; Schally, 1978).

The basic insight of their discovery has to do with coordination of the body. The cells must "talk" to each other in some way. The molecular and cellular components must function as a whole, particularly in adapting to changes in life conditions. In this view, the brain and endocrine system are a functional unit in adaptation. Schally, Guillemin, and collaborators helped make this integration of the nervous and endocrine systems a major object of research.

The research on hypothalamic hormones provided not only new insights but also better methods for peptide analysis. These new techniques, coinciding with the discovery of receptors in the brain and other related advances, have led to a burst of neuropeptide research in the past few years. In addition to their intrinsic worth, the discoveries being made have major implications for clinical pharmacology and other therapies in the remainder of this century, based not only on the new technologies but also on a deeper understanding of adaptation.

A particularly interesting direction of neuroendocrine research has involved the elucidation of influences of higher brain centers via the hypothalamus on the anterior pituitary/adrenocortical system (Sowers, 1980). Attention has been centered chiefly on the limbic system. Several workers have shown that stimulation of some limbic areas with chronically implanted electrodes in awake mammals, including primates, can substantially increase or decrease the circulating concentrations of adrenal and other hormones. There is a growing body of information on the neural circuitry underlying influences on endocrine and autonomic responses of varying external and internal circumstances (Sawchenko and Swanson, 1981).

Of special importance in stress responses are the hypothalamic-limbic-midbrain circuits (Usdin et al., 1980). They strongly affect the endocrine system and autonomic nervous system, and hence the cardiovascular, gastrointestinal, and immune systems. Thus, they provide a physiological mechanism through which psychosocial factors can affect the health of the body. But the details of the ways in which specific stressful situations contribute to cetain pathologies in specific individuals remain to be worked out. These circuits also are involved substantially in mediating adaptive functions of memory, appraisal, and motivational-emotional responses. Acting in concert with the greatly developed neocortex in human beings, they play a vital role in appraising the functional significance of ongoing events and thereby paving the way for adaptive responses.

During the last three decades, significant progress has been made in understanding the role of the central nervous system in controlling normal cardiovascular function (Institute of Medicine, 1981; Solomon et al., 1981). This knowledge enhances appreciation of ways in which environmental or behavioral factors can contribute to disease. A wealth of evidence suggests that the origins of common cardiovascular diseases are multifactorial. Thus, the effects of stress on the pathogenesis of cardiovascular disorders must be viewed in the context of other metabolic or circulatory abnormalities that contribute to the disease process. Repeated, sustained, stressful experiences well may affect the cardiovascular system in such ways that some people—especially those genetically predisposed—develop high blood pressure (Shapiro et al., 1979). In this context, it is important to note that circulatory changes associated with alarm reactions to severe stressors resemble those that accompany the development of experimental and human hypertension. This suggests, but does not prove, that stimuli that bring about the onset of hypertension have an effect on brain mechanisms that regulate cardiovascular function. Animal experiments and human clinical research increasingly point toward involvement of brain and behavior in a sizable fraction of cardiovascular diseases (Jenkins, 1976). Neuroendocrine responses under consideration here are pertinent to cardiovascular responses under stress. These problems are considered further in Chapter 7.

Because it controls the adrenal cortex, ACTH has been of special interest to stress researchers in recent years, as studies of it have become technically feasible. ACTH is present in many neurons in various brain regions. The work on "releasing factors" in the brain that led to the discovery of the hypothalamic hormones began several decades ago in the search for the ACTH-releasing factor, while trying to understand the psychobiology of stress. It is ironic that this hypothalamic hormone has been the most difficult to characterize chemically. Recently, there have been reports of the exact structure of a peptide that stimulates secretion of ACTH both in cultured anterior pituitary cells and in whole animals (Vale et al., 1981). The authors suggest that this molecule is likely to be a key signal in mediating and integrating an organism's endocrine, visceral, and behavioral responses to stress. This hypothesis opens possibilities for clarifying the mechanisms of that stress response and for developing drugs to modify it.

Of additional interest is the discovery that ACTH is closely linked to beta-endorphin, one of a family of recently discovered peptides that have actions resembling those of morphine or heroin (cf. Chapter 1). ACTH and beta-endorphin share a common precursor whose structure has very recently been established by use of recombinant DNA techniques. Thus, it may well be that ACTH and endorphins are secreted together under conditions appraised by a subject as dangerous. This suggests that they may mediate a closely related set of adaptive functions. Probably, they facilitate the organism's ability to respond to stress, withstand pain, mobilize for action, and do what is necessary to cope with the challenge (Snyder, 1980; Bloom, 1981; Krieger and Martin, 1981).

Biobehavioral Aspects of Stress

Clinical observations and animal experiments have long suggested that intensely stressful experiences can have long-lasting effects on behavior. In some respects, people learn best when they are alert, attentive, and aroused. When severely threatened, they often learn indelibly to avoid a similar situation in the future. Such avoidance responses are crucial for survival. They are easy to learn and hard to forget (Hamburg, 1963). There is now evidence that hormones released into the blood during stress facilitate such learning and may have a role in chemical storage of memory (McGaugh et al., 1980).

In one line of inquiry, it has been shown that an animal's memory can be influenced by altering the activity of various neuroregulators. Memory can be impaired by inhibiting the synthesis of epinephrine and norepinephrine and improved by stimulating their secretion or injecting norepinephrine directly into the brain (McGaugh et al., 1980). Retention of newly learned responses can be influenced by peptide hormones and catecholamines, as well as by drugs that affect hormone metabolism (de Wied and Bohus, 1979; Bloom, 1981; Iversen, 1981). These findings provide support for the view that processes associated with emotional responses modulate memory storage (Kety, 1970).

Two peptides are of special interest in this context: ACTH and vasopressin, a stress-responsive hormone of the posterior pituitary (de Wied and Bohus, 1979). ACTH enhances avoidance learning and prolongs avoidance after the noxious stimulus has been removed. Moreover, an active molecular fragment of ACTH facilitates learning and remembering in some animal studies, although findings in human subjects are less clear. Vasopressin produces a long-term delay in extinction of avoidance responses that have been learned in stressful conditions. Recent neuroanatomical and neurochemical studies suggest that vasopressin interacts with norepinephrine in the hypothalamus and limbic system to influence learning. In addition, the effect of vasopressin on the peripheral autonomic nervous system, including its effects in elevating blood pressure, may also influence learning under stress.

Converging evidence suggests that vasopressin and other neuropeptides act at both peripheral and central nervous system sites in an integrated fashion (Bloom, 1981; Iversen, 1981). Under stress, both central and peripheral components of the nervous system, acting jointly with elements of the endocrine system, induce behavioral arousal and concomitant visceral arousal. Vasopressin, ACTH, and norepinephrine may all be involved, in the brain and elsewhere, to produce a coordinated physiological and behavioral response. One aspect of this response is a central feature of human adaptation—learning how to deal with the problem in the future.

Recent research has helped greatly to clarify the nature of receptors in the nervous and endocrine systems. Studies of receptor interactions of agonists and antagonists are uncovering the mechanisms of action of neuroregulators in synaptic transmission. Conditions influencing receptor function are being worked out, as are the consequences of a substance binding to a receptor. Both pre- and post-synaptic receptors are of intense interest. This research has direct implications for development of more effective drugs in treatment of cardiovascular disorders (Frishman, 1981).

In this context, a line of inquiry of both basic and clinical interest involves the analysis of benzodiazepine receptors in the brain (Snyder, 1981). Several drugs of this class are useful clinically to stop seizures, to diminish anxiety, and to facilitate sleep. A recent Institute of Medicine study documented the great extent to which these drugs are prescribed in medical practice (Institute of Medicine, 1979; Solomon et al., 1979). A conservative estimate is that 8,000 tons of benzodiazepines were consumed in the United States in 1977. For some years, benzodiazepine antianxiety drugs have been the most widely prescribed of all drugs. Can a deeper understanding of the mechanism of action of such drugs clarify the psychobiology of anxiety and related stress responses?

In the late 1970s, investigators discovered highly specific binding sites in the brain for benzodiazepines (Braestrup and Squire, 1978). Techniques developed earlier for opiate receptors were used to show that binding occurred with several benzodiazepines and that the binding sites were specific for this class of drugs. Moreover, there was a close parallel between the binding affinity of different benzodiazepines and their therapeutic potencies. Further research has suggested a link between the anatomical distribution of benzodiazepine receptors and the pharmacological effects of these drugs (Tallman et al., 1978). Particularly high concentrations are found in portions of the limbic system involved in regulation of emotional responses.

Behavioral, electrophysiological, pharmacological, and biochemical evidence now indicates that the benzodiazepines act at specific receptor sites differentially distributed in the brain (Tallman et al., 1978). The benzodiazepine receptor interacts with a receptor for the major inhibitory neuroregulator gamma-aminobutyric acid (GABA), enhancing its inhibitory properties. These receptors also may interact with an endogenous benzodiazepine-like substance, but this has yet to be isolated. Recent research suggests that these receptors have two recognition sites: one for benzodiazepines and another for GABA. Their interaction is currently being analyzed. This work has stimulated the development of new measurement tools that are useful clinically and for basic research. The search for an endogenous antianxiety substance is a matter of great interest for fundamental behavioral biology and for clinical medicine.

Individual Differences in Vulnerability to Stress

Everyone is exposed to stressful experiences; yet for any noxious agent (biological or psychosocial), individuals can have markedly different responses. Pertinent genetic and environmental influences are beginning to be understood, and studies of such factors will deserve attention in the years ahead, especially in view of the advances occurring in genetics. Applications of these advances to human problems are increasing sharply.

Genetic Factors

Studies of how genetic factors affect elements of response to stressful experience require identification of the genes involved in susceptibility and resistance to particular diseases and conditions. Research on interactions of such genes with specific environmental factors may suggest sharply focused preventive interventions.

More information is needed about how various types of stress alter rates of synthesis or utilization of brain neuroregulators and whether there are times when synthesis cannot keep up with demand. The same consideration applies to the adrenocortical response to stress. Some clinical disorders are characterized by an inability to respond to stress. Genetically determined biochemical regulation of brain amine metabolism or corticosteroid metabolism could prove to be of clinical significance.

Early studies of the genetics of brain amine biochemistry found differences in brain concentrations of serotonin and norepinephrine in the brain for some inbred strains of mice and rats (Barchas et al., 1975). There have followed investigations to determine whether these differences result from genetically controlled changes in synthesis, metabolism, utilization, or responses to stress (Ciaranello, 1979). Although little research has yet been done on these problems, there is reason to believe that genetic factors may affect aspects of these mechanisms. Thus, it is possible that two people might send the same number of nerve impulses to the adrenal medulla; yet, because of a genetic difference, one might secrete much more epinephrine than the other. Such a difference might have behavioral consequences when the epinephrine reaches various target organs, including adaptively critical brain cells of the hypothalamus.

Genetically determined variations in the biogenic amines or corticosteroids and their physiological regulation might create substantial individual differences in emotional and endocrine responses to stressful situations (Vogel and Motulsky, 1979). Some individuals may, in the face of severe life stresses, be genetically predisposed to depressive reactions, intense anxiety, or elevated blood pressure. A variety of clinical disorders arise partly from genetically determined alterations in normal biochemical processes that must interact in complex ways with environmental factors such as jeopardy to crucial human relationships.

An understanding of stress genetics requires investigation of the genetic basis for differences in the endocrine and behavioral reactions to stress and its consequences (Gershon et al., 1981). These reactions range from effects on perception of external and internal stimuli to influences on the responses of body tissues and brain function to the hormones released during stress. Most research in this area has focused on adrenal corticosteroids and catecholamines. Equally important, however, are the neuroregulators in the brain and in the peripheral nervous system that modulate stress responses.

What is needed is the identification of genes responsible for observed differences. The effects on the stress response for each identified gene then must be investigated to establish which are regulatory and which are structural. Genetic mapping of these variants can identify regulatory sites. Dynamic processes such as enzyme induction or the modulation of receptor molecules also merit study. The systems should be examined in developing and in mature animals, because stress susceptibility changes during development. Research into major pathological mutations affecting the stress response systems of experimental animals deserves high priority; such studies can provide useful animal models of specific human diseases.

There is a great need for integration of genetic research with studies of environmentally caused variation in responses to stress. Individuals can respond to the same environmental variable quite differently, and the patterns of immediate and delayed responses to stressors also may differ markedly.

Psychosocial Factors

Another set of factors that affect vulnerability to stressful life experiences lies in the social environment (Rahe and Arthur, 1978). Epidemiological studies of varying design—using different populations, health outcome measures, and stress indicators—suggest that life events can increase the risk of a variety of disorders (Elliott and Eisdorfer, 1982). Studies of the effects on health of natural or man-made disasters suggest that about half of physically unharmed survivors experience an acute emotional, physical, or psychosomatic consequence; many suffer long-term changes in health. More common events such as bereavement, physical injury, or retirement also are associated with an increased risk for becoming ill. Illness rates are elevated among workers in jobs involving very high levels of workload, responsibility, and interpersonal or role conflicts. Community disintegration, a lack of social supports, and the number of recent stressful events in an individual's life also can affect health, productivity, and even life expectancy.

Physical disorders in which stressors have been implicated as risk factors include bronchial asthma, influenza, peptic ulcers, hypertension, hyperthyroidism, and sudden cardiac death. Stressors also seem to be risk factors in the precipitation of such mental disorders as depression, schizophrenia, alcoholism, and drug abuse. This does not mean that stressful experience is the sole or even the primary cause of these disorders. Historically, simple cause-effect hypotheses of stress and disease have been prominent in stress research (Elliott and Eisdorfer, 1982). Such concepts ignore factors that mediate steps between being exposed to a stressor and consequently developing a disease. Both genetic and environmental mediators shape the biological reactions and clinical consequences of stressful experience. The relations doubtless will be difficult to disentangle, but the problems are too important and the prospects too promising to justify neglect.

A recent body of research into the relationship between human attachments, illness, and mortality is providing a growing amount of evidence that people whose human attachments are weak also are more prone to illness and early death (Berkman and Syme, 1979; Berkman, 1981). Although mechanisms of such vulnerability are not yet firmly established, it appears that support systems can buffer stressful experiences. Such networks also can influence the use of health services and adherence to medical regimens. This is pertinent to the requirements for behavior change in smoking cessation, weight control, or long-term adherence to antihypertensive medication. Social support systems facilitate the development of coping strategies that help people contain distress within tolerable limits, maintain self-esteem, preserve interpersonal relationships, meet requirements of new situations, and prepare for the future (Hamburg and Killilea, 1979). An interesting area for future research will be the experimental construction of social support networks where natural ones are lacking.

Coping Strategies

Studies of coping behavior in distressing circumstances fall mainly into three classes: (1) people in life-threatening situations, such as serious injury (Hamburg, 1974; Cohen and Lazarus, 1979); (2) people in drastic psychosocial transitions such as that from high school to college or a major personal loss (Coelho et al., 1963; Glick et al., 1974); (3) people experiencing a major transition of the life course such as puberty or pregnancy (Shereshefsky and Yarrow, 1973; Hamburg, 1980). A literature on coping, adaptation, and health has emerged over the past 30 years (Coelho et al., 1970; Coelho et al., 1974; Frankenhaeuser, 1980; Levine and Ursin, 1980; Miller, 1980; Coelho, 1981).

One striking observation by many investigators is that individuals evince a great diversity of responses under a given set of environmental conditions. The perception of threat depends on cognitive processes of appraisal, through which the events take on personal meaning. Among fundamental motivations that affect such meaning are those concerned with individual survival, self-esteem, close attachment with significant others, and a sense of belonging in a valued group.

Coping Tasks

The individual in stressful circumstances needs to accomplish the following tasks: (1) contain distress within tolerable limits; (2) maintain self-esteem; (3) preserve interpersonal relationships; and (4) meet the conditions of the new situation. Behavior under stress tends to convert the unfamiliar to a familiar condition, thus making the environment predictable. Greater predictability enhances the feasibility of making adaptive responses. These may be somatic, cognitive, emotional, interpersonal, or organizational, and they may proceed on various levels of awareness. Psychological preparation for stressful transitions offers some promise for preventing human suffering. For each of the four tasks mentioned above, multiple strategies can be employed at various levels of awareness. These strategies reflect not only the developmental history of the person but also the different circumstances surrounding each transitional situation, as well as cultural influences that indicate preference for certain strategies. Some are readily drawn from cultural prescriptions or institutional arrangements; others require much improvising by the individual.

Individual Aspects of Coping Strategies

Observational studies have been carried out in clinical and field settings where people must cope with very difficult questions of survival and physical impairment. For example, studies of badly burned patients and of patients with severe poliomyelitis (Hamburg et al., 1953; Visotsky et al., 1961; Friedman et al., 1963; Schoenberg et al., 1974) probed questions about the difficult and disturbing aspects of the adaptive problems faced by these severely ill patients and the psychological strategies such patients utilized in attempting to cope with these problems.

The psychological threats of a nearly fatal injury or severe prolonged illness place patients in danger of being overwhelmed by emotional distress. Many patients at first tend to keep unpleasant thoughts and feelings out of awareness by minimizing painful stimuli through tight control of all emotions. The patient's attitude is, in effect, "I will not think about any of these unpleasant things; if I cannot avoid them, I will not allow myself to have any feelings about them." A few patients go so far as to deny any recognition of injury altogether.

Short-term coping strategies usually are replaced by processes that help the individual face threatening implications and deal with them. Most patients eventually face the actual conditions of their illness, seek information about the factors relevant to recovery, and assess probable long-term limitations (Hamburg and Adams, 1967). The time of transition from avoidance behavior to acceptance varies greatly from patient to patient—from a few weeks to a much longer period. A variety of coping strategies, employed at every level of awareness, are used in making this transition. The importance of close, emotionally supportive relationships during this transition is manifested in many ways. In general, the effectiveness of coping behavior is strongly related to feelings not only of being valued by significant other people but of being indispensable to them.

Intermediate goals are typical and useful steps in trying to achieve a long-term physical goal. They share certain features: (1) the time unit is relatively short term (weeks or months); (2) the goal is readily visible, bearing a recognizable relation to existing capabilities; and (3) the goal is probably attainable. Attainment of such goals is intrinsically rewarding. Most patients undergo a series of successive approximations through which they eventually face and accept the physical limitations that they would have much preferred to avoid. These approximations amount to a series of small steps leading to ultimate recognition of a painful reality. With this recognition usually comes heightened ability to adapt to the new situation and make use of whatever potentialities it offers for dependable gratification, self-respect, and reliable relationships with significant other people.

A few studies have followed severely injured patients and their families over several years (Andreasen et al., 1972). These studies indicate that mastery of profoundly stressful challenges ultimately can strengthen personal resourcefulness. Concern with the welfare of others, enhanced solidarity in family relations, and renewed religious faith enter prominently into follow-up accounts. Many handicapped patients take pride in self-rehabilitation, exercising for long hours and meticulously following rehabilitation plans. As their strength improves, such patients immerse themselves in work, thus rebuilding self-esteem and distracting their own attention from intensely anxiety-provoking areas.

Common, though not universal, patterns of effective coping have repeatedly been observed in natural settings of formidable difficulty (Edwards and Kelly, 1980; Hamburg and Hamburg, 1980). Listed somewhat in sequential order in Table 3.1, they focus on the individual process of working out a coping strategy, or an interrelated set of strategies. These observations reflect what people tend to do under stress, even if they do not realize it. The time scale usually is months. Usually, this sequence of events is fully observable within a year after onset of a major stressful transition. Each basic theme has many specific variations.

Social Aspects of Coping Strategies

Much coping behavior involves individual improvizations to work out an implicit strategy for mastering a set of difficult tasks; but it almost always

TABLE 3.1   Common Steps in Effective Coping with Severely Stressful Circumstances

---

1. People under stress tend to regulate timing and dosage of awareness of threat; they seek a gradual transition from avoidance to recognition, if the threat is highly distressing.
2. People under stress tend to handle multiple, concurrent stresses by processing them sequentially, one at a time.
3. People under stress seek information regarding the task from multiple sources.
4. People under stress create expectations, hopeful if possible.
5. People under stress will delineate manageable units, focusing on intermediate goals that are visible and probably reachable.
6. People under stress rehearse task-specific behavior; they trend to practice in a safe situation. This often involves restoration of an affectionate, respectful relationship with a person who has previously been important in the person's life.
7. Task-specific behavior is then tested in relevant situations, preferably of no more than moderate risk.
8. As new behavior patterns are tested, feedback is appraised for adequacy of performance and personal satisfaction.
9. More than one approach is tried, often a predominant and subsidiary approach.
10. In due course, commitment is made to a promising approach; it is pursued with vigor and persistence.
11. Buffers are constructed against disappointment; contingency plans are made for the inevitable disappointments of living.

SOURCE: Hamburg and Hamburg (1980).

occurs in social context, and that context makes a difference. Under stress, the first response is often one of seeking affiliation. Established attachments are most highly valued under these conditions, but many other affiliations are useful. For really stressful experiences, almost any affiliation will help, at least transiently. With human anchorage, information seeking can proceed in a supportive context. Individuals tend to use such social contexts to: (1) clarify channels available; (2) guide priorities; (3) provide structured preparation; and (4) obtain specific prescriptions for behavior.

Prevention Aspects of Coping Strategies

In studies of people in life-threatening situations and other major transitions, observers have been impressed by the diversity of patterns of coping behavior that prove to be useful to different persons and to the same person in different circumstances. Such observations suggest a certain durability in those patterns that prove personally rewarding. There is often a cumulative quality to the progression of coping sequences through different stresses over an extended time. Within a moderate range of severity, resolution of earlier disappointments tends to be helpful in coping with problems encountered later in life. So it is useful to view coping behavior in psychosocial transitions as complex skills acquired through long sequences of experiences, with considerable transfer of learning from one stressful episode to another. One contributory factor is the enhancement of self-esteem that tends to result from mastery of difficult and distressing experiences. In general, mastery tends to contribute to a sense of efficacy or resourcefulness, based partly on the development of specific skills and partly on confidence from dealing effectively with earlier similar situations.

It should be feasible to use knowledge of tasks and strategies in a situation of major transition in ways that heighten the ability of many individuals to cope with difficult aspects of their experiences (Moos, 1976). Future research must identify useful strategies and determine how they relate to an individual's available repertoire.

Several attempts have been made to apply concepts of coping to disease prevention and health promotion. One direction of inquiry involves the 10- to 15-year-old age group (Institute of Medicine, 1978). Early adolescence is an important and neglected phase of human development that lends itself to analysis in terms of developmental tasks and coping strategies. It is a phase during which drastic changes occur internally and externally at about the same time. Many adolescents are not prepared to cope with this conjunction of stressful events. It is also a time characterized by exploratory behavior, including the use of intoxicating substances, cigarettes, and vehicles (cf. Chapter 14). One approach to preparing adolescents to cope uses peer counseling in junior and senior high schools; this approach rests on an analysis of developmental tasks and coping strategies (Hamburg and Hamburg, 1975). Relying on the credibility of peers in adolescence, such programs train students to help other students. This may be done by clarifying the tasks and available strategies in a particular social setting, by providing information on basic processes of interpersonal relationships, and by providing continuing supervision to the student counselors. The approach has been employed successfully, for example, in prevention of heavy smoking (cf. Chapter 5).

Enough experience has accumulated for careful innovations with systematic assessment at predictable major transitions for every age group. In essence, this involves anticipating drastic changes in life experience and helping individuals prepare for them. To be effective, preparation must entail accurate information from credible sources in a way that is personally meaningful. Moreover, such information is most likely to be applied if there is opportunity first to test and try its utility in relative safety and then gradually to apply it in less structured settings that still provide feedback to the individual of improved knowledge and skill.

Decision Making in Stressful Health-Related Circumstances

One fruitful line of inquiry places adaptive behavior in the context of decision making and problem solving. Health-related decisions usually require a conflict of motivations, often in the face of incomplete or unclear choices. Decisions about treatment of illness often involve acceptance of short-term losses such as the physical discomforts of surgery in order to attain the long-term goal of counteracting a structural defect or a disease. Decisions are particularly threatening when all available alternatives present severe anticipated losses and uncertain expected gains.

Patterns of Decision Making

Janis and Mann (1977) describe five basic patterns of coping with realistic threats (Table 3.2). These patterns were derived from an analysis of the research literature on how people react to emergency warnings and public health messages that urge protective actions. The first two patterns may save time and emotional distress, but they often are inadequate for a crucial choice. Similarly, defensive avoidance and hypervigilance can be adaptive, but they are more often inadequate if the problem involves serious threats over a long period of time. Consequently, all four tend to be defective decision-making modes. The fifth pattern, vigilance, may be maladaptive if danger is imminent and an immediate response is required but usually leads to valid decisions if time is available.

TABLE 3.2 Patterns of Coping with Realistic Threats

Unconflicted Persistence The decision maker complacently carries on with established behavior, ignoring information about the risk of losses.

Unconflicted Change The decision maker uncritically adopts a new course of salient or strongly recommended action.

Defensive Avoidance The decision maker avoids conflict by delaying, shifting responsibility to someone else or constructing wishful rationalizations that bolster one attractive option while ignoring others.

Hypervigilance The decision maker searches frantically for a way out of the dilemma and hastily adopts one course of action that seems to promise immediate relief, giving little consideration to the consequences of that action.

Vigilance The decision maker searches carefully for relevant information and appraises options deliberately before making a choice.

SOURCE: Janis and Mann (1977).

In this framework, the coping pattern is determined by the presence or absence of three conditions: awareness of substantial risks for whichever alternative is chosen; hope of finding a better alternative; and belief that there is adequate time to search and deliberate before a decision is required. The approach is relevant to a variety of health-related decisions. For example, it suggests the value of intervening to overcome defensive avoidance of health-relevant information via the technique of "emotional role playing." Emotional role playing in antismoking clinics can produce long-term changes in attitudes of personal vulnerability and cigarette consumption among heavy smokers (Janis and Mann, 1977). The technique also has promise for other health-relevant decisions, including alcohol intake (Toomey, 1972).

Facilitation of Decision Making

How can health-relevant information be used effectively to change behavior for health? Warnings can increase motivation for decision making and behavior change. Information about illness, treatment, or prevention can prepare a person for what lies ahead. Much research has attempted to clarify the conditions under which warnings and other information are most likely to be effective.

Field experiments indicate that advance warnings combined with accurate reassurances can serve to "inoculate" people against coming stressful experiences. Such preparation can enhance adherence to difficult decisions. In one approach, stress inoculation is given shortly after a decision is made but before it is implemented. Such accurate preparatory information helps the individual to anticipate a threat, start working through anxiety or grief, and make plans for coping effectively. Such information also helps give the individual a sense of control over threatening events.

Much of the evidence on effectiveness of stress inoculation comes from studies of patients voluntarily undergoing abdominal surgery or painful medical treatments. Laboratory studies indicate that people are less likely to experience intense distress or extreme changes in attitude when confronted with an unpleasant experience if they can anticipate the unpleasant event. But some studies reveal that such information alone, without coping recommendations, is ineffective (Janis, in press). Future research must determine ways in which preparation can best be achieved for different populations and different health-relevant conditions. Such decisions may involve adherence to a difficult but valuable therapeutic regimen or involve giving up enjoyable habits in the interest of disease prevention.

Importance of Perceived Control

The tendency to deal actively with environmental conditions and threatening events is a fundamental aspect of human adaptability. A promising line of inquiry recently has related this tendency to health in novel ways in the form of perceived control (Janis and Rodin, 1979).

A personal sense of control entails expectations of having the power and opportunity to select preferred goals and means of gaining those goals. Perceived control also refers to a belief that the individual's actions will influence valued outcomes. Perceived control is important for health-relevant behavior because strong social constraints and physical restrictions tend to increase psychological stress, whereas adequate control tends to enhance coping skills. Control processes also are important in achieving commitment to health-enhancing behavior patterns. In the research literature on actual and perceived control over present or impending harm, two directions of stress reduction emerge: self-regulated administration, which fosters control, is personally rewarding and encouraging; a sense of control in the face of uncertain threats leads to increased predictability and hence more effective action.

Some serious problems in caring for the elderly are examined elsewhere in this report (Chapter 11). One application of control-oriented coping is of special interest in that population (Langer and Rodin 1976; Rodin, 1980). A field study used an intervention to encourage elderly nursing home residents to make a greater number of choices and feel more in control of day-to-day events. The study attempted to determine whether the decline in health, alertness, and activity that so often occurs among the aged in nursing homes could in this way be ameliorated. Residents in the study group became more active and reported feeling less unhappy than did members of the comparison group, who were encouraged to assume that the staff would care for them. Patients given responsibility for making their own decisions also were significantly more alert and involved in many different kinds of activities, especially social activities. A physician's "blind" evaluations of patient medical records showed that, during the six months after the intervention, the experimental group had significantly greater improvement in health than did the comparison group. The difference between the groups was apparent even in terms of death rates during the 18 months after the original intervention: 15 percent in the intervention group died, as compared with 30 percent in the control group.

Similar interventions, enhancing the sense of personal control by providing adequate information and freedom for informed choices, may be applicable to other problems in the years ahead. The approach might be used to improve adherence to proven therapeutic or preventive plans.

Feelings of personal responsibility are especially relevant to long-term regimens that are not easily monitored, for example, antihypertensive drugs.

Coping and Learning

Effective coping strategies often are described as actions that eliminate, modify, or avoid problem situations (White and Watt, 1981). On reflection, this clearly implies complex learning processes. Earlier in this chapter, basic processes of avoidance learning were mentioned in the context of advances in neuroendocrinology, but human beings draw on the full range of learning capabilities for adaptation.

There is a long tradition of research on learning, including problem solving (Hilgard and Bower, 1975; Estes et al., 1981). A principal direction of the field of psychology since its inception as a science has been to understand basic processes of learning and their application. In recent years, a theory has emerged that emphasizes the social context of human learning (Bandura, 1977a). For example, fundamental elements of conditioning occur in a social context that strongly influences the shaping of behavior through experience. This theory is a balanced synthesis of cognitive psychology and behavior modification—both areas in which much progress has been made. It draws on experimentally verified principles of learning to describe in detail how a set of social and personal competences could develop out of the social conditions within which the learning occurs. It also deals explicitly with application of these principles to problems of health.

Much human learning occurs through observing another person making skilled responses, for example, driving a car in a way that avoids accidents. The sequence of observation/initiation/practice is a major pathway to learning in nonhuman primates such as chimpanzees and is greatly enriched in humans, especially by the use of language. Experiments employing the imitation of a human model by children have confirmed this pattern of learning. So too have systematic, quantitative studies of health-relevant behavior change in adults. The use of learning principles and technologies to help children and adolescents acquire coping skills has emerged in recent years as a promising line of inquiry (Bandura, 1977b).

The potential uses of principles of cognitive problem solving for health-relevant behavior change is of considerable interest in medicine and public health. Therapeutic and preventive procedures often require changes in behavior in order to be effective. The question of patient adherence to treatment and prevention regimens, for example, may be approached from a problem-solving perspective (Benfari et al., 1981). In one study, only about half of the patients on long-term medication regimens were adherent

(Sackett and Haynes, 1976). Individualized approaches may be necessary, because some patients are totally nonadherent and others are partially adherent. A substantial amount of research has been done on factors relevant to adherence, and insights on this pervasive problem are emerging (cf. Chapter 16).

Abilities to deal with stressful life events have been related in recent research to personal qualities of willingness to face challenge, internal locus of control, and commitment to the task at hand (Kahn, 1981). Why these abilities develop in some individuals but not others needs further study, as do ways of implementing such processes in people who lack them.

The formulation of maladaptive coping behaviors and their underlying cognitive processes should be studied in relation to sociocultural influences. For example, cigarette smoking, excessive use of alcohol, and drug abuse may be socially induced, especially by peer group pressures. Social isolation has a profoundly adverse effect on health (Berkman and Syme, 1979), although some individuals cope effectively with social isolation (Berkman, 1981). How does this occur? Migrants from other cultures or from rural to urban settings are especially at risk, because they must cope with drastic changes in psychosocial and cultural modes (Berkman, 1981).

Adaptive behaviors also may be socially induced, and intimate social relationships such as with a spouse can promote coping ability and favorably influence cognition of stressful events (Brown, 1981). Social influences on health are being studied effectively by social network indices (Berkman, 1981). Application of such techniques to doctor-patient relationships may help to enhance the efficacy of future therapeutic and preventive efforts.

Conclusions

On the whole, determining how individuals attempt to cope with stress has been a neglected area of great potential importance. In years to come, better understanding of human coping behavior can be useful in improving treatment and preventive interventions. The promise of such interventions is clearest with respect to mental health but is directly relevant to general health. Failure of coping to reduce stress can contribute to physical illness, and coping efforts that harm health, including smoking, alcohol use, and risky driving, weigh heavily in the burden of illness.

Further application of basic learning principles such as operant conditioning, cognitive problem solving, and social learning to the highly practical problems of coping with stressful life experiences is a line of inquiry well worth pursuing in years to come. At least partly in the context of stress research, there have been major advances both in the biological sciences and in the behavioral sciences. These advances now can help to solve stress problems in ways that were largely unimaginable when stress first came into scientific focus several decades ago.

References

Andreasen, N., Noyes, R., Hartford, C. Factors influencing adjustment of burn patients during hospitalization. *Psychosom. Med.* 34:517–525, 1972

Bandura, A. *Social Learning Theory* Englewood Cliffs, N.J.: Prentice-Hall, 1977a.

Bandura, A. Self-efficacy: Toward a unifying theory of behavioral change. *Psychol. Rev.* 84:191–215, 1977b.

Barchas, J., Ciaranello, R., Kessler, S., and Hamburg, D. Genetic aspects of the synthesis of catecholamines in adrenal medulla. *Psychoneuroendocrinology* 1:103–113, 1975.

Barchas, J. D., Akil, H., Elliott, G. R., Holman, R. B., and Watson, S. J. Behavioral neurochemistry: Neuroregulators and behavioral states. *Science* 200:964–973, 1978.

Benfari, R., Eaker, E., Stall, J. Behavioral intervention and compliance to treatment regimes. *Annu. Rev. Publ. Health* 2:431–471, 1981.

Berkman, L. Physical health and the social environment: A social epidemiological perspective. IN: *The Relevance of Social Science for Medicine* (Eisenberg, L., and Kleinman, A., eds.) New York: D. Reidel, 1981, pp. 51–76.

Berkman, L. F., and Syme, S. L. Social networks, host resistance, and mortality: A nine-year follow-up study of Alameda County residents. *Am. J. Epidemiol.* 109:186–204, 1979.

Bloom, F. E. Neuropeptides. *Sci. Am.* 243:148–168, 1981.

Braestrup, C., and Squire, R. F. Brain specific benzodiazepine receptors. *Br. J. Psychiatry* 133:249–260, 1978.

Brown, G. S. Presentation given at the conference on stress, coping and development at the Center for Advanced Study in the Behavioral Sciences, Stanford, California, 1981.

Ciaranello, R. D. Genetic regulation of the catecholamine synthesizing enzymes. IN: *Genetic Variation in Hormone Systems, Vol. 2* (Shire, J. G. M., ed.) Boca Raton: CRC Press, 1979, pp. 49–61.

Coelho, G. *Coping and Adaptation: An Annotated Bibliography* Washington, D.C.: U.S. Government Printing Office, 1981, DHHS Publ. No. (ADM) 81–863.

Coehlo, G., Hamburg, D., and Adams, J. *Coping and Adaptation* New York: Basic Books, 1974.

Coelho, G., Hamburg, D., Moos, R., and Randolph, P. (Eds.) *Coping and Adaptation: A Behavioral Sciences Bibliography* Washington, D.C.: U.S. Government Printing Office, 1970.

Coelho, G. V., Hamburg, D. A., and Murphey, E. B. Coping strategies in a new learning environment. *Arch. Gen. Psychiatry* 9:433–443, 1963.

Cohen, F., Lazarus, R. Coping with the stress of illness. IN: *Health Psychology—A Handbook* (Stone, G., Cohen, F., Adler, N., eds.) San Francisco: Jossey-Bass, 1979, pp. 217–254.

de Wied, D., and Bohus, B. Modulation of memory processes by neuropeptides of hypothalamic-neurohypophyseal origin. IN: *Brain Mechanisms in Memory and Learning* (Brazier, M. A. B., ed.) New York: Raven Press, 1979, pp. 139–149.

Dimsdale, J. E., and Moss, J. Plasma catecholamines in stress and exercise. *J. Am. Med. Assoc.* 243:340–342, 1980.

Edwards, D. W., and Kelly, J. G. Coping and adaptation: A longitudinal study. *Am. J. Commun. Psychol.* 8:203–215, 1980.

Elliott, G. R., and Eisdorfer, C. *Stress and Human Health* New York: Springer, 1982.

Estes, W. K., Shiffrin, R. M., Simon, H. A., and Smith, E. E. The science of cognition. IN: *Outlook for Science and Technology: The Next Five Years* (National Academy of Sciences) San Francisco: Freeman, 1981, pp. 157–190.

Frankenhaeuser, M. Psychobiological aspects of life stress. IN: *Coping and Health* (Levine, S., and Ursin, H., eds.) New York: Plenum Press, 1980, pp. 203–223.

Friedman, S. B., Chodoff, P., Mason, J. W., and Hamburg, D. A. Behavioral observations on parents anticipating the death of a child. *Pediatrics* 32:610–625, 1963.

Frishman, W. H. Beta-adrenoceptor antagonists: New drugs and new indications. *N. Engl. J. Med.* 305:500–506, 1981.

Gershon, E., Matthysse, S., Breadefield, X., and Ciaranello, R. (Eds.) *Genetic Research Strategies in Psychobiology and Psychiatry* Pacific Grove, Calif.: Boxwood Press, 1981.

Glick, I. O., Weiss, R. S., Parkes, M. C. *The First Year of Bereavement* New York: Wiley, 1974.

Guillemin, R. Peptides in the brain: The new endocrinology of the neuron. *Science* 202:390–402, 1978.

Hamburg, B. A. Early adolescence as a life stress. IN: *Coping and Health* (Levine, S., and Ursin, H., eds.) New York: Plenum Press, 1980, pp. 121–143.

Hamburg, B. A., and Hamburg, D. Stressful transitions of adolescence—endocrine and psychosocial aspects. IN: *Society, Stress, and Disease, Vol. 2* (Levi, L., ed.) London: Oxford University Press, 1975, pp. 93–106.

Hamburg, B. A., and Killilea, M. Relation of social support, stress, illness, and use of health services. IN: *Healthy People. Background Papers* (United States Department of Health, Education, and Welfare) Washington, D.C.: U.S. Government Printing Office, 1979, pp. 253–276.

Hamburg, D. Plasma and urinary cortico-steroid levels in naturally occurring psychologic stresses. *Assoc. Res. Nerv. Ment. Dis.* 40:406–413, 1962.

Hamburg, D. Emotions in the perspective of human evolution. IN: *Expression of the Emotions in Man* (Knapp, P., ed.) New York: International Universities Press, 1963, pp. 300–317.

Hamburg, D. Coping behavior in life-threatening circumstances. *Psychother. Psychosom.* 23:13–25, 1974.

Hamburg, D., and Hamburg, B. A lifespan perspective on adaptation and health. IN: *Family and Health: Epidemiological Approach, Vol. II* (Kaplan, B., and Ibrahim, M., eds.) Chapel Hill: University of North Carolina Press, 1980.

Hamburg, D. A., and Adams, J. E. A perspective coping behavior: Seeking and utilizing information in major transitions. *Arch. Gen. Psychiatry* 17:277–284, 1967.

Hamburg, D. A., Artz, C. P., Reiss, E., Amspacher, W. H., and Chambers, R. E. Clinical importance of emotional problems in the care of patients with burns. *N. Engl. J. Med.* 248:355–359, 1953.

Harris, G. W. *Neural Control of the Pituitary Gland* London: Edward Arnold, 1955.

Hilgard, E., and Bower, G. *Theories of Learning* 4 New Jersey: Prentice-Hall, 1975.

Hubel, D. H. The brain. *Sci. Am.* 241:44, 1979.

Institute of Medicine *Adolescent Behavior and Health: A Conference Summary* Washington, D.C.: National Academy of Sciences, 1978.

Institute of Medicine *Sleeping Pills, Insomnia, and Medical Practice* Washington, D.C.: National Academy of Sciences, 1979.

Institute of Medicine *Research on Stress and Human Health* Washington, D.C.: National Academy Press, 1981.

Iversen, S. D. Neuropeptides: Do they integrate body and brain? *Nature 291*:454, 1981.

Janis, I. Improving adherence to medical recommendations: Descriptive hypotheses derived from recent research in social psychology. IN: *Handbook of Medical Psychology, Vol. 4* (Baum, A., Singer, J. E., and Taylor, S. E., eds.) Hillsdale, N.J.: Lawrence Erlbaum, in press.

Janis, I., and Mann, L. *Decision Making: A Psychological Analysis of Conflict, Choice, and Commitment* New York: Free Press, 1977.

Janis, I., and Rodin, J. Attribution, control, and decision making: Social psychology and health care. IN: *Health Psychology—A Handbook* (Stone, G., Cohen, F., and Adler, N., eds.) San Francisco: Jossey-Bass, 1979, pp. 487–521.

Jenkins, C. D. Recent evidence supporting psychologic and social risk factors for coronary heart disease. *N. Engl. J. Med. 294*:987–994, 1976.

Kahn, R. L. *Work and Health* New York: Wiley Interscience, 1981.

Kety, S. S. The biogenic amines in the central nervous system: Their possible roles in arousal, emotion, and learning. IN: *The Neurosciences* (Schmitt, F. O., ed.) New York: Rockefeller University Press, 1970.

Krieger, D. T., and Hughes, J. C. (Eds.) *Neuroendocrinology* Boston: Sinauer Associates, 1980.

Krieger, D. T., and Martin, J. B. Brain peptides. *N. Engl. J. Med. 304*:944–951, 1981.

Langer, E. J., and Rodin, J. The effects of choice and enhanced personal responsibility for the aged: A field experiment in an institutional setting. *J. Pers. Soc. Psychol. 34*:191–198, 1976.

Levine, S., and Ursin, H. (Eds.) *Coping and Health* New York: Plenum Press, 1980.

Luria, S. E., Gould, S. J., and Singer, S. *A View of Life* New York: Benjamin/Cummings, 1981.

McGaugh, J. L., Martinez, J. L., Jr., Jensen, R. A., Messing, R. B., and Vasquez, B. J. Central and peripheral catecholamine function in learning and memory processes. IN: *Neural Mechanisms of Goal-Directed Behavior and Learning* (Thompson, R. F., Hicks, L. H., and Shyrkov, V. B., eds.) New York: Academic Press, 1980, pp. 75–91.

Miller, N. E. A perspective on the effects of stress and coping on disease and health. IN: *Coping and Health* (Levine, S., and Ursin, H., eds.) New York: Plenum Press, 1980, pp. 323–353.

Moos, R. H. (Ed.) *Human Adaptation: Coping with Life Crises* Lexington, Mass.: Heath, 1976.

Nauta, W., and Feritag, M. The organization of the brain. *Sci. Am. 241*:88–111, 1979.

Rahe, R. H., and Arthur, R. J. Life change and illness studies: Past history and future directions. *J. Hum. Stress 4*:3–15, 1978.

Rodin, J. Managing the stress of aging: The role of control and coping. IN: *Coping and Health* (Levine, S., and Ursin, H., eds) New York: Plenum Press, 1980, pp. 171–202.

Rose, R. M. Endocrine responses to stressful psychological events. *Psychiatr. Clin. N. Am. 3*:251–276, 1980.

Sackett, D. L., and Haynes, R. B. *Compliance with Therapeutic Regimens* Baltimore: Johns Hopkins University Press, 1976, p. 23.

Sawchenko, P. E., and Swanson, L. W. Central noradrenergic pathways for the integration of hypothalamic neuroendocrine and autonomic responses. *Science* 214:685, 1981.

Schally, A. Aspects of hypothalamic regulation of the pituitary gland. *Science* 202:18–28, 1978.

Schoenberg, B., Carr, A., Kutcher, A., Peretz, D., and Goldberg, I. (Eds.) *Anticipatory Grief* New York: Columbia University Press, 1974.

Selye, H. *The Physiology and Pathology of Exposure to Stress* Montreal: Acta, 1950.

Shapiro, A. P., Benson, H., Chobanian, A. V., Herd, J. A., Julius, S. Kaplan, N., Lazarus, R. S., Ostfeld, A. M., and Syme, S. L. The role of stress in hypertension. *J. Hum. Stress* 5:7–26, 1979.

Shereshefsky, P., and Yarrow, L. *Psychological Aspects of a First Pregnancy and Early Postnatal Adaptation* New York: Raven Press, 1973.

Snyder, S. H. Benzodiazepine receptors. *Psychiatr. Ann.* 11:19–23, 1981.

Snyder, S. H. Brain peptides as neurotransmitters. *Science* 209:976–983, 1980.

Solomon, F., White, C. C., Parron, D. L., and Mendelson, W. Sleeping pills, insomnia, and medical practice. *N. Engl. J. Med.* 300:803–808, 1979.

Solomon, F., Parron, D. L., and Dews, P. B. (Eds.) *Biobehavioral Factors in Sudden Cardiac Death. Interim Report No. 3., Health and Behavior: A Research Agenda* Washington, D.C.: National Academy Press, 1981.

Sowers, J. R. (Ed.) *Hypothalamic Hormones* Stroudsburg: Dowden, Hutchinson and Ross, 1980.

Tallman, J. F., Thomas, J. W., and Gallager, D. W. GABAergic modulation of benzodiazepine binding site sensitivity. *Nature* 274:383–384, 1978.

Toomey, M. Conflict theory approach to decision making applied to alcoholics. *J. Pers. Soc. Psychol.* 24:199–206, 1972.

Usdin, E., Kvetnansky, R., and Kopin, I. J. (Eds.) *Catecholamines and Stress: Recent Advances* New York: Elsevier/North-Holland, 1980.

Vale, W., Spiess, J., Rivier, C., and Rivier, J. Characterization of a 41-residue ovine hypothalamic peptide that stimulates secretion of corticotropin and beta-endorphin. *Science* 213:1394–1397, 1981.

Visotsky, H. M., Hamburg, D. A., Goss, M. E., and Lebovits, B. Z. Coping behavior under extreme stress: Observations of patients with severe poliomyelitis. *Arch. Gen. Psychiatry* 5:423–448, 1961.

Vogel, F., and Motulsky, A. G. *Human Genetics: Problems and Approaches* Berlin: Springer-Verlag, 1979.

White, R. W., and Watt, N. F. *The Abnormal Personality, 5th Ed.* New York: Wiley, 1981.

4
Alcoholism, Alcohol Abuse, and Health

As detailed in Chapter 2, an estimated 13 million people in the United States misuse alcohol, and about 50,000 to 200,000 die each year of alcohol-related illness, accidents, and violence. Alcohol contributes to pancreatitis, brain and liver damage, several types of cancer, cardiac myopathy, and physical and mental abnormalities in the children of alcoholic women. Perhaps half of the 55,000 motor vehicle deaths each year and 10 to 30 percent of vehicular injuries are related to alcohol. There also are injuries from fires, other accidents, and violence. The total direct and indirect costs of alcohol abuse have been estimated to be $43 billion for 1975.* Beyond these are such costs as family disruption that are even more difficult to quantitate (National Institute on Alcoholism and Alcohol Abuse, 1979).

There has been a worldwide trend toward increased per capita consumption of alcohol and a parallel increase in the use of other mood-modifying substances. These trends, coupled with a shift in lifestyle that makes it more likely that an individual will drink at times of significant demand on psychomotor and cognitive skills, suggest a need for timely research on the use of alcohol and the effects of that use (Straus, 1981).

Recognition of the physical, emotional, and economic costs of alcoholism and alcohol abuse led to the establishment in the United States of the National Institute on Alcohol Abuse and Alcoholism in 1971, in part to

*There is not complete agreement on this aggregate cost figure. There are reasons to believe that it overestimates some component costs and underestimates others (Institute of Medicine, 1980; Moore and Gerstein, 1981).

88

support and stimulate research into the extent, etiology, prevention, and treatment of alcohol-related problems. Alcohol abuse and related problems have biological, psychological, and social dimensions; no single discipline or research approach explains the progression toward abuse and its consequent problems. Many questions remain, but a number of promising lines of inquiry have been identified.

Recently, the Institute of Medicine (1980) completed the study *Alcoholism, Alcohol Abuse, and Related Problems: Opportunities for Research*, which identified areas of research of particular promise over the next five years. Research opportunities were assessed across six areas: biochemical and genetic, neuropharmacological, clinical and epidemiological, psychosocial, prevention, and treatment. Another survey of some research opportunities relating to alcohol was done at a workshop held in conjunction with the conference *Health, Behavior, and Aging* as part of the Health and Behavior project (Parron et al., 1981). The Institute of Medicine (1981) conference *Health Promotion and the Mass Media* was another valuable resource: alcohol advertising and the portrayal of drinking-related behaviors in prime-time television programs were considered as special focus topics of the conference.

Prominent among the recurrent themes at these Institute of Medicine activities was the interaction of extrinsic influences with factors unique to an individual in the etiology of problem drinking and associated adverse health effects. An individual's physiological predispositions are shaped by and continue to interact with psychosocial influences from family, school, work place, community, and other social institutions. In each case, a given factor places an individual at greater or lesser risk and alters that person's susceptibility to the sum of interacting risks. No single cause of alcohol abuse or particular clinical complications from its abuse has been found, or indeed is ever likely to be found.

The importance of combining the questions, methodologies, and insights of various biobehavioral science disciplines also was emphasized. The phenomenon of intoxication is a case in point. It has both physiological and cultural dimensions, and personal beliefs about the effects of alcohol can modify its pharmacological effects. Thus, continued basic research in the biomedical and psychosocial sciences, as well as research combining these two lines of inquiry, should help to provide knowledge needed to design more effective and appropriately targeted prevention and therapy programs.

Genetic Risk

Sons of alcoholics are twice as likely as others to become alcoholics. Because parents provide both social environment and genetic endowment, it is necessary to distinguish between these two influences. Available studies of twins and of adopted children support the existence of risk in part based on genotype. Even when raised from very early infancy by people who do not abuse alcohol, adopted males with an alcoholic biological parent have an alcoholism rate that is about the same as that for males raised by their own alcoholic parents. Also, identical twins have greater concordance for alcoholism than do fraternal twins. These data, together with clear-cut evidence from animal studies of genetic components to the response to alcohol, are sufficiently persuasive to stimulate a search for a specific gene or combination of genes that place an individual at higher-than-average risk of alcoholism (Goodwin, 1971; Goodwin et al., 1974; Reed, 1977).

The search for genetic markers of predisposition to alcoholism has focused mainly on biochemical and physiological differences between alcoholics and nonalcoholics. Studies of the enzymes and pathways of alcohol metabolism, the structure and composition of membranes, and changes in neurotransmitters and their receptors may offer insights into apparent differential susceptibilities and their possible genetic basis. Alcoholics are an obvious study group, but continuing abuse of alcohol may produce effects such as malnutrition that obscure significant biochemical differences. Therefore, other study populations are needed. Children and first-degree relatives of alcoholics and some tribes of American Indians with high or low frequencies of abuse may be appropriate (Institute of Medicine, 1980). In all cases, attention to possible confounding effects of cigarette smoking and other drug use is vital. Characterization of genetic influences would also facilitate research on environmental factors that promote or deter development of alcohol-related problems in predisposed individuals.

Just as persons in the general population vary in their responses to alcohol, alcoholics show diversity in developing clinical problems such as cirrhosis of the liver. These differences also may depend on genetic predisposition, and biochemical/genetic studies similar to those mentioned above might elucidate factors underlying the diversity of clinical expressions of alcohol-related health problems (Institute of Medicine, 1980).

Psychosocial Risk

Although twin studies indicate a possible genetic component of alcoholism, they support the importance of nongenetic factors, because not all identical twins are concordant for the disorder. Nonconcordant identical twins and "successful" children in alcoholic families are especially interesting for study of psychosocial risk factors. The relationships among the stress of life events, social supports, and various styles of coping, either on the family level or the individual level, are a rich area for research. For example, what coping styles are likely to be learned or transmitted within families, considering both promotors and deterrents of alcoholism? Research also should be encouraged on the formative factors for successful outcomes in children of alcoholic parents.

Alcoholism is less frequent in populations in which drinking customs, values, and sanctions are well known, agreed to by all, and consistent with the rest of the culture. Research on socialization, family dynamics, and parenting reveals that basic attitudes and values start developing early in life and are directly related to the way a parent behaves with a child (Sears et al., 1957; Stolz, 1967; Parron, 1979). What drinking means to someone is largely a function of the social expectations that are shared with other members of the person's current peer group. Thus, of what significance are social norms and group pressures as factors that motivate individuals to drink beyond comfortable capacities? Many sociological factors contribute to self-regulation of alcohol intake and to self-medication with alcohol, for example, as an antidote for depression (more in men than women) or for sleep disorders.

Age Groups of Special Interest

Adolescents

Young adolescents (10–15 years old) are an important high-risk group. Recent surveys report that drinking patterns among young people (10–15) have changed markedly over the past generation. A greater percentage of them drink, they have their first drinking experience earlier, they drink larger quantities, and they report more frequent intoxications (Rachal et al., 1975; Fishburne et al., 1980). Although girls still drink less than do boys, the percentage who drink and who report intoxication has increased more rapidly for girls than for boys (Wechsler and McFadden, 1976). Similar patterns obtain for cigarette smoking (National Institute of Education, 1979). Because of the overlap among problems related to alcohol, abuse of other drugs, cigarette smoking, and mental disorders, coordinated research efforts addressing parental behavior, cognitive development, and risk-taking behaviors in young adolescents are likely to be fruitful (Hamburg, 1979; McAlister, 1979). Among factors that can influence the quality of adolescent assessments of personal risk are: (1) understanding and believing outcomes, (2) having an immediate time perspective, (3) being influenced by peers or significant others, and (4) having a sense of personal worth. Insight into influences on these factors can be important to efforts to promote adolescent health by reducing the need for drinking alcohol or engaging in other risky behavior.

Normal individuals differ considerably in their rates of cognitive, affective, neuroendocrine, skeletal, and genital development. Interrelationships among these and implications for health of variations in developmental rates should be elucidated. Research on the cognitive development of young adolescents and its relation to other behaviors is directly relevant to alcoholism. For example, adolescents under 15 are relatively poor at using symbols, making valid generalizations, and objectively processing information (Karplus et al., 1975; Hurd, 1978). Surveys indicate that they systematically overestimate the prevalence of certain behaviors in peers. Thus, one study found that, when the actual rate of smoking in a school was 15 percent, most students estimated the rate to be over 80 percent (Fishbein, 1977). Consistent overgeneralization may help explain the powerful impact of peer and media influences on young adolescents. Even when more abstract levels of cognitive functioning develop, there is a strong tendency for reversion to concrete information processing at times of stress and anxiety.

Research also is needed on the apparent egocentrism of adolescence. This cognitive stance has been reported to reach a peak in early adolescence (Elkind, 1967). Egocentrism appears to underlie a "here and now" time perspective in which long-term consequences and future happenings have little impact. It may also explain ideas of invulnerability that allow young adolescents to persuade themselves that they can safely take a known risk. When this immediate time perspective and sense of invulnerability are coupled with failure to understand laws of probability and to make accurate estimates, young adolescents may be especially likely to engage in unprotected sexual encounters, to use drugs, and to use alcohol with a false sense of confidence. It may be that teenagers convince themselves that "it won't happen to me"; that adverse consequences will occur much later, so "no need to worry now"; and that reversibility is possible, therefore, "I can stop whenever I want to." This is an important area for study. In addition, research on exploratory behaviors and factors that help make those behaviors permanent in some young people but not in others may be crucial for developing effective prevention programs.

Because of its importance to their behavior, it is particularly vital for young adolescents to learn to resist peer pressure. Research should continue on ways to teach young people how to resist peer pressure under a variety of conditions and on positive uses of peer pressure. Social support networks are tremendously important, and much work is needed on ways to strengthen and restructure such networks. Adding to the difficulties in preventing alcohol abuse and other destructive behavior is the increase in the effective length of adolescence. Physical maturation now occurs earlier than it did a few generations ago, and the period of social dependency now is prolonged to the late teens or early twenties. In the face of these realities, building a sense of worth in young adolescents that will remain through the 10 or more years of dependency and form a solid foundation for responsible maturity remains a major problem.

Adolescent risk assessment of alcohol use offers an instructive vignette. Understanding factors that influence such assessments is crucial to developing effective interventions for prevention, early detection, and treatment of alcohol abuse. Much more needs to be learned about alcoholism, and this knowledge needs to be transmitted in a manner that can be used effectively to improve the quality of risk assessment by all persons, adults and adolescents.

The Elderly

Interest in research on alcohol-related problems among the elderly is growing, partly because of the increasing numbers and proportion of elderly persons in the population of the United States (cf. Chapter 11). In addition, study of the impact on drinking behavior of the physiological changes and often abrupt changes in life situations experienced by the elderly may yield new insights.

At a given blood alcohol concentration, the elderly appear to be less aware than younger persons of changes in cognitive and psychomotor ability. This blunting of the perceived effect may help to explain why some elderly people stop drinking and others drink more: perhaps the former abandon a no-longer-effective action and the latter try to recapture desired effects. Studies of these phenomena could provide important clues to major determinants of drinking patterns.

Many other fruitful areas of inquiry, focusing on responses to stress, sleep disorders, the interaction of alcohol with medications, the importance of alcohol for socialization, and the efficacy of treatment modalities, were identified in the Institute of Medicine studies (Institute of Medicine, 1980; Parron et al., 1981).

Biochemical Effects of Special Interest

Alcohol abuse combines high toxicity with long-term exposure. Better knowledge of the intermediate steps from exposure to disease should aid in the design of therapeutic and preventive interventions.

Membranes

Among the most promising lines of inquiry are studies of the effects on cell membranes of acute and chronic alcohol consumption (Institute of Medicine, 1980). Alcohol alters membrane fluidity, chemical composition (lipids and proteins), and function (transport and membrane-bound enzyme activity) (Chin et al., 1978; Johnson et al., 1979; Kalant et al., 1979). Chronic exposure to alcohol alters membrane structure and function in such a way that some of the structure and function effects typical of acute exposure to alcohol are altered; this may be significant to the tolerance and dependence that are characteristic of alcoholism (Curran and Seeman, 1977).

The implications and potential applications of this reseach are far-reaching. Studies of the chemical, physical, biochemical, and electrophysiological parameters of membranes, especially neuronal membranes, in animals, isolated cells, and cell cultures may suggest candidates for genetic markers of persons especially susceptible to becoming alcoholics or developing adverse effects from alcohol abuse. The research also may provide a useful assay for studying sobering or antiaddiction agents.

Neuropharmacology

Studies of neurotransmitters and their receptors, as influenced by both acute and chronic consumption of alcohol, also show promise for the near future (Institute of Medicine, 1980). Improved methods for detecting and quantitating minute amounts of biological substances have revealed many previously unsuspected neuroregulators in the past decade (cf. Chapter 9). Similar advances have greatly facilitated measurements of specific neuroregulator concentration, localization, and turnover and have enhanced understanding of the role of receptors in membranes.

Membrane changes in target organ cells may be highly relevant to the pathogenesis of disorders associated with alcohol abuse. In addition, the hypothalamus regulates the secretion of pituitary hormones that in turn regulate hormone secretion by peripheral glands. Alcohol-induced disturbances in hormone balance via the hypothalamus may underlie some clinical and behavioral problems associated with abuse. Thus, studies of brain function hold long-range promise not only for understanding the behavioral effects of alcohol but also for preventing or treating clinical disorders such as liver cirrhosis, pancreatitis, and oral cavity cancers that are associated with chronic excessive consumption of alcohol.

The neuroendocrine effects of alcohol, with potential impact on every organ system, have received little attention. Research in that area holds promise for understanding and dealing both with long-term biomedical complications and with acute behavioral effects (Cicero, in press). Of special interest would be studies of neuroendocrine, neurochemical, and neuro-physiological mechanisms of tolerance and dependence. Brain reinforcement that leads to alcoholism brings together psychological and biochemical mechanisms; coordinated research efforts are most likely to make progress.

Metabolism of Alcohol

Study of the enzymes important in the metabolism of alcohol may be relevant to both biomedical and behavioral effects of alcohol consumption. Several enzymes (alcohol dehydrogenase [ADH], microsomal ethanol oxidizing system, and catalase) are known to accept alcohol as a substrate. Alcohol dehydrogenase is probably the major enzyme for oxidation of alcohol, but the physiological significance and the relative roles of other enzymes and of particular forms of ADH are not fully resolved (Li, 1977; Harada et al., 1980). This is a research area of importance, because the oxidation of alcohol or the induction, activation, or inhibition of these enzymes by alcohol potentially could lead to a cascade of effects, such as altered redox potential in the cell or altered ability to oxidize steroids or other hormones (Higgins, 1979). Metabolites of alcohol such as acetaldehyde might react to form neuroregulator analogues of importance in the behavioral effects of alcohol (Cohen, 1976). Some individuals and ethnic groups have variants of these enzymes, called isozymes, that may be markers of genetic predisposition to alcohol abuse or one of the clinical complications of that abuse.

Screening Tests

Reliable, sensitive, and accurate screening tests are needed for early signs of alcohol abuse. Most available screens have been developed and validated for alcoholics. It may be possible to modify some existing psychological and biochemical tests developed to identify individuals at high risk for abuse before drinking problems have appeared. People identified to be at high risk would be priority targets for such preventive interventions as education and counseling. It seems likely that interventions will have greater success if they can be applied early.

The work place has emerged as a major and effective focal point for prevention and treatment programs. Early programs were directed toward identifying and treating alcoholism; more recently, the trend has been toward a "troubled-employee" approach (Schramm, 1977). Employees with problems of whatever origin are identified by a drop in the quality of their performance on the job or by patterns of absenteeism; after consultation and counseling, they can be referred to support programs outside of the work place, as appropriate. Some work place programs report "success" rates of up to 60 percent, which is rather high compared with those of other treatment programs (Von Wiegand, 1972). This is, however, consistent with the generally better prognosis with any treatment approach for those who are employed as opposed to those who are not.

Research questions of interest include the benefits of a narrow focus on alcohol-related problems compared with a broader troubled-employee approach. With increasing numbers of women in the work place, it also would be timely to determine whether these programs serve men and women equally effectively.

Altering Patterns of Drinking

Drinking behavior does not remain constant, but determinants of change are poorly understood. The natural history of alcohol-related problems deserves careful study. Spontaneous remission, for example, occurs, but study of its frequency and "triggers" is needed. What conflicts, supports, and environmental changes are associated with alterations in drinking patterns? Does the individual learn other, better coping mechanisms, or have other maladaptive behaviors been substituted for drinking?

Some studies have looked for good predictors of success in a treatment program, but how well this correlates with characteristics of "spontaneous" remitters is unknown. Given that only a minority of alcoholics seek treatment and that only about one third of those who are treated obtain long-term control over their drinking, study of the determinants of remission merits greater attention.

Some insight into ways to alter patterns of drinking and the behaviors associated with drinking may be gained from the research on methods for helping individuals (or groups) by means of mass media, for example, to change such health-relevant behaviors as diet and cigarette smoking (cf. Chapter 15). Existing studies have focused on cardiovascular risk, but those protocols may productively be modified, expanded, or copied by alcohol researchers.

Further insights also may be provided by an international perspective. Clues to understanding the etiology of problem drinking or the potential effect on drinking behavior of public policies may be found in comparisons of experiences among different countries.

References

Chin, J. H., Parsons, L. M., and Goldstein, D. B. Increased cholesterol content of erythrocyte and brain membranes in ethanol-tolerant mice. *Biochem. Biophys. Acta* 513:358–363, 1978.

Cicero, T. J. Common mechanisms underlying the effects of ethanol and the narcotics on neuroendocrine function. *Adv. Substance Abuse,* in press.

Cohen, G. Alkaloid products in the metabolism of alcohol and biogenic amines. *Biochem. Pharmacol.* 25:1123–1128, 1976.

Curran, M., and Seeman, P. Alcohol tolerance in a cholinergic nerve terminal: Relation to the membrane expansion-fluidization theory of ethanol action. *Science* 197:910–911, 1977.

Elkind, D. Egocentrism in adolescence. *Child Dev.* 38:1025–1034, 1967.

Fishbein, M. Consumer beliefs and behavior with respect to cigarette smoking: A critical analysis of the public literature. IN: *Report to Congress Pursuant to the Public Health Cigarette Smoking Act for the Year 1976* (Federal Trade Commission) Washington, D.C.: U.S. Government Printing Office, 1977.

Fishburne, P. M., Abelson, H. I., and Cisin, I. *National Survey on Drug Abuse: Main Findings, 1979* Rockville, Md.: National Institute on Drug Abuse, 1980.

Goodwin, D. W. Is alcoholism hereditary? *Arch. Gen. Psychiatry* 25:545–549, 1971.

Goodwin, D. W., Schulsinger, F., Moller, N., Hermansen, L., Winokur, G., and Guze, S. B. Drinking problems in adopted and nonadopted sons of alcoholics. *Arch. Gen. Psychiatry* 31:164–169, 1974.

Hamburg, B. A. Developmental issues in school-age pregnancy. Paper presented at the International Conference on Aspects of Psychiatric Problems of Childhood and Adolescence, Paris, November, 1979.

Harada, S., Misawa, S., Agarwal, D. P., and Goedde, H. W. Liver alcohol dehydrogenase and aldehyde dehydrogenase in the Japanese: Isozyme variation and its possible role in alcohol intoxication. *Am. J. Hum. Genet.* 32:8–15, 1980.

Higgins, J. J. Control of ethanol oxidation and its interaction with other metabolic systems. IN: *Biochemistry and Pharmacology of Ethanol, Vol. 1* (Majchrowicz, E., and Noble, E. P., eds.) New York: Plenum Press, 1979, pp. 249–351.

Hurd, P. D. *Early Adolescence: Perspectives and Recommendations to the National Science Foundation* Washington, D.C.: U.S. Government Printing Office, 1978.

Institute of Medicine *Alcoholism, Alcohol Abuse, and Related Problems: Opportunities for Research* Washington, D.C.: National Academy Press, 1980.

Institute of Medicine *Health Promotion and the Mass Media* Washington, D.C.: National Academy Press, 1981.

Johnson, D. A., Lee, N. M., Cooke, R., and Loh, H. H. Ethanol-induced fluidization of brain lipid bilayers: Required presence of cholesterol in membranes for the expression of tolerance. *Mol. Pharmacol.* 15:739–746, 1979.

Kalant, H., Rangaraj, N., Woo, N., and Endrenyi, L. Effects of ethanol on neuronal membrane transport systems. IN: *Progress in Neurotoxicology* (Manzo, L., et al., eds.) Oxford: Pergamon Press, 1979.

Karplus, R., Karplus, E., Formisano, M., et al. *Proportional Reasoning and Control of Variables in Seven Countries: Advancing Education Through Science Oriented Programs* Berkeley, Calif.: Lawrence Hall of Science, 1975, Report 10–25.

Li, T. K. Enzymology of human alcohol metabolism. *Adv. Enzymol.* 45:427–484, 1977.

McAlister, A. L. Tobacco, alcohol, and drug abuse: Onset and prevention. IN:

Healthy People. Background Papers (United States Department of Health, Education, and Welfare) Washington, D.C.: U.S. Government Printing Office, 1979, DHEW (PHS) Publ. No. 79–55071A, pp. 197–206.

Moore, M. H., and Gerstein, D. R. (Eds.) *Alcohol and Public Policy: Beyond the Shadow of Prohibition* Washington, D.C.: National Academy Press, 1981.

National Institute of Education *Teenage Smoking: Immediate and Long-Term Patterns* Washington, D.C.: U.S. Government Printing Office, 1979.

National Institute on Alcoholism and Alcohol Abuse *Third Special Report to the U.S. Congress on Alcohol and Health. Technical Support Document* Washington, D.C.: U.S. Government Printing Office, 1979, DHEW Publ. No. (ADM) 79–832.

Parron, D. L. Black parents' concept of parenthood. *World J. Psychosyn. 11*:7–12, 1979.

Parron, D. L., Solomon, F., and Rodin, J. (Eds.) *Health, Behavior, and Aging. Interim Report No. 5, Health and Behavior: A Research Agenda* Washington, D.C.: National Academy Press, 1981.

Rachal, J. V., Williams, J. R., Brehm, M. L., et al. *A National Study of Adolescent Drinking Behavior, Attitudes and Correlates* Washington, D.C.: National Institute on Alcoholism and Alcohol Abuse, 1975, No. PB–246–002.

Reed, T. E. Three heritable responses to alcohol in a heterogeneous randomly mated mouse strain: Inferences for humans. *J. Stud. Alcohol 38*:618–632, 1977.

Schramm, C. J. *Alcoholism and Its Treatment in Industry* Baltimore: Johns Hopkins University Press, 1977.

Sears, R., Maccoby, E., and Levin, H. *Patterns of Child Rearing* Evanston, Ill.: Row, Peterson, 1957.

Stolz, L. M. *Influences on Parent Behavior* Stanford, Calif.: Stanford University Press, 1967.

Straus, R. Types of alcohol dependence. IN: *Biology of Alcoholism, Vol. 7* (Kissin, B., ed.) New York: Plenum, 1981.

Von Wiegand, R. A. Alcoholism in industry (USA). *Br. J. Addic. 67*:181–187, 1972.

Wechsler, H., and McFadden, M. Sex differences in adolescent alcohol and drug use: A disappearing phenomenon. *J. Stud. Alcohol 27*:1291–1301, 1976.

5
Smoking and Health

Of all the major risk factors for serious illness, disability, and premature death in the United States, smoking may be the most important preventable one (U.S. Public Health Service, 1979). There is convincing evidence that amount of smoking correlates closely with increased risk of lung cancer and coronary heart disease. In 1975, the effects of smoking accounted for $5 to $8 billion in health care costs, including 10 percent of all hospital costs (Rice et al., 1977). Information about adverse effects of smoking has been public knowledge for more than 15 years; yet many people continue to smoke, and a large number of teenagers and young adults still are taking up the habit. As part of the Health and Behavior project, the Institute of Medicine (1980) held the conference *Smoking and Behavior* in September 1979. Participants examined contributions of the biobehavioral sciences to explaining why smoking is such an attractive and intractable behavior; they also identified promising directions for research on initiation, development, maintenance, and quitting of the smoking habit.

Prevention

The tenacity of the smoking habit causes most experts to concur that preventing the initiation of smoking is preferable to getting people to quit. Most people begin smoking in adolescence and early adulthood. Despite the widespread publicity about the dangers, some 4,000 youngsters in the United States each day begin smoking for the first time. Encouragingly, overall rates of teenage smoking declined between 1974 and 1979 (National

99

Center of Health Statistics, 1979) and current data reflect a continuing decline. However, rates for women age 17–24 rose during that time and now exceed those for young men (U.S. Department of Health and Human Services, 1980). Of particular concern is the observation that teenagers who smoke more than a few casual cigarettes are at tremendous risk of escalating to regular smoking (National Institute on Drug Abuse, 1979). Factors that encourage smoking initiation and adoption urgently need to be identified, as do methods for preventing such behaviors.

What distinguishes the 20 percent of 17- and 18-year-olds in the United States who smoke from the 80 percent who do not? Several factors are associated with an increased risk of cigarette smoking, including a high propensity for aggressiveness and risk taking early in life, stresses of puberty, parents and siblings who smoke, peer pressure to smoke, parental acceptance of a child's smoking, and messages in the mass media (Evans et al., 1978). By the seventh grade, nearly all children now are aware that smoking is dangerous; yet, for some, fear of adverse consequences is insufficient to prevent smoking adoption. For example, if both an older sibling and a parent smoke, a child is four times more likely to smoke than if no one in the family uses cigarettes. Furthermore, the incidence of smoking is much greater in junior high schools attached to senior high schools than in those physically separate from one. Other variables include low self-esteem, social anxiety, and poor social skills. One potential influence on smoking adoption that merits more study is the impact of low-tar, low-nicotine cigarettes. Such cigarettes may produce fewer unpleasant effects in first users than do stronger brands. If so, their widespread use may have removed a major barrier against smoking. Research on risk factors is vital to prevention efforts, because it highlights those factors most central to inducing young people to try smoking their first few cigarettes.

Several learning theories are useful in designing effective smoking prevention campaigns. Social learning theory (Bandura, 1977) helps to explain when onset of smoking is likely to occur. Both personal and social expectations may be important. If an adolescent expects to win friends but has not done so, low self-esteem may interact with social expectations to promote the use of cigarettes. In contrast, a teenager with many friends and high self-esteem is less likely to adopt smoking, even with social pressures to do so. This theory suggests that one prevention method could be to help adolescents increase their self-esteem. Cognitive models (McGuire, 1974) suggest that it may be possible to design verbal "inoculations" against the influence of persuasive communications, and thus help teenagers resist pressures to smoke.

Several investigators have studied the preventive effects of thorough information about the hazards of cigarette smoking, along with peer role modeling of ways to resist common pressures to try it (Evans et al., 1978; McAlister et al., 1979; Botvin, 1980; Hurd et al., 1980). Successful programs have in common active involvement of young people in developing strategies to counteract pressures from peers, media, and adults. These programs use such techniques as role playing and peer counseling. Adolescents may view films of or model situations in which they are pressured to try a cigarette, so that they can learn to resist such inducements. The programs also emphasize immediate physiological consequences of smoking, such as increased heart rate, rather than long-term dangers like lung cancer. Two-year follow-up studies indicate that the incidence of smoking adoption among students exposed to such programs is about half that of controls (Telch et al., in press), suggesting that they at least can delay the onset of smoking and may prevent its occurrence altogether for many young people.

A major deterrent to prevention research is the lack of cheap, reliable, and sensitive ways to determine who has been smoking and how much. Most studies rely on self-reporting, which can be affected by such factors as the way in which questions are asked or the circumstances of reporting. A number of biological measures have been used; all have serious limitations (Institute of Medicine, 1980). This is an instance in which behavioral research could be enhanced by a contribution from the biological sciences.

Also of importance are potential interactions among cigarette smoking and other forms of teenage risk taking, including alcohol intake, drug use, reckless driving, and premarital sex. These various behaviors usually are of interest to different types of investigators and funding sources. Little information is available about common themes and significant overlaps among populations at risk. A more unified approach to considering risky behavior could be very informative.

Maintenance

Of everyone in the United States regularly smoking cigarettes, approximately 60 percent have tried to quit at some time; another 30 percent would like to quit. Of an estimated 30 million smokers in the United States each year who attempt to stop smoking, only about 3 million achieve long-term abstinence (National Center of Health Statistics, 1979). A better understanding of this powerful and persistent addiction to cigarette smoking would be invaluable in efforts to combat it. Obtaining such knowledge requires collaboration between the biological and behavioral sciences.

Cigarette smoking is an impressively effective drug delivery mechanism (Russell, 1978). Peak concentrations of substances in tobacco smoke reach the brain within 6 to 8 seconds after the smoke is inhaled. Any compounds that have tension-relieving or other reinforcing properties could produce conditioned behavior. The immediacy of the reinforcement might permit even a relatively weak reinforcer to sustain the 70,000 puffs per year averaged by a one-pack-per-day smoker. Even the short interval between inhalation of smoke and brain effects is bridged by nearly instantaneous effects on mucous membranes and by the sensations and movements associated with lighting the cigarette, holding it, and feeling it on the lips. Linked with pharmacological effects of smoking, these become powerful secondary reinforcers. There also are environmental and social contributors to smoking, such as particular places and situations in which smoking usually is a part of the activity. Smoking has identifiable social consequences, both good and bad, that vary with age, gender, economic status, and profession. Any of these may help maintain or inhibit smoking by a particular person.

Every attempt to replace regular cigarettes with tobacco-free substitutes has failed, emphasizing the importance of tobacco's pharmacological properties. Most researchers believe that nicotine or a metabolite is the main unconditioned reinforcer in cigarette smoke; people gain little satisfaction from smoke lacking nicotine, even if it contains carbon monoxide, tars, and other products of burning tobacco (Krasnegor, 1979). Animals generally do not inhale tobacco smoke or self-inject nicotine as a reinforcer, so a good animal model of smoking addiction has not been available. Such a model would be extremely useful in clarifying the role of nicotine in smoking. Recent research on combining nicotine injections with visual stimuli suggests one approach to resolving that obstacle (Goldberg et al., 1981).

There is a surprising paucity of information on the pharmacology of nicotine, particularly regarding its behavioral effects. Recent advances in drug analysis and drug delivery systems have yet to be used to determine effects of nicotine at concentrations commonly found in smokers, nor have sophisticated behavioral methods been used to assess its actions on the brain. Research on nicotine and sugar intake provides an example of the potential of such research (Grunberg, 1980). Rats receiving constant nicotine infusions over several weeks decreased their sugar intake without compensating for lost calories from other food sources. Human subjects who had been abstinent from cigarettes overnight showed an increased preference for sweet foods. This work has obvious, direct implications for commonly observed weight changes that accompany smoking cessation and often deter smokers from attempting to quit.

Also requiring study are the many other agents in cigarettes, including menthol and flavorings that are becoming increasingly important in low-tar, low-nicotine, heavily filtered brands. Good studies of these substances, and of nicotine, will require better assay techniques. For instance, nicotine lasts such a short time in blood that it gives no information about long-term smoking habits. Ways are needed to determine how much someone has smoked and how much of certain substances a person has inhaled and metabolized. Such technical measures should be feasible with existing technology.

Behavioral factors may be particularly important in initiating the smoking habit and modulating such aspects as day-to-day changes in smoking, choice of cigarette brands, and the situations in which smoking occurs. Use of existing theories to analyze behaviors associated with smoking may provide helpful insights. How important to smoking habits are adjunctive behaviors that foster the smoking habit indirectly? How often is cigarette smoking entrained in common activities such as coffee breaks or in responses to a stress? Of special interest are efforts to identify different subgroups of smokers. Research on plasma nicotine suggests at least three types of smoking patterns: trough maintainers, who maintain their concentrations above some minimum; peak seekers, who repeatedly seek brief periods of high concentrations; and noninhalers, who never achieve very high concentrations (Russell, 1979).

Of particular importance is research that unites smoking pharmacology with smoking behavior. This may require studies in which pharmacological agents are infused into subjects while behavioral variables such as number of cigarettes smoked and puff rate and force are monitored. Other aspects of cigarettes that should be considered are burn characteristics, which affect the time course of nicotine delivery; temperature and acidity, which alter the effect on mucous membranes; smoke dilution, which changes the relative proportion of carbon monoxide to tar and nicotine; and draw resistance, which determines the ease with which smoke is inhaled. Interactions between cigarette design and smoking styles also may be important. For example, are low-tar, low-nicotine cigarettes smoked in ways that increase the delivery of tar and nicotine to the lungs?

Quitting

Over 90 percent of people who try to quit smoking do so without using any formal cessation program. About two thirds of them quit for at least one month, but only one third succeed for at least one year (Schwartz and Rider, 1978). For the Smoking and Behavior conference, Orleans (1980) reviewed the relative success rates of a variety of cessation programs. Many treatments can help a high percentage of smokers reach initial abstinence, but few help them stay off cigarettes permanently. In general, media campaigns and physician advice show low one-year abstinence results. An exception to this is physician advice to patients recovering from a recent heart attack: over 50 percent of those patients still are not smoking at least one year after quitting (Croog and Richards, 1977). Most formal quit clinics, both at medical centers and in voluntary organizations, achieve good initial results, ranging as high as 70 percent; however, long-term quit rates do not differ from spontaneous quit rates. Hypnosis, behavior modification, and psychotherapy also have disappointing long-term quit rates. In contrast, several more recent behavioral approaches, including rapid smoking and smoke holding with rapid puffing, have somewhat better—30 to 50 percent—quit rates at one year.

A key research issue about quitting is better identification of those who can stop smoking on their own: why can some people quit while others cannot? Detailed study of factors that contribute to successful quitting might suggest ways of helping others to stop. Some behavioral theories are helpful. For example, belief in self-efficacy may be a major predictor of success. In one study, smokers given self-control instructions and pills that they were told would help them stop smoking all decreased their smoking (Chambliss and Murray, 1979). Half then were told correctly that the pills were placebos and that any reduction in smoking resulted from their own efforts; the other half thought that their success came from the pill. At one month, all of the latter group had returned to earlier levels of smoking; those who had received the attribution of self-efficacy sustained a reduction in smoking. Perhaps people who believe they can quit smoking permanently are more likely to succeed than are those who harbor doubts.

Methods must be found to enhance the ability of large portions of the population to quit smoking if they wish to do so. Sheer numbers of the smoking population make infeasible the use of formal cessation programs, except for the relatively few persons who cannot stop smoking otherwise. Even relatively ineffective methods may be useful if they can be applied to large groups of individuals at little cost. For example, if a physician advises well patients to stop smoking, about 5 percent will quit who otherwise would not (Russell et al., 1979). Consistent physician advice nationwide could significantly reduce the number of smokers. Yet in 1975 two thirds of adults with a smoking history denied ever having a physician tell them to quit (U.S. Department of Health, Education, and Welfare, 1976). Similarly, mass media campaigns might reach a percentage of the smoking population who otherwise would continue to smoke. A media campaign in Finland not only emphasized the need to stop smoking but also taught skills for stopping (McAlister et al., 1980). Groups of smokers watched a series of television shows in which a panel was taught how to stop smoking; each group also received pamphlets and tried to mimic the techniques shown on television. Of 100,000 smokers exposed to the shows, 10 percent were abstinent from cigarettes six months later. Of particular interest would be incorporation of self-efficacy attributions, emphasizing the need for viewers to control their own lives and the possibility of stopping if they wish to do so.

For those wanting to use formal programs, research is needed to match individual needs with program offerings. To date, the only behavioral treatments clearly better than spontaneous quitting involve aversive conditioning. In one of the first, called rapid smoking, the client inhales every smoke six seconds during clinical sessions, continuing to smoke until it becomes intolerable; clients do not smoke between sessions (Hall et al., 1979). The procedure produces marked physiological side effects, including increases in heart rate, blood pressure, and carboxyhemoglobin concentrations. As a result, many people who most need such a treatment cannot use it because of lung or heart dysfunctions. Variations of the basic method have been introduced. For example, in normal-paced aversive smoking, subjects concentrate on unpleasant sensations of cigarette smoke as they smoke in their usual fashion. Long-term quit rates do not seem to be as good for this method as for rapid smoking but are superior to no treatment (Danaher, 1977). More research is needed to assess the efficacy and safety of this and similar techniques such as noninhaling puffing and smoke holding (Orleans, 1980).

Regardless of how someone quits smoking, relapse rates are high. Studies of predisposing factors to relapse and of ways to maintain abstinence from smoking are vital. Relapse curves for smokers in quit-smoking programs are similar to those for alcoholics and heroin addicts after abstinence-oriented treatments. This observation has led to efforts to apply learning theory to the problem of relapse. For all three kinds of addiction, negative emotional states such as anger or frustration account for many first slips back to addictive patterns. Smokers often reported slipping because of social pressure to smoke or because of interpersonal conflicts. Of those who slipped once, 74 percent eventually resumed smoking; 91 percent of those who slipped a second time began smoking again (Marlatt and Gordon, 1979). Research is needed to discover how to help exsmokers avoid slipping and to teach them not to give up if they do slip. Raising social supports in the exsmoker's natural environmental may be useful (Janis and Hoffman, 1970). Such work ties in nicely with self-efficacy research for helping people quit smoking initially.

Finally, the value of individualizing treatment should be examined for a variety of programs. In many instances, success rates for therapies might be much greater for targeted populations. As mentioned earlier, recent heart attack patients are much more susceptible to physician advice to quit smoking than are healthy people. Women who smoke also are an important target. The four million women who smoke and use oral contraceptives have especially high rates of stroke and heart attacks (U.S. Public Health

Service, 1979). Risks of smoking and benefits of quitting are greatest during pregnancy (Danaher, 1978). Pregnant women may be more susceptible to efforts to get them to quit if they understand that their baby's life is in danger. However, they also pose special problems about how to help them quit, if they need a formal program, because most aversive therapies are inappropriate. Blue collar workers also are an important target group, particularly when occupational risks compound smoking risks, as for asbestos workers (Ellis, 1978). Furthermore, they are not high users of existing quit clinics, preventive health services, or university-based smoking control programs. Work-site initiatives are needed to reach them in ways that are most likely to help them quit smoking.

References

Bandura, A. *Social Learning Theory* Englewood Cliffs, N.J.: Prentice-Hall, 1977.

Botvin, G. J., Eng, A., and Williams, C. L. Preventing the onset of cigarette smoking through life skills training. *Prev. Med.* 9:135–143, 1980.

Chambliss, C., and Murray, E. J. Cognitive procedures for smoking reduction: Symptom attribution versus efficacy attribution. *Cog. Ther. Res.* 3:91–95, 1979.

Croog, S. H., and Richards, N. P. Health beliefs and smoking patterns in heart patients and their wives: A longitundinal study. *Am. J. Publ. Health* 67:921–929, 1977.

Danaher, B. Research on rapid smoking: Interim summary and recommendations. *Addict. Behav.* 2:151–166, 1977.

Danaher, B. G. Ob-gyn intervention in helping smokers quit. IN: *Progress in Smoking Cessation: International Conference on Smoking Cessation* (Schwartz, J., ed.) New York: American Cancer Society, 1978.

Ellis, B. How to reach and convince asbestos workers to give up smoking. IN: *Progress in Smoking Cessation: International Conference on Smoking Cessation* (Schwartz, J., ed.) New York: American Cancer Society, 1978.

Evans, R. I., Rozelle, R. M., Mittlemark, M. D., Hansen, W. B., Bane, A. L., Harris, J. Deterring the onset of smoking in children: Knowledge of immediate physiological effects and coping with peer pressure, media pressure, and parent modeling. *J. Appl. Soc. Psychol.* 8:126–135, 1978.

Goldberg, S. R., Spealman, R. D., and Goldberg, D. M. Persistent behavior at high rates maintained by intravenous self-administration of nicotine. *Science* 214:573–575, 1981.

Grunberg, N. E. The effect of nicotine on food consumption and taste preference. Unpublished dissertation, Columbia University, 1980.

Hall, R. G., Sachs, D. P. L., and Hall, S. M. Medical risk and therapeutic effectiveness of rapid smoking. *Behav. Ther.* 10:249–259, 1979.

Hurd, P., Johnson, C. A., Pechecek, T., Bast, L. P., Jacobs, D. R., and Leupker, R. V. Prevention of smoking in seventh grade students. *J. Behav. Med.* 3:15–28, 1980.

Institute of Medicine *Smoking and Behavior. Interim Report No. 1, Health and Behavior: A Research Agenda* Washington, D.C.: National Academy of Sciences, 1980.

Janis, I. L., and Hoffman, D. Facilitating effects of daily contact between partners who make a decision to cut down on smoking. *J. Pers. Soc. Psychol.* 17:25–35, 1970.

Krasnegor, N. A. (Ed.) *Cigarette Smoking as a Dependence Process* Research Monograph No. 23. Washington, D.C.: U.S. Government Printing Office, 1979, DHEW Publ. No. (ADM) 79–800.

McAlister, A. L., Perry, C., and Maccoby, N. Adolescent smoking: Onset and prevention. *Pediatrics* 63:650–658, 1979.

McAlister, A., Puska, P., Koskela, K., Pallonen, U., and Maccoby, N. Mass communication and community organization for public health education. *Am. Psychol.* 35:375–379, 1980.

McGuire, W. J. Communication-persuasion models for drug education: Experimental findings. IN: *Research on Methods and Programs of Drug Education* (Goodstadt, M., ed.) Toronto: Addiction Research Foundation, 1974.

Marlatt, G. A., and Gordon, J. R. Determinants of relapse: Implications for the maintenance of behavior change. IN: *Behavioral Medicine: Changing Health Lifestyles* (Davidson, P., and Davidson, S. M., eds.) New York: Brunner Mazel, 1979.

National Center of Health Statistics *Advance Data from Vital and Health Statistics (No. 54)* Hyattsville, Md.: National Center for Health Statistics, 1979.

National Institute on Drug Abuse *Technical Review on Cigarette Smoking as an Addiction: Report of the Task Force on Smoking* Rockville, Md.: National Institute on Drug Abuse, 1979.

Orleans, C. S. Quitting smoking: Overview and critical issues. IN: *Smoking and Behavior* (Institute of Medicine) Washington, D.C.: National Academy of Sciences, 1980.

Rice, D. P., Feldman, J. J., and White, K. L. *The Current Burden of Illness in the United States* Washington, D.C.: National Academy of Sciences, 1977.

Russell, M. A. H. Smoking problems: An overview. IN: *Research on Smoking Behavior* (Jarvik, M. E., Cullen, J. W., Vogt, E. R., and West, L. J., eds) Research Monograph No. 17. Washington, D.C.: U.S. Government Printing Office, 1978, DHEW Publ. No. (ADM) 78–581.

Russell, M. A. H. Tobacco dependence: Is nicotine rewarding or aversive? IN: *Cigarette Smoking as a Dependence Process* (Krasnegor, N. A., ed.) Research Monograph No. 23. Washington, D.C.: U.S. Government Printing Office, 1979, DHEW Publ. No. (ADM) 79–800.

Russell, M. A. H., Wilson, C., Taylor, C., and Baker, C. D. The effect of general practitioner's advice against smoking. *Br. Med. J.* 2:231–235, 1979.

Schwartz, J. L., and Rider, G. *Review and Evaluation of Smoking Control Methods: The United States and Canada, 1969–1977* Washington, D.C.: U.S. Government Printing Office, 1978, DHEW Publ. No. (CDC) 79–8369.

Telch, M. J., Killen, J. D., McAlister, A. L., Perry, C. L., and Maccoby, N. Long-term follow-up of a pilot project on smoking prevention with adolescents. *J. Behav. Med.*, in press.

United States Department of Health, Education, and Welfare *Adult Use of Tobacco— 1975* Washington, D.C.: U.S. Government Printing Office, 1976.

United States Department of Health and Human Services *The Health Consequences of Smoking for Women* Washington D.C.: U.S. Government Printing Office, 1980.

United States Public Health Service *Smoking and Health: A Report of the Surgeon General* Washington, D.C.: U.S. Government Printing Office, 1979, DHEW Publ. No. (PHS) 79–50066.

6
Sleep, Biological
Clocks, and Health

Sleep disturbance or insomnia is a widespread problem among adults. Between 29 and 39 percent of individuals over age 18 in the United States (or 45 to 60 million persons) perceive themselves as having had trouble sleeping within a given year (Institute of Medicine, 1979). Of these, 8 to 12 million seek help from a physician, and an estimated 4 to 6 million receive a prescription for sleeping pills. The Institute of Medicine report *Sleeping Pills, Insomnia, and Medical Practice* raised questions about this extensive use of drugs in the treatment of insomnia. There were 25.6 million prescriptions for sleep medications in 1977 alone, in addition to the estimated 30 million packages of over-the-counter sleep aids purchased annually. A survey of 4,500 physicians showed that when patients complain to a doctor about trouble with sleeping, about 55 percent are routinely given a prescription. Such practices would not have been continued over the years if patients did not often report benefit, but the scientific basis for this clinical judgment is modest.

The evidence for efficacy and safety of sleep drugs in long-term use is limited. There even is evidence suggesting that chronic use may exacerbate rather than ameliorate the difficulties of some insomniac patients. There are significant hazards associated with their use, including the dangerous interaction of such drugs with alcohol, their interference with daytime performance, rebound insomnia leading to habitual drug use, and the easy availability of such drugs for suicide. The costs to society may include increased mortality from their use in suicide or accidental overdose; costs of treatment for nonfatal overdose emergencies; morbidity, mortality, lost productivity, and even increased crime because of addiction to some of these drugs; and potential safety hazards from persons operating machinery or driving while still under the influence of sleep medication (Institute of Medicine, 1979; Solomon et al., 1979).

Insomnia is not a unitary disorder, and there is a need for development of specific modes of treatment—both pharmacological and nonpharmacological—for different forms of insomnia. A paucity of existing knowledge currently prevents selection of one treatment approach over another, or even one drug over another, although several useful interventions are available. Further progress will depend heavily on basic research on the neurobiology and psychology of sleep. One area—biological rhythms—is examined here as a case study for basic, clinical, and epidemiological research.

Sleep and Biological Rhythms

The relationship of sleep to biological rhythms is a promising area of basic research that may be fundamental to understanding and classifying some forms of insomnia. Recently, the Association of Sleep Disorders Centers (1979) has recognized in its classification of sleep and arousal disorders that "sleep scheduling disorders" are a distinct subtype of insomnia.

The daily cycle of sleep and wakefulness normally is synchronized to the periodic external environment by an internal biological clock. This physiological timing system shares the properties of similar circadian rhythms in a wide array of life forms, from single-cell algae to the entire plant and animal kingdom (Moore-Ede et al., 1982). In human beings, each day's sleep and wakefulness normally are consolidated into separate blocks, with sleep occurring at night and wakefulness occurring during the daytime.

Over the past decade, the merger of research findings from two disciplines—circadian physiology and sleep disorders medicine—has yielded greater understanding of the physiological and behavioral processes that affect the timing of the sleep-wake cycle and its relationship to the environmental day-night cycle. Acute phase shift experiments that put subjects to bed at an unaccustomed time of day have demonstrated that sleep disturbance results if sleep is shifted by 6 to 12 hours from the habitual time. The disturbance is characterized by awakening toward the end of sleep, together with an abnormal progression of sleep stages within the sleep time and an increased fragmentation of sleep patterns (Webb et al., 1971; Taub and Berger, 1973; Hume, 1978; Weitzman and Kripke, 1981). This confirms reports by shift workers and persons suffering from "jet-lag." Although most shift workers attribute disturbances in daytime sleep that follows nighttime work to daytime noise (Knauth and Rutenfranz, 1972a,b), sleep at that time of day would be disturbed even in the absence of noise.

Insight into the environmental factors that affect the timing of sleep has been achieved through studies of human beings living in schedule-free environments such as deep within caves, isolated from the periodic day-night changes of the environment, or in controlled laboratory settings designed to achieve the same results (Zulley et al., 1981). In such constant conditions, the timing of the sleep-wake cycle and of a variety of other physiologic functions continues to be periodic. Researchers have found that the length of unrestricted sleep varies with the phase of the self-sustained circadian rhythm of body temperature (Czeisler, 1978; Zulley, 1979; Czeisler et al., 1980). Furthermore, in a well-designed study simulating sleep after a night of shift work, Akerstedt and Gillberg (1981) verified the previously unexplained report of Foret and Lantin (1972) that major reductions occur in the duration of sleep of train drivers working at night and trying to sleep by day. They concluded that the primary determinant of the length of sleep was the phase of the body temperature cycle at bedtime rather than the length of prior wakefulness.

The results of this basic and applied research help explain why shift workers are only able to sleep a short time when they go to sleep at 8 to 10 a.m. They are trying to sleep at the "wake-up phase" of their internal biological clock. Not only is sleep cut short but the temporal organization of the sleep stages also is altered (Czeisler and Guilleminault, 1980).

Treatment of Sleep Scheduling Disorders

The impact of *when* bedtime occurs on *whether* sleep can occur prompted Czeisler et al. (1981a) to apply the properties of basic research on biological clocks to the diagnosis and treatment of the Delayed Sleep Phase (DSP) type of insomnia, a sleep scheduling disorder. They noted that patients with DSP insomnia were able to sleep well, but only if they slept at the "wrong" time of day (e.g., 4 a.m. to noon). They hypothesized that DSP insomnia was due to a specific abnormality of the system that regulates the time of sleep, rather than to a dysfunction of the sleep-generating process itself. This led to the development of a successful nonpharmacological treatment for DSP insomnia that employs the best method effectively to reset the biological clock responsible for timing the occurrence of sleep. Such studies emphasize the importance of recognizing the impact of biological clocks on the timing of sleep and other processes.

Properties of Biological Clocks

Human beings, like most other species on earth, have evolved in a regular 24-hour light-dark cycle. Although the earth's daily spin on its axis has been slowing down over the past one million years (Coale, 1974), the day length when humanlike forms first appeared was only 20 seconds shorter than it is now (Rosenberg and Runcorn, 1975). In comparison, environmental changes of the last 100 years have been immense. With the invention of the light bulb and the airplane, superimposed on the industrial revolution, there have been unprecedented changes in the temporal environment to which humans are exposed. Only since the invention of artificial light sources have human beings attempted on a large scale to manipulate the timing of the sleep-wake cycle to accommodate socioeconomic needs.

Travel to the east or west used to be sufficiently slow so that the daily light-dark cycle rarely deviated by more than an hour—well within the capacity of the body to adjust. Today, however, millions of people are abruptly subjected to shifts in environmental time cues when they work on shift work schedules or fly across time zones. Still others are in settings such as a hospital intensive care ward, where they are largely isolated from daily time cues.

In the absence of periodic environmental time cues, the cycle length or the free-running period length of circadian rhythms is no longer synchronized or entrained to a 24-hour period. Whether the free-running period is greater or less than 24 hours depends on the species; nonetheless, it remains close to 24 hours in all species. In normal human subjects, the average free-running period of the sleep-wake cycle is approximately 25 hours. In other words, in constant conditions the internal biological clock runs a little slower than its mechanical or geophysical counterparts. Therefore, successful synchronization of human circadian rhythms (including that of the sleep-wake cycle) to the 24-hour day requires that the biological clock be "reset" by an average of one hour each day.

It is generally accepted that the most important periodic environmental stimulus for entraining circadian rhythms in nearly all species is the daily alternation of light and dark (Rusak and Zucker, 1975). However, the effectiveness of a light-dark cycle alone as the synchronizer of circadian rhythms in human beings has been shown only recently (Czeisler, 1978; Czeisler et al., 1981b). The relative importance of different synchronizers to the human system remains unknown. Still, it is clear that the combination of an imposed light-dark cycle with scheduling of the time available for sleep and waking is a very effective synchronizing cue for all measurable human circadian rhythms.

Nearly 10 years ago, a specific area of the brain—the suprachiasmatic nucleus (SCN) of the hypothalamus—was identified as a central neural pacemaker responsible for the generation of many overt circadian rhythms such as the rest-activity cycle and many neuroendocrine rhythms (Moore and Eichler, 1972; Stephan and Zucker, 1972). A newly discovered monosynaptic pathway from the retina to the hypothalamus, the so-called ret-inohypothalamic tract, enabled researchers to locate the SCN. The tract appears to be responsible for transmitting photic stimuli for synchronization of this neural system with the external light-dark cycle (Moore, 1974). The human circadian system is, however, a multioscillator system (Wever, 1979). Under certain conditions, it reliably splits into two separate groups of rhythms that appear to be driven by separate pacemakers. Lesioning of the SCN in primates results in the loss of rhythmicity in certain functions such as activity while rhythms in functions such as body temperature persist (Fuller et al., 1981). Recently, Kronauer et al. (1982) have developed a mathematical model of the human circadian timing system using two interacting sinusoidal oscillators. This model system has successfully explained a number of results of the interaction between the human circadian timing system and periodic environmental time cues. These results imply the existence of a second pacemaker within the human brain, although its location has yet to be identified.

Voluntary Disruptions of the Sleep-Wake Cycle

In addition to patients who present with the primary complaint of insomnia due to an intrinsic disorder of the sleep timing process, many persons have had disruptions of the timing of their normal sleep-wake cycles by altered work or travel schedules.

Occupational Schedules (Shift Work)

There has been a dramatic increase over the past 20 years in the prevalence of shift work throughout industrialized nations. Though it has always been an integral part of most military operations, recent increases in the civilian sector have been striking. In France, shift work rose from 10 percent to 22 percent between 1957 and 1974. In the United States, shift work in man-ufacturing centers has been increasing about 3 percent every five years; full-night-shift workers rose 13 percent over the last three-year period reported (Johnson et al., 1981). Some major industries have more than half their workers on shifts.

Shift work has developed to such an extent because of the demand in modern societies for use of expensive equipment around the clock; the need for continuous attention to technological processes in the chemical, steel, and energy industries; and the demand for 24-hour services from hospitals, transportation, and emergency services. Shift work schedules vary greatly; working shifts may be from 6 to 12 hours in length (Tasto and Colligan, 1977). When the sequence of shifts changes frequently, the shift worker is exposed to an average day length that is significantly different from 24 hours. An extreme example is the work pattern of the men in the U.S. Navy who operate nuclear submarines (Schaeffer et al., 1979), who typically work with 6 hours duty and 12 hours of rest—an 18-hour day-night cycle. The rationale from the Navy's viewpoint is that 8-hour duty spans are too long for peak vigilance to be maintained and there is only space on the submarine to carry three shifts of men. This solution ignores the fact that an 18-hour day-night cycle exceeds the range to which the human sleep-wake cycle can adapt.

Some schedules may have permanent assignment to a given shift, others may rotate rapidly (every one to two days) or slowly (every week or month) (Rutenfranz et al., 1977). Some have the crews rotating to earlier shift hours; others, to later ones. Even those who always work on the night shift may still be subject to changing environmental schedules if they adopt daytime activities for social reasons during weekends or vacation.

Transmeridian Travel (Jet-Lag)

Since the 1950s and the advent of widespread commercial jet travel, increasing numbers of persons have been exposed to the effect of rapid movement across time zones. Most international air routes are in an east-west direction, rather than a north-south direction, because many of the major centers of international commerce are in Europe, the United States, and Japan—all located at similar latitudes. Airline flight crews are exposed to particularly irregular schedules; they are subjected to a combination of the effects of shift work and jet-lag (Institute of Medicine, 1981a).

Health Consequences of Abnormal Work Schedules

Despite substantial increases both in the number of people exposed to abnormal temporal work-rest schedules and in the extent to which such schedules deviate from the regular 24-hour day, there has been relatively little effort to explore physiological, medical, economic, or psychosocial consequences of these major variations in work-sleep schedules. The rapid pace of the investigation and convergence of research findings in sleep, biological rhythms, and behavior recently led the National Institute of Occupational Health and Safety (NIOSH) to hold a symposium on the 24-hour workday entitled *Variations in Work-Sleep Schedules* (Johnson et al., 1981). This symposium brought together experts in sleep research, biological rhythm research, and occupational medicine.

Long-Term Effects of Shift Work

There are significant differences in the tolerance that people have for working or sleeping on abnormal schedules (Reinberg et al., 1978, 1981). Differences may be related to properties of their circadian timing system such as the amplitude of the oscillation. When schedules entailing night work were first adopted by the armaments industry in World War I, an especially large number of stomach disorders occurred among night-shift workers (Vernon, 1921). In 1939, Duesberg and Weiss calculated that the risk of stomach ulcer was eight times greater for such workers than for those on day schedules. However, since World War II, comparisons of the health of shift workers with the general population have not been so striking. This is probably because a constant process of selection takes place among shift workers. Few now are forced onto night-shift schedules, although economic need may implicitly pressure people into accepting such work. Those who cannot cope with night-shift schedules often switch to another job. Thus, statistical comparisons between night workers and day workers are biased against finding any differences.

The long-term health consequences of abnormal work and sleep schedules in human beings are unknown. No long-term human studies have been conducted on the effects of extended exposure to night-shift work, with the cumulative sleep deprivation and disruption of the sleep-wake cycle that this entails. Animal studies document the need for research. For example, laboratory animals subjected to a 6-hour phase shift of the light-dark cycle every week (similar to a rotating shift work system) had a 20 percent shorter life span than did those kept on a normal 24-hour schedule (Aschoff et al., 1971). Naturally, these animals did not choose to participate in the shift routine, whereas workers do have a choice. Careful long-term follow-up studies of chronic shift workers are needed to see if there are similar long-term consequences to such altered routines in humans.

Abnormal sleep duration is reported to correlate with disease consequences, although the data are hard to interpret. In a large prospective study, Kripke et al. (1979) found that otherwise healthy individuals who initially reported that they habitually slept much less or more than average were more likely than controls to have died by the six-year follow-up. There are many potential explanations for this finding, including possible effects of long-term use of sleep medications; but all explanations imply a complex relationship between sleep habits and general health. As noted earlier, a major topic is the appropriate use and long-term effects of drugs for those who are unable to sleep.

A big problem in conducting epidemiological studies of shift work is in comparability of study samples. There is a surprisingly wide array of shift work schedules currently in use (Tasto and Colligan, 1977). Some of them, though classified as shift work, never involve night work. Furthermore, the U.S. Labor Department's Bureau of Labor Statistics monitors only the starting times of workers for the major U.S. industries (Colligan, 1981). Thus, little information currently is available on the number of people who rotate shifts; even the sketchy information that is available only describes workers in major industries, which may or may not correlate with practices elsewhere. The extent of the problem, however, is indicated by a recent interview survey that showed that 27 percent of employed men reported jobs involving work shifts, including both day and night shifts (National Center for Health Statistics, 1981).

Thus, the objective health status of shift workers and the long-term health consequences of shift work require investigation. The mortality and morbidity rates associated with exposure to shift work could be collected in relation to the differing categories of shift schedules worked. An international classification system of shift work schedules together with an international shift work registry could be established. The World Health Organization and the International Labor Organization might be enlisted to facilitate international cooperation.

At present, the best-documented health consequences of night-shift work are disorders of sleep and disorders of digestion (Rutenfranz et al., 1976). There also are reports of respiratory problems and lower back pain (Japan Association of Industrial Health, 1979; Kogi, 1981). However, the incidence of cardiovascular disease and neurological disorders among shift workers seems not to be greater than for the general population (Rutenfranz et al., 1977).

Sleep Disorders

Night duty, whether scheduled on a permanent or rotating basis, results in the most disruption of the sleep-wake cycle. Foret and Lantin (1972) reported major reductions in the duration of sleep in train drivers working at night and trying to sleep during the day; the drivers had great difficulty sleeping past noon, regardless of when they went to bed. A survey of 1,200 factory workers in St. Louis reported a 15 to 20 percent decrease in the reported duration of sleep following night duty, with nearly half the workers having difficulty in falling or staying asleep (Tepas et al., 1978). Averaging results of 198 surveys of a total of 4,500 shift workers conducted over the past 25 years, about 62 percent of those working at night complained of sleep disturbance (Rutenfranz et al., 1981).

A retrospective study of 115 former shift workers indicated that 90 percent considered their sleep while working shifts to have been disturbed

(Aanonsen, 1964). This is markedly greater than the one third of the overall adult population who report some sleep disturbance within a given year (Institute of Medicine, 1979). It is unknown to what extent the 14 million shift workers in the United States contribute to the estimated 50 million adults who have trouble sleeping. Similarly, it is unclear to what extent imposed variations in sleep by work schedules, leisure activities, or social demands contribute to the 8 to 10 million people who annually bring their sleep complaints to the attention of a physician.

Disorders of Digestion

Digestive problems associated with shift work include gastric and peptic ulcers, gastritis, and various intestinal disorders (Japan Association of Industrial Health, 1979; Kogi, 1981). Again, worker self-selection appears to play a major role in studies of the relation of digestive disorders to shift work. A study of 128 shift workers found they had a two- to fourfold increased incidence of gastrointestinal disorders such as peptic ulcers when compared with a general population of workers who had never been on shift work (Aanonsen, 1959, 1964). About 10 to 20 percent of workers who began shift work reacted to shift work with gastrointestinal diseases. Hence, shift work may only be well tolerated by a segment of the population. Although more than half of shift workers surveyed in various studies complained of disrupted eating habits and 20 to 40 percent complained of gastrointestinal disturbances (Rutenfranz et al., 1981), results of studies of gastric ulcer disease in shift workers have varied from an eightfold increase over day workers (Duesberg and Weiss, 1939) to an equal ulcer incidence (Aanonsen, 1959, 1964). These findings led the NIOSH symposium to recommend a concerted international effort to establish an international classification system for shift work schedules, together with national shift work registries in each of the major industrialized countries based on that classification scheme.

Other Potential Hazards

There are also potential dangers associated with shift work due to the hazards of operating complex equipment, monitoring safety indicators, or making important decisions while operating on a disrupted routine. This is particularly true as the demands of continuous industrial processes have required the performance of complex cognitive tasks at all hours (Wojtczak-Jaroszowa, 1977). Few data are available from field studies, but laboratory studies indicate significant time-of-day effects in performance measures (Folkard, 1981). Field studies that have been done indicate that the incidence of errors at work is much higher in the early morning hours (3 to 5 a.m.) than at any other time of day by people who have not fully synchronized to the new schedule—and most shift workers on rapidly changing schedules do not become synchronized. The delay before telephone calls are answered (Browne, 1949), the errors in reading meters (Bjerner et al., 1955), and the number of errors in answering warning signals (Hildebrandt et al., 1974) all increase during the early morning hours. Similarly, truck drivers have an extraordinarily elevated risk of having single-vehicle accidents at 5 a.m., compared with other times (Harris, 1977).

Human errors by pilots or air traffic controllers contribute to aircraft accidents. To what extent does this reflect incomplete adjustment to their shift work schedule? The exact contribution of their disrupted duty-rest schedule is hard to ascertain, because the extensive accident reports that the National Transportation Safety Board prepares after an aircraft accident do not evaluate the prior work-rest schedule of the crew or air traffic controllers involved (Moore-Ede and Fuller, 1980).

It is of interest to note that the nuclear power plant accident at Three Mile Island in 1979 occurred at 4 a.m.—in the middle of the night shift of 11 p.m. to 7 a.m.—with a crew that had been on night duty for only a few days and had been rotating on a weekly basis around the clock for the previous six weeks. Ehret (1981) has pointed out how the nuclear power plant operator is confronted by a complex array of instruments and instrument panels in a monotonous environment. A decrease of vigilance or performance of psychomotor tasks such as reading meters (Bjerner, et al., 1955) and responding to emergency calls (Hildebrandt et al., 1974) could contribute to a sequence of events that precipitates accidents.

Psychological Stress

Shift workers report serious disruptions of social life because their free time is not coordinated with that of family and friends. This causes stresses in family life (Japan Association of Industrial Health, 1979; Kogi, 1981), especially because of conflicting demands on the shift workers who may want to sleep during the daytime, when their spouses and children are awake and making noise.

The commonplace experience of sleep disturbances following acute stressors has been confirmed experimentally (Lester et al., 1967; Goodyear, 1973). In addition, Healey (1976) found that, compared with controls, chronic insomniacs reported significantly more stressful life events during the year in which insomnia began, suggesting that acute stressors may allow wakefulness to intrude into sleep and might induce long-term sleep disturbances. On the other hand, sleep may have a protective role in certain stressful situations. For example, Cohen (1975) noted that subjects who underwent mildly threatening experiences before bedtime had increased amounts of rapid-eye-movement (REM) sleep and suggested that sleep might provide a psychological defense. Aakvaag et al. (1978) showed that even short periods of sleep during a five-day military exercise could reverse stress-related changes in growth hormone, prolactin, and testosterone. Perhaps altered sleep is a physiological response to physical or psychological stressors that lead to actual sleep disturbances only under certain extreme conditions (Institute of Medicine, 1981b; Elliott and Eisdorfer, 1982).

Sleep deprivation is psychologically and physiologically stressful. Prolonged sleep deprivation can produce marked decrements in performance, coordination, motivation, and concentration. Yet in psychiatric patients it can have activating effects. Mendelson et al. (1977) reported that one third to one half of severely depressed patients showed a transitory antidepressant response after a full night of sleep deprivation. An increased appreciation for the importance of biological rhythms has encouraged a reexamination of the effects of sleep deprivation, because of its impact on the circadian timing system. For example, Taub and Berger (1976) described performance deficits in normal subjects whose sleep was displaced forward or backward by three hours, even though their total sleep time was essentially unchanged. Furthermore, Wehr et al. (1979) have shown that shifting the sleep-wake cycle by six hours to earlier clock hours (a phase advance) can act as an antidepressant. This may be one route by which sleep deprivation achieves its previously noted antidepressant effect (Mendelson et al., 1977).

Conclusions

The disruption of mealtimes and rest periods is the most obvious putative cause of the gastrointestinal and sleep disorders associated with disrupted work-rest schedules. Food is provided at times of day when the endogenous circadian rhythmicity of the gastrointestinal tract does not anticipate it (Suda and Saito, 1979). Similarly, shift workers often cannot sleep when their circadian system would normally precipitate it and instead try to sleep near the maximum of their endogenous rhythm of alertness. Hence, they fail to obtain needed rest. Also, they are trying to function at maximum capacity when their physiological systems are geared down to minimum levels of alertness and cognitive functioning.

With frequently changing shifts, the body is in a constant state of forced internal desynchronization. The cycles in the environment such as light-dark, social cues, and food availability, which normally synchronize the circadian system, are disrupted and may even provide conflicting phase information. Hence, predictability of internal physiological events is constantly disrupted. Studies in primates have demonstrated failures of homeostatic mechanisms when periodic environmental time cues are disrupted (Fuller et al., 1978). It would not be surprising if there were long-term health consequences from living on disrupted schedules. The main task ahead is to determine more precisely the costs of such practices, so that they can be weighed against the benefits. At the same time, a concerted effort must be made to determine the best way to minimize disruptions to the human physiological timing system caused by needed round-the-clock duty scheduling.

Given the multidisciplinary nature of the problem, a broadly based approach to research would be most helpful. The types needed would include investigations into:

- basic neuroanatomy, neurophysiology, and neuropharmacology both of the sleep-wake cycle and of the circadian timing system in human beings;
- temporal organization of the circadian timing system, including the behavioral physiology and neuroendocrinology, with mathematical modeling of the system;
- basic physiology of sleep and wakefulness and their synchronization by the environment;
- medical and psychological effects of altered environments;
- optimal design of shift work schedules to minimize disruption of the circadian sleep-wake cycle and other timing systems;
- development of an international classification system for shift work schedules; and
- studies of workers entering shift work, with special emphasis on the interaction of different shift schedules with other hazards and protective factors in the work place, as probed by prospective epidemiological methods.

References

Aakvaag, A., Sand, T., Opstad, P. K., and Fonnum, F. Hormonal changes in serum in young men during prolonged physical strain. *Eur. J. Appl. Physiol.* 39:283–291, 1978.

Aanonsen, A. Medical problems of shift work. *Ind. Med. Surg.* 28:422–427, 1959.

Aanonsen, A. *Shift Work and Health*. Oslo: Universitetsforlaget, 1964.

Akerstedt, T., and Gillberg, R. The circadian pattern of unrestricted sleep and its relation to body temperature, hormones and alertness. IN: *The Twenty-Four Hour Workday: Proceedings of a Symposium on Variations in Work-Sleep Schedules* (Johnson, L. C., Tepas, D. I., Colquhoun, W. P., and Colligan, M. J., eds.) Washington, D.C.: U.S. Government Printing Office, 1981, DHHS Publ. No. (NIOSH) 81–127.

Aschoff, J., Saint-Paul, U., and Wever, R. Die lebensdauer von fliegen unter dem einfluss von zeit-verschiebungen. *Naturwissenschaften 58*:574, 1971.

Association of Sleep Disorders Centers. Diagnostic classification of sleep and arousal disorders, 1st Ed. *Sleep 2*:1–137, 1979.

Bjerner, B., Holm, A., and Swensson, A. Diurnal variation in mental performance— A study of three-shift workers. *Br. J. Ind. Med. 12*:103–110, 1955.

Browne, R. C. The day and night performance of teleprinter switchboard operators. *Occup. Psychol. 23*:1–6, 1949.

Coale, A. J. The history of the human population. *Sci. Am. 231*:40–51,1974.

Cohen, D. B. Eye movements during REM sleep: The influence of personality and presleep conditions. *J. Pers. Soc. Psychol. 32*:1090–1093, 1975.

Colligan, M. Methodological and practical issues related to shift work research. IN: *The Twenty-Four Hour Workday: Proceedings of a Symposium on Variations in Work-Sleep Schedules* (Johnson, L. C., Tepas, D. I., Colquhoun, W. P., and Colligan, M. J., eds.) Washington, D.C.: U.S. Government Printing Office, 1981, DHHS Publ. No. (NIOSH) 81–127, pp. 261–268.

Czeisler, C. A. Human circadian physiology: Internal organization of temperature, sleep-wake and neuroendocrine rhythms monitored in an environment free of time cues. Unpublished doctoral dissertation, Stanford University, 1978.

Czeisler, C. A., and Guilleminault, C. *REM Sleep: Its Temporal Distribution* New York: Raven Press, 1980.

Czeisler, C. A., Weitzman, E. D., Moore-Ede, M. C., Zimmerman, J. C., Knauer, R. S. Human sleep: Its duration and organization depend on its circadian phase. *Science 210*:1264–1267, 1980.

Czeisler, C. A., Richardson, G. S., Coleman, R. M., Zimmerman, J.C., Moore-Ede, M. C., Dement, W. C., and Weitzman, E. D. Chronotherapy: Resetting the circadian clocks of patients with delayed sleep phase insomnia. *Sleep 4*:1–21, 1981a.

Czeisler, C. A., Richardson, G. S., Zimmerman, J. C., Moore-Ede, M. C., and Weitzman, E. D. Entrainment of human circadian rhythms by light-dark cycles: A reassessment. *Photochem. Photobiol. 34*:239–247, 1981b.

Duesberg, R., and Weiss, W. Statistische Erhebungen uber Haufigkeit des Magengeschwurs unter verschiedenen Berufsbedingungen. *Reichsarbeitsblatt III*:272–273, 1939.

Ehret, C. F. New approaches to chronohygeine for the shift worker in the nuclear power industry. IN: *Night- and Shift-Work. Biological and Social Aspects* (Reinberg, A., Vieux, N., and Andlauer, T., eds.) Oxford: Pergamon Press, 1981, pp. 263–270.

Elliott, G. R., and Eisdorfer, C. (Eds.) *Stress and Human Health* New York: Springer, 1982.

Folkard, S. Shiftwork and performance. IN: *The Twenty-Four Hour Workday: Proceedings of a Symposium on Variations in Work-Sleep Schedules* (Johnson, L. C., Tepas, D. I., Colquhoun, W. P., and Colligan, M. J., eds.) Washington, D.C.: U.S. Government Printing Office, 1981, DHHS Publ. No. (NIOSH) 81–127.

Foret, J., and Lantin, G. IN: *Aspects of Human Efficiency* (Colquhoun, W. P., ed.) London: English University Press, 1972, pp. 273–282.

Fuller, C. A., Sulzman, F. M., and Moore-Ede, M. C. Thermoregulation is impaired in an environment without circadian time cues. *Science 199*:794–796, 1978.

Fuller, C. A., Lydic, R., Sulzman, F. M., Albers, H. E., Tepper, B., and Moore-

Ede, M. C. Circadian rhythm of body temperature persists after suprachiasmatic lesions in the squirrel monkey. *Am. J. Physiol. 241*:R385–R391, 1981.

Goodyear, M. D. E. Stress, adrenocortical activity, and sleep habits. *Ergonomics 16*:679–681, 1973.

Harris, W. Fatigue, circadian rhythm, and truck accidents. IN: *Vigilance Theory, Operational Performance, and Physiological Correlates* (Mackie, R., ed.) New York: Plenum Press, 1977, pp. 133–146.

Healey, E. S. The onset of chronic insomnia and the role of life-stress events. Unpublished doctoral dissertation, Ohio State University, 1976.

Hildebrandt, G., Rohmert, W., and Rutenfranz, J. 12 and 24h rhythms in error frequency of locomotive drivers and the influence of tiredness. *Int. J. Chronobiol. 2*:175–180, 1974.

Hume, K. I. Some electrophysiological studies of sleep from subjects on varying sleep-wakefulness schedules. Unpublished doctoral dissertation, Victoria University of Manchester, England, 1978.

Institute of Medicine *Sleeping Pills, Insomnia, and Medical Practice* Washington, D.C.: National Academy of Sciences, 1979.

Institute of Medicine *Airline Pilot Age, Health, and Performance* Washington, D.C.: National Academy Press, 1981a.

Institute of Medicine *Research on Stress and Human Health* Washington, D.C.: National Academy Press, 1981b.

Japan Association of Industrial Health (Shift Work Committee). Opinion of night and shift work. *J. Sci. Labour 55(Part II)*:1–36, 1979.

Johnson, L. C., Tepas, D. I., Colquhoun, W. J., and Colligan, M. J. (Eds.) *The Twenty-Four Hour Workday: Proceedings of a Symposium on Variations in Work-Sleep Schedules* Washington, D.C.: U.S. Government Printing Office, 1981, DHHS Publ. No. (NIOSH) 81–127.

Knauth, P., and Rutenfranz, J. Untersuchungen zum Problem des Schlafverhaltens bei experimenteller Schichtarbeit. *Int. Arch. Arbeitsmed. 30*:1–22, 1972a.

Knauth, P., and Rutenfranz, J. Untersuchungen uber die Beziehungen zwischen Schichtform und Tagesaufteilung. *Int. Arch. Arbeitsmed. 30*:173–191, 1972b.

Kogi, K. Research motives and methods in field approaches to shift work. IN: *The Twenty-Four Hour Workday: Proceedings of a Symposium on Variations in Work-Sleep Schedules* (Johnson, L. C., Tepas, D. I., Colquhoun, W. P., and Colligan, M. J., eds.) Washington, D.C.: U.S. Government Printing Office, 1981, DHHS Publ. No. (NIOSH) 81–127.

Kripke, D. F., Simons, R. N., Garfinkel, L., and Hammond, E. L. Short and long sleep and sleeping pills: Is increased mortality associated? *Arch. Gen. Psychiatry 36*:103–116, 1979.

Kronauer, R. E., Czeisler, C. A., Pilato, S. F., Moore-Ede, M. C. and Weitzman, E. D. Mathematical model of the human circadian system with two interacting oscillators. *Am. J. Physiol., 11*:R3–R17, 1982.

Lester, B. K., Burch, N. R., and Dossett, R. C. Nocturnal EEG-GSR profiles: The influence of pre-sleep states. *Psychophysiology 3*:238–248, 1967.

Mendelson, W. B., Gillin, J. C., and Wyatt, R. J. *Human Sleep and Its Disorders* New York: Plenum Press, 1977.

Moore, R. Y. Visual pathways and the central neural control of diurnal rhythms. IN: *The Neurosciences: Third Study Program* (Schmitt, F. O., and Worden, F. G., eds.) Cambridge: MIT Press, 1974, pp. 537–542.

Moore, R. Y., and Eichler, V. B. Loss of a circadian adrenal corticosterone rhythm following suprachiasmatic lesions in the rat. *Brain Res.* 42:201–206, 1972.

Moore-Ede, M. C., and Fuller, C. A. Evaluation of aircraft accident reports. *Forum Int. Soc. Air Safety Invest.* 13:13–15, 1980.

Moore-Ede, M. C., Sulzman, F. M., and Fuller, C. A. *The Clocks that Time Us: Physiology of the Circadian Timing System* Cambridge, Mass.: Harvard University Press, 1982.

National Center for Health Statistics *Basic Data from Wave I of the National Survey of Personal Health Practices and Consequences: United States, 1979* (Schoenborn, C. A., ed.) Washington, D.C.: U.S. Government Printing Office, 1981, DHHS Publ. No. (PHS) 81–1163.

Reinberg, A., Vieux, N., Ghata, J., Chaumont, A. J., and Laporte, A. Circadian rhythm amplitude and individual ability to adjust to shift work. *Ergonomics* 21:763–766, 1978.

Reinberg, A., Andlauer, P., and Norbert, V. Circadian temperature rhythm amplitude and long term tolerance of shift working. IN: *The Twenty-Four Hour Workday: Proceedings of a Symposium on Variations in Work-Sleep Schedules* (Johnson, L. C., Tepas, D. I., Colquhoun, W. P., and Colligan, M. J., eds.) Washington, D.C.: U.S. Government Printing Office, 1981, DHHS Publ. No. (NIOSH) 81–127.

Rosenberg, G. D., and Runcorn, S. K. Conclusions. IN: *Growth Rhythm and the History of the Earth's Rotation* (Rosenberg, G. D., and Runcorn, S. K., eds.) London: Wiley, 1975, pp. 535–538.

Rusak, B., and Zucker, I. Biological rhythms and animal behavior. *Ann. Rev. Psychol.* 26:137–171, 1975.

Rutenfranz, J., Knauth, P., and Colquhoun, W. P. Hours of work and shift work. *Ergonomics* 19:331–340, 1976.

Rutenfranz, J., Colquhoun, W. P., Knauth, P., and Ghata, J. N. Biomedical and psychosocial aspects of shift work: A review. *Scand. J. Work Environ. Health* 3:165–182, 1977.

Rutenfranz, J., Knauth, P., and Angersbach, D. IN: *The Twenty-Four Hour Workday: Proceedings of a Symposium on Variations in Work-Sleep Schedules* (Johnson, L. C., Tepas, D. I., Colquhoun, W. P., and Colligan, M. J., eds.) Washington, D.C.: U.S. Government Printing Office, 1981, DHHS Publ. No. (NIOSH) 81–127.

Schaeffer, K. E., Kerr, C. M., Buss, D., and Haus, E. Effect of 18–h watch schedules on circadian cycles of physiological functions during submarine patrols: Circadian cycles in submarine patrols. *Undersea Biomed. Res.* S81–S90 (submarine supplement), 1979.

Solomon, F., White, C., Parron, D. L., and Mendelson, W. Sleeping pills, insomnia, and medical practice. *N. Engl. J. Med.* 300:803–808, 1979.

Stephan, F. K., and Zucker, I. Circadian rhythms in drinking behavior and locomotor activity of rats are eliminated by hypothalamic lesions. *Proc. Natl. Acad. Sci. USA* 69:1583–1586, 1972.

Suda, M., and Saito, M. Coordinative regulation of feeding behavior and metabolism by a circadian timing system. IN: *Biological Rhythms and Their Central Mechanism* (Suda, M., Hayaishi, O., and Nakagawa, H., eds.) New York: Elsevier North-Holland, 1979, pp. 263–271.

Tasto, D. L., and Colligan, M. J. *Shift Work Practices in the United States* Washington, D.C.: U.S. Government Printing Office, 1977, DHEW Pub. No. (NIOSH) 77–148.

Taub, J. M., and Berger, R. J. Sleep stage patterns associated with acute shifts in the sleep-wakefulness cycle. *Electroencephalogr. Clin. Neurophysiol.* 35:613–619, 1973.

Taub, J. M., and Berger, R. J. The effects of changing the phase and duration of sleep. *J. Exp. Psychol. Hum. Percep. Perform.* 2:30–41, 1976.

Tepas D. I., Stock, C. G., Maltese, J. W., and Walsh, J. K. Reported sleep of shift workers: A preliminary report. *Sleep Res.* 7:313, 1978.

Vernon, H. M. *Industrial Fatigue and Efficiency* New York: E. P. Dutton, 1921.

Webb, W. B., Agnew, H. W., Jr., and Williams, K. L. Effect on sleep of a sleep period time displacement. *Aerospace Med.* 42:152–155, 1971.

Wehr, T. A., Wirz-Justice, A., Goodwin, F. K., Duncan, W., and Gillin, J. C. Phase advance of the circadian sleep-wake cycle as an antidepressant. *Science 206*:710–713, 1979.

Weitzman, E. D., and Kripke, D. Experimental 12–hour shift of the sleep-wake cycle in man: Effects on sleep and physiologic rhythms. IN: *The Twenty-Four Hour Workday: Proceedings of a Symposium on Variations in Work-Sleep Schedules* (Johnson, L. C., Tepas, D. I., Colquhoun, W. P., and Colligan, M. J., eds.) Washington, D.C.: U.S. Government Printing Office, 1981, DHHS Publ. No. (NIOSH) 81–127.

Wever, R. *The Circadian System of Man* New York: Springer, 1979.

Wojtczak-Jaroszowa, J. *Physiological and Psychological Aspects of Night and Shift Work* Washington, D.C.: U.S. Government Printing Office, 1977, DHEW Publ. No. (NIOSH) 78–113.

Zulley, J. *Der Einfluss von Zeitgebern auf den hlaf des Menschen* Frankfurt: Rita G. Fischer-Verlag, 1979.

Zulley, J., Wever, R., and Aschoff, J. The dependence on onset and duration of sleep on the circadian rhythm of rectal temperature. *Pflugers Arch. 391*:314–318, 1981.

7
Cardiovascular Disease and Behavior

Diseases associated with atherosclerosis and hypertension are the most important component of the burden of illness in the United States today, causing more deaths, disabilities, and economic loss than any other category of acute or chronic diseases (National Heart, Lung, and Blood Institute, 1981). In 1977, cardiovascular diseases caused 873,000 deaths—almost half of all deaths in the United States. Their economic cost was an estimated $39 billion in health expenditures and lost productivity. In addition, these diseases exact a massive personal toll both on life expectancy and on the quality of life (cf. Chapter 2).

Epidemiological research has led to recognition that cardiovascular disease is not an inevitable result of the aging process and that behavioral factors are significant in its etiology and course. The Framingham, Massachusetts, study of coronary heart disease has been especially enlightening. Designed as a prospective study of a large population, it has examined associations of various genetic, physiological, and behavioral factors with the incidence of myocardial infarctions and sudden cardiac death (Kannell et al., 1966; Dawber, 1980). The study demonstrated for the first time correlations between cardiovascular disease and such behavior-related factors as cigarette smoking, obesity, and hypertension.

Through the 1940s and 1950s, premature death from coronary heart disease increased to become the major health problem for adults in the United States. However, since about 1968, there has been a decline in the death rate from coronary heart disease; that decline has been particularly steep during the past decade (National Heart, Lung, and Blood Institute, 1981). As a direct result, average life expectancy has improved. But the United States continues to have one of the highest coronary death rates among middle-aged men in the world; coronary heart disease alone is responsible for about 640,000 deaths annually. Many factors may have contributed to the decline in mortality—for example, nation-wide programs for control of hypertension and advances in treating and managing cardiovascular disease. Still, it seems likely that voluntary changes in lifestyle also have had an effect. Over two thirds of American families have appreciably altered certain habits during these years. These changes in diet, smoking, and exercise were paralleled by remarkable decreases in deaths from cardiovascular disorders such as coronary heart disease and stroke. In 1978 alone, an estimated 114,000 fewer deaths occurred among people age 35–74 than expected, based on 1968 mortality rates (National Heart, Lung, and Blood Institute, 1981).

Pathogenesis of Cardiovascular Disease

Clinical manifestations of coronary heart disease are cardiac ischemia, including angina pectoris; acute myocardial infarction; sudden cardiac death; and congestive heart failure. The underlying pathological condition usually is atherosclerosis, a specific type of hardening of the arteries that affects large arteries.

Atherogenesis is the process that culminates in atherosclerosis (National Heart, Lung, and Blood Institute, 1981). In early stages, the inner layer of an affected artery thickens with deposition of fat, together with an increase in the number of cells in the innermost layer of the artery. In advanced stages, mounds of tissue called fibrous plaques form on the lining of the artery, most frequently and severely in the arteries of the heart, brain, and legs. Although people often begin to develop plaques in their twenties, resulting local disturbances in blood flow usually are clinically silent for years. The rate at which plaques grow large enough to produce symptoms varies from one individual to another. On average, plaques are more extensive and larger in Americans than in persons from nonindustrialized countries (McGill, 1968).

Conditions closely associated with more extensive and advanced fibrous plaques are also associated with high rates of cardiovascular disease—the major risk factors discussed below. The variety of conditions that accelerate the process suggests that several mechanisms such as potential interactions with behavior may be involved on several levels.

Risk Factors of Cardiovascular Disease

The concept of risk factors in cardiovascular disease was an outgrowth of prospective epidemiological studies begun in the late 1950s. An association was noted between certain characteristics of individuals who were apparently healthy when first seen in the health care system and their risk for subsequently developing coronary heart disease. Among the established risk factors are hypertension (high blood pressure), hypercholesterolemia (high concentration of cholesterol in blood), advanced age, maleness, cigarette smoking, diabetes, and marked obesity. Suspected risk factors include physical inactivity, personality behavior type, and a high concentration of glucose without overt diabetes mellitus (National Heart, Lung, and Blood Institute, 1981).

Cigarette Smoking

The association between cigarette smoking and cardiovascular disease is strong and consistent. In the Framingham study, cigarette smoking was the strongest observed risk factor for sudden cardiac death. Among cigarette smokers, the rate of sudden cardiac death in the youngest decade was almost four times greater than that found in nonsmokers; in older age groups, smoking was associated with a twofold greater incidence of sudden cardiac death (Dawber, 1980).

Cigarette smoking also is associated with an increased risk of ischemic heart disease and its complications. A pack-a-day smoker has about twice the risk of a heart attack as the nonsmoker; a two-pack-a-day smoker has about three times the risk (National Heart, Lung, and Blood Institute, 1981). People who stop smoking may have an immediate decline in their risk of atherosclerotic disease, with an eventual return to disease rates resembling those of nonsmokers. As emphasized in Chapter 5, smoking may be the most important preventable behavioral factor contributing to illness, disability, and premature death.

Hypertension

Blood pressure is an important indicator of cardiovascular function. Both systolic blood pressure, more affected by cardiac output, and diastolic blood pressure, more affected by peripheral resistance, change markedly as a function of physical and psychological status. Definitions of high blood pressure are statistical, constituting a deviation from the population average or values known to be deleterious to health (Hypertension Detection and Follow-Up Program, 1979). Techniques for measuring blood pressure and characterizing variations in it have advanced greatly in recent years. Application of those advances to elucidating the role of behavioral factors in hypertension has moved more slowly.

In the United States, hypertension affects 23 to 60 million people, depending on the criteria used to define it (Rice and Kleinman, 1980). More than 60 million people have had at least a one-time blood pressure measurement of 140/90 or greater. Blood pressure varies from minute to minute and day to day; for persons whose pressures are close to 140/90, definition of who is a "case" is problematic. Approximately 35 million Americans have definite high blood pressure (blood pressure of 160/95 or greater); another 25 million are estimated to have borderline hypertension (blood pressure of 140/90 to 159/94). These figures, in aggregate, account for almost one quarter of the entire U.S. population.

As chronic blood pressure rises, so does the risk for ischemic heart disease and its complications. In younger men followed for 24 years in the Framingham study, hypertensives had twice the risk of developing coronary heart disease as did normotensive subjects. Blood pressure also was related to the development of myocardial infarction and angina pectoris.

Two recent Institute of Medicine activities considered issues in hypertension that are related to the biobehavioral sciences. One Health and Behavior conference examined research opportunities in combined drug and psychosocial treatments of hypertension, including problems of adherence to long-term drug treatment (Parron et al., 1981). Some of these issues are discussed in Chapter 16. In a major Institute of Medicine study— *Research on Stress and Human Health*—the evidence that stressful environmental conditions play a role in the etiology or course of hypertension was examined (Bunney et al., 1982).

Stress and Hypertension   Clinical evidence of an association between chronic stressors and hypertension is suggestive but not definitive (cf. Chapter 3). Hypertensives have been characterized as tending to be withdrawn, uncommunicative, and anxious to avoid confrontation even when it is appropriate. An early hypothesis was that hypertension was a result of "anger directed inward," caused by an inability to express anger properly to others (Alexander, 1950). Kalis et al. (1957) proposed that such behavior could be beneficial to the hypertensive because it minimizes situations in which rage reactions occur. In accord with this hypothesis, Weiner et al. (1962) demonstrated that hypertensives tend to respond in ways that avoid involvement. Similarly, Sapira and colleagues (1971) found that, in contrast to normotensives, hypertensives failed to perceive obvious conflicts when viewing movies of a "good" and "bad" doctor-patient relationship. A prospective study of air traffic controllers showed that this array of personality and behavioral characteristics precede the rise of blood pressure into hypertensive range. Although the roots of the hypertension no doubt antedated the psychosocial measurements, it is unknown whether they precede development of the personality pattern. This study does show that the behavioral features are not the result of being clinically hypertensive (Rose et al., 1978).

Some studies suggest that hypertension also may be affected by acutely stressful events. Weiner (1970) has reviewed several such studies. Unfortunately, all were retrospective and used observers who knew which patients were hypertensive. Under such experimental conditions, observers may unconsciously continue to focus on the time around the onset of hypertension until a plausibly stressful event is uncovered. Thus, the current trend toward doing such research prospectively has powerful methodological advantages.

The few available controlled clinical studies suggest that even simple stimuli, such as having blood drawn or performing mental calculations, can increase blood pressure, changing cardiovascular output and peripheral resistance (Shapiro, 1961). Evidence suggests that hypertensives and normotensives with a family history of hypertension are more responsive to environmental and behavioral stressors than are normotensive controls (Shapiro, 1960; Falkner et al., 1981). However, it is unclear whether such transient effects play any role in the etiology of hypertension. Animal experiments have helped to confirm some of the effects of stressors on the cardiovascular system (Ciaranello et al., 1982). Those that result in sustained hypertension require animals to adjust to situations that are filled with threat and uncertainty, such as avoidance conditioning in monkeys (Benson et al., 1969) and social crowding in mice (Henry et al., 1975).

Heterogeneity Among Hypertensives   An important development in the past decade is the accumulating evidence of different physiological types of hypertensives (Julius, 1981; Weiner, 1981). A substantial subset of borderline hypertensives may be characterized as having both high plasma renin concentrations and high cardiac output; others are average in both these respects. It is possible that such physiological heterogeneity is accompanied by psychological heterogeneity. For example, Esler et al. (1977) studied a subgroup of borderline hypertensives with high renin excretion and cardiac output. These patients exhibited the same types of withdrawal and submissiveness mentioned earlier for people with established hypertension. Borderline hypertensives with normal renin values resembled normotensive controls and did not exhibit those types of behaviors. The normal-renin hypertensive group differed from normotensive controls only in appearing to be more resentful.

Julius and Esler (1975) have argued that high-renin, high-cardiac-output borderline hypertension results from increased sympathetic nervous system activity alone or with diminished parasympathetic inhibition. The latter would suggest a disturbance in central autonomic regulation and could indicate a condition of increased sensitivity to stressors (Julius, 1981).

Mechanisms Connecting Behavior and Hypertension In the past few decades, scientists have learned much about the effects of stressors on the cardiovascular function of animals and man (Elliott and Eisdorfer, 1982), but much remains to be learned. Particular attention should be given to the neuroanatomy and the neurochemistry of the cardiovascular system. The breadth of skills needed to work in this area of research has caused some to call for the creation of a new field, cardiovascular neurobiology (Cohen, 1981).

Ways in which behavior affects hypertension have yet to be explained. Continuous monitoring of blood pressure in freely moving subjects has shown that blood pressures fluctuate widely over time in both hypertensives and normotensives. Transient changes may or may not play a role in the etiology, perpetuation, or exacerbation of the disease. Animals in which sensory nerves from the cardiovascular system have been severed exhibit exaggerated responses to stimuli, suggesting important interactions between behavior and cardiovascular pressure receptors. For example, a primary or secondary receptor dysfunction might increase cardiovascular responsiveness, amplifying reactions to usual life events beyond normal limits (Folkow and Rubinstein, 1966). This could, in turn, damage blood vessels and cause cardiovascular hypertrophy and hypertension.

Responses to behavioral events may not only alter the immediate level of blood pressure but may carry over and affect the normal 24-hour pattern of blood pressure. It is now possible to monitor arterial pressure and heart rate continuously in man (Richardson et al., 1964; Harshfield et al., 1979), and this technique should be applied to hypertensives to determine if their responses to stressors have effects that carry over into other times of day, such as during sleep. It is possible, for example, that some apparently normotensive patients do not experience the normal nocturnal fall in blood pressure, which could predispose them to cardiovascular disease.

Hypercholesterolemia

A strong body of evidence supports an association between an elevated concentration of cholesterol in blood and the progression of atherosclerosis (National Heart, Lung, and Blood Institute, 1981). Average serum cholesterol is higher for people in the United States and in other relatively affluent nations than it is for those in less affluent countries. This difference arises in early childhood and persists throughout life. Although the chain of phys-iological steps leading from high serum cholesterol concentration to for-mation of atherosclerotic plaques has yet to be fully explained, there are plausible mechanisms for a causal relationship. The strength and consistency of this association have led to studies of whether reducing cholesterol concentrations can retard the progression of atherosclerosis and reduce the incidence of clinically manifest cardiovascular disease (cf. Chapter 15).

The average concentration of cholesterol in the plasma of middle-aged American men is presently about 220 mg/dl of blood. Risk of premature coronary heart disease and its consequences, especially acute heart attacks, increases rapidly when cholesterol exceeds 220 mg/dl. Men from 40 to 49 years of age with cholesterol levels above 240 mg/dl have more than twice the risk of developing premature coronary heart disease of men in the same age group whose cholesterol levels are less than 220 mg/dl; men with levels of 270 mg/dl and higher have almost three times the risk. The relationship is similar for women (National Heart, Lung, and Blood Institute, 1981).

Blood cholesterol is part of lipoprotein complexes that can be categorized according to their density: high density lipoprotein (HDL), low-density lipoprotein (LDL), and very low density lipoprotein (VLDL). Each complex has a distinct chemical composition and a unique role in the body's uptake and deposition of cholesterol. Studies suggest that risk of cardiovascular disease is directly related to total cholesterol and cholesterol as LDL and inversely related to HDL. That means that a high total cholesterol or a high proportion of cholesterol as LDL is a risk factor of atherosclerotic heart disease; HDL-cholesterol may be "protective" (National Heart, Lung, and Blood Institute, 1981).

Only part of blood cholesterol is derived from dietary intake of choles-terol; there also is important endogenous synthesis. Still, controlled ex-periments carried out in metabolic wards and recent epidemiological studies with a 20-year follow-up period indicate that the amount of dietary intake of cholesterol correlates with blood cholesterol levels (McGill, 1979; Na-tional Heart, Lung, and Blood Institute, 1981). Cross-sectional data from epidemiological studies done in the United States and in Israel have not, however, confirmed this association. Consumption of saturated and poly-unsaturated fatty acids also appears to influence the amount of cholesterol present in blood and its distribution among HDL and LDL fractions (Glueck, 1979; Shekelle et al., 1981), with saturated fatty acids such as those found in dairy and meat products being a greater health risk.

It now is recognized that dietary factors interact with individual phys-iological and genetic traits, along with exercise habits and other behaviors, in determining blood cholesterol levels (Glueck, 1979; National Heart,

Lung, and Blood Institute, 1981). There is considerable evidence that certain types of behavioral challenge raise blood cholesterol levels (Jenkins et al., 1969; Rahe et al., 1972; Eliot, 1979).

An important research question is how to reduce cholesterol effectively in large populations. A possible answer lies in the major voluntary changes in American diets that have occurred since 1950 (cf. Chapter 15). For example, consumption of eggs, the single largest dietary source of cholesterol, has dropped 30 percent (Stamler, 1978). Per capita consumption of butter has declined by 55 percent (Page and Friend, 1978), and use of margarines and vegetable oils low in saturated fats and high in polyunsaturated fats has markedly increased. As a result, intake of saturated fat and cholesterol has declined (Rizak and Jackson, 1980). In keeping with these changes in diet, the mean serum cholesterol of middle-aged men in the United States decreased from about 235 mg/dl in the 1950s and early 1960s to less than 220 mg/dl in the 1970s (National Heart, Lung, and Blood Institute, 1981). Much more needs to be known about factors that fostered these marked shifts from well-established eating habits of large numbers of people.

Behavioral Patterns

In recent years, most research on behavior patterns and cardiovascular disease has related to "Type A" behavior. Two cardiologists, Friedman and Rosenman (1959), became interested in behavior because of certain commonalities they saw in patients who had heart attacks. They characterized these Type A people as being strongly competitive, unusually aggressive, highly work-oriented, and having a persistent sense of time urgency. People in whom such behaviors were not as prevalent were called "Type B." Several scales are available to distinguish Type A from Type B behavior patterns (Jenkins, 1978). There are significant relationships among the scales, but it seems likely that each measures unique aspects of the interrelated factors that constitute Type A behavior (Rosenman and Friedman, 1974).

Excellent prospective studies have shown that Type A people have a much higher incidence of heart attacks than do Type B people (Rosenman, 1978). At present, however, that information has only limited clinical value. The behavior pattern is quite common among males in Western cultures, only some of whom develop cardiovascular disease—a finding that is also true for hypertension and hypercholesterolemia. At present, it also is unclear whether Type A behaviors can be changed in ways that reduce risk of cardiovascular disease, although some small pilot studies suggest that changes can be made (Rahe et al., 1975, Roskies et al., 1978).

A critical review of available research and theory recently was conducted by the Review Panel on Coronary-Prone Behavior and Coronary Heart Disease (1981) for the National Heart, Lung, and Blood Institute. The panel concluded that "Type A behavior . . . is associated with an increased risk of clinically apparent CHD [coronary heart disease] in employed, middle-aged U.S. citizens." The report further states that the Type A risk contribution appears to be of the same order of magnitude as other standard risk factors and in addition to them. They called for research into: (1) more precise delineation of associations of coronary-prone behavior and coronary heart disease; (2) better methods for assessing the Type A behavior pattern; (3) identification of physiological mechanisms that link behavior to coronary heart disease; (4) exploration of cultural and developmental factors that might influence expression of consequences of Type A behavior; and (5) more definitive tests of possible intervention strategies.

Obesity

Marked obesity is a risk factor for ischemic heart disease, at least in early middle age. Much of the effect is attributable to the association of obesity with several of the other risk factors of cardiovascular disease, including hypercholesterolemia, hypertension, and diabetes. Diabetes is now established as one of the chief health hazards of being markedly obese. Obese individuals are more likely to have elevated concentrations of atherogenic lipoproteins and lower levels of HDL than nonobese persons. Sedentary habits may add to the risk. In fact, weight gain was the only environmental factor in the Framingham study related to ultimate elevation of blood pressure. Biobehavioral research opportunities related to obesity are discussed in Chapter 8.

Familial Incidence

A family history of premature and often fatal heart attack is associated with an increased risk of ischemic heart disease (National Heart, Lung, and Blood Institute, 1981). This association may be due to genetic or environmental factors. Several types of abnormal patterns of metabolizing lipoproteins are inherited biologically, and some of them predispose to more severe atherosclerosis and to more frequent ischemic heart disease. However, familial predisposition to atherosclerosis may also arise from a common diet and lifestyle. In most persons, atherosclerosis and its complications probably result from interactions between both behavioral and genetic characteristics and the external environment. Much more work is needed on factors affecting health outcomes of such interactions.

Physical Inactivity

Several carefully executed studies indicate that physical activity independently decreases the risk of developing clinical complications of atherosclerosis (Thomas et al., 1981). The Framingham study showed that the rate of coronary disease for men with sedentary lifestyles was about three times higher than that for active men (Dawber, 1980). Also, the age of onset of cardiovascular disease typically was earlier in the least active individuals. However, the mechanism by which physical activity may affect morbidity and mortality from cardiovascular disease remains to be determined. Conducting a well-designed population study involving exercise has proved to be very difficult. Therefore, although it is likely that a sedentary lifestyle is a significant risk factor in cardiovascular disease, further research is necessary to determine whether exercise interacts with other risk factors and by what mechanism.

Case Study of Sudden Cardiac Death

Sudden cardiac death as a specific disease entity is the major cause of mortality among Americans 20 to 64 years old. It was a topic for one of the Health and Behavior conferences (Solomon et al., 1981). Sudden cardiac death claims the lives of about 400,000 persons annually (DeSilva and Lown, 1978; Cobb et al., 1980). It is the principal terminal event for coronary deaths, accounting for 65 percent of the total; it affects persons so young that many potential years of vigorous life are lost. Considerations of relationships between behavioral factors and cardiovascular disease in general are relevant to understanding the influence of those factors on sudden cardiac death. But abundant evidence suggests that there may, in addition, be a specific emotional role in processes leading to sudden cardiac death.

Definition of Sudden Cardiac Death

The general definition of sudden cardiac death is unexpected death that occurs within 24 hours in a previously fully ambulatory person. Deaths that occur instantly or within an hour of the onset of symptoms appear to result mainly from cardiac arrhythmias incompatible with a life-sustaining cardiac output (Iseri et al., 1978). Deaths that occur after several hours of symptom onset may result from ischemia, myocardial infarction, or failure of the heart as a pump. Most of the emphasis of the conference was on deaths that result from disturbances of normal cardiac rhythms.

At autopsy, 75 percent of sudden cardiac death victims have advanced coronary artery disease (Reichenbach and Moss, 1975), compared with the usual incidence of 38 percent for autopsy patients of all types. Although the heart is almost invariably diseased in sudden cardiac death, the type of disease typically is compatible with many years of active and satisfactory life. Thus, behavioral factors may trigger an attack of sudden cardiac death in an individual who might otherwise have many years of life remaining.

Settings in Which Sudden Cardiac Death Occurs

Studies of the circumstances surrounding sudden cardiac death provide clues to its etiology. Nearly 75 percent of sudden deaths occur at home (Kuller et al., 1967; Wikland, 1968). In contrast to acute myocardial infarction, sudden cardiac death most commonly occurs during waking hours. Epidemiological surveys have established that sudden cardiac deaths are overrepresented on Saturdays and Mondays, strongly suggesting a behavioral component in the etiology (Myers and Dewar, 1975). Also, intense and unusual fatigue is a common precursor to sudden cardiac death (Kuller, 1978).

Both pathological and epidemiological studies support the possibility of an emotional role in sudden cardiac death. Cardiac histology of sudden death differs from that of myocardial infarction. In the former, the lesion has been described as coagulative myocytolysis (Baroldi et al., 1979; Cebelin and Hirsch, 1980). The most commonly observed finding in myocardial infarction is coagulative necrosis secondary to ischemia. Pathological findings similar to those in sudden cardiac death victims are found in patients with pheochromocytomas, which secrete large amounts of catecholamines, in chronic alcoholics, in animals given pharmacological doses of catecholamines, and in mugging victims who have died suddenly after experiencing a seemingly minor trauma (Connor, 1968; Engel, 1971; Baroldi, 1975; Eliot et al., 1978; Cebelin and Hirsch, 1980).

In regard to a biobehavioral contribution to the generation of sudden cardiac death, interest has centered on (1) the long-term personal and societal factors that contribute to the development of a diseased heart and (2) the short-term factors that facilitate the physiological disturbances leading to a fatal arrhythmia.

Mechanisms of Sudden Cardiac Death

Although there probably are numerous forms of arrhythmic death, researchers have emphasized two: asystolic deaths mediated by altered vagal function via the parasympathetic nervous system (Richter, 1957) and deaths from ventricular fibrillation mediated by the sympathetic nervous system (Lown, 1973). Any of three physiological routes may be involved in initiation of these disturbances: factors related to the load on the myocardium, including volume and pressure demands; direct nervous influences on the heart through vagus and sympathetic nerves; and blood-borne chemical influences, including oxygen and carbon dioxide pressures, ions required for cardiac contractility, energy-supplying compounds, hormones, and recreational pharmacological substances. These three routes are plausibly related to one another by direct actions and by reflex arcs involving the central nervous system.

A better understanding of neural controls of the heart relating to sudden cardiac death include:

• description of neural pathways involved;
• determination of the discharge patterns that are associated with the initiation of an arrhythmia;
• description of the influence of both internal and external stimuli upon these discharge patterns;
• delineation of the extent to which neuronal changes can produce persistent abnormal cardiac rhythms; and
• exploration of the means by which manipulation of relevant neural pathways may prevent or reverse the pathological response to the processes involved.

Although sudden cardiac death may result from vagal mediation causing asystolic death (Richter, 1957), the preponderance of such deaths appears to be the result of ventricular fibrillation (Lown, 1973; Cobb et al., 1975; Iseri et al., 1978). Sympathetic denervation protects animals against ventricular fibrillation (Rosenfeld et al., 1978). Conversely, animals are at increased risk when they are behaviorally aroused (DeSilva et al., 1978; Liang et al., 1979).

The primary technique for documenting changes in heart electrical activity originated with Lown et al. (1973), who studied the threshold necessary to evoke repetitive ectopic activity as a precursor to ventricular fibrillation. In the ischemic heart, a unilateral increase in sympathetic outflow or an imbalance between left and right sympathetic cardiac influences can predispose the heart to ventricular fibrillation. The central nervous system probably controls these patterns of activity. Thus, Rabinowitz and Lown (1978) showed in dogs that increasing brain concentrations of the neuroregulator serotonin raise the threshold for ventricular fibrillation and reduce sympathetic outflow. This analysis suggests an important role for stress responses in the mechanisms of sudden cardiac death and rational approaches to prevention.

In accord with the above experiments, Cohen and Cabot (1979) found that the most prominent area of serotonergic neurons in the brain, the raphe nuclei, has cell groups that project directly to the sympathetic pre-ganglionic neurons. Stimulation of this region suppresses neuronal firing and produces a fall in both systolic and diastolic pressure as well as changes in the heart rate. Lesions in this raphe-spinal system alter heart rate re-sponses to various stimuli. The raphe-spinal system may serve a rate-limiting function, inhibiting sympathetic preganglionic activity and thereby reducing sympathetic outflow. More work is necessary to confirm and extend these experiments; but relationships among behavioral, anatomical, physiological, and pharmacological factors can now be envisioned.

Some investigators believe that activation of the sympathetic nervous system by stressful experiences may be only a "trigger," albeit a clinically significant one. In this view, the trigger may relate to altered platelet func-tion, inducing a hypercoagulable state fostering transient platelet plugs, ischemia, and then heightened vulnerability to arrhythmic events (Haft et al., 1972a,b; Haft and Fani, 1973; Harker and Ritchie, 1980). In contrast, some have pointed to the effect of sympathetic nervous stimulation not on the heart rhythm centers per se but on the coronary vascular bed itself. This vascular bed is richly innervated, and coronary spasm can be induced rather easily by alpha-adrenergic stimulation (Mudge et al., 1976a,b; Hillis and Braunwald, 1978). The possibility that coronary spasm is a key me-diating event in sudden death suggests that there may be a direct benefit from using calcium channel blocking agents, which decrease coronary vas-cular resistance (Antman et al., 1980). In any event, it appears that brain and behavior may be involved in sudden cardiac death via several pathways and processes.

Since the earliest investigations documenting a relationship between be-havioral state and physiological function, considerable evidence has impli-cated the adrenal medulla and cortex as central to the physiological response to changes in emotional state, especially involving danger and alarm. Most evidence points to the adrenal medullary sympathetic nervous system as one connection between behavior and cardiac function (cf. Chapter 3). Along with studies of the precise neural involvement in cardiac functioning, epidemiological data are needed for a better understanding of psychosocial factors that precipitate sudden death and to point to new directions in research.

Risk Factors in Sudden Cardiac Death

Careful examination of the risk factors associated with sudden cardiac death reveals both similarities to and differences from those for myocardial in-farction. Heavy smoking, obesity, and hypercholesterolemia are consistent risk factors for cardiovascular disease, whether resulting in sudden cardiac death or myocardial infarction (Gordon et al., 1977). Severe fatigue is more common than chest pain as a precursor to sudden death (Kuller, 1978), and hypertension and excessive alcohol use are more commonly associated with sudden cardiac death than with myocardial infarction (Weinblatt et al., 1978). In the United States, sudden cardiac death victims typically come from lower socioeconomic classes and have lower educational achievement. Interestingly, the opposite pattern is seen for sudden cardiac victims in developing countries.

Many investigators have pointed to stress, anxiety, anger, hopelessness, and emotional arousal in general as precursors to sudden death (Dimsdale, 1977; Engel, 1976; Reich et al., 1981). Female sudden death victims often are divorced or single, have a history of psychiatric treatment, or have experienced the death of a close friend or relative in the six months preceding their death (Talbott et al., 1977; Cottington et al., 1980). A relative risk factor calculation cannot be determined, because the incidence of similar stressors in the general population was not measured.

Research Opportunities in Sudden Cardiac Death

A wide variety of studies indicate that the nervous system helps regulate the heart. In physiological models, brain stimulation, brain lesions, and drugs reliably produce cardiovascular pathology. Studies in cardiovascular neuropharmacology have demonstrated the involvement of biogenic amines and neuropeptides in the control of cardiovascular physiology (cf. Chapters 3 and 9). Behavioral models have been used to study stimulus-induced cardiovascular changes and the potential importance of learning. Finally, epidemiological studies have implicated environmental, social, and psychological factors in the etiology of sudden cardiac death.

Based on considerations at the Health and Behavior conference *Biobehavioral Factors in Sudden Cardiac Death*, studies should be initiated in at least four major areas (Solomon et al., 1981):

- *cardiovascular neurobiology*, with special emphasis on elucidating the neurobiological pathways that control cardiac function;
- *cardiovascular psychobiology*, involving both more precise definition of cardiovascular reflexes and studies of such systems in awake, behaving animals and in man;
- *cardiovascular sociobiology*, emphasizing the role of social factors in determining the timing and severity of arrhythmias; and
- *epidemiology*, extending currently accepted techniques to a wider pop-

ulation sample to clarify relationships between cardiovascular disease and behavior.

Conclusions

From the earliest days of medicine, physicians have recognized that behavioral activities and social context can profoundly affect a person's health, well-being, productivity, and longevity. Discovery of the mechanisms of behavioral and social influence on disease have lagged far behind elucidation of infective, nutritional, and some other mechanisms of disease. Although health professionals often acknowledged the influences of behavioral and social factors on physical illness, lack of information about mechanisms has limited the ability of medicine to intervene. In the case of cardiovascular disease, behavioral influences on pathophysiology and its outcome have recently been the subject of extensive study.

Some contributions that behavioral factors make to the etiology of cardiovascular disease are well documented. Many risk factors, including cigarette smoking and dietary intake of cholesterol, have been implicated directly as etiological agents. There is evidence that certain patterns of lifestyle are pathogenetic and that these components may be relatively discrete. If so, it may be possible to help individuals alter them without requiring a major reordering of society. Cardiovascular disease is so prevalent that recognition of even modest behavioral influences, if they can be beneficially influenced, may be of considerable usefulness.

Diet, exercise, and use of tobacco and alcohol are types of behaviors that influence the development of cardiovascular pathology. Thus, the stage is set for the application of this information in disease prevention. Chapter 15 considers issues in biobehavioral research involved in modifying the pathogenic patterns of such behaviors. An increased research effort must be made to better understand ways in which behavioral factors relate to cardiovascular disease and mechanisms by which they exert their effects.

References

Alexander, F. *Psychosomatic Medicine, Its Principles and Applications* New York: Norton, 1950.

Antman, E., Muller, J., Goldberg, S., MacAlpin, R., Rubenfire, M., Tabatznik, B., Liang, C., Heupler, F., Achuff, S., Reichek, N., Geltman, E., Kerin, N. Z., Neff, R. K, and Braunwald, E. Nifedipine therapy for coronary artery spasm. *N. Engl. J. Med.* 303:1269–1273, 1980.

Baroldi, G. Different types of myocardial necrosis in coronary heart disease: A pathophysiologic review of their functional significance. *Am. Heart J.* 89:742–752, 1975.

Baroldi, G., Falzi, G., and Mariani, F. Sudden coronary death: A postmortem study in 208 selected cases compared to 97 "control" subjects. *Am. Heart J.* 98:20–31, 1979.

Benson, H., Herd, J. A., Morse, W. H., and Kelleher, R. T. Behavioral induction of arterial hypertension and its reversal. *Am. J. Physiol.* 217:30–34, 1969.

Bunney, W., Jr., Shapiro, A., Ader, R., Davis, J., Herd, A., Kopin, I. J., Krieger, D., Matthysse, S., Stunkard, A., Weissman, M., and Wyatt, R. J. Panel report on stress and illness. IN: *Stress and Human Health* (Elliott, G. R., and Eisdorfer, C., eds.) New York: Springer-Verlag, 1982.

Cebelin, M. S., and Hirsch, C. S. Human stress cardiomyopathy. Myocardial lesions in victims of homicidal assaults without internal injuries. *Hum. Pathol.* 11:123–132, 1980.

Ciaranello, R., Lipton, M., Barchas, J., Barchas, P. R., Bonica, J., Ferrario, C., Levine, S., and Stein, M. Panel report on biological substrates of stress. IN: *Stress and Human Health* (Elliott, G. R., and Eisdorfer, C., eds.) New York: Springer, 1982, pp. 189–254.

Cobb, L. A., Baum, R. S., Alvarez, H., and Schaffer, W. A. Resuscitation from out-of-hospital ventricular fibrillation: Four years follow-up. *Circulation 52(Suppl. III)*:223–228, 1975.

Cobb, L. A., Werner, J. A., and Trobaugh, G. B. Sudden cardiac death. I. A decade's experience with out-of-hospital resuscitation. *Mod. Concepts Cardiovasc. Dis.* 49:31–36, 1980.

Cohen, D. H. Toward a cardiovascular neurobiology. IN: *Biobehavioral Factors in Sudden Cardiac Death* (Solomon, F., Parron, D. L., and Dews, P. B., eds.) Washington, D.C.: National Academy Press, 1981, pp. 77–81.

Cohen, D. H., and Cabot, J. B. Toward a cardiovascular neurobiology. *Trends Neurosci.* 2:273–276, 1979.

Connor, R. C. R. Heart damage associated with intracranial lesions. *Br. Med. J.* 3:29–31, 1968.

Cottington, E. M., Matthews, K. A., Talbott, P. H., and Kuller, L. H. Environmental events preceding sudden death in women. *Psychosom. Med.* 42:567–574, 1980.

Dawber, T. *The Framingham Study: Epidemiology of Atherosclerotic Disease* Cambridge, Mass.: Harvard University Press, 1980.

DeSilva, R. A., and Lown, B. Ventricular premature beats, stress and sudden death. *Psychosomatics* 19:649–659, 1978.

DeSilva, R. A., Verrier, R. L., and Lown, B. Effect of psychological stress and vagal stimulation with morphine sulfate on ventricular vulnerability to ventricular fibrillation (VF) in the conscious dog. *Am. Heart J.* 95:197–203, 1978.

Dimsdale, J. E. Emotional causes of sudden death. *Am. J. Psychiatry* 134:1361–1366, 1977.

Eliot, R. S., Todd, G. L., Clayton, F. C., and Pieper, G. M. Experimental catecholamine-induced acute myocardial necrosis. *Adv. Cardiol.* 25:107–118, 1978.

Eliot, R. S. *Stress and the Major Cardiovascular Disorders* Mount Kisco, N.Y.: Futura, 1979.

Elliott, G. R., and Eisdorfer, C. (Eds.) *Stress and Human Health* New York: Springer-Verlag, 1982.

Engel, G. L. Sudden and rapid death during psychological stress. Folklore or folk wisdom? *Ann. Intern. Med.* 74:771–782, 1971.

Engel, G. L. Psychologic factors in instantaneous cardiac death. *N. Engl. J. Med.* 294:664–665, 1976.

Esler, M., Julius, S., Zweifler, A., Randall, O., Harburg, E., Gardiner, H., and

DeQuattro, V. Mild high-renin essential hypertension. Neurogenic human hypertension? *N. Engl. J. Med. 296*:405–411, 1977.

Falkner, B., Kushner, H., Onesto, G., and Angelanos, E. T. Cardiovascular characteristics in adolescents who develop essential hypertension. *Hypertension 3*:521–527, 1981.

Folkow, B., and Rubinstein, E. H. Cardiovascular effects of acute and chronic stimulations of the hypothalamic defense area in the rat. *Acta Physiol. Scand. 68*:48–57, 1966.

Friedman, M., and Rosenman, R. H. Association of specific overt behavior pattern with blood and cardiovascular findings. *J. Am. Med. Assoc. 169*:1286–1296, 1959.

Glueck, C. J. Dictary fat and atherosclerosis. *Am. J. Clin. Nutr. 32*:2703–2711, 1979.

Gordon, T., Casteilli, W. P., Hjortland, M. C., Kannel, W. B., and Dawber, T. R. Predicting coronary heart disease in middle-aged and older persons: The Framingham study. *J. Am. Med. Assoc. 238*:497–499, 1977.

Haft, J. I., and Fani, K. Stress and the induction of intravascular platelet aggregation in the heart. *Circulation 48*:164–169, 1973.

Haft, J. I., Gershengorn, K., Kranz, P., and Oestreicher, R. Protection against epinephrine-induced myocardial necrosis by drugs that inhibit platelet aggregation. *Am. J. Cardiol. 30*:838–843, 1972a.

Haft, J. I., Kranz, P. D., Albert, F. J., and Fani, K. Intravascular platelet aggregation in the heart induced by norepinephrine: Microscopic studies. *Circulation 46*:698–708, 1972b.

Harker, L. A., and Ritchie, J. L. The role of platelets in acute vascular events. *Circulation 62(Suppl. V)*:13–18, 1980.

Harshfield, G. A., Pickering, T. G., and Laragh, J. H. A validation study of the Del Mar Avionics ambulatory blood pressure instrument. *Ambulatory Electrocardiography 1*, 1979.

Henry, J. P., Stephens, P. M., and Santisteban, G. A. A model of psychosocial hypertension showing reversibility and progression of cardiovascular complications. *Circ. Res. 36*:156–164, 1975.

Hillis, L. D., and Braunwald, E. Coronary-artery spasm. *N. Engl. J. Med. 299*:695–702, 1978.

Hypertension Detection and Follow-Up Program Cooperative Group. Five-year findings of the Hypertension Detection and Follow-Up program. I. Reduction in mortality of persons with high blood pressure, including mild hypertension. *J. Am. Med. Assoc. 242*:2562–2571, 1979.

Iseri, L. T., Humphrey, S. B., and Siner, E. J. Prehospital brady-asystolic cardiac arrest. *Ann. Intern. Med. 88*:741–745, 1978.

Jenkins, C. D. A comparative review of the interview and questionnaire methods in the assessment of the coronary-prone behavior pattern. IN: *Coronary-Prone Behavior* (Dembroski, T. M., Weiss, S. M., Shields, J. L., Haynes, S. G., and Feinleib, M., eds.) New York: Springer-Verlag, 1978, pp. 71–88.

Jenkins, C. D., Hames, D. G., Zyzanski, S. J., Rosenman, R. H., and Friedman, M. Psychological traits and serum lipids. *Psychosom. Med. 31*:115–128, 1969.

Julius, S. The psychology of borderline hypertension. IN: *Brain, Behavior, and Bodily Disease* (Weiner, H., Hofer, M. A., and Stunkard, A. J., eds.) New York: Raven Press, 1981.

Julius, S., and Esler, M. Autonomic nervous cardiovascular regulation in borderline hypertension. *Am. J. Cardiol. 36*:685–696, 1975.

Kalis, B. L., Harris, R. E., Sokolow, M., and Carpenter, L. G. Response to psychological stress in patients with essential hypertension. *Am. Heart J.* 53:572–578, 1957.

Kannel, W., Dawber, T., and McNamara, P. Detection of the coronary-prone adult: The Framingham study. *J. Iowa Med. Soc.* 56:26, 1966.

Kuller, L. H. Prodramata of sudden death and myocardial infarction. *Adv. Cardiol.* 25:61–72, 1978.

Kuller, L., Lilienfeld, A., and Fisher, R. An epidemiological study of sudden and unexpected deaths in adults. *Medicine* 46:341–361, 1967.

Liang, B., Verrier, R. L., Melman, J., and Lown, B. Correlation between circulating catecholamine levels and ventricular vulnerability during psychological stress in conscious dogs. *Proc. Soc. Exp. Biol. Med.* 161:266–269, 1979.

Lown, B. Sudden death from coronary heart disease. IN: *Early Phases of Coronary Heart Disease* (Waldenstrom, J., Larsson, T., and Ljungstedt, J., eds.) Stockholm: Nordiska Bokhandelns Forlag, 1973.

Lown, B., Verrier, R. L., and Corbalan, R. Psychologic stress and threshold for repetitive ventricular response. *Science* 182:834–836, 1973.

McGill, H. C. (Ed.) *The Geographic Pathology of Atherosclerosis* Baltimore: Williams and Wilkins, 1968.

McGill, H. C. The relationship of dietary cholesterol to serum cholesterol concentration and to atherosclerosis in man. *Am. J. Clin. Nutr.* 32:2664–2702, 1979.

Mudge, G. H., Grossman, W., Mills, R. M., Lesch, M., and Braunwald, E. Evidence for reflex coronary artery spasm in patients with ischemic heart disease. *Trans. Assoc. Am. Physicians.* 89:225, 1976a.

Mudge, G. H., Grossman, W., Mills, R. M., Lesch, M., and Braunwald, E. Reflex increase in coronary vascular resistance in patients with ischemic heart disease. *N. Engl. J. Med.* 295:1333–1337, 1976b.

Myers, A., and Dewar, H. A. Circumstances attending 100 sudden deaths from coronary artery disease with coroner's necroposies. *Br. Heart J.* 37:1133–1143, 1975.

National Heart, Lung, and Blood Institute *Arteriosclerosis, 1981* Washington, D.C.: U.S. Government Printing Office, 1981, DHHS Publ. No. (NIH) 81–2034.

Page, L., and Friend, B. The changing United States diet. *BioScience* 28:192–197, 1978.

Parron, D. L., Solomon, F., and Haggerty, R. J. (Eds.) *Combining Psychosocial and Drug Therapy: Hypertension, Depression, Diabetes Interim Report No. 2, Health and Behavior: A Research Agenda* Washington, D.C.: National Academy Press, 1981.

Rabinowitz, S. H., and Lown, B. Central neurochemical factors related to serotonin metabolism and cardiac ventricular vulnerability for repetitive electrical activity. *Am. J. Cardiol.* 41:516–522, 1978.

Rahe, R. H., Rubin, R. T., and Gunderson, E. K. E. Measures of subjects' motivation and affect correlated with their serum uric acid, cholesterol and cortisol. *Arch. Gen. Psychiatry* 26:357–359, 1972.

Rahe, R. H., O'Neill, T. O., Hagan, A., and Arthur, R. J. Brief group therapy following myocardial infarction. Eighteen month follow-up of a controlled trial. *Int. J. Psychiatry Med.* 6:349–358, 1975.

Reich, P., DeSilva, R. A., Lown, B., and Murawski, B. J. Acute psychological disturbance preceding life-threatening ventricular arrhythmias. *J. Am. Med. Assoc.* 246:233–235, 1981.

Reichenbach, D. D., and Moss, N. S. Myocardial cell necrosis and sudden death in humans. *Circulation 52(Suppl. III)*:60–62, 1975.

Review Panel on Coronary-Prone Behavior and Coronary Heart Disease. Coronary-prone behavior and coronary heart disease: A critical review. *Circulation* 63:1199–1215, 1981.

Rice, D. P., and Kleinman, J. C. National health data for policy and planning. *Health Policy Educ. 1*:129–141, 1980.

Richardson, D. W., Honour, A. J., Fenton, G. W., Stott, F. H., and Pickering, G. W. Variation in arterial pressure throughout the day and night. *Clin. Sci.* 26:445–460, 1964.

Richter, C. P. On the phenomenon of sudden death in animals and man. *Psychosom. Med.* 19:191–198, 1957.

Rizak, R. L., and Jackson, E. M. Current food consumption practices and nutrient sources in the American diet. Hyattsville, Md.: Consumer Nutrition Center—Human Nutrition Science and Education Administration, U.S. Department of Agriculture, 1980.

Rose, R. M., Jenkins, C. D., and Hurst, M. W. *Air Traffic Controller Health Change Study*. Washington, D.C.: U.S. Department of Transportation, Federal Aviation Agency, 1978, Document No. FAA-AM-78-39.

Rosenfeld, J., Rosen, M. R., and Hoffman, B. F. Pharmacologic and behavioral effects on arrhythmias which immediately follow abrupt coronary occlusion: A canine model of sudden coronary death. *Am. J. Cardiol.* 41:1075–1082, 1978.

Rosenman, R. H. Role of Type A behavior pattern in the pathogenesis of ischemic heart disease and modification for prevention. *Adv. Cardiol.* 25:35–46, 1978.

Rosenman, R. H., and Friedman, M. Neurogenic factors in pathogenesis of coronary heart disease. *Med. Clin. N. Am.* 58:269–279, 1974.

Roskies, E., Spevack, M., Surklis, A., Cohen, C., and Gilman, S. Changing the coronary-prone (Type A) behavior pattern in a nonclinical population. *J. Behav. Med. 1*:201–216, 1978.

Sapira, J. D., Scheib, E. T., Moriarty, R., and Shapiro, A. P. Differences in perception between hypertensive and normotensive populations. *Psychosom. Med. 33*:239–250, 1971

Shapiro, A. P. Psychophysiologic mechanisms in hypertensive vascular disease. *Ann. Intern. Med.* 53:64–83, 1960.

Shapiro, A. P. An experimental study of comparative responses of blood pressure to different noxious stimuli. *J. Chronic Dis. 13*:293–311, 1961.

Shekelle, R. B., Shryock, A. M., Paul, O., Lepper, M., Stanler, J., Liu, S., and Raynor, W. J. Diet, serum cholesterol, and death from coronary heart disease. The Western Electric study. *N. Engl. J. Med.* 304:65–70, 1981.

Solomon, F., Parron, D. L., and Dews, P. B. (Eds.) *Biobehavioral Factors in Sudden Cardiac Death. Interim Report No. 3, Health and Behavior: A Research Agenda* Washington, D.C.: National Academy Press, 1981.

Spain, D. M. Anatomical basis for sudden cardiac death. IN: *Sudden Cardiac Death* (Surawicz, B., and Pellegrino, E. E., eds.) New York: Grune and Stratton, 1964.

Stamler, J. Introduction to risk factors in coronary artery disease. IN: *Baylor College of Medicine Cardiology Series. Vol. 1, Part 3* (McIntosh, H. D., ed.) Northfield, Tex.: Medical Communications, 1978.

Talbott, E., Kuller, L. H., Detre, K., and Perper, J. Biologic and psychosocial risk factors of sudden death from coronary disease in white women. *Am. J. Cardiol.* 39:858–864, 1977.

Thomas, G. S., Lee, P. R., Franks, P. L., and Paffenbarger, R., Jr. (Eds.) *Exercise and Health: The Evidence and the Implications* Cambridge: Oelgeschlager, Gunn, and Hain, 1981.

Weinblatt, E., Ruberman, W., Goldberg, J. D., Frank, C. W., Shapiro, S., and Chaudhary, B. S. Relation of education to sudden death after myocardial infarction. *N. Engl. J. Med. 299*:60–65, 1978.

Weiner, H. Psychosomatic research in essential hypertension: Retrospect and prospect. IN: *Psychosomatics in Essential Hypertension* (Koster, M., Musaph, H., and Visser, P., eds.) Basel: S. Karger, 1970, pp. 58–116.

Weiner, H. Summary. IN: *Brain, Behavior, and Bodily Disease* (Weiner, H., Hofer, M. A., and Stunkard, A. J., eds.) New York: Raven Press, 1981.

Weiner, H., Singer, M. T., and Reiser, M. F. Cardiovascular responses and their psychological correlates. I. A study in healthy young adults and patients with peptic ulcer and hypertension. *Psychosom. Med. 24*:477–498, 1962.

Wikland, B. Death from arteriosclerotic heart disease outside hospitals. *Acta Med. Scand. 184*:129–133, 1968.

8
Diabetes and Behavior

The isolation of insulin in 1921 by Banting and Best (1922) was heralded as a therapeutic milestone for persons with diabetes, and countless lives have been saved. Nonetheless, 60 years later, diabetes mellitus ranks among the nation's leading medical problems. Therapy still depends on diet modification, insulin replacement, and adherence to a demanding medical regimen. Although present therapies can control certain symptoms, they cannot cure the disease or its complications that impair both the quality and length of life.

Approximately five million Americans (2.3 percent of the population) are known to have diabetes; another five million people may have undiagnosed or latent diabetes (National Diabetes Data Group, 1978). Among persons age 45–64 years, the annual prevalence rate is 5 percent; for those over 65, the rate is one in every 12 persons.

Diabetes, the fifth ranking cause of death by disease, accounted for 35,000 deaths in 1976 and is a contributing factor in another 90,000 deaths each year. Blindness is 25 times more common in the diabetic than in the nondiabetic population; each year, about 5,000 diabetics become blind. About 500,000 women of childbearing age have diabetes. During pregnancy, such women face a probability of fetal death that is five times greater than for nondiabetic women and a risk of bearing an infant with congenital abnormalities that is three times greater. About 25 percent of diabetics are under treatment for heart disease, and diabetes is one of the four major risk factors for heart disease.

Diabetes is the fourth leading cause of visits to general and family practice

144

physicians. About 90 percent of diabetics see a physician at least once a year, and one third of all diabetics have been hospitalized because of their disease. Many have repeated and frequent hospital admissions. In 1977, annual direct and indirect costs of diabetes mellitus were estimated at $6.8 billion. This amount does not include the costs of complications of diabetes, which have been estimated at $297 million for direct costs alone (Diabetes Mellitus Coordinating Committee, 1979).

Clinical Aspects of Diabetes

Of the 5.2 million Americans with diagnosed diabetes, 5 to 10 percent require one or more daily injections of insulin. This form of the disease is commonly called juvenile-onset diabetes or insulin-dependent diabetes mellitus (IDDM) and usually develops before age 20. It is the most common endocrine disease in childhood. Maturity-onset noninsulin-dependent diabetes mellitus (NIDDM) constitutes more than 80 percent of the diabetic population. NIDDM typically develops after age 40, usually in individuals who are overnourished or obese; symptoms often can be controlled by oral hypoglycemics, exercise, and restricted diet. More than one million NIDDM patients take insulin for better control of their symptoms and blood glucose.

Diabetes originally was viewed as a simple hormone deficiency caused by the failure of the beta cells of the pancreas to produce enough insulin. It now is thought to be a group of diseases with a variety of causes—genetic, environmental, and immunological—all of which result in an inability to utilize glucose normally. Recent advances in diabetes have established that there is multifactorial control of glucose regulation. The most prominent regulators of glucose metabolism also are significantly responsive to stress. Some of those that increase blood sugar are catecholamines, cortisol, growth hormone, and glucagon. The neuropeptide somatostatin can be a powerful inhibitor of both growth hormone and glucagon. So far, little is known about patterns of physiological response to stress as a factor in the metabolism of blood glucose.

Emotional stress (Koski, 1969), psychosocial factors (Garner and Thompson, 1978; Johnson, 1980), and familial factors (Baker et al., 1975) are all thought to influence the course of diabetes. Only recently have systematic interdisciplinary efforts begun to investigate those possibilities (Hamburg et al., 1980).

Clinical Course

Complications of diabetes are devastating, and all systems of the body can be affected. The most feared complications are blindness, atherosclerosis, and gangrene. Atherosclerosis affects the large blood vessels (cf. Chapter 7). This complication is especially prominent in maturity-onset diabetes but occurs with both types. The greater the atherosclerosis, the greater the incidence of coronary heart disease and strokes. Diabetics also have a 100-fold increase in the prevalence of peripheral vascular problems as compared with nondiabetics. The major blood vessels of diabetics with atherosclerosis show premature aging. If the individual is 50 years old, the blood vessels have the same appearance as vessels from a 60- or 70-year-old. According to Joslin Clinic data, even with the best current therapies for diabetes, coronary heart disease acccounts for more than 50 percent of the deaths in diabetes mellitus. Gangrene of the lower extremities, which often leads to amputation, is a major cause of hospitalization of diabetic patients.

Juvenile-onset or insulin-dependent diabetics suffer from disease of the tiny blood vessels (capillaries) as well as the major ones. Capillaries in the retina of the eye and in the kidneys are especially affected. The average life span for a juvenile diabetic is about 35 years from the time of diagnosis. About 50 percent of juvenile diabetics who developed diabetes between 5 and 15 years of age will have died of renal failure by 40 and 50 years of age, because of specific small vessel complications in the kidney. About 20 percent of the same population will be legally blind, and all will have evidence of nerve damage due to the vascular lesions.

Treatment

Pharmacological approaches to therapy for diabetic patients are more extensive than ever before. Recent advances involve efforts to define more accurately the specifics of abnormal metabolic actions in relation to the various diabetic syndromes and their complications. New forms of insulin act more efficiently at the cell level and show less tendency to provoke allergic reactions. Single-peak insulin and monocomponent insulin are examples of two very pure forms of insulin. The major therapeutic advance along these lines for the future will be the production of human insulin using recombinant DNA techniques.

There have also been advances in the delivery of insulin. Most IDDM patients now inject themselves daily with a combination of intermediate- and short-acting insulins. Therapeutic trials are under way using preprogrammed insulin infusion pumps that deliver insulin automatically via a subcutaneously placed needle. Although continuous infusion pumps offer the potential of more precise titration, there are problems about delivery of appropriate insulin doses. At times, there is pooling of insulin in the tissues. There also are risks of infection with implanted needles. Nor does preprogramming conform to unexpected needs. Also, for many women, the pump and tubing are not cosmetically acceptable. Although the pumps are about the size of a small transistor radio and fit nicely on the belt and under a suit jacket, women can find them obtrusive and unwieldy. Certain kinds of activities are limited or prevented while wearing the insulin pump. For all of these reasons, the insulin infusion pump will not release the IDDM diabetic patient from a demanding therapeutic regimen.

Despite medical advances, following the diagnosis of diabetes the patient and family still must adapt to a radically altered life. There are continuing stresses such as living with the foreboding of a shortened life span for the patient; the specter of severe complications that may result in coronary disease, blindness, stroke, amputation, or other major physical handicaps; apprehension over unpredictable occurrence of insulin reactions or life-threatening crises related to ketoacidosis; and pervasive concern over ability to handle these crises. At best, there are daily problems of fitting a personal and family lifestyle around monitoring and regulating the diet, exercise, and medication of the diabetic patient.

Important Issues in Diabetes for the Biobehavioral Sciences

Three broad areas have emerged to command the attention of biobehavioral scientists for collaborative efforts with biomedical scientists in diabetes research:

- *Coping with the emotional burden of diabetes* A conceptual model and empirical data base are needed concerning the processes of coping with the predictable crises and daily demands of diabetes. The repertoires of coping skills and strategies that will be effective under diverse conditions and for persons of varying ages and social circumstances must be identified and incorporated into the lives of diabetics and their families. The uses of networks of social support in preventing and buffering the harmful effects of life stress need to be understood.

- *Effective use of health services and adherence to treatment* More information is needed about factors that influence the development of responsible self-care and enhance the adoption of behavior and lifestyle that reduce health risk and maximize functional health status. The potential of the health care delivery system for providing effective patient education and social support as an adjunct of good medical care must be utilized. Research of this kind in diabetes can be a prototype for other chronic diseases. Promotion of increased individual health care responsibility has broad implications for improving the overall health status in other medical conditions.

- *Physiological-behavioral interactions* Interactive metabolic effects of biomedical and psychosocial variables should be studied more closely. There is a need to differentiate subsets of diabetic patients for whom the profiles of these interactive effects show distinctive patterns in response to social and environmental factors. This knowledge could have great significance for the management of diabetes.

There is now a substantial body of concepts, methodology, and data in the biobehavioral sciences that would seem to have great potential for transfer to diabetes-related problems. As an initial step in this direction, the National Institutes of Health convened a conference of behavioral scientists, diabetologists, and biomedical investigators to foster an exchange of information and perspectives (Hamburg et al., 1980). The goals of the conference were to:

1. identify existing behavioral knowledge and techniques and suggest methods of applying them to problems of diabetics and their families;
2. identify research areas of most need and promise;
3. actively encourage the interface between biomedical and behavioral researchers and clinicians;
4. attract both new and established behavioral investigators into the diabetes research area; and
5. develop new models and approaches for the study of adherence and outcome in diabetes.

Coping with the Emotional Burdens of Diabetes

The human capacity for coping with adversity is immense (cf. Chapter 3). Nevertheless, living with diabetes can impose challenges that test the limits of endurance. Outcomes for diabetic patients and their families depend on the nature and extent of the burdens imposed, the context in which stresses are experienced (Lazarus, 1977), and the coping ability of the specific persons involved. For some, relatively minor stresses precipitate unmanageable physical and emotional responses. Techniques are needed to identify readily these high-risk individuals and families, so that needed support can be offered. Most manage to adapt with reasonable success, but often at great personal costs. For a fortunate few, even experiences that appear to be disastrous are managed; and, in the coping process, certain individuals actually seem to gain in overall strength and competence. Garmezy (1980) and others have emphasized that the medical profession has much to learn from studying these stress-resistant, highly effective copers. Existing research indicates that the coping skills of the more typical, less competent persons can be improved substantially by appropriate interventions. Cohen and Lazarus (1979) have summarized concepts, issues, and research data in an excellent overview of the current state of knowledge pertaining to coping with physical illness.

Coping can be anticipatory; that is, preparatory and adaptive strategies can be initiated prior to a stressful confrontation that is predictable. When the predictions are valid and the preparatory actions are appropriate, potential harm is markedly diminished. Although it has not been generally specified as such, health care professionals have long used effective anticipatory coping to help diabetics avoid or minimize medical problems due to hypoglycemia, poor foot care, and intercurrent infections. Risks are explained, preventive measures are detailed, early warning signals of pathology are specified, and plans for prompt treatment are explained clearly. As a result, diabetics and their families often handle disturbances in these areas with competence and relatively minor anxiety. When comparable health disturbances arise from unknown cause, ambiguity, ignorance, and lack of a clear plan of action can lead to great emotional distress. In these situations, the amount of distress may seem to be out of proportion to the degree of illness. High anxiety may, in turn, aggravate the medical condition.

There are predictable crises related to the course of diabetes and to the effects of developmental transitions and stage of the life span on events of the illness. Many of the adaptive challenges that the diabetic patient must face also are posed for family and friends. Effective anticipatory coping for these situations could lessen distress and improve health outcomes (Hamburg et al., 1980).

For most persons, a diagnosis of diabetes comes as an unexpected, devastating development; it may start with an acute life-threatening illness that requires hospitalization. For others, the onset is insidious and less dramatic. Regardless of severity of onset, most patients experience an initial disbelief and deep concern about the prospects for the quality of life in the future. They also feel anxious about the impact on meaningful interpersonal relationships. The overall appraisal of these issues and initial coping experiences may affect life-long patterns of coping strategies as well as health attitudes and behaviors. Existing research shows that there is a danger of information overload during the initial IDDM episode. The only immediate knowledge that parents or family can absorb is survival information, because of the overwhelming trauma of the initial diagnosis. It is still unclear how the handling of events of the initial episode affect the degree to which persons incorporate diabetes as a tolerable routine of daily life or adopt a sick role.

Diabetic patients and families must cope with many predictable medical events. The physical well-being, energy level, and mood of diabetic patients may be affected by blood sugar level and metabolic status, which can fluctuate widely and rapidly. At times, efforts to control blood sugar closely can lead to high frequency of hypoglycemic episodes that have mood and behavior components. Failure of the patient or significant others to understand such side effects can be a source of needless personal distress and interpersonal tension. A major task of the care provider is to work out a medical regimen that balances the patient's psychosocial well-being with the medical goal of maintenance of appropriate glucose levels.

The complications of diabetes are another predictable source of adaptive challenge. The potential for severe complications resulting in major handicap or death threatens all diabetic patients; however, perceptions of personal vulnerability and coping demands can vary tremendously. Parents typically are more concerned about complications than are their young diabetic children. Adult crises occur when the first symptoms of a complication are confirmed or following a personal encounter with another diabetic who has a complication.

Individuals with diabetes must confront the same life course changes that others do. For them, however, adolescence, marriage, pregnancy, and career decisions may be unusually stressful (Pearlin, 1975; Mattson, 1980). There are recent efforts to develop behavioral assessments of coping competence in the diabetic patient and family. The battery includes ratings by diabetic educators of knowledge and skills of diabetes management, assessment of family coping styles, and a measure of family adjustment and patient self-concept. The aim is to identify families in need of additional help and competent families whose strengths can be monitored and reinforced (Baker et al., 1975).

The medical care system may be the only resource some people have in times of stress. Research on the pathways to care and studies of the utilization of health services have highlighted the potential importance of the lay referral network (family, friends, community influentials) and the lay treatment network (family, personal social networks, natural helpers in neighborhoods, community care givers such as clergy and teachers, mutual help groups). The relationship between these social support systems and utilization of medical care services is complex. Absence of an adequate social support network can inhibit the entry into the system to obtain needed medical care and increase the use of health services when the major problem is the need for human support. The social support capabilities of the medical care settings may need to be enhanced, but an equally important strategy may be to devise ways of increasing interactions between the health service providers and social support systems in communities. Models of such strategies are only recently becoming available. An important development for diabetics has been the recognition by health professionals of the importance of peer groups of diabetic patients and families. Many physicians and clinics now refer patients to existing self-help diabetes groups or sponsor such groups in their own offices.

Development of Responsible Self-Care

There is considerable biobehavioral science research under way on the determinants of adherence behavior (cf. Chapter 16). Evidence strongly suggests that the diverse abnormal phenomena characterizing the diabetic state are partly or completely reversed with control of aberrant glucose levels. Historically, manipulation of diet has been a key in attempting to treat diabetes. Behavioral treatment of obesity is important in its own right and even more so as a model system for studying what may be the single most important psychosocial and behavioral factor in diabetes—adherence to therapeutic regimens. In its study of adherence to diet and exercise programs, behavioral treatment of obesity has had access to the most reliable, valid, and economic-dependent variable in behavioral research—change in weight. Determination of the major results of behavioral treatment of obesity show it to be a modest improvement over traditional methods of outpatient treatment with respect to decreased attrition, decreased symptomatology, and increased weight loss. Weight loss, although small, has been clinically useful in control of hypertension and could be significant in control of diabetes.

What is being learned in this model system is beginning to be applied to adherence to therapeutic regimens, particularly to taking medications. Recent studies of home glucose monitoring suggest that providing information about blood glucose levels can enhance the level of personal responsibility taken for adherence to the regimen and maintenance of good diabetic control (Stunkard, 1980).

Until recently, the metabolic effects of exercise and its appropriate use in treating diabetes have not been well understood. Research has helped to define hormonal and metabolic consequences of exercise in diabetes mellitus and obesity. The status of diabetic control or degree of insulin deficiency appears to determine the glucose response to acute exercise. In poorly regulated insulin-dependent diabetics, acute exercise results in a rise in blood sugar; but in moderately well controlled IDDM or NIDDM patients, acute exercise leads to a fall in blood glucose. The mechanisms of exercise-induced hypoglycemia in insulin-treated IDDM diabetics have also been clarified. Acute exercise increases the availability of insulin from exercised sites, which may cause hypoglycemia by interfering with hepatic glucose production. Recent data suggest that, in nondiabetic subjects, acute exercise increases insulin binding; this may also be of importance in the blood glucose response. In obese subjects, ketones and fatty acids replace glucose as the major substrates for muscle during starvation or treatment with protein diets. The effects of physical training on insulin and glucose homeostasis have been examined in normal, obese, and NIDDM diabetics. In very well trained athletes, hypoinsulinemia has been documented, suggesting an increased insulin sensitivity. In obese subjects, physical conditioning lowers plasma insulin. In NIDDM diabetics, the data are conflicting as to whether there is an improvement in insulin sensitivity or glucose tolerance.

There is a need to encourage interdisciplinary research in which are established biochemical, physiological, and behavioral aspects of effects of exercise on stress reduction, insulin sensitivity and availablity, and other relaxed metabolic factors such as lipoproteins. Such basic research would be invaluable in designing useful exercise training programs for diabetics that take into account both risks and benefits (Diabetes Mellitus Coordinating Committee, 1979).

Use of Health Services

No physical disease demands a stronger partnership between patient and therapist than diabetes. Education in self-care has been a hallmark of successful management. Successfully managing day-to-day details of diabetes creates a healthier and more secure diabetic person. Denial of the disease, hostility toward everyone involved, and rigid resistance to advisable change can lead to dangerous situations for the patient. Self-care education is a continuing process that should occur whenever patient and therapist meet.

A relatively new area being explored in behavioral medicine is the interaction of the personality of the patient and the type of treatment. Some treatments in themselves appear to be more conducive to adherence than are others. However, adherence may be facilitated further by a match between the personality, goals, and needs of the patient and the type of treatment (Eisenthal et al., 1979). In this context, treatment is used broadly to refer to all demands made on the patient by physicians, nurses, dietitians, educators, and others in the health care system. Attempts to match patient needs and treatment characteristics should include:

• *Determining the patient's needs*, which may be influenced by such variables as type and stage of illness; age, sex, and socioeconomic level of patient; family constellation and amount of available social support; and concurrent life stresses. Needs of the patient also vary in terms of personal motivations and ethnic and cultural qualities that characterize the person and family.

• *Assessing the potential demands* that are traditionally imposed on the patient by each type of treatment. This involves fully understanding the consequences of what a patient is asked to do or to sacrifice when following a proposed regimen.

• *Evaluating the context* in which the demands are made. Variables include health-professional supportiveness, type and quality of educational programs, and attributes such as warmth or continuity of care of the clinic setting. The success of adding services such as telephone hotlines and individualized education programs has been described (Miller and Goldstein, 1972; Giordano et al., 1977). Innovations in service delivery have led to decreased hospitalization, better control, and substantial cost savings.

Within the broad domain of therapeutic strategies are various concepts, programs, and innovative procedures. How these elements are integrated into the life of a person with diabetes will vary according to health beliefs, state of health, perceived efficacy of therapy, and access to health care services and resources.

Physiological Behavioral Interactions in Diabetes

During the past five years, remarkable strides have been made in understanding basic cellular mechanisms underlying the production of insulin, glucagon, and a variety of other important peptide hormones and neuroregulators. These advances have been made possible by the development of several important basic techniques, most notably the advent of methods for isolating and translating messenger RNA in cell-free systems in vitro and the remarkable breakthroughs in gene isolation, nucleotide sequencing, and recombinant DNA technology.

A number of examples can be cited to highlight this progress. Several early precursors of important hormones have been identified and partially or completely characterized, including preproinsulin, the initial translation product of the insulin gene, and proglucagon, a larger precursor peptide from which glucagon and other, larger glucagon-related peptides probably derive. As discussed in Chapter 3, interconnections have been found among adrenocorticotropic hormone (ACTH), melanocyte stimulating hormone (MSH), and the potent morphinelike peptide beta-endorphin, all of which derive from a large polypeptide precursor that is fragmented by mechanisms similar to those that convert proinsulin to insulin. Analysis of these mechanisms may help to explain how the entire body is recruited in complex reactions such as the stress response. There is also evidence that mutations in the proinsulin molecule occur in the human population and may in some instances give rise to diabetic syndromes.

The proinsulin-related insulinlike growth factor (IGF) has been isolated and characterized. It is partly under the control of growth hormone and thus may be one of a number of factors (somatomedins) that, along with insulin, control physical growth. This demonstration, along with parallel studies on relaxation and nerve growth factor, indicate that the insulin gene has diversified by means of gene duplications occurring early in evolution into a family of structurally related peptides that play varied integrative roles. Such studies have been made possible by techniques for cloning and nucleotide sequencing of cDNA copies of messenger RNA for hormones such as insulin, growth hormone, chorionic gonadotropin, placental lactogen, parathyroid hormone, and the ACTH-endorphin precursor from both animal and human sources.

This recent and continuing explosion of knowledge is paralleled by comparable advances in understanding brain neuroregulation (cf. Chapter 9). Taken together, there are remarkable opportunities for behavioral and biomedical researchers in diabetes, particularly in relation to stress responses, pain, glucose metabolism, control of appetite, and direct effects of hypoglycemia on mood and behavior.

Issues Relating to the Control of Obesity

A research focus of special interest is obesity, which is a risk factor both of diabetes and cardiovascular disease. About 90 percent of people who become diabetic are overweight. Thus, for those who get diabetes, a crucial problem is how to control excessive caloric intake.

How excessive caloric intake influences the onset and course of diabetes is a focus of current research. The beta cells of the pancreas have a remarkable capacity to increase insulin production when body weight increases; at higher weights, more insulin is needed to keep a blood sugar level normal, partly because the fat cells become relatively insensitive to insulin. But beta cells cannot expand secretory capacity indefinitely. Furthermore, overweight people have a decreased number of insulin receptors. Fasting or weight loss results in a return of the number of insulin receptors to normal or near normal and an increased insulin sensitivity.

One approach to the treatment of obesity in maturity-onset diabetes is illustrated by the Diabetes Unit of Emory University. (Davidson, 1976; Davidson and Goldsmith, 1979). A team (physician, podiatrist, dietician, and nurse) evaluates and educates patients and provides continuous follow-up care. Physicians take personal responsibility for prescribing diet. They work closely with dieticians to teach the patient how to regulate intake. This group uses a stepped approach to treating obese diabetics. The first step is conventional low-calorie diets. If the patient loses weight, a low-calorie diet is maintained along with an exercise routine and continuous follow-up care. If the low-calorie diet does not work, a fast is instituted with close medical supervision. Follow-up of fast-induced weight loss includes a low-calorie diet and exercise routine with continuous support. The continuity of care has been found critically important. From 1970 to 1978, patients at Emory have lost an average of 20 pounds each, constituting 40 percent of the excess weight. About 80 percent of their patients are on diet therapy alone; 20 percent are on insulin. Other approaches to patient education facilitated by social reinforcement have shown similar promise.

In other research, a group of patients taken off oral agents in 1970 were followed until 1978. Those who lost the most weight had the greatest lowering of plasma glucose. The group placed on insulin transiently and then on diet alone lost an average of 33 pounds, and their average plasma glucose in 1978 was 100 mg/dl lower than it had been on oral agent therapy in 1971. Patients who were on insulin in 1978 and who were the most above ideal body weight had the greatest plasma glucose increase from 1971 to 1978 (Davidson, 1981). This, again, tends to indicate that control of plasma glucose entails more than giving insulin.

Careful attention to nutrition can be an important component of a coordinated care program for diabetics by helping to promote continuity of care. In an interesting innovation showing the ingenuity that can be applied in health education, one group approached the problem of getting patients involved in nutritional planning by producing a *Diabetes Guidebook: Diet Section* (Davidson and Goldsmith, 1979). The book is color coded to simplify use by patients who cannot read or write. Special efforts were made to choose foods preferred by that patient population. The original basic nutritional care program is expensive, but long-term savings can be effected by reducing the need for insulin and diabetes-induced illnesses.

In the conference *Combining Psychosocial and Drug Therapy*, there was a broad consensus that research on treatment of obesity in relation to diabetes and hypertension is a matter of high priority (Parron et al., 1981). Special attention was directed to principles of social learning and factors influencing long-term maintenance of weight loss, as well as to conditions in which relapse occurs. This latter focus is also a priority consideration in research on smoking cessation (cf. Chapter 5).

Conclusions

Diabetes is a classic example of a chronic disorder with a clear biological origin that nonetheless has major behavioral components. To ignore its psychosocial aspects is to risk treatment failure. For obese patients with adult-onset diabetes, successful biobehavioral interventions may alleviate the diabetes.

Psychosocial aspects of treatment also can be crucial for diabetics without weight problems, helping them to understand better how the disease affects their lives and the lives of those around them. Integrated health care systems focus both on controlling the physical manifestation of elevated blood sugar and on the particular needs of the patients as they cope with demands of their disorder. Application of the biobehavioral sciences to gaining better insights into factors that affect the ability of individuals to adapt already is proving to be a rewarding and enlightening direction for research.

References

Baker, L., Minuchin, S., Milman, L., et al. Psychosomatic aspects of juvenile diabetes mellitus: A progress report. IN: *Diabetes in Juveniles: Medical and Rehabilitation Aspects. Modern Problems in Pediatrics, Volume 12* (Laron, Z., ed.) New York: Karger, 1975, pp. 332–343.

Banting, F. G., and Best, C. H. The internal secretion of the pancreas. *J. Lab. Clin. Med.* 7:251–266, 1922.

Cohen, F., and Lazarus, R. S. Coping with the stresses of illness. IN: *Health Psychology—A Handbook: Theories, Applications and Challenges of a Psychological Approach to the Health Care System* (Stone, G. C., Cohen, F., and Adler, N. E., eds.) San Francisco: Jossey-Bass, 1979, pp. 217–254.

Davidson, J. K. Controlling diabetes mellitus with diet therapy. *Postgrad. Med.* 59:114–122, 1976.

Davidson, J. K. Management of maturity onset diabetes. IN: *Combining Psychosocial and Drug Therapy. Interim Report No. 2, Health and Behavior: A Research Agenda* (Parron, D. L., Solomon, F., and Haggerty, R. eds.) Washington, D.C.: National Academy Press, 1981

Davidson, J. K., and Goldsmith, M. P. *Diabetes Guidebook: Diet Section, Edition Three* Columbus, Ga.: Litho-Krome, 1979.

Diabetes Mellitus Coordinating Committee, *Fifth Annual Report to the Director of N.I.H., Fiscal Year, 1978* NIH Publ. No. 79–1956, June 1979.

Eisenthal, S., Emery, R., Lazare, A., and Udin, H. "Adherence" and the negotiated approach to patienthood. *Arch. Gen. Psychiatry 36:*393–398, 1979.

Garner, A. M., and Thompson, C. W. Juvenile diabetes. IN: *Psychological Management of Pediatric Problems, Volume One* (Magrab, P. R., ed.) Baltimore: University Park Press, 1978, pp. 221–258.

Garmezy, N. Behavioral issues in chronic illness. IN: *Behavioral and Psychosocial Issues in Diabetes* (Hamburg, B., Lipsett, L., Inoff, G., and Drash, A., eds.) Washington, D.C.: U.S. Department of Health and Human Services, 1980, NIH Publ. No. 80–1993.

Giordano, B., Rosenbloom, A. L., Heller, D., Weber, F. T., Gonzalez, R., and Grgic, A. Regional services for children and youth with diabetes. *Pediatrics 60:*492–498, 1977.

Hamburg, B. A., Lipsett, L. F., Inoff, G. E., and Drash, A. L. (Eds.) *Behavioral and Psychosocial Issues in Diabetes* Washington, D.C.: U.S. Department of Health and Human Services, 1980, NIH Publ. No. 80–1993.

Johnson, S. B. Psychosocial factors in juvenile diabetes: A review. *J. Behav. Med.* 3:95–116, 1980.

Koski, M. L. The coping process in childhood diabetes. *Acta Paediatr. Scand. 198 (Suppl.):*1–56, 1969.

Lazarus, R. S. Psychological stress and coping in adaptation and illness. IN: *Proceedings of the National Heart, Lung, and Blood Institute Working Conference on Health Behavior* (Weiss, S. M., ed.) Washington, D.C.: U.S. Government Printing Office, 1977, DHEW Publ. No. (NIH) 77–868, pp. 199–214.

Mattson, A. Juvenile diabetes: Impacts in life stages and systems. IN: *Behavioral and Psychosocial Issues in Diabetes.* (Hamburg, B., Lipsett, L. F., Inoff, G. E., and Drash, A. L., eds.) Washington, D.C.: U.S. Department of Health and Human Services 1980, NIH Publ. No. 80–1993.

Miller, L.V. and Goldstein, J. More efficient care of diabetic patients in a county-hospital setting. *N. Engl. J. Med., 286:*1388–1391, 1972.

National Diabetes Data Group. *Diabetes Data Compiled 1977* Washington, D.C.: U.S. Government Printing Office, 1978, DHEW Publ. No. (NIH) 78–1468.

Parron, D. L., Solomon, F., and Haggerty, R. (Eds.) *Combining Psychosocial and Drug Therapy. Interim Report No. 2, Health and Behavior: A Research Agenda* Washington, D.C.: National Academy Press, 1981.

Pearlin, L. I. Status inequality and stress in marriage. *Am. Sociol. Rev.* 40:344–357, 1975.

Stunkard, A. J. Adherence to treatment for diabetes. IN: *Behavioral and Psychosocial Issues in Diabetes* (Hamburg, B., Lipsett, L. F., Inoff, G. E., and Drash, A. L., eds.) Washington, D.C.: U.S. Department of Health and Human Services, 1980, NIH Publ. No. 80–1993.

9
Major Mental Disorders
and Behavior

Great advances in the understanding and treatment of severe mental illness have occurred in the past 25 years. Before World War II, a diagnosis of schizophrenia or psychotic depression produced feelings of fear and hopelessness similar to those that many people still associate with a diagnosis of cancer. The favorable investigative climate fostered primarily through governmental programs like those of the Alcohol, Drug Abuse, and Mental Health Administration (ADAMHA) has helped to improve the treatment of the most disabling mental disorders.

The population in American psychiatric hospitals increased for many years, peaking in 1955 at over 500,000. Since then, it has declined steadily as wider application has been made of new drug and psychosocial treatments; by 1973, the number of patients hospitalized for mental illnesses had fallen to only half of the 1955 figure (Berger et al., 1977). This decrease in the hospitalized patient population has continued, despite a growing total population and rising admission rates to mental hospitals. Yet it is only one aspect of the impact of effective treatments. The existence of psychoactive agents has molded basic research on brain physiology, pharmacology, and biochemistry; and requirements for precise evaluation of new drugs have fostered major improvements in clinical research methodology (cf. Chapter 19).

The Institute of Medicine has conducted several activities in the past few years that addressed the role of biobehavioral sciences in improving treatment of major mental illnesses. To assist the President's Commission on Mental Health, the Institute invited several papers assessing scientific advances and research needs in psychobiological and psychosocial treatments of major mental disorders (Parloff et al., 1978; Berger et al., in press). The Institute also convened a conference to explore issues in the provision of care for mental disorders in general health care systems, where the majority of people needing mental health care interact with health professionals (Parron and Solomon, 1980). More recently, as part of the study Research on Stress in Health and Disease, a group evaluated evidence that life events and other psychological and social influences are risk factors of mental and physical disorders (Elliott and Eisdorfer, 1982). This chapter presents some highlights of these projects.

Basic Concepts of Brain Function

In vertebrates, including human beings, the brain and spinal cord form a continous structure, the central nervous system (CNS) (Kandel and Schwartz, 1981). The peripheral nervous system connects the central nervous system with other organs in the body, conveying information to the brain through sensory nerves and from the brain through motor nerves. The brain also monitors the blood for information in the form of chemicals that are released elsewhere in the body, and it sends out chemical signals that influence the activity of specific organs such as the heart, adrenals, and thyroid (National Academy of Sciences, 1979).

As many as 100 billion nerve cells make up the human brain. Each cell interconnects with many other neurons, receiving and sending information that can facilitate or inhibit cell action. For most neurons, specific compounds transmit information between cells and regulate such transmissions. Until recently, scientists thought that only a small number of chemicals were involved in neuronal regulation. However, in the past few years, many investigators have added to the list of such compounds (Barchas et al., 1978). Rapid developments in this area have necessitated reevaluations of ways in which chemicals could regulate neuronal activity. A number of nomenclatures have been proposed (Dismukes, 1979), one of which is shown in Table 9.1. The term *neuroregulators* emphasizes that the compounds all have in common the ability to regulate communication among nerve cells. These are subdivided into two broad categories: neurotransmitters actually convey discrete messages between two nerve cells, and neuromodulators modify the effectiveness of such neurotransmission.

Neurotransmission

Neurons characteristically have a central cell body containing the nucleus and much of the enzymes and other biochemical machinery needed to

TABLE 9.1   Categories of Neuroregulators

Neuroregulators: substances involved in interneuronal communication.

Neurotransmitters: neuroregulators that act at a neuronal synapse to transmit a presynaptic signal to a postsynaptic neuron.

Neuromodulators: neuroregulators that affect neuronal communication through mechanisms other than synaptic transmission.

   Hormonal neuromodulators: substances that alter neuronal activity at a distance from the site of release, possibly at many targets simultaneously; they exert their effects either via specific membrane receptors or by selectively interfering with some aspect of neurotransmission.

   Synaptic neuromodulators: substances that affect neuronal function locally by altering neurotransmitter activity at the synapse through a specific site, possibly a membrane receptor.

---

maintain their function. From this body extend many fibers, some short and others much longer. Most of the fibers, called dendrites, receive information from other cells. One, the axon, sends signals out from the cell body; it may extend relatively short distances to convey messages to other neurons in the brain or as far as 3 ft in man to provide information to an end organ such as a muscle. An electrical signal is conveyed along the axon until it reaches a synapse—a specialized structure in which two neurons come into very close contact. Only a small gap, the synaptic cleft, separates them. The neurotransmitter conveys the signal across that cleft. The main known features of neurotransmission are identified in a representation of a dopamine synapse (Figure 9.1).

In the presynaptic terminal, the neurotransmitter dopamine is synthesized in two steps from tyrosine, its amino acid precursor. The enzyme tyrosine hydroxylase catalyzes the first reaction; it is present only in neurons in which dopamine and related neuroregulators are formed. A second enzyme, dopa decarboxylase, completes the synthesis, and dopamine is stored in presynpatic vesicles, or granules.

An electrical signal along the axon depolarizes the presynaptic membrane and initiates a chain of events that releases dopamine into the synaptic cleft. The neurotransmitter then diffuses across this gap and interacts with specific membrane receptors on the postsynaptic side in a "lock and key" fashion. Interaction with postsynaptic receptors probably produces conformational changes in the receptor that result in a number of changes in the postsynaptic neuron. There also appear to be presynaptic receptors for dopamine that may form part of a feedback loop to regulate neuronal activity.

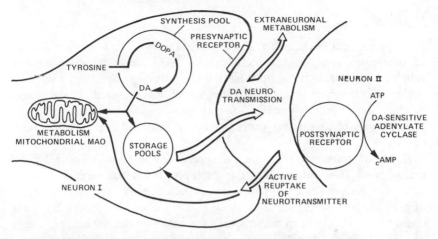

FIGURE 9.1   Idealized representation of a dopaminergic synapse. Dopamine (DA) is synthesized in two steps from the amino acid tyrosine and then stored in synaptic vesicles. An action potential depolarizes the presynaptic membrane, resulting in the release of dopamine into the synaptic cleft. The neurotransmitter then interacts with specific postsynaptic receptors, initiating a complex series of events that includes changes in membrane permeability to specific ions and cyclic AMP (cAMP) formation. The latter, in turn, facilitates other intracellular processes. There also is some evidence for presynaptic receptors, which may alter dopamine synthesis as a function of synaptic activity. The neuronal signal is terminated when dopamine is cleared from the synaptic cleft, primarily through an active reuptake mechanism that returns it to the presynaptic terminal, where it is either metabolized by monoamine oxidase (MAO) or restored in vesicles for future use. Reproduced with permission of authors from Barchas et al. (1978). Copyright © 1978 by the American Association for the Advancement of Science.

Depending on the synapse, the neurotransmitter may either excite or inhibit activity of the neuron on which it acts. The signal, once sent, must end rapidly; signal termination is accomplished by removing the transmitter from the synaptic cleft. As with several other transmitters, dopamine has a specific reuptake mechanism that rapidly returns most of it to the presynaptic terminal, where it is stored again in vesicles for later use or destroyed enzymatically.

A number of other important neuroregulators are thought to act as neurotransmitters in some parts of the brain and peripheral nervous system, including serotonin, norepinephrine, gamma-aminobutyric acid (GABA), and acetylcholine. Each has comparable systems of synthesis, storage, release, and inactivation. All of those mentioned have been implicated in hypotheses about major mental disorders.

Neuromodulation

More precise understanding about neuronal function has suggested that not all neuroregulators are neurotransmitters. Exploration of other ways in which they might act on neurons has led to the concept of neuromodulation (Elliott and Barchas, 1980). There are several hypotheses about alternative mechanisms for precisely controlling communication among groups of nerve cells. Tentatively, neuromodulators can be subdivided into two broad categories.

Hormonal neuromodulators affect neuronal activity at locations relatively distant from their release site. For example, hormonal neuromodulators might be released from peripheral or central neurons or from other types of cells in the body and produce widespread effects throughout the brain (Figure 9.2). Unlike neurotransmitters, hormonal neuromodulators can have prolonged effects, altering baseline activity of spontaneously firing neurons or affecting responses to other neuronal input. Such a mechanism could enable precise modulation of the activity of an entire group of nerve cells.

Synaptic neuromodulators affect neuronal function secondarily by altering the activity of a neurotransmitter at sites of synthesis, release, receptor interactions, reuptake, or metabolism (Figure 9.2). This concept is being developed, and much more research on examples is needed to support the data recently obtained. Investigators have found that some neurons contain more than one potential neuroregulator. This conflicts with earlier suggestions that a single neuron could only contain one neurotransmitter. Perhaps one substance is a neurotransmitter and the others are synaptic neuromodulators.

Newly Discovered Neuroregulators

Discovery of a number of previously unsuspected neuroregulators in the brain has generated much interest in the field. Perhaps the most widely known of the discoveries are the endorphins, a class of polypeptide substances that possess analgesic activity like that of morphine and other opiates (cf. Chapter 1). These opioid peptides now have been found in the brain, pituitary, spinal cord, adrenals, and blood. They are involved in the perception of and reaction to pain. They also are intimately entwined with the adrenocortical stress response, which suggests that their physiological role may extend beyond pain (cf. Chapter 3). The peptides are much more difficult to study than other substances, but new methodologies are being developed (Snyder, 1980).

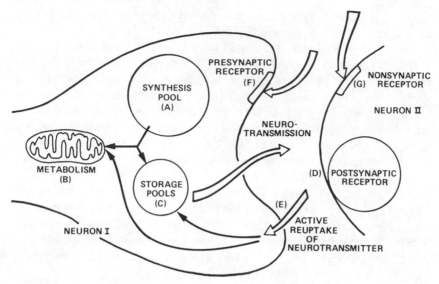

FIGURE 9.2   Possible sites of action of neuromodulators. Each letter indicates a potential site for synaptic or hormonal neuromodulation of neuronal activity:

   A. inhibition or stimulation of neurotransmitter synthesis;
   B. blockade or induction of neurotransmitter metabolism;
   C. interference with neurotransmitter storage, possibly by replacing it with a less active analogue (false transmitter);
   D. inhibition at postsynaptic neurotransmitter receptor sites;
   E. blockade of reuptake mechanisms;
   F. competitive or noncompetive inhibition at presynaptic neurotransmitter receptor sites; and
   G. interaction with specific nonsynaptic receptors that affect basal neuronal activity or alter neuronal responsiveness to other input.

Reproduced with permission of authors from Elliott and Barchas (1980).

Analytic Techniques

A contributing factor to the surge of knowledge within the neurosciences has been the many technological innovations developed in the past few years. For example, recent discoveries of neuroregulators can be traced directly to application of fluorimetric, enzymatic, gas chromatographic, mass spectometric, and radioimmunologic techniques for their detection and quantitation. Many of the substances of interest are present only in minute amounts. It is not at all unusual for the quantity of a substance to be reported as picograms (10^{-12} g) per gram of brain tissue.

Among important recent advances have been improved techniques for obtaining anatomical maps of neuroregulator distribution in the brain (National Academy of Sciences, 1979). More has been learned in the past ten years about how neurons connect with each other than in all previous history. For example, it is possible to trace neuronal pathways in undamaged animal brains by utilizing the neuron's own transporting mechanisms. Radiolabeled amino acids injected near cell bodies are taken up into the cell and transported along the axon. Other methods enable investigators to trace backward from the synapse to the cell body. One recently developed technique with great potential takes advantage of the fact that neurons use glucose for energy. A chemical called deoxyglucose is taken up by neurons but cannot be metabolized, so that its accumulation correlates with neuronal activity. Positron labeling makes it possible to use this method in human beings and other mammals to localize changes in neuronal activity during the performance of specific behaviors.

Affective Disorders

The affective disorders of depression and manic psychosis are probably the most destructive group of emotional illnesses in the United States in terms of prevalence, economic cost, impact on families, and even mortality. "Depression" is used to describe both a normal mood and a serious mental or emotional disorder (Berger, 1977). As a normal mood, it refers to transitory feelings of sadness or discouragement that everyone feels during difficult times. As a mental disorder, depression has many symptoms, only one of which is sadness. People with severe depression are profoundly pessimistic and often feel unworthy of the good things they have enjoyed in life; they tend to feel helpless and lose interest in their work and social activities. Often, they feel guilty about not living up to expectations of others. Some depressed people are anxious or fearful and may be physically active without accomplishing much. Others feel tired and weak, have trouble concentrating, and move quite slowly. Common physical symptoms include headaches, backaches, or gastrointestinal distress and, in cases of severe depression, insomnia and loss of appetite and weight. Suicidal thinking and attempts are the most dangerous depressive symptoms. Collectively these symptoms are called the depression syndrome, which is quite variable from person to person. Some feel more emotional distress, others suffer primarily from physical symptoms.

Mania is a severe emotional disorder that seems to be, in many ways, the opposite of depression (Sack and De Fraites, 1977). The symptoms of mania can be divided into changes in mood, thought, motor activity, and behavior. Manics often are elated—sometimes euphoric, overconfident or superficially carefree. They exude optimism and may feel particularly attractive, desirable, efficient, and alert. However, their mood tends to yield readily to irritability if they are frustrated. The thought patterns of manics are disturbed, flitting rapidly from one thought to another. Ideas of potency, knowledge, and special abilities also appear in severe mania. Motor activity is accelerated, and manics work energetically, although they may move restlessly from project to project, unable to complete one. Drastic decisions may be made without preparation. As a result, severe mania can be as devastating to personal relationships and careers as is depression.

About 1.5 million people are being treated for depression today, and perhaps three or even five times that number may need such treatment (President's Commission on Mental Health, 1978). Thus, there may be from 4.5 to 7.5 million individuals in the United States who currently suffer the psychic pain, life disruptions, and risk of suicide associated with depression. As many as 15 percent of the population will have at least one depressive episode during their lifetime. There is good evidence that genetic and biological factors are important in some forms of depression, especially bipolar depression, in which patients experience recurrent bouts of depression and mania (Nurenberger and Gershon, in press). But psychosocial factors also appear to play a significant role in many cases.

Psychosocial Risk Factors

Predisposition   Brown and Harris (1978) found a strong inverse association between social class and unipolar depression. Weissman and Myers (1978) reported a similar association between lower social class and depression for prevalence in the community but not for lifetime incidence of depression in the subjects studied. Reasons for these differences are the subject of debate. One contributing factor may be that subtypes of depression are associated with social class to different degrees. No available studies have had enough subjects across diagnostic subgroups to test this possibility.

Only a few studies have assessed associations between chronic stressors and depression. Brown and Harris (1978) found that people who spent two years in situations they perceived as threatening were at increased risk of developing depression. Rates of depression are much higher for women than for men, particularly for mothers and young wives (Weissman and Klerman, 1977). It could be valuable to explore biological, psychological, and sociological sex differences to help account for these differences in depression rates.

Precipitation and Perpetuation   A number of well-done studies have tested the belief that at least some depressions are a reaction to an individual's recent experiences (Paykel, in press). Two large projects concluded that, compared with the general population, depressed patients experience many more life events just prior to the onset of a depressive episode (Paykel et al., 1969; Brown et al., 1973). Depressed patients report the occurrence of a wide range of events preceding a depressive episode, particularly the loss of someone important and threats to self-esteem. Marital disharmony also occurs frequently prior to the onset of depression.

Little information is available about the influence of life events on the likelihood of relapse in depression. As with onset of depression, the occurrence of undesirable life events during the preceding three months appears to increase the risk of relapse (Paykel and Tanner, 1976). Also, depressed patients who live in families that have high expressed emotion may be more likely to relapse than are those living in families with low expressed emotion (Vaughan and Leff, 1976). The condition of high expressed emotion is characterized by high involvement of the family with the patient, usually in a critical or hostile context (Brown et al., 1972).

Suicide, the most dramatic manifestation of depression, may be especially affected by outside events. Successful and attempted suicides correlate with the intensity and the timing of threatening life events (Paykel, 1976). As appears to be true more generally, the type of life event that is personally significant may differ widely from one individual to another. Still, loss of a significant relationship is particularly common. Vulnerability may be a crucial concept for understanding the relationship between life events and suicide attempts. Pokorny and Kaplan (1976) compared successful suicides with controls matched for type and severity of depression and for other socioeconomic factors. Based on information obtained at the last hospital admission before they committed suicide, subjects had a high "defenseless score," consisting of feelings of anxiety, depressed mood, inferiority, guilt, and suicidal ideation. Detection of such feelings could alert health professionals to patients who are in special danger of attempting suicide.

Pharmacological Treatments

Much of the change in treating people with affective disorders springs directly from the introduction of effective antidepressant and antimanic drugs. Although these treatment modalities now are widely accepted, considerable ingenuity was required to prove their efficacy in treating severe affective disorders. This effort provided valuable experimental tools to clinical research. One of the best examples of such secondary contributions was the incorporation into psychiatric research of the double-blind design, which now is a standard for rigorous tests of any new medical treatment (Kraemer, 1977). Using this design, one or more drugs are compared either to a medically inert placebo or to a drug with proven efficacy. The minimal requirement is that both patient and investigator be "blind to," i.e., unaware of the identity of, the medication being given. Use of the double-blind technique greatly eases problems of unconscious bias of patient and physician in evaluating drug effects.

The need for accurate measures of treatment effects was especially great in depression, because many patients have a spontaneous remission. Well-controlled studies estimate placebo response rates to be about 16 percent for chronically depressed and 46 percent for acutely ill patients (Klerman, 1972; Davis, 1976). Even with this high spontaneous remission rate, antidepressants have consistently proven to be effective treatments for depression. For example, tricyclic antidepressants, the most widely used class of antidepressant drugs, are more effective than placebo for acute treatment of a depressive episode in about two thirds of studies (Berger, 1977). About 80 percent of acutely depressed patients respond to available pharmacological ther·pies and psychotherapies. As another aspect of efficacy, investigators have shown that maintenance treatment with tricyclics for up to a year significantly decreases the relapse rate of depressed patients. Thus, tricyclics both provide acute relief of depressive symptoms and delay or prevent their return.

Despite the success of the tricyclics, the drugs are not ideal. They take at least two and up to six weeks to begin relieving the symptoms of depression. They also have numerous side effects that, in some patients, can be severe enough to prohibit their continued use (Berger, 1977). An especially unfortunate feature of tricyclics is their toxicity at high doses: overdoses can be fatal, making the drugs particularly dangerous for exactly the patients who need them most urgently—namely, depressed patients with suicidal ideation. Also, tricyclics cannot help every patient, and as yet there is no way to predict who will respond. Some patients fail to respond to one antidepressant but have a dramatic response to a second type. During the two to three months necessary to find the correct drug, patients continue to suffer and remain at risk of suicide. The search for new and better drugs continues (Feighner, 1981).

The discovery that lithium salts are an effective treatment of mania has had an impact both at a clinical and at a basic science level (Gershon and Shopsin, 1973). By means that still are unclear, lithium provides selective relief from the severe symptoms of manic psychosis and may also be of benefit in treating some subgroups of depressed patients. Clinical effects are truly dramatic. Lithium is considerably safer than the antidepressants but can produce serious side effects and is potentially fatal in excessive doses. Therefore, further research also is needed into the etiology of mania and into the mechanisms by which lithium exerts its effects, so that more effective and safer treatments can be devised.

Psychosocial Treatments

Psychosocial interventions continue to be of major importance in the treatment of affective disorders. As mentioned earlier, drugs must be given for several weeks before they begin to produce the desired therapeutic effect. At a minimum, psychosocial interventions are needed to help depressed patients get through the waiting period. This is especially true of suicidal patients, who may need hospitalization and close supervision. In addition, available drugs are not effective for everyone, nor do they always alleviate all symptoms even when they are effective. Some patients simply refuse to take medications or are unable to tolerate their side effects. Also, evidence suggests that drugs act primarily by reducing depressive symptoms, with much less effect on improving social functioning or general adjustment, for which psychosocial treatments may have their strongest impact. This last point argues for the value of combined approaches to treatment, using both drug and psychosocial interventions as appropriate (cf. Chapter 16).

Many different types of psychotherapies are used to treat depression, either alone or in combination with antidepressant drugs. Psychodynamic therapy attempts to explore the childhood events and current intrapsychic conflicts that make a person vulnerable to depression. Interpersonal therapy assumes that depression is caused by strains in relationships with people who are important in a patient's social and interpersonal context; it seeks to improve coping strategies and interpersonal functioning. Cognitive therapy attempts to alleviate depressive symptoms by helping the patient correct negative self-concepts. Marital therapy tries to improve interactions between husband and wife as a way to remove causes of the depression. Supportive psychotherapy focuses on recent events that led to the current depression; it uses reassurance and advice and allows the patient to ventilate and rationally discuss feelings and fears. Group therapy is a generic term for approaches having in common simultaneous treatment of a number of patients by one or a few therapists; a variety of theoretical orientations can be applied to this format. Behavior therapy also is a generic term, referring to therapies based on learning theory; they concentrate on relieving symptoms, rather than on underlying psychodynamics.

All of these types of psychotherapy are widely used in treating depression. However, systematic efforts to document their efficacy and to determine which types of patients are most likely to respond to a particular modality have been under way on a fairly large scale only in the past few years. Such studies have formidable difficulties, including marked variability of approaches even among practitioners of the same treatment orientation.

A number of studies have compared the efficacy of psychotherapy alone with low-contact or other appropriate control groups (Weissman, 1979). Therapies included cognitive, behavior, interpersonal, marital, and group. All of the studies support the conclusion that people who receive psychotherapy do better than those who receive minimal interventions. Several studies have compared psychotherapy to antidepressants, again with a range of treatment modalities represented (Weissman, 1979). In one, cognitive therapy was superior to a fixed drug dose in reducing symptoms in acutely depressed patients. In another, psychotherapy was equal to drug treatment in reducing such symptoms. In other studies, drugs were superior in preventing relapse or symptom reduction, but psychotherapy was slightly better in enhancing social functioning. Possible benefits of combined treatments are particularly important, as discussed in Chapter 16.

Basic and Clinical Research

By studying the pharmacological and biobehavioral effects of antidepressant and antimanic agents, scientists have made progress in uncovering the basis of the disorders that these drugs treat. In turn, identification of disturbed neuroregulator systems should offer new clues for developing better diagnostic and therapeutic tools. Most biochemical hypotheses of depression have invoked abnormalities in brain neuroregulators, particularly norepinephrine and serotonin (Berger and Barchas, 1977). The known antidepressants have been found to have activities that could increase the brain activity of either or both of these compounds. Efforts to establish whether depression actually results from a defect in neuroregulator function continues to stimulate advances in knowledge about the brain and already has suggested new directions in the search for safer and more effective drug treatments.

Studies of electrical activity of the brain have shown that depressed patients have markedly abnormal patterns, some of which are associated with altered sleep cycles. Because some of these abnormalities resolve as patients improve, future developments in this area may provide a sensitive and objective measure of the severity of depression. Equally important will be studies of the psychosocial components of depression; studies of coping mechanisms, developmental processes, social behavior, and basic social processes can help to define the role of loss, stress, and social interactions in producing depression and in aiding or hindering its resolution.

Several animal models of depression have been developed. In one interesting model, animals are exposed to uncontrollable, adverse events; this treatment produces increased passivity, decreased aggression and dominance, slowed thinking, and decreased appetite (Seligman, 1975). The model is especially relevant to reactions of persons who repeatedly face situations for which all responses are futile. Of great potential interest for prevention is evidence that the expected symptoms do not occur in animals "immunized" by prior exposure to bad events over which they can exert control (Hannum et al., 1976). Social separation of young rhesus and pigtail monkeys from their mothers provides another animal model of depression; separation results in disoriented locomotion, lack of play, lethargy, passivity, social withdrawal and self-absorption, and sleep changes (Mineka and Suomi, 1978). Exposure to socially rich environments prior to separation can prevent the occurrence of symptoms; contact with older peers during the depression may ameliorate them. Both of these models should provide tools for researchers trying to identify specific biological and psychological mechanisms by which behavioral or psychological events can precipitate depression. They also should be useful in studies of early environmental risk factors for depression and of prevention and treatment strategies.

The advantages of a diverse but firm research base already are manifest in several recent improvements in the treatment of affective disorders. Efforts to devise increasingly specific diagnostic categories have facilitated separation of depressed patients into more clinically homogeneous subgroups. As mentioned earlier, at least one group, bipolar depressives, has a strong genetic component to the depression and is particularly responsive to lithium. As studies are made of the relationship between potential genetic components and the environmental and behavioral factors that are so important in the illness, it seems reasonable to anticipate the development of diagnostic and therapeutic refinements.

Schizophrenia

Schizophrenia usually begins with a gradually increasing sense of inner turmoil and ill-being (Hollister, 1977). As the schizophrenic episode evolves, more specific symptoms appear, including severe problems with thinking. Individuals feel flooded with thoughts and fear a loss of control. Frequently, they begin to act compulsively, performing painstaking, repetitious, often meaningless tasks. Further difficulty is manifested by increasingly distorted concept formation, bizarre speech, and illogical thinking. Often schizophrenics form paranoid delusions, ranging from pervasive suspiciousness to beliefs in complex but highly improbable plots against them. Emotional expression may be completely absent or inappropriate. Many schizophrenics report hallucinations, but this symptom is not an essential feature. Generally, hallucinations are auditory, with one or more berating or threatening voices; however, they can occur in any sensory systems.

In the United States, 300,000 new cases of schizophrenia are diagnosed each year, and there is about a 1 percent chance that a person will be hospitalized for schizophrenia sometime during his life (President's Commission on Mental Health, 1978). However, the impact of schizophrenia on society is much higher than these figures initially suggest. Even with available forms of treatment, schizophrenics occupy about half of the hospital beds for mentally ill and mentally retarded patients—or one fourth of *all* available hospital beds. Thus, 200,000 hospitalized patients in the United States carry a diagnosis of schizophrenia, and another 400,000 schizophrenics are either being seen as outpatients or receiving no medical attention. Available evidence indicates that the incidence of schizophrenia has been constant in the United States for the past 100 years. So far, the incidence does not appear to be strongly influenced by culture or nationality. Cultural influences on symptoms are striking and may be important for the course of the disorder. A substantial number of twin and adoptive studies provide compelling evidence that genetic factors are important in the etiology of schizophrenia (Kety, 1980). Environmental influences also are undoubtedly important, but specific factors still are incompletely understood.

Psychosocial Influences

Predisposition The only consistently strong correlations with the occurrence of the first episode of schizophrenia have been lower socioeconomic status and prolonged exposure to seriously disordered family relationships. Schizophrenics are present disproportionately in the lowest socioeconomic classes (Kohn, 1973). Investigators have hypothesized downward social drift, downward genetic drift, and negative impact of poverty to explain the association (cf. Chapter 12). There also may be a connection with disordered families. For example, fathers are more likely to be absent in low-status families.

Some families can be characterized as having inappropriate communication, deviant or atypical role structures, and a negative emotional environment. Individuals who go through crucial developmental stages in such a setting appear to be at particular risk of later developing schizophrenia. In a five-year prospective study, Doane et al. (1981) identified deviant communication patterns within the family and parental expression of sustained negative feelings toward an adolescent as risk factors of schizophrenia. Although useful, such a study cannot prove that these factors increase the risk of becoming schizophrenic. For example, perhaps genes that create vulnerability to schizophrenia also cause deviant communication patterns in the family. Studies of adopted or cross-fostered subjects could help to distinguish among alternative explanations.

One of the best-documented environmental influences on a mental disorder is that of disordered family relationships on schizophrenia relapse. As with depression, schizophrenics in remission are more likely to relapse if they return to family settings with high expressed emotion. Thus, over 50 percent of schizophrenic patients returning to such a home relapsed, compared with 13 percent of patients returning to a home with low expressed emotion (Brown et al., 1972). A more complete understanding of the effects of family relationships on the course of schizophrenia might suggest new preventive approaches for breaking the familiar cycle of hospitalization, remission, relapse, and rehospitalization.

Precipitation and Perpetuation   The importance of stressful life events in precipitating a schizophrenic episode remains controversial (Rabkin, 1980; Dohrenwend and Egri, 1981). In the best-controlled studies (Brown et al., 1972; Jacobs and Myers, 1976), schizophrenics were much more likely than controls to have experienced major life events during the reporting period; but most of the events might have resulted from early effects of the mental disorder. Schizophrenics may be more likely to generate major life events as they enter a schizophrenic episode (Fontana et al., 1972). However, there also may be an excess of independent events during the three weeks before the onset of an episode (Brown and Birley, 1968). A similar buildup of independent events preceding relapse was found by Leff et al. (1973), who studied schizophrenics being treated in the community with antipsychotic drugs.

Pharmacological Treatments

Schizophrenic episodes usually are treated with antipsychotics and supportive psychotherapy. Taken together, the evidence overwhelmingly confirms that antipsychotics are effective treatments for schizophrenia. Among patients receiving an antipsychotic, only 10 percent fail to show some improvement and nearly 70 percent improve significantly; by contrast, 50 percent of patients on placebo are unchanged or become worse, and only 25 percent improve substantially (Davis and Cole, 1975). Typically, major improvement occurs during the first six weeks. Antipsychotics appear to act with relative specificity on the fundamental features of schizophrenia, with more variable effects on less closely related symptoms. Thus, the drugs decrease the severity of thought disorders and increase the level of social interaction, with no consistent effects on levels of anxiety. The value of antipsychotic drugs in long-term maintenance treatment of schizophrenia remains unresolved. Although they can delay recurrence of symptoms in some patients, they have no beneficial effect or are unneccessary in others (Morgan and Cheadle, 1974). At present, it is impossible to predict the needs of a given patient.

Antipsychotic drugs are relatively safe, particularly compared with antidepressants. Still, they can have serious side effects. One important set of side effects is the tendency of these drugs to cause disorders of movement (Hollister, 1977). Many of the disorders resolve spontaneously or can be alleviated pharmacologically; others can, in some patients, cause prolonged disability. The potentially irreversible motor defect called tardive dyskinesia can result from long-term treatment with antipsychotics. Efforts to prevent and treat side effects and to develop more specific treatments for schizophrenia continue to be important areas of research.

Psychosocial Treatments

Nonpharmacological aspects of treating schizophrenics appear to influence outcomes for some patients. In general, research evidence suggests that such approaches are most useful in combination with appropriate drug therapy. Psychosocial interventions have proved of value for hospital and post-hospital treatment. An important advance has been the development of systematic assessment instruments for characterizing the psychosocial environment (Moos, 1975). Four aspects of the treatment milieu have been identified as positive factors for post-hospital psychosocial adjustment: small treatment community size; positive expectations among staff; high staff morale, with active involvement in the treatment process; and a problem-solving, practical orientation (Will et al., in press).

Institutional Treatment   Hospital programs for schizophrenics have changed markedly over the past 25 years. Patients now are treated as adults, allowed and expected to share in activities and decision-making processes of their hospital unit. Acute schizophrenics seem to respond best to stimulus-decreasing environments that provide active, involved staff who are accepting and supportive. Even without antipsychotic drugs, some acute patients who stay in such a setting for three to five months have rehospitalization rates and post-hospital social adjustments that are comparable with those of patients on drugs (Rappaport et al., 1980). Given the dangerous side effects of the antipsychotics, it would be highly desirable to have ways of identifying patients likely to respond to such an environment. For chronic schizophrenics, effective therapeutic environments are highly structured and organized, with expectations oriented toward specific behavior changes (Paul and Lentz, 1977). Evidence suggests that, with a program using behavior therapy with continued aftercare and active community residential care, institutions can discharge more than 90 percent of chronic schizophrenics into the community with a two-year rehospitalization rate of less than 5 percent (Paul and Lentz, 1977). Only 10 percent of these patients can live completely independently; but all should be able to fulfill basic needs of food, shelter, socialization, and recreation.

Community Treatment   One consequence of effective drug treatments for schizophrenia has been an increased emphasis on returning patients to the community as quickly as practicable. This has created a clear need for psychosocial interventions to help recovered patients enter situations that will minimize the chances of relapse while maximizing their independence and function. Such patients often have only limited social and interpersonal skills with which to seek and maintain adequate community adjustment. Patients who receive both drugs and assistance from a social worker have significantly better social adjustment than do those receiving only drugs. Transitional facilities such as halfway houses also help reduce relapses, but only while the patients remain in contact with the facility (Rog and Raush, 1975). This suggests the value of creating supportive environments in which schizophrenics can live in the community (cf. Chapter 18). The research cited earlier about effects of life stressors on relapse also supports such an approach to long-term care (Wing, 1978). However, few tests have so far been made of the effectiveness of such environments.

Basic and Clinical Research

Research in schizophrenia has taken many routes, but none has had more impact than have efforts to discover why antipsychotic drugs work and how this information can be applied to improving diagnosis and therapy of schizophrenia. Two current major hypotheses about schizophrenia form the nexus of much of the present research into the biological causes of this disorder. The dopamine hypothesis of schizophrenia postulates a relative excess of specific brain pathways that utilize dopamine as a neurotransmitter (Snyder, 1976). A second hypothesis suggests that schizophrenia arises from production in the body of a substance that produces psychosis, i.e., a psychotogen; this is referred to as the psychotogen hypothesis of schizophrenia (Koslow, 1977). A number of other hypotheses about roles in schizophrenia of other neuroregulators have also been made (Berger et al., 1978a). Research into these hypotheses and the production of basic information that will open up far-reaching new possibilities constitute an urgent need. Required for the validation of such hypotheses will be studies of basic neurobiology and psychopharmacology, genetic studies of neuroregulators, investigations of behavioral and biochemical interactions, and exploration of neurophysiological and neuropsychological components of schizophrenia.

The schizophrenic state appears to be a uniquely human disorder, but animals manifest behavior patterns that are similar in some respects. Animal models continue to be controversial but valuable in schizophrenia research. Amphetamines can produce a psychotic state in human beings that closely resembles paranoid schizophrenia and that antipsychotic drugs can partially reverse. In animals, amphetamines produce bizarre, stereotypic behaviors reminiscent of human paranoid behavior; these effects also are blocked by antipsychotics (Borison and Diamond, 1978). The importance of behavioral and environmental factors on the effects of amphetamines in animals has only begun to be explored (Haber et al., 1977). Such studies may contribute greatly to efforts to better understand ways in which life events exacerbate or alleviate schizophrenic symptoms.

Clinical studies of schizophrenia also are of great importance. More precise diagnostic categories could improve diagnosis and treatment. Reliable and specific diagnostic categories are particularly important to studies of genetic components of schizophrenia and of their important but unstudied interactions with behavior.

Markers of Vulnerability

A variety of evidence suggests that the occurrence of a mental disorder results from a combination of physiological and psychosocial factors. It seems reasonable that, at least for some individuals, a vulnerability must be present before environmental factors can precipitate a disorder. Discovery of an objective marker for such vulnerability would be of great value for both basic research and clinical applications.

Several biological abnormalities are associated with depression in at least some patients. As noted earlier, some forms of depression are thought to result from a breakdown in the usual function of brain norepinephrine and serotonin. Some depressed patients have a relatively low urinary excretion of 3–methoxy–4-hydroxyphenylglycol (MHPG), a norepinephrine metabolite; this is of particular interest, because such people may respond especially well to antidepressants that enhance the activity of norepinephrine neurons in the brain (Maas, 1975). Some depressed patients also seem to have a defect in the brain regulation of the adrenal glands; they have relatively high blood concentrations of corticosteroids and fail to suppress steroid secretion appropriately (Carroll, 1972). This surprising discovery has held up well under continuing scrutiny. Such an abnormality might greatly alter responses to stressful events, suggesting a possible connection between environmental events and depression.

A few physiological measures in some schizophrenics differ from those for nonschizophrenics. For example, average platelet activity of the metabolic enzyme monoamine oxidase (MAO) for chronic schizophrenics is below the average for appropriate controls (Berger et al., 1978b). More recently, new techniques have enabled investigators to discover that some chronic schizophrenics have enlarged brain ventricles suggestive of cortical and cerebellar atrophy (Weinberger et al., 1979); these changes are accompanied by measurable decreases in psychological function (Golden et al., 1980). Other neurological abnormalities also may be present. Rochford et al. (1970) found neurological abnormalities in two thirds of their schizophrenic subjects and in none of the control subjects who had affective disorders. Perhaps even more compelling is a study of identical (monozygotic) twins, in which 73 percent of the schizophrenic twins had signs of a neurological deficit, yet virtually none of the nonschizophrenic cotwins had such signs (Mosher et al., 1971). Also of interest are studies of an eye-tracking dysfunction found in a high proportion of schizophrenics and in their nonschizophrenic relatives (Holzman et al., 1974), again suggesting the possibility of a neurophysiological defect.

Some events at birth may predispose an individual to the later development of schizophrenia. Obstetrical complications were more frequent and severe for subjects who have been diagnosed as being schizophrenic than for matched controls (Kinney and Jacobsen, 1978). Prolonged labor was particularly common in the schizophrenic group, suggesting that perinatal brain injury through anoxia might play a role. In another approach, Dalen (1975) found that 5 to 15 percent more schizophrenics are born during the winter or spring than during the summer or fall. Among interesting possibilities, such a seasonal variation in disease incidence might reflect the action of an infectious agent such as a slow virus (Matthysse and Matthysse, 1978) or changes in nutritional status of essential vitamins and minerals that might influence the occurrence of intracranial bleeding at birth (Kinney and Jacobsen, 1978).

Some studies have examined factors that might increase the risk of developing any kind of mental illness. For example, Buchsbaum et al. (1976) assessed platelet MAO activity in college student volunteers. Comparing the 10 percent having lowest activities with the 10 percent having highest, they found that the suicide rate of families of low-MAO subjects was eight times higher than that of families of high-MAO subjects. These researchers later measured cortical average evoked potentials in the same subjects. (Haier et al., 1980). Repeated presentations of evoked potentials resulted in an increased response for some people (augmenters) and in a reduced response in others (reducers). Among the subjects, the combination of augmenters with low MAO activity or of reducers with high MAO activity was associated with a markedly increased risk of being diagnosed as having major depression sometime during the 18 months following the measurements. Such studies reflect beginning efforts to apply increasingly sophisticated techniques for assessing human neurophysiology to the task of identifying people who may be at special risk of developing mental disorders. Ready identification of high-risk subgroups would be tremendously useful in designing targeted interventions.

Conclusions

The involvement of the biobehavioral sciences in investigating and treating major mental disorders has been markedly productive. The discovery of successful drug treatments for depression, mania, and schizophrenia provided invaluable tools for neuroscientists trying to decipher brain mechanisms. In turn, their basic research has provided insights into possible mechanisms for these disorders and has suggested ways in which treatment might be improved.

Similarly, the psychological and social sciences have greatly expanded the range of treatment options for patients with a severe mental illness, either as an alternative to drugs or in combination with them. It is encouraging that biologically and psychosocially oriented investigators and clinicians have begun to seek ways to explore the interface between their fields. Instead of being viewed as competitive approaches, these viewpoints now are being approached as complementary perspectives of the complex interactions between an individual's internal and external environments.

References

Barchas, J. D., Akil, H., Elliott, G. R., Holman, R. B., and Watson, S. J. Behavioral neurochemistry: Neuroregulators and behavioral states. *Science 200*:964–973, 1978.

Berger, P. A. Antidepressant medications and the treatment of depression. IN: *Psychopharmacology: From Theory to Practice* (Barchas, J. D., Berger, P. A., Ciaranello, R. D., and Elliott, G. R., eds.) New York: Oxford University Press, 1977, pp. 174–207.

Berger, P. A., and Barchas, J. D. Biochemical hypotheses of affective disorders. IN: *Psychopharmacology: From Theory to Practice* (Barchas, J. D., Berger, P. A., Ciaranello, R. D., and Elliott, G. R., eds.) New York: Oxford University Press, 1977, pp. 151–173.

Berger, P. A., Hamburg, B. A., and Hamburg, D. A. Mental health: Progress and problems. *Daedalus 106*:261–276, 1977.

Berger, P. A., Elliott, G. R., and Barchas, J. D. Neuroregulators and schizophrenia. IN: *Psychopharmacology: A Generation of Progress* (Lipton, M. A., Dimascio, A., and Killam, K. F., eds.) New York: Raven, 1978a, pp. 1071–1082.

Berger, P. A., Elliott, G. R., and Barchas, J. D. *Treatment of Mental Disorders: Pscyhobiological Approaches* New York: McGraw-Hill, in press.

Berger, P. A., Ginsburg, R. A., Barchas, J. D., Murphy, D. L., and Wyatt, R. J. Platelet monoamine oxidase in chronic schizophrenic patients. *Am. J. Psychiatry* 135:95–99, 1978b.

Borison, R. L., and Diamond, B. I. A new animal model for schizophrenia: Interactions with adrenergic mechanisms. *Biol. Psychiatry* 13:217–225, 1978.

Brown, G. W., and Birley, J. L. T. Crises and life changes and the onset of schizophrenia. *J. Health Soc. Behav.* 9:203–214, 1968.

Brown, G. W., and Harris, T. *Social Origins of Depression: A Study of Psychiatric Disorder in Women* London: Tavistock, 1978.

Brown, G. W., Birley, J. L. T., and Wing, J. K. Influence of family life on the course of schizophrenic disorders: A replication. *Br. J. Psychiatry* 121:241–258, 1972.

Brown, G. W., Sklair, F., Harris, T. O., and Birley, J. L. T. Life events psychiatric disorders. Part I: Some methodological issues. *Psychol. Med.* 3:74–87, 1973.

Buchsbaum, M. S., Coursey, R. D., and Murphy, D. L. The biochemical-high-risk paradigm: Behavioral and familial correlates of low platelet monoamine oxidase activity. *Science* 194:339–341, 1976.

Carroll, B. J. Control of plasma cortisol levels in depression: Studies with the dexamethasone suppression test. IN: *Depressive Illness: Some Research Studies* (Davies, B., Carroll, B. J., and Mowbray, R. M., eds.) Springfield, Ill.: Charles C. Thomas, 1972, pp. 87–148.

Dalen, P. *Season of Birth: A Study of Schizophrenia and Other Mental Disorders* Amsterdam: North-Holland, 1975.

Davis, J. M. Tricyclic antidepressants. IN: *The Drug Treatment of Mental Disorders* (Simpson, L. L., ed.) New York: Raven Press, 1976, pp. 127–146.

Davis, J. M., and Cole, J. O. Antipsychotic agents. IN: *Comprehensive Textbook of Psychiatry, 2nd Ed.* (Freedman, A. M., Kaplan, H. I., and Sadock, B. J., eds.) Baltimore: Williams and Wilkins, 1975.

Dismukes, R. K. New concepts of molecular communication among neurons. *Behav. Brain Sci.* 2:409–448, 1979.

Doane, J. A., West, K. L., Goldstein, M. J., Rodnick, E. H., and Jones, J. E. Parental communication deviance and affective style: Predictors of subsequent schizophrenia spectrum disorders in vulnerable adolescents. *Arch. Gen. Psychiatry* 38:679–685, 1981.

Dohrenwend, B. P., and Egri, G. Recent stressful life events and episodes of schizophrenia. *Schiz. Bull.* 7:12–23, 1981.

Elliott, G. R., and Barchas, J. D. Changing concepts about neuroregulation: Neurotransmitters and neuromodulators. IN: *Hormones and the Brain* (de Wied, D., and van Keep, P. A., eds.) Lancaster: MTP Press, 1980, pp. 43–52.

Elliott, G. R., and Eisdorfer, C. (Eds.) *Stress and Human Health* New York: Springer, 1982.

Feighner, J. P. Clinical efficacy of the newer antidepressants. *J. Clin. Psychopharmacol.* 1:23S–26S, 1981.

Fontana, A. F., Marcus, J. L., Noel, B., and Rakusin, J. M. Prehospitalization coping styles of psychiatric patients: The goal-directedness of life events. *J. Nerv. Ment. Dis.* 155:311–321, 1972.

Gershon, S., and Shopsin, B. (Eds.) *Lithium: Its Role in Psychiatric Research and Treatment* New York: Plenum, 1973.

Golden, C. J., Moses, J. A., Zelazoski, R., Graber, B., Zatz, L. M., Horvath, T. B., and Berger, P. A. Cerebral ventricular size and neuropsychological impairment in young chronic schizophrenics: Measurement by the standardized Luria-Nebraska neuropsychological battery. *Arch. Gen. Psychiatry* 37:619–623, 1980.

Haber, S., Barchas, P. R., and Barchas, J. D. Effects of amphetamine on social behaviors of rhesus macaques: An animal model of paranoia. IN: *Animal Models in Psychiatry and Neurology* (Hanin, I., and Usdin, E., eds.) New York: Pergamon Press, 1977, pp. 107–115.

Haier, R. J., Buchsbaum, M. S., and Murphy, D. L. An 18–month followup of students biologically at risk for psychiatric problems. *Schiz. Bull.* 6:334–337, 1980.

Hannum, R. D., Rosellini, R. A., and Seligmann, M. E. P. Learned helplessness in the rat: Retention and immunization. *Dev. Psychol.* 12:449–454, 1976.

Hollister, L. E. Antipsychotic medications and the treatment of schizophrenia. IN: *Psychopharmacology: From Theory to Practice* (Barchas, J. D., Berger, P. A., Ciaranello, R. D., and Elliott, G. R., eds.) New York: Oxford University Press, 1977, pp. 121–150.

Holzman, P. S., Proctor, L. R., Levy, D. L., Yasillo, N. J., Meltzer, H. Y., and Hurt, S. W. Eye-tracking dysfunctions in schizophrenic patients and their relatives. *Arch. Gen. Psychiatry* 31:143–151, 1974.

Jacobs, S., and Myers, J. Recent life events and acute schizophrenic psychosis: A controlled study. *J. Nerv. Ment. Dis.* 162:75–87, 1976.

Kandel, E. R., and Schwartz, J. H. (Eds.) *Principles of Neural Science* New York: Elsevier/North-Holland, 1981.

Kety, S. S. The syndrome of schizophrenia: Unresolved questions and opportunities for research. *Br. J. Psychiatry* 136:421–436, 1980.

Kinney, D. K., and Jacobsen, B. Environmental factors in schizophrenia: New adoption study evidence and its implications for genetic and environmental research. IN: *The Nature of Schizophrenia* (Wynne, L. C., Cromwell, R. L., and Matthysse, S., eds.) New York: Wiley, 1978, pp. 38–51.

Klerman, G. L. Drug therapy of clinical depressions—current status and implications for research on the neuropharmacology of affective disorders. *J. Psychiatr. Res.* 9:253–270, 1972.

Kohn, M. L. Social class and schizophrenia: A critical review and a reformulation. *Schiz. Bull.* 7:60–79, 1973.

Koslow, S. Bio-significance of N- and O-methylated indoles to psychiatric disorders. IN: *Neuroregulators and Psychiatric Disorders* (Usdin, E., Hamburg, D. A., and Barchas, J. D., eds.) New York: Oxford University Press, 1977, pp. 210–219.

Kraemer, H. C. Methodological aspects of psychopharmacology. IN: *Psychopharmacology: From Theory to Practice* (Barchas, J. D., Berger, P. A., Ciaranello, R. D., and Elliott, G. R., eds.) New York: Oxford University Press, 1977, pp. 504–513.

Leff, J. P., Hirsch, S. R., Gaind, R., Rohde, P. D., and Stevens, B. C. Life events and maintenance therapy in schizophrenic relapse. *Br. J. Psychiatry* 123:659–660, 1973.

Maas, J. W. Biogenic amines and depression: Biochemical and pharmacological separation of two types of depression. *Arch. Gen. Psychiatry* 32:1357–1361, 1975.

Matthysse, A. G., and Matthysse, S. W., Bacteriophage models of neurotropic virus specificity. *Birth Defects* 14:111–121, 1978.

Mineka, S., and Suomi, S. J. Social separation in monkeys. *Psychol. Bull.* 85:1376–1400, 1978.

Moos, R. H. *Evaluating Correctional and Community Settings* New York: Wiley, 1975.

Morgan, R., and Cheadle, J. Maintenance treatment of chronic schizophrenia with neuroleptic drugs. *Acta Psychiatr. Scand.* 50:78–85, 1974.

Mosher, L. R., Pollin, W., and Stabenau, J. R. Identical twins discordant for schizophrenia: Neurologic findings. *Arch. Gen. Psychiatry* 24:422–30, 1971.

National Academy of Sciences *Science and Technology: Five-Year Outlook* San Francisco: Freeman, 1979.

Nurenberger, J., and Gershon, E. Genetics of affective disorders. IN: *Depression and Antidepressants: Implications for Cause and Treatment* (Friedman, E., ed.) New York: Raven Press, in press.

Parloff, M. B., Wolfe, B., Hadley, S., and Waskow, I. E. Assessment of psychosocial treatment of mental disorders: Current status and prospects. An invited paper of the Advisory Committee on Mental Health of the Institute of Medicine, 1978.

Parron, D. L., and Solomon, F. (Eds.) *Mental Health Services in Primary Care Settings* Report of a Conference, April 2–3, 1979. Washington, D.C.: U.S. Government Printing Office, 1980, DHHS Publ. No. (ADM) 80–995.

Paul, G. L., and Lentz, R. J. *Psychosocial Treatment of Chronic Mental Patients: Milieu Versus Social-Learning Programs* Cambridge, Mass.: Harvard University Press, 1977.

Paykel, E. S. Life stress, depression, and attempted suicide. *J. Hum. Stress* 2:3–10, 1976.

Paykel, E. S. Life events and early environment. IN: *Handbook of Affective Disorders* Edinburgh: Churchill Livingstone, in press.

Paykel, E. S., and Tanner, J. Life events, depressive relapse and maintenance treatment. *Psychol. Med.* 6:481–485, 1976.

Paykel, E. S., Myers, J. K., Dienelt, M. N., Klerman, G. L., Lindenthal, J. J., and Pepper, M. P. Life events and depression: A controlled study. *Arch. Gen. Psychiatry* 21:753–760, 1969.

Pokorny, A. D., and Kaplan, H. B. Suicide following psychiatric hospitalization. *J. Nerv. Ment. Dis.* 162:119–125, 1976.

President's Commission on Mental Health *Report to the President, Vol. I* Washington, D.C.: U.S. Government Printing Office, 1978.

Rabkin, J. G. Stressful life events and schizophrenia: A review of the research literature. *Psychol. Bull.* 87:408–425, 1980.

Rappaport, M., Hopkins, H. K., Hall, K., Belleza, T., and Silverman, J. Schizophrenics for whom phenothiazines may be contraindicated or unnecessary. IN: *Controversy and Psychiatry* (Brodie, H. K. H., and Brady, P., eds.) Philadelphia: Saunders, 1980.

Rochford, J. M., Detre, T., Tucker, G. J., and Harrow, M. Neuropsychological impairments in functional psychiatric disease. *Arch. Gen. Psychiatry* 22:114–119, 1970.

Rog, D. J., and Raush, H. L. The psychiatric half-way house. How is it measuring up? *Community Ment. Health J.* 11:155–162, 1975.

Sack, R. L., and De Fraites, E. Lithium and the treatment of mania. IN: *Psychopharmacology: From Theory to Practice* (Barchas, J. D., Berger, P. A., Ciaranello, R. D., and Elliott, G. R., eds.) New York: Oxford University Press, 1977, pp. 208–225.

Seligman, M. E. P. *Helplessness: On Depression, Helplessness, and Death* San Francisco: Freeman, 1975.

Snyder, S. H. The dopamine hypothesis of schizophrenia: Focus on the dopamine receptor. *Am. J. Psychiatry* 133:197–202, 1976.

Snyder, S. H. Brain peptides as neurotransmitters. *Science* 209:976–983, 1980.

Vaughn, C. E., and Leff, J. P. The influence of family and social factors on the course of psychiatric illness: A comparison of schizophrenic and depressed neurotic patients. *Br. J. Psychiatry* 129:125–137, 1976.

Weinberger, D. R., Torrey, E. F., Neophytides, A. N., and Wyatt, R. J. Lateral cerebral ventricular enlargement in chronic schizophrenia. *Arch. Gen. Psychiatry* 36:735–739, 1979.

Weissman, M. M. The psychological treatment of depression: Evidence for the efficacy of psychotherapy alone, in comparison with and in combination with pharmacotherapy. *Arch. Gen. Psychiatry* 36:1261–1269, 1979.

Weissman, M. M., and Klerman, G. L. Sex differences and the epidemiology of depression. *Arch. Gen. Psychiatry* 34:98–111, 1977.

Weissman, M. M., and Myers, J. K. Affective disorders in a U.S. urban community: The use of research diagnostic criteria in an epidemiological survey. *Arch. Gen. Psychiatry* 35:1304–1311, 1978.

Will, O. A., Gunderson, J. G., and Mosher, L. R. (Eds.) *Psychiatric Milieu and the Therapeutic Process* New York: Jason Aronson, in press.

Wing, J. K. *Reasoning about Madness* Oxford: Oxford University Press, 1978.

III
SCIENTIFIC OPPORTUNITIES: SPECIAL LIFE CONSIDERATIONS

10
Work and Health

People's roles and identities in society relate to the type of work they do (Kahn, 1981). Jobs differ greatly, and work has correspondingly different meanings in people's lives. For some, it is threatening and unpleasant; for others, it is engrossing and self-fulfilling, providing social contacts and supports. Financial rewards of working enable people to acquire necessities for health and survival. But, beyond money, most people want challenge and variety in the content of their jobs and positive relationships with others at work. The work people do and the way they relate to it are among the most important predictors of well-being.

A number of investigators have looked at factors that affect work productivity and satisfaction (Kahn, 1981). One interesting example of such work was done by Coch and French (1948). They were trying to discover why changes in job specifications often resulted in reductions in productivity, increases in turnover, and prolonged learning time. They hypothesized that these behaviors were manifestations of psychological "resistance to change" and that increased participation of workers in the decisions leading to change would reduce such resistance. In one experimental group, all workers were consulted and involved in decisions about the introduction of the proposed change; in the second, representatives of the workers were involved, and they reported back to the larger group. For a control group, management explained the changes and the reasons for them. Full involvement maximized productivity and speed of learning; partial involvement produced similar but attenuated effects.

Physical characteristics of organizations influence worker relationships, which, in turn, influence organizational function and efficiency. However, these features do not account totally for worker motivation. The characteristics of the individual and his or her personal relationships also affect reactions to psychosocial influences in the environment (Bromet and Moos, 1976). Competent people are less likely to perceive conditions as stressful (Pearlin and Johnson, 1977), and people with supportive relationships are less likely to experience adverse health outcomes in response to perceived stress (Cassel, 1976; Cobb and Kasl, 1977).

Several Institute of Medicine projects considered the importance of work in relation to individual health. The study *Research on Stress in Human Health* (Elliott and Eisdorfer, 1982) examined both ways in which organizational settings produced or avoided stressing individuals associated with them and methods for systematically altering such settings to reduce their stressfulness. Also, the Institute of Medicine (1981) sponsored a conference that explored the potential role of the work place in health promotion.

Stressful Components of Working Life

Work organizations differ in their stage of development, size, and role and in the personalities involved. They may be split into subsystems that reflect different functions such as production, maintenance, research, and management. These subsystems may differ in the level of stress involved in their tasks. The stress also relates to the type of activity, usually being greater if the activity involves people rather than things (Kahn, 1981). Physical size of organizations has been related to productivity of coal miners and aircraft factory employees, to indices of employee satisfaction, to absenteeism, and to turnover rates in industrial organizations (Porter and Steers, 1973).

Stress Related to the Physical Environment

Stress can arise from exposure to odors, glare, noise, low levels of illumination, and extreme conditions with regard to ventilation, temperature, and humidity. Secondary distress can arise from fear of being exposed to life-threatening substances or situations (Levi et al., 1981). Such conditions usually involve a combination of many exposures, and such combinations may lead to complex interactions and problems that are difficult to foresee from the outset. Positive aspects may counterbalance adverse ones. Overcrowding or high-density populations of workers in particular settings may be less stressful if there is open space, gardens, or quiet surroundings (Rappoport, 1975).

Stress Related to Mass-Production Technology

Most work organizations have a long chain of command between the individual worker and management (Levi et al., 1981) and a wide gap between workers and consumers (Maule et al., 1973). Such separations may foster feelings of remoteness between one's work and its outcome. Workers may have very little control over the work, especially if the work is done mainly by machines. Such situations may result in restricted movements, lack of stimulus variation and control, shift work, and work loads that are not suited to individual capacity. All of these factors may have long-term effects on health and well-being (Levi et al., 1981).

In a study conducted by Frankenhaeuser and Gardell (1976), a group of workers classified as being at high risk on the basis of the extremely constricted, machine-paced nature of their assembly line task was compared with a control group of workers at the same mill whose jobs were not as constricted. Urine epinephrine secretion was used as a measure of stress. The high-risk group showed a significantly higher average epinephrine excretion than did controls and a much higher catecholamine buildup during the working day. Controls decreased catecholamine secretion toward the end of the day, whereas the high-risk group increased it. High-risk individuals also found it more difficult to relax after work and reported a greater frequency of psychosomatic symptoms. Absenteeism in this group was exceptionally high.

Tasks producing high epinephrine excretion were highly repetitious and machine-paced and required the worker to maintain the same posture throughout the workday. These features are representative of many mass-production industries; but whether strain on workers will decrease with a change to full automation needs assessment (Frankenhaeuser, 1981). One advantage of fully automated systems is that many of the remaining tasks require skill, and supervisory roles may enable greater control over work pace. Operators also may be relatively free to move about and interact socially. All of these features increase the sense of active participation in the work role. However, monitoring requires an unusual combination of constant high levels of attention and readiness with few actual demands for action. The brain needs to be stimulated to maintain attention. For example, the ability to detect critical signals in a monotonous environment decreases rapidly within the first half hour (Broadbent, 1971). The task of monitoring may be particularly stressful when a failure to pay attention and to react immediately may result in major machine damage, financial loss, or danger to people. Decision making may be hampered under such conditions (Frankenhaeuser, 1981).

Air traffic control is an excellent example of jobs that combine long periods of low activity with the need for constant preparedness. Rose et al. (1978) showed that air traffic controllers have a greater incidence of a variety of illnesses than do second-class airmen, who undergo the same sorts of government-mandated physical examinations and meet the same physical standards. An association with hypertension was most marked, but incidences of peptic ulcer disease and diabetes mellitus also were higher than in other workers under less stressful conditions. The effects appeared to be dose-dependent, illness incidences being greater for air traffic controllers at high-traffic centers than for those at low-traffic ones.

One typical concomitant of being stressed is an elevation of blood catecholamines, secreted from the adrenals (cf. Chapter 3). The relevance of increased levels of catecholamines to health outcome is uncertain, but findings suggest that prolonged or exceptionally high secretion may produce damage to various organ systems (Raab, 1971; Eliot et al., 1977). The speed with which a person exposed to high-stress situations unwinds after the experience will influence the "wear" on biological systems. Individuals who are rapid catecholamine decreasers usually are more efficient and maintain a more healthy state than are slow catecholamine decreasers (Johansson and Frankenhaeuser, 1973). A quick return to baseline after energy mobilization in response to stress implies an economical mode of response (Frankenhaeuser, 1981).

Workers involved in tasks that require overtime may need to adapt to the extra demands. A study of female office workers in an insurance company revealed that epinephrine secretion was markedly increased throughout the overtime period, both during the day and in the evening (Rissler, 1977). Effects of overtime spread to leisure hours, in that the women reported irritability and fatigue during these relaxed hours and showed elevated heart rates. Such effects may accumulate gradually, delaying recognition of their magnitude (Frankenhaeuser, 1981).

Shift work is another demand placed on an increasing number of employees. Shift workers report high frequencies of sleep, mood, digestive, and social disorders (Levi et al., 1981). Irregular shifts are the most disruptive, especially if work context changes also. Closer attention should be given to the importance of biological rhythms of activity in humans and to ways in which work demands may be modified to minimize disruptions (cf. Chapter 6).

The reward system is very important in determining work outcome and worker efficiency and health. Many mass-production industries use piece wages, at least in part as incentives for productivity. Such pay systems are associated with higher sick leave and injury rates and may be especially stressful for handicapped workers and in jobs involving risk of injury (Levi et al., 1981). Substitution of fixed wages in such a setting is associated with greater worker satisfaction, fewer sick leaves, and fewer work-related injuries; but productivity also decreases (Levi et al., 1981). There is continuing debate about how to balance these conflicting outcomes. More exploration is needed of alternative pay schedules that may be more satisfactory to both employer and employee.

The social climate in work organizations can affect employee health. Variables involved have been related to health indicators such as complaints of physical symptoms, absenteeism, and sick-call rates, as well as to outcome of psychiatric treatments (Moos, 1976). Military basic training companies that emphasize strict organization and officer control and deemphasize personal status tend to have high sick-call rates. Psychiatric wards with few social activities, little emphasis on involving patients in programs, and staff who discourage criticism and are unwilling to act on patient suggestions have higher treatment failures (Moos, 1979).

Additional sources of stress may relate to accessibility of the work situation. Commuting to and from work can add to the stress experienced by the worker. Lundberg (1976) studied stressful aspects of commuting between a suburban home and central-city job under different conditions of crowdedness. Commuters showed an increase in epinephrine excretion and reported feelings of discomfort in relation to an increase in crowding. Passengers who boarded the train midway, when conditions were more crowded and seat selection was more restricted, had higher epinephrine excretion rates than did those who boarded the train at the onset of the route (Singer et al., 1978). Psychological factors, including controllability, were more influential determinants of stress than were the length and duration of the trip.

Conditions at the work site can have pervasive effects in the life of the worker. Workers who have very little control and are under heavy work load show little involvement in organized activities outside work, as well as in work. As workers gain more perceived control and feel less pressured, they show more involvement in leisure and organizational activities (Karasek, 1981).

The relations between these variables in the work setting and their health outcomes are only associational as yet, but they offer interesting insights. Human beings appear to need a moderately varied flow of stimuli and events, as well as opportunities for supportive social interaction and for a measure of control over their activities. Elaboration of work conditions under which such needs can be met while maintaining acceptable levels of productivity and cost effectiveness would greatly benefit both industries and workers.

Individual Vulnerability

Individuals differ widely in their susceptibility to stress in daily life, reflecting both genetic and developmental influences (cf. Chapter 3). Flexible, extroverted individuals report more symptoms when faced with role conflicts than do more rigid, introverted types (Kahn et al., 1964). In studies of people undergoing life changes, those who remained healthy were emotionally insulated, showed a lack of concern for others, and had little involvement in life affairs as compared with those who became ill (Hinkle, 1974). On the other hand, Kobasa (1979) found that those who did not get ill despite stressful life events had a strong sense of commitment to self, a vigorous attitude to life, and an internal locus of control. It is, as yet, unclear which response is more appropriate. Studies are needed of long-term consequences of different types of reactions to potentially stressful situations.

Other aspects of personal predisposition also may increase an individual's vulnerability to work stress. Type A behavior may be such a factor. This behavior pattern is strongly associated with heart disease (Chapter 7). People who are characterized as Type A have high levels of job involvement and occupational pressure (Friedman and Rosenman, 1971). They also have a strong sense of time urgency, great impatience, and harsh competitiveness, compared with Type B individuals (Jenkins, 1976). Among men and women in white collar jobs, the incidence of heart disease is twice as high for Type A individuals as for Type B individuals; this relative risk is independent of other risk factors such as smoking, diet, and blood pressure (Haynes et al., 1980). Personality factors were also important in reactions of air traffic controllers to occupational stress. Rose et al. (1978) found that air traffic controllers who were extremely conscientious and eager to perform well when first employed tended to show higher rates of "burn out" and distress symptoms than did more typical workers.

In exploring the effects of personality factors on health, it is important to consider that associations with other characteristics may help to explain why seemingly unhealthful behaviors are present. Thus, they may be assets in one context and serious vulnerabilities in another. For example, Type A behavior patterns may result in personal satisfaction, goal attainment, and community respect.

Social Factors Influencing Individual Susceptibilities

Social factors outside work can influence individual reactions to occupational stresses (Levi et al., 1981). For example, poor-quality day care for preschool children may add considerably to the stress experienced by working parents, especially single parents, and their children. The importance of this factor was illustrated in a longitudinal, interdisciplinary evaluation of the effects of introducing more nurses per child in a day-care setting (Kagan et al., 1978). Epinephrine excretion and behavioral deviations among the children decreased sharply, as did absenteeism among the nurses. There also were suggestions of secondary effects on the health of the parents.

Many kinds of organizational stress are less severe for people who have supportive family relationships than for those who do not. Among stresses studied in this context are administrative responsibilities (French, 1974), monotonous work situations (House and Wells, 1978), and unemployment (Cobb and Kasl, 1977). What remains to be learned are what forms of support are effective under what conditions and for which individuals. Research on the buffering effect of social support has produced sufficiently consistent findings to merit further study into these aspects of the problem.

Special Conditions

Handicapped people are especially likely to be adversely affected by such environmental conditions as physical discomfort, crowding, and work pressures that may arise in systems that utilize piece wages (Lawton and Nahemow, 1973; Levi et al., 1981). Organizations should give more attention to special conditions that would enable such individuals to work effectively (Goldstein et al., 1980).

Migrant workers with language problems may also be under great stress through lack of effective communication abilities. Employers of such individuals may find it useful to anticipate and attempt to help them overcome their special difficulties. Migrants may be under stress from cultural change and relocation. Traditionally, immigrants to the United States have been expected to abandon their old customs and adopt those of their new country; yet some groups, such as orientals, have resisted such pressures. The long-term consequences of either approach have yet to be defined.

School Settings

Organizational behavior begins to develop in school (Kahn et al., 1981). School settings have many similarities to work settings and are, in a sense, training grounds for them. Rutter (1979) found that financial resources, school and class size, organizational structure, and punishment had little effect on academic performance. Features contributing to pupil success included rewards and praise, opportunities for students to assume responsibilities, emphasis on academic progress, positive models provided by teachers, group management style in the classroom, and staff organization. It would be useful to include schools in studies of organizational influences on health (Kahn et al., 1981). Further research should focus on schools as people-processing institutions. Long-term studies are needed to identify risk factors in school settings for adverse health outcomes both immediately and later at adult stages (Kahn et al., 1981).

Stress Related to Lack of Work

Unemployment

Job loss can create a marked loss of self-esteem and security. Such feelings may become apparent only following initial, highly motivated attempts to find a new job (Powell and Driscoll, 1973). Failure to find employment and continuing depletion of financial resources may lead to prolonged depression, apathy, loss of occupational identity, and disorganization in time and space. In a recent study of unemployed men, loss of a stable daily routine frequently appeared to disrupt the ability to estimate the passage of time, not only in days and weeks, but also in minutes and hours (Levin, 1975). Work routine may provide a standard by which daily activities are ordered. When this structure is missing, absence of a behavioral routine is accompanied by distortions in time perception.

Timing of unemployment is important. Its effects can differ both as a function of the stage in life at which it occurs (Minkler, 1981) and in relation to political and socioeconomic conditions. Young workers in their first job may be discouraged by unemployment, even though they are likely to be able to find new jobs and develop new goals. Middle-aged workers will be under extreme stress by job loss, especially if they have families to raise and children to send to school. These workers may find it harder to get new jobs or change life goals. Older workers may suffer from reduced incomes just when extra finances are needed for retirement; but these workers may more easily translate unemployment into the retired role (Minkler, 1981).

Brenner (1976) has examined a variety of aggregate time series data that suggest that an increase in unemployment is associated with subsequent increases in mortality rates and increased rates of hospitalization for psychiatric disorders. However, these associations, based on time-lagged analyses of population data, are open to a variety of alternative explanations.

Unemployed workers often report major changes in lifestyle while unemployed; they also report feeling insecure and fearful (Liem, 1981). It remains to be determined which of these factors bear on health outcomes. In one study, men who lost their jobs due to plant closure evidenced more psychological and physical illnesses than did men employed in similar but stable work settings (Cobb and Kasl, 1977). Disorders included stomach upsets, joint swelling, high cholesterol levels, and hypertension. Depression and anxiety also occurred more frequently in the unemployed group. Unemployed men who have high levels of emotional support from their wives and families report fewer illness symptoms and have lower blood cholesterol and uric acid levels than do men lacking such supports (Gore, 1973). Komorovsky (1940) found during the Great Depression that unemployed men with primarily utilitarian marriages suffered more distress than did men with loving, supportive marital relationships.

Retirement

The timing of retirement is important. Those who are forced to retire are less likely to experience the "honeymoon" phase that follows planned retirement (Atchley, 1976). Enforced retirement may result from general high unemployment and a major recession, in which case older workers may be even more resistant to retirement because of their own economic needs (Harris, 1976). Early retirement may also be due to illness, in which case it may produce improved health and a sense of well-being (Minkler, 1981). However, among men who had open heart surgery, forced early retirement was associated with poorer emotional and social adjustment than that seen in cases of voluntary retirement (Zyzanski et al., 1981). These effects lasted years after the retirement occurs and may result from lack of control over life events (cf. Chapter 11).

The suicide rate for men is particularly high at retirement age, perhaps as a result of loss of role and of meaningful social contacts (Minkler, 1981). The suicide rate for women now is highest at age 45–54, which coincides with children leaving home and with menopause. It will be interesting to see if there is a second peak in the suicide rate for women at retirement when employment becomes a more major part of their definition of self (Minkler, 1981).

Stress Related to Other Nonwork Roles

Available evidence suggests that nonwork roles of housewives or the handicapped are neither more nor less stressful than organizational roles. Gove and Geerken (1977) found that married women who do not work outside the home show as many psychiatric symptoms as do employed women. Haynes and Feinleib (1980) found that housewives evidenced the same rate of incidence of cardiovascular disease as women who are employed outside the home.

Strategies for Alleviating Excessive Work Stress

Interventions to reduce stress in the work place can occur at both individual and organizational levels. Given the advantages mentioned earlier of having active worker participation, it seems likely that the most successful programs have strong worker involvement. In Scandinavia and some other countries, such involvement has been fostered by legislation that permits workers to seek changes in work conditions that they think are hazardous (Levi et al., 1981).

Interventions at the individual level could involve instruction in healthy practices or include retraining or placement into more suitable types of work. Measures of personality traits (Jenkins, 1976), social networks (Mitchell, 1969), and family functioning (Haggerty et al., 1975) may be useful indicators of individuals at particular risk for adverse health consequences. More precise quantitation of such risk factors is needed. However, as measures are developed, it will be important to balance efforts to exclude people from jobs in which they are exposed to risk with the rights of those individuals to make decisions about their own priorities.

Specific Research Needs

Research Needs Related to Decreasing Work Stress

Among interventions for which preliminary evidence suggests the value of further research are (Levi et al., 1981):

- increasing the workers' control over the work arrangements;
- providing chances for worker participation in decision making;
- avoiding monotonous, machine-paced, or short but frequent work tasks;
- maintaining attentional processes and reaction requirements within the range of human effectiveness and capability;
- helping workers see the relevance of their work;
- avoiding over- and under-work load;
- avoiding social isolation and facilitating support systems and social contacts among workers; and
- allowing greater freedom of movement in work tasks.

As more information about these interventions becomes available, it should be possible to balance appropriately between organizational needs for productivity and individual needs for physical and mental health. Evidence suggests that, at least in certain contexts, an adequate understanding of what makes a setting stressful may make it feasible to optimize conditions for both the workers and the organization (Levi et al., 1981).

Research Needs Related to Retirement

Some major areas for research on retirement are indicated below. Such studies also may relate to problems and health outcomes in the unemployed. Physiological and psychosocial influences should be assessed frequently, and morbidity and mortality rates should be checked through different stages of unemployment. Background socioeconomic changes also should be evaluated in relation to health outcome in the retired and unemployed.

* Prospective studies are needed of workers approaching retirement, using physiological indices of health status.
* Analyses of yearly morbidity and mortality rates for older workers and retirees might help to identify differentially stressful phases in the retirement process.
* Comparisons of those retiring involuntarily with those retiring voluntarily could elucidate the influence of self-control in retirement onset.
* Research could usefully define the role of psychosocial variables that may affect health before, during, and after retirement.
* Exploration of the relationship between retirement effects and depression and suicide in older persons might help to identify people at especially high risk of having such reactions.
* Experiments on the effects of gradually reducing work loads, rather than insisting on abrupt retirement, might suggest ways of avoiding some of the more deleterious concomitants of retiring.

Health Promotion

The work place offers exceptional opportunities for fostering health among employees, and certain industries already are strongly interested in health promotion techniques. Evaluation of such services is essential to determine if the objectives are being met and to discover optimal facilities for attaining these goals. Promotion of health practices in the work place is much more likely to be effective if it is based on scientifically sound data. The following ideas for further investigations were developed from the Institute of Medicine (1981) conference Evaluation of Health Promotion in the Workplace:

* What are the costs and benefits of preventive services, and what kinds of data are needed to measure them?
* How should such programs influence corporate planning?

- How can unions and workers be involved in evaluating prevention programs?
- What ethical and legal difficulties are likely to arise from health-related information about employees?
- What constitutes a target population?
- What types of health promotion activities are effective?
- To whom do the evaluation results apply?

Goals of program evaluation will differ from site to site, given the diversity of objectives. However, to ensure reliability and replication of results, evaluations must (1) define the context in which the program was instituted and the types of interventions that were employed; (2) identify all participants and specific target groups; (3) determine what changes in personal behavior occurred as a result of the interventions; (4) evaluate effects of the program on a variety of measures such as self-reports of health status, health services utilization, productivity, disability, and mortality; and (5) measure direct and indirect costs involved in instituting the program, including medications, instruction time, and time lost from work (Institute of Medicine, 1981).

A number of factors may facilitate good employee participation in prevention programs. It may be most cost effective to involve only those identified as "at risk," so that those unlikely to benefit are not urged to participate. It is vital to ensure confidentiality of health records, especially concerning mental health. If programs involve financial or time costs, less affluent workers may require some form of financial assistance. Reasons for resistance to health promotion programs and ways to overcome that resistance are areas in which much good research is needed.

Conclusions

Organizational settings such as the work place are rich sources of research opportunities. Changes in a particular factory or an industry may create "natural experiments" in which researchers can study the effects of stressful conditions in a reasonably controlled and well-defined setting. Examples of potential experiments include plant automation, changes in the timing of shift schedules, and layoffs due to company decline or general recession.

The important contributions of the individual to work stress need further elucidation. Studies should look for interactions between work demands and worker abilities. Such assessments offer the possibility of developing an interactive formulation of ways in which occupational stress can affect health. That formulation could form the basis for creating more effective ways of identifying and alleviating unnecessarily stressful conditions.

References

Atchley, R. C. *The Sociology of Retirement* New York: Holstead Press, 1976.

Brenner, M. H. *Estimating the Social Costs of National Economic Policy: Implications for Mental and Physical Health and Criminal Aggression* Washington, D.C.: U.S. Government Printing Office, 1976.

Broadbent, D. E. *Decision and Stress* New York: Academic Press, 1971.

Bromet, E., and Moos, R. The impact of organizational structure and change. IN: *The Human Context: Environmental Determinants of Behavior* (Moos, R. H., ed.) New York: Wiley, 1976, pp. 248–283.

Cassell, J. C. The contributions of the social environment to host resistance. *Am. J. Epidemiol* 104:107–123, 1976.

Cobb, S., and Kasl, S. *Termination: The Consequences of Job Loss* Washington, D.C.: U.S. Government Printing Office, 1977, DHEW Publ. No. (NIOSH) 77–224.

Coch, L., and French, J. R. P., Jr. Overcoming resistance to change. *Hum. Relations* 1:512–532, 1948.

Eliot, R. S., Clayton, F. C., Pieper, G. M., and Todd, G. L. Influence of environmental stress on the pathogenesis of sudden cardiac death. *Fed. Proc.* 36:1719–1724, 1977.

Elliott, G. R., and Eisdorfer, C. (Eds.) *Stress and Human Health* New York: Springer, 1982.

Frankenhaeuser, M. Coping with stress at work. *Int. J. Health Ser.* 11:491–510, 1981.

Frankenhaeuser, M., and Gardell, B. Underload and overload in working life: Outline of a multidisciplinary approach. *J. Hum. Stress* 2:35–46, 1976.

Friedman, M., and Rosenman, R. H. Type A behavior pattern: Its association with coronary heart disease. *Ann. Clin. Res.* 3:300–312, 1971.

French, J. R. P., Jr. Person-role fit. IN: *Occupational Stress* (McLean, A. A., ed.) Springfield, Ill.: Charles C. Thomas, 1974, p. 70–79.

Goldstein, M. J., Baker, B. L., and Jamison, K. R. *Abnormal Psychology: Experiences, Origins and Interventions* Boston: Little, Brown, 1980.

Gore, S. The influence of social support and related variables in ameliorating the consequences of job loss. Unpublished doctoral dissertation, University of Michigan, 1973.

Gove, W. R., and Geerken, M. R. The effect of children and employment on the mental health of married men and women. *Soc. Forces* 56:66–76, 1977.

Haggerty, R. J., Boghmann, K. J., and Pless, I. B. *Child Health and the Community* New York: Wiley, 1975.

Harris, L. *The Myth and Reality of Aging in America* Washington, D.C.: National Council on Aging, 1976.

Haynes, S. G., and Feinlab, M. Women, work, and coronary heart disease: Prospective findings from the Framingham heart study. *Am. J. Publ. Health* 70:133–141, 1980.

Haynes, S. G., Levine, S., Scotch, N., Feinlieb, M., and Kannell, W. B. The relationship of psychosocial factors to coronary heart disease in the Framingham study I. Methods and risk factors. *Am. J. Epidemiol.* 107:362–383, 1980.

Hinkle, L. E., Jr. The effect of exposure to cultural change, social change, and changes in interpersonal relationships on health. IN: *Stressful Life Events: Their Nature and Effects* (Dohrenwend, B. S., and Dohrenwend, B. P., eds.) New York: Wiley, 1974, pp. 9–44.

House, J. S., and Wells, J. A. Occupational stress, social support, and health. IN: *Reducing Occupational Stress: Proceedings of a Conference* (McLean, A., Black, G., and Colligan, M., eds.) Washington, D.C.: U.S. Government Printing Office, 1978, DHEW Publ. No. (NIOSH) 78–140, pp. 8–29.

Institute of Medicine *Evaluating Health Promotion in the Workplace* Washington, D.C.: National Academy Press, 1981.

Jenkins, C. D. Recent evidence supporting psychologic and social risk factors for coronary disease. *N Engl. J. Med. 294*:987–994 and 1033–1038, 1976.

Johansson, G., and Frankenhaeuser, M. Temporal factors in sympathoadrenome-dullary activity following acute behavioral activation. *Biol. Psychol. 1*:63–73, 1973.

Kagan, A. R., Cederblad, M., Hook, B., and Levi, L. Evaluation of the effect of increasing the number of nurses on health and behavior of 3-year-old children in day care, satisfaction of their parents and health and satisfaction of their nurses. *Reports from the Laboratory for Clinical Stress Research* (Stockholm) No. 89, 1978.

Kahn, R. L. *Work and Health* New York: Wiley Interscience, 1981.

Kahn, R. L., Wolfe, D. M. Quinn, R. P., and Snock, J. D. *Organizational Stress* New York: Wiley, 1964.

Kahn, R., Hein, K., House, J., Kasl, S., and McLean, A. Stress in organizational settings. IN: *Research on Stress in Human Health* (Institute of Medicine) Washington, D.C.: National Academy Press, 1981, pp. 63–93.

Karasek, R. Job socialization and job strain. The implications of two related psychosocial mechanisms for job design. IN: *Working Life: A Social Science Contribution to Work Reform* (Gardell, B., and Johansson, G., eds.) London: Wiley, 1981.

Kobasa, S. C. Stressful life events, personality and health: An inquiry into hardiness. *J. Pers. Soc. Psychol. 37*:1-11, 1979.

Komorovsky, M. *The Unemployed Man and His Family* New York: Dryden Press, 1940.

Lawton, M. P., and Nahemow, L. Eidology and the aging process. IN: *The Psychology of Adult Development and Aging* (Eisdorfer, C., and Lawton, P., eds.) Washington, D.C.: American Psychological Association, 1973, pp. 619–674.

Levi, L., Frankenhaeuser, M., and Gardell, B. Work stress related social structures and processes. IN: *Research on Stress in Human Health* (Institute of Medicine) Washington, D.C.: National Academy Press, 1981, pp. 95–117.

Levin, H. Work: The staff of life. Paper presented at the annual convention of the American Psychological Association, Chicago, September, 1975.

Liem, R. Economic change and unemployment: Contexts of illness. IN: *Social Contexts of Health, Stress and Patient Care* (Mishler, E. G., Amarasnigham, L. R., Hauser, S. T., Liem, R., Osherson, D., and Waxler, N. E., eds.) Cambridge: University Press, 1981, pp. 54–78.

Lundberg, U. Urban community: Crowdedness and catecholamine excretion. *J. Hum. Stress 2*:26–32, 1976.

Maule, H. G., Levi, L., McLean, A., Pardon, N., and Savicevic, M. *Occupational Mental Health* Geneva: World Health Organization, 1973.

Minkler, M. Research on the health effects of retirement: An uncertain legacy. *J. Health Soc. Behav. 22*:117–130, 1981.

Mitchell, J. C. The concept and use of social networks. IN: *Social Networks in Urban Situations* (Mitchell, J. C., ed.) Manchester: University Press, 1969, pp. 1–50.

Moos, R. H. *The Human Context: Environmental Determinants of Behavior* New York: John Wiley and Sons, 1976.

Moos, R. H. Social-ecological perspectives on health. IN: *Health Psychology—A*

Handbook (Stone, G. C., Cohen, F., and Adler, N. E., eds.) San Francisco: Jossey-Bass, 1979, pp. 523–547.

Pearlin, L. I., and Johnson, J. S. Marital status, life strains and depression. *Am. Sociol. Rev. 42*:704–715, 1977.

Porter, L. W., and Steers, R. M. Organizational work and personal factors in employee turnover and absenteeism. *Psychol. Bull. 80*:151-176, 1973.

Powell, D., and Driscoll, P. Middle class professionals face unemployment. *Society 10*:18–26, 1973.

Raab, W. Cardiotoxic biochemical effects of emotional-environmental stressors—fundamentals of psychocardiology. IN: *Society, Stress and Disease, Vol. 1: The Psychosocial Environment and Psychosomatic Diseases* (Levi, L., ed.) London: Oxford University Press, 1971, pp. 331–337.

Rappoport A. Toward a redefinition of density. *Environ. Behav. 7*:133–158, 1975.

Rissler, A. Stress reactions at work and after work during a period of quantitative overload. *Erogonomics 20*:13–16, 1977.

Rose, R. M., Jenkins, C. D., and Hurst, M. W. *Air Traffic Controller Health Change Study* A report to the Federal Aviation Administration on research perfomed under Contract No. DOT–FA3WA3211, 1978.

Rutter, M. *Changing Youth in a Changing Society: Patterns of Adolescent Development and Disorder* London: Nuffield Provincial Hospital, 1979.

Singer, J. E., Lundberg, V., and Frankenhaeuser, M. Stress on the train: A study of urban commuting. *Adv. Environ. Psychol. 1*:41–56, 1978.

Zyzanski, S. J., Stanton, B. A., Jenkins, C. D., and Klein, M. D. Medical and psychosocial outcome in survivors of major heart surgery. *J. Psychosom. Res. 25*:213–221, 1981.

11
Aging and Health

An important consequence of improvements in sanitation, disease prevention, and medical care is an extraordinary increase in both the number and proportion of elderly individuals in the population. In developed countries, most individuals now are likely to attain old age, with the social, psychological, and biological problems that often accompany it. This "aging population" challenges research and clinical activities. Much of the current knowledge about health and bodily functions derived from studies of the behavior, physical characteristics, and function of younger individuals. This knowledge is not readily generalizable to older adults because of a variety of age-related changes and generational differences.

Efforts are under way to understand better the changes that accompany the aging process. In 1974, Congress passed the Research on Aging Act to support research with multidisciplinary focus on the diverse problems affecting the elderly population. A selection of these research areas was addressed at the Health and Behavior conference *Health, Behavior, and Aging* (Parron et al., 1981).

From the broad range of potential topics reflecting the influence of aging on the interaction of health and behavior, the conference focused on three areas as examples of the various stages of development of new knowledge and its potential for clinical applications: (1) health and behavior in the elderly; (2) alcohol use as a health problem in aging; and (3) immunology and behavior in the elderly. This chapter conveys highlights of research opportunities in each of these areas to demonstrate the many important questions about aging that must be answered.

200

Issues in Aging Research

Those who wish to do research on aging encounter substantial procedural problems. It is impossible to know what patterns of health and behavior are peculiar to older people without dynamic studies of people as they are aging and of the variations of the aging process under differing social and historical conditions. Of utmost importance are clarification and specification of those social conditions and mechanisms that influence the aging process and its linkages to health.

Two major types of misinterpretation beset the literature on aging (Riley, 1978). First, there is the "life course fallacy," which erroneously interprets cross-sectional data as if they described the aging process. In cross-section, for example, old people in the United States have lower educational attainment than young people. The apparent "decline" reflects the fact that young people now are more likely to have advanced education than were young people years ago. In cross-section, older people generally score lower on intelligence tests than do teenagers. In the past, these findings have been interpreted as a decline in intelligence *because* of growing older—an interpretation now widely disputed (Horn and Donaldson, 1980; Schaie, 1981). What had been overlooked were the cohort differences in life course patterns, including experience with testing and educational attainment. Also based on cross-sectional data, but attributed to the aging process, are declines in many physiological functions such as nerve conduction velocity, maximum breathing capacity, and fasting blood glucose (Shock, 1977). Is the simplistic interpretation of these data as inevitable accompaniments of the process another instance of a life course fallacy? Pertinent research of this question is under way (Riley, 1981).

To avoid the life-course fallacy, longitudinal studies often are used to focus directly on the aging process; here too, however, there are dangers of misinterpretation. A second fallacy, "cohort centrism," can arise through overgeneralizing from the experience of a single cohort. A cohort—a group born during the same period—may differ from other cohorts not only in size and other demographic characteristics but also in the social and historical conditions that influence the aging process (Elder, 1974). For example, members of different cohorts are likely to have had different educational histories, exposure to diseases, health care, and exercise and nutritional patterns during their lives (Uhlenberg, 1979). Thus, people who are growing old today may experience the process of aging quite differently from earlier cohorts of old people and from cohorts who will grow old in the future (Ryder, 1965).

To address such fallacies, attention has been given to conceptual and methodological methods to overcome the inherent problems of aging research (Riley, 1976; National Academy of Sciences, 1979). Further development is needed, but these approaches offer several advantages (Bielby and Hauser, 1977; Hannan and Tuma, 1979; Nesselroade and Baltes, 1979):

- use of data from multiple cohorts and from multiple points in time, not only at the beginning and end of an interval;
- causal analysis of relationships among a complex array of biological, psychological, and social variables;
- paths of relative influence from one set of variables through mediating variables to a third set of measures;
- options of different measurement models; and
- distinction, under certain circumstances and assumptions, among the effects of aging, cohort membership, and historical periods.

Methodological efforts currently under way center on the problems of analyzing continuous life histories, of linking social change to the lives of individuals, and of estimating causal relationships in cohort-longitudinal designs.

Age-relevant designs for research on health and behavior can make use of an accumulating body of technical sophistication. Research designs should include consideration of sampling problems, which have tended to place undue emphasis on readily accessible subjects such as institutional populations or comparatively healthy old people living at home; of special problems of questioning older people; of ethical issues in designing research, particularly on the cognitively impaired; and of sensitivity to ageism.

Physical Changes, Immunology, and Behavior in the Aged

A new biology has developed in recent years with the potential of resolving long-standing questions about human aging and age-related disorders. New methods of genetic analysis and molecular biology enable researchers to trace the roles of genes, their protein products, and their control mechanisms. For example, more than 100 distinct genetic sites of potential importance in modulating the development rates of age-related disabilities in humans have been identified thus far.

Cultivation of human cells in vitro provides a model for studying cellular changes in aging, because these normal cells appear to have a finite life. For at least some cell types, the older the donor, the shorter the life span of cells in culture (Finch and Hayflick, 1977). Steps are now being taken to confirm these findings and to find the basis for the differences in longevity between cell types and among cells from individuals of various ages. Using cell fusion, investigators are beginning to determine the extent to which longevity is programmed in the nucleus or in the cytoplasm. Finally, cells from patients with conditions associated with premature aging may provide important clues to the genetic basis of aging.

Immunology and Behavior

A core question in gerontological research is the degree to which a change in function or biochemistry of an aging tissue is due to shifts in the mixture of cell types or to alterations in individual cells. Such advances as monoclonal antibodies and other identification techniques may help determine the specific cellular components in aging tissues. The immune system, which produces antibodies in response to invading antigens, deteriorates with age; the decline can lead to increased susceptibility to infection and possibly to tumors (Walford, 1969; Fabris et al., 1972; Nandy and Sherwin, 1977; Makinodan and Raye, 1980; Walford, 1980).

Autoimmunity, or immune responses to one's own tissues, usually increases with age in both experimental animals and human beings. Animal studies have shown that increases in autoantibodies and abnormal immunoglobulins can be slowed by manipulating diet and other environmental factors (Walford et al., 1973). The potential reversibility of these immunological changes suggests that research may be able eventually to lessen age-related susceptibility to specific autoimmune diseases.

Psychosocial events appear to affect immune function. Experimental studies show a complex interaction between psychosocial factors and cell-mediated immunity. A variety of stresses such as loud noise and electric shock have variable effects on T-cell activity in laboratory animals (Johnson et al., 1963; Mettrop and Visser, 1971; Amkraut and Solomon, 1972; Solomon et al., 1974; Joasoo and McKenzie, 1976; Monjan and Collector, 1977). A limited number of human studies have shown transient depression of T-cell function following the death of a spouse (Bartrop et al., 1977; Schleifer et al., 1980).

At present, only limited data are available about changes in the nervous system in later life. There have been few investigations of neuroanatomical changes in older people, but preliminary findings provide evidence of changes in gross brain structure. Among these changes are decreased brain weights, signs of cortical atrophy, and ventricular enlargement (Brody and Vijayashankar, 1977). The computed tomographic (CT) scan demonstrates evidence of atrophic changes in the brain that are only weakly related, if at all, to cognitive impairment (Ford and Winter, 1981). Thus, even if gross structural changes in the nervous system are found, such changes may predict little about brain function and behavior.

In recent years, the focus of reseach on the biological basis of behavioral change during aging has expanded from an exclusive focus on regional cell loss to include the study of neuroregulators in the nervous system (Samarajski, 1975). It is possible that alterations of certain neuroregulators underlie common mental health problems in older people.

There appear to be age-related changes in visual, auditory, and tactile receptors in most adults. There also appear to be changes in skeletal muscle fibers, thereby limiting quick movement. Most pathological changes of aging occur very slowly over a long period of time, thereby allowing ample opportunity for adjustment and compensation (Klisz, in press). Also, the nervous system appears to have a large reserve capacity and a great amount of structural redundancy (Finger, 1978).

Senile dementia, ranging from mild to severe, occurs in about 15 percent of those over age 65 (Kay, 1977) and has pathological features distinct from normal aging. This condition is characterized by loss of initiative, decrease in judgment, difficulty in selecting appropriate words, severe loss of recent memory, difficulty in doing calculations, disorientation, and personality deterioration. One interesting focus of recent biological research on senile dementia is on changes in choline acetyltransferase, the enzyme involved in synthesizing the neuroregulator acetylcholine. Although the levels of this enzyme decline in normal aging, the decline is greatly accelerated with patients who have senile dementia of the Alzheimer type, as compared with age-matched controls (Perry, 1980; Perry et al., 1980). The receptors for acetylcholine are present in normal quantity even in the absence of the enzyme, raising the possibility that providing an appropriate substitute substance could arrest the decline in function associated with the disorder.

Other neurobiological research has demonstrated age-related changes in neurotransmitter uptake that may contribute to the higher incidence of parkinsonism in older patients. Various hormones and hormone fragments are being studied with respect to brain function, including learning and memory. A new approach to the treatment of senile brain disease involves the use of a hormone fragment that seems to improve memory in certain behavioral tests in animals (deWied et al., 1976). The substance ACTH (4–10) is a fragment of a stress-related human pituitary hormone; it is being studied in patients with defective memory.

Pharmacology

Age has been shown to affect the pharmacokinetics of and responses to some drugs (Vestal, 1978). Dosages that are effective and safe in young adults may not be appropriate for the elderly, because of changes in circulation, metabolism, excretion, or other systemic functions. It is well known that diseases of certain organ systems, which are common in elderly people (e.g., renal disease), alter rates of metabolism and excretion of drugs and therefore affect pharmacokinetics. Adverse reactions to prescribed and over-the-counter drugs have been associated with prolonged hospitalization of the elderly; recent medical research has found some major drugs to be ineffective or unnecessarily risky in the elderly (Seidl et al., 1966; Bellville et al., 1971; Berkowitz et al., 1975; Law and Chalmers, 1976; Richey and Bender, 1977; Vestal, 1978). Information is accumulating about changes in enzyme and organ function, effects of drug interactions, and difficulties in adhering to therapeutic regimens because of poor memory and altered eating habits. Most pharmaceutical studies are performed using young people as subjects; the applicability of these studies to older populations is limited (Institute of Medicine, 1979). Research in clinical pharmacology will benefit from a perspective that considers the entire life span.

Alcohol Abuse as a Health Problem in Aging

Alcohol use peaks between the ages of 35 and 50; yet alcoholism is estimated to be present in 2 to 10 percent of the population over the age of 55. It has been reported to be a problem in as many as 60 percent of patients over age 60 who are in general hospitals and psychiatric facilities (Locke et al., 1960; Baily et al., 1965; Drew, 1968; Simon et al., 1968; Gaitz and Baer, 1971; McCusker et al., 1971; Siassi et al., 1973). These estimates, if correct, are a strong indication of ineffective identification and treatment of alcohol abuse in the aged.

Research is needed to develop and validate measures of alcohol abuse in the elderly. Problems with current methodology include: (1) the criteria for defining alcoholism were developed in studies of younger and middle-aged individuals and may not be valid for the elderly; (2) there is a non-random distribution of those with alcohol-related problems in the settings used for the studies, for example, municipal rather than private hospitals; and (3) invalid responses to survey questions stem from misperceptions, inaccurate memory, or intentional distortions.

Reasons for alcohol abuse by the elderly are not understood. Several ideas have been put forth, including multiple stresses from job loss, death of close friends and family, economic constraints, and poor health (Harrington and Price, 1962; Graux; 1969, Zimberg, 1974; Haglund and Schuckit, 1977). However, it is unclear what factors distinguish those who respond to stresses by abusing alcohol from those who do not. There is often an altered perception among the elderly of the effects of alcohol. They typically are more sensitive to the effects of alcohol than are younger people, but these effects are not as readily perceived by older persons. This "blunting" may lead to cessation of drinking for lack of the desired effect, or it may increase drinking behavior in an attempt by the individual to recapture expected effects of alcohol consumption (Kissin, 1974). Clearly, this is an important area for further research and investigation.

As is the case for other drugs, the pharmacokinetics of alcohol metabolism in the elderly are not well understood. Further confounding this issue is the greater likelihood of elderly individuals to be taking other drugs that in combination with alcohol, may produce adverse consequences. Changes in sleep-wake mechanisms with aging are poorly understood, but complaints of insomnia among older people are common. These complaints often lead to self-treatment with alcohol or sleeping agents, which may in turn lead to a toxic effect or "carryover" from night to day without producing significant improvement in sleep patterns (Institute of Medicine, 1979).

In addition to these direct effects, alcohol alone or in combination with prescription or over-the-counter drugs may be particularly dangerous as a contributor to instability of motion, leading to morbidity from falls (Institute of Medicine, 1979). Because of the greater severity of fall-related injuries among the elderly, and the apparent link of fall injuries and rapid general decline in their health, this aspect of alcohol pharmacology deserves serious consideration.

Even moderate amounts of alcohol may produce behavioral and cognitive impairment in the normal elderly individual. It can lead to a diminished cardiac efficiency in those with heart disease and impair respiratory functioning in those with pulmonary disease (Gould et al., 1971; Phillipson, 1976). The potential problems that result from alcohol abuse in the elderly make it important to identify and help those with a drinking problem. As compared with the young, the elderly are more likely to complete treatment and derive benefit from treatment of alcoholism (Baekeland and Lundwall, 1977; Schuckit, 1977; Pattison, 1979; Glaser, 1980). Paradoxically, professionals often regard the elderly as inappropriate candidates for treatment. Careful methodological studies are needed to characterize the patterns and consequences of geriatric alcohol use, abuse, and treatment. The psychobiological approach in examining the predisposing, precipitating, and perpetuating causes of these abuse behaviors is essential (cf. Chapter 4).

There also is a possibility some beneficial effects of moderate alcohol use in the elderly. Moderate alcohol intake in social encounters, as an aperitif or as a pleasurable ritual, may have profound effects on the mental well-being of elderly persons and may be associated with unusual longevity. For example, consumption of alcohol in a cabaret-type setting has been shown to promote socialization and reduce isolation among elderly patients in long-term care facilities (Chien et al., 1973).

Health Behavior in the Elderly

Several factors are now converging to emphasize the importance and feasibility of a thorough evaluation of the relation of age, behavior, and health. Geriatrics, perhaps the most neglected area of modern medicine, is receiving increased attention. There is a rapidly increasing understanding of the influence of age on physiological, sociological, and psychological processes and the impact of these age-related changes on the presentation of disease, its response to treatment, and the complications that ensue.

One fundamental aspect of aging is that it is a psychosocial as well as a biological process. As people age, they develop attitudes and patterns of behavior, learn the expectations of their culture, enter a sequence of social roles, interact with other people, and form a social self. These psychosocial changes in older people may affect the processes and outcomes of diseases in the elderly.

A pervasive behavioral phenomenon partly responsible for advanced disease states in the frail elderly is their failure to report illness. Legitimate symptoms heralding serious but often treatable disease are concealed, or at least not reported, by elderly patients (Williamson et al., 1964; Anderson, 1966). The most common explanation for this apparently self-destructive behavior is the pervasive belief that old age is inextricably associated with illness, functional decline, and feeling sick. This view guarantees that older persons, even when afflicted with the same symptoms that impel the middle-aged sick into the mainstream of the health care system, will not seek care or will suffer in silence the progression of many diseases and will endure the functional losses engendered by untreated illness. It is unfortunate that many physicians also view the aging process as one of inevitable and universal biological deterioration and have been shown to spend less time in office visits with older than with younger patients (Coe and Brehn, 1972; Kane et al., 1980).

Other explanations for the under-reporting of illness in the elderly population include: (1) a high prevalence of depression, which interferes with the desire to retain vigor; (2) the increasing prevalence of cognitive loss with age, which causes both a diminished ability to complain and elicits an unsatisfactory medical evaluation for potentially reversible problems; and (3) fear that diagnostic or therapeutic techniques could generate functional loss or jeopardize independent living (Parron et al., 1981).

Another factor that predisposes elderly individuals to functional decline based on late detection of potentially treatable disease is the common occurrence of illness clustering in aged patients. Usually termed multiple pathology, the existence of several concurrent diseases in an old person who either is not obviously ill or is under treatment for a separate problem has profound negative influence on health and functional independence in old age. If the entire spectrum of pathological conditions is not identified and considered, diagnostic or therapeutic initiatives may be as likely to produce harm as benefit (Korenchevsky, 1961; Besdine, 1980).

These issues are especially dangerous when coupled with the existing American organizational structure of health care delivery. The health care system relies on the patient or patient-advocate to initiate care and enter the medical system. Entrance into the health care system is a great obstacle to the elderly who have preconceived notions regarding infirmity as an obligate part of old age, lack a strong family network, or have infrequent health service contacts. New techniques for health assessment and surveillance of older persons could bridge the gaps in our health care system and provide the elderly with earlier disease intervention (Wetle and Whitelaw, 1977).

Some diseases that increase in prevalence with aging affect behavior and mental health both by direct deleterious effects on the nervous system and by placing additional stresses on the individual. For example, diseases of the cardiopulmonary system occur more frequently in later life, and these diseases often compromise the functional integrity of the nervous system. Renal diseases can also lead to personality and intellectual disturbances, as evidenced by patients maintained on renal dialysis for long periods of time who are prone to develop dementia (Libow, 1977). Biological changes that occur with aging and changes in health status may produce changes in behavior that further alienate the patient from adequate medical care.

Long-Term Care

Nursing home costs place an enormous burden on the individual, the family, and public resources. The three most common reasons for nursing home admissions are incontinence, immobility, and impairment of cognitive function (Parron et al., 1981). Research aimed at preventing and improving the treatment of these disorders should be a high priority. Although the prevalent notion is that family members are deserting their elder relatives at nursing homes, research has shown that even though the elderly and their children may prefer to live separately, they tend to keep in touch and participate in each other's lives, often making major sacrifices to delay or avoid institutionalization.

Because family relationships are important in maintaining the ill or frail elderly outside of institutions, research into the dynamics of such relationships is important. Policy makers, for example, should know how desirable changes in family behavior may be promoted by public and private systems of health care, income maintenance, housing, and support services.

Current practice and reimbursement policy emphasize skilled institutional care for the elderly. Many individuals require and benefit from institutional care, but the lack of alternative types of care can result in inappropriate use of high-intensity facilities. Studies have demonstrated that dependence is enhanced by providing unnecessary services (Wack and Rodin, 1978). Elderly persons who find themselves in mutual aid, social support networks with meaningful tasks and a basis for self-respect may function effectively at very advanced ages (Langer and Rodin, 1976; Rodin and Langer, 1977).

It must be remembered that the elderly population is diverse. Some individuals in advanced age are frail; others have physical and behavioral performance levels on a par with or exceeding those of much younger persons. This diversity indicates that decline and dependence are not universal, inevitable results of aging, and that sociobehavioral factors have important influences on the course and outcome of physical changes.

Conclusions

There are many promising directions for future research into aging, health, and behavior. Although aging is likely to bring some decline, many elderly persons function well until death. For those who are functionally disabled, the rate of decline may be minimized or decreased substantially through early detection and appropriate assistance. Promoting independence among the elderly will entail an improved ability to identify environmental, genetic, social, and behavioral risk factors for the development of functional dependence.

A sustained effort is required to meet the health needs of older people in this country. Their rising numbers and special problems offer challenges in basic science, clinical investigation, service delivery, and social organization. Studies of health and behavior in the elderly must take into account not only environmental and social conditions but also the underlying physical and psychological changes that occur with age and that serve as a substrate of the influence on the presentation of disease, its response to treatment, and the complications that ensue. Research is needed to specify the interactions among historical events and societal, sociobehavioral, and biological processes.

Opportunities are at hand for obtaining needed information of the desired scope. An expanding number of longitudinal and cohort studies are becoming available for secondary analysis or for use as supplementary information. Unfortunately, current systems are not designed to facilitate integration across biomedical and psychosocial disciplines. Computer-based bibliographies and inventories of research on aging, health, and behavior are needed.

It is important to recognize the heterogeneity of the elderly population in designing research. A full range of ages among the elderly should be included in studies, as should those elderly who are more resistant to the vulnerabilities of advancing age. Studies of aging should include subjects from across the adult age range and, where possible, should use longitudinal study designs with special attention to the influence of cohort effects.

Studies of health and behavior in the elderly should take into account underlying physical, social, and psychological changes that accompany age. Long-term follow-up, including data on morbidity and mortality, is especially important for understanding the impact of intervention. Morbidity measures should include socioeconomic and psychological measures.

The need for and potential benefits of carefully designed research into the relationships of health, behavior, and aging are clear. The early steps along these pathways have demonstrated the beneficial outcomes of better health for older persons, better family relationships, enhanced effectiveness of interventions, and, most important, improved quality of life for older individuals.

References

Amkraut, A., and Solomon, G. F. Stress and murine sarcoma virus (Moloney)-induced tumors. *Cancer Res. 32*:1428–1433, 1972.

Anderson, W. F. The prevention of illness in the elderly: The Rutherglen experiment in medicine in old age. Proceedings of a conference held at the Royal College of Physicians of London, Pitman, London, 1966.

Baekeland, F. and Lundwall, L. K. Engaging the alcoholic in treatment and keeping him there. IN: *The Biology of Alcoholism: Treatment and Rehabilitation of the Chronic Alcoholic, Vol. 5* (Kissin, B., and Begleiter, H., eds.) New York: Plenum Press, 1977, pp. 161–195.

Baily, M. B., Haberman, P. W., and Alksne, H. The epidemiology of alcoholism in an urban residential area. *Q. J. Stud. Alcohol 26*:19–40, 1965.

Bartrop, R. W., Lazarus, L., Luckhurst, E., Kiloh, L. G., and Penny, R. Depressed lymphocyte function after bereavement. *Lancet 1*:834–836, 1977.

Bellville, J. W., Forrest, W. H., Jr., Miller, E., and Brown, B. W., Jr. Influence of age on pain relief from analgesics. *J. Am. Med. Assoc. 217*:1835, 1971.

Berkowitz, B. A., Ngai, S. H., Yang, J. C. Hempstead, J., and Spector, S. The disposition of morphine in surgical patients. *Clin. Pharmacol. Ther. 17*:629, 1975.

Besdine, R. W. Geriatric medicine: An overview. *Annu. Rev. Gerontol. Geriatr. 1*:135–153, 1980.

Bielby, W. T., and Hauser, R. M. Structural equation models. *Annu. Rev. Sociol. 3*:137–161, 1977.

Brody, H., and Vijayashankar, N. Anatomical changes in the nervous system. IN: *Handbook of the Biology of Aging* (Finch, C. E., and Hayflick, L., eds.) New York: Van Nostrand Reinhard, 1977.

Chien, C. P., Stotsky, B. A., and Cole, J. O. Psychiatric treatment for nursing home patients: Drug, alcohol and milieu. *Am. J. Psychiatry* 130:543–548, 1973.

Coe, R. M., and Brehn, H. P. *Preventive Health Care for Adults: A Study of Medical Practice* New Haven: College and University Press, 1972.

deWied, D., Bohus, B., Gispen, W. H., Urban, I., and van Wimersma Greidanus, T. B. Hormonal influences on motivational learning and memory processes. IN: *Hormones, Behavior and Psychopathology* (Sachar, E., ed.) New York: Raven Press, 1976, pp. 1-14.

Drew, L. R. H. Alcoholism as a self limiting disease. *Q. J. Stud. Alcohol* 29:956–967, 1968.

Elder, G., Jr. *Children of the Great Depression* Chicago: University of Chicago Press, 1974.

Fabris, N., Pierpaoli, W., and Sorkin, E. Lymphocytes, hormones and aging. *Nature* 240:557–559, 1972.

Finch, C. E., and Hayflick, L. *Handbook of the Biology of Aging* New York: Van Nostrand Reinhold, 1977.

Finger, S. (Ed.) *Recovery from Brain Damage: Research and Theory* New York: Plenum Press, 1978.

Ford, C. V., and Winter, J. Computerized axial tomograms and dementia in elderly patients. *J. Gerontol.* 36:164–169, 1981.

Gaitz, C. M., and Baer, P. E. Characteristics of elderly patients with alcoholism. *Arch. Gen. Psychiatry* 24:372–378, 1971.

Glaser, F. B. Anybody got a match? Treatment research and the matching hypothesis. IN: *Alcoholism Treatment in Transition* (Edwards, G., and Grant, M., eds.) London: Croom Helm, 1980, pp. 178–196.

Gould, L., Zahir, M., DeMartino, A. and Gomprecht, R. F. Cardiac effects of a cocktail. *J. Am. Med. Assoc.* 218:1799–1802, 1971.

Graux, P. Alcoholism of the elderly. *Rev. Alcohol* 15:61–63, 1969.

Haglund, R. M. J., and Schuckit, M. A. The epidemiology of alcoholism. IN: *Alcoholism: Development, Consequences and Interventions* (Estes, N., and Heinemann, E., eds.) St. Louis: Mosby, 1977, pp. 28–43.

Hannan, M. T., and Tuma, B. B. Methods for temporal analysis. *Annu. Rev. Sociol.* 5:303–328, 1979.

Harrington, L. G., and Price, A. C. Alcoholism in a geriatric setting. I. Disciplinary problems, marital status and income level. *J. Am. Geriatr. Soc.* 10:197–200, 1962.

Horn, J. L., and Donaldson, G. Cognitive development in adulthood. IN: *Constancy and Change in Human Development* (Brim, O. G., and Kagan, J., eds.) Cambridge Mass.: Harvard University Press, 1980.

Institute of Medicine *Sleeping Pills, Insomnia, and Medical Practice* Washington, D.C.: National Academy of Sciences, 1979.

Joasoo, A., and McKenzie, J. M. Stress and the immune response in rats. *Int. Arch. Allergy Appl. Immunol.* 50:659–663, 1976.

Johnson, T., Lavendar, J. F., Hultin, E., and Rasmussen, A. F., Jr. The influence of avoidance-learning stress on resistance to coxsacle B virus in mice. *J. Immunol.* 91:569–573, 1963.

Kane, R. D., Solomon, D., Beck, J., Keeler, E., and Kane, R. The future need for geriatric manpower in the United States. *N. Engl. J. Med.* 302:1327–1332, 1980.

Kay, D. W. The epidemiology of brain deficit in the aged problems in patient identification. IN: *Cognitive and Emotional Disturbance in the Elderly: Clinical Issues*

(Eisdorfer, C., and Friedel, R. O., eds.) New York: Yearbook Medical Publishers, 1977.

Kissin, B. The pharmacodynamics and natural history of alcoholism. IN: *The Biology of Alcoholism, Vol. 3* (Kissin, B., and Begleiter, H., eds.) New York: Plenum Press, 1974, pp 1–36.

Klisz, D. Knowledge base in biology for training mental health workers to work with the elderly. IN: *Conference on Training Psychologists for Work in Aging* (Vanden Bos, G., ed.) Washington, D.C.: American Psychological Association, in press.

Korenchevsky, V. *Physiological and Pathological Aging* New York: Basel/Karger, 1961.

Langer, E. J., and Rodin, J. The effects of choice and enhanced personal responsibility for the aged: A field experiment in an institutional setting. *J. Pers. Soc. Psychol.* 34:191-198, 1976.

Law, R., and Chalmers, C. Medicines and elderly people: A general practice survey. *Br. J. Med.* 1:565–571, 1976.

Libow, L. S. Senile dementia and pseudosenility: Clinical diagnosis. IN: *Cognitive and Emotional Disturbance in the Elderly: Clinical Issues* (Eisdorfer, C., and Friedel, R. O., eds) New York: Yearbook Medical Publishers, 1977, pp. 75–88.

Locke, B. Z., Kramer, M., and Pasamamick, B. Alcoholic psychoses among first admissions to public mental hospitals in Ohio. *Q. J. Stud. Alcohol* 21:457–474, 1960.

McCusker, J., Cherubin, C. F., and Zimberg, S. Prevalence of alcoholism in general municipal hospital population. *N.Y. State J. Med.* 71:751–754, 1971.

Makinodan, T., and Raye, M. M. B. Age influence on the immune system. *Adv. Immunol.* 29:287–333, 1980.

Mettrop, P. J. G., and Visser, P. Influence on the induction and elicitation of contact-dermatitis in guinea pigs. *Psychophysiology* 8:45–53, 1971.

Monjan, A. A., and Collector, M. I. Stress-induced modulation of the immune response. *Science* 196:307–308, 1977.

Nandy, K., and Sherwin, I. (Eds.) *The Aging Brain and Senile Dementia* New York: Plenum Press, 1977.

National Academy of Sciences. *Science and Technology: A Five-Year Outlook* San Francisco: Freeman, 1979.

Nesselroade, J. R., and Baltes, P. B. (Eds.) *Longitudinal Research in the Study of Behavior and Development* New York: Academic Press, 1979.

Parron, D. L., Solomon, F., and Rodin, J. (Eds.) *Health, Behavior, and Aging. Interim Report No. 5, Health and Behavior: A Research Agenda* Washington, D.C.: National Academy Press, 1981.

Pattison, E. M. The selection of treatment modalities for the alcoholic patient. IN: *The Diagnosis and Treament of Alcoholism* (Mendelson, J. H., and Mello, N. K., eds.) New York: McGraw-Hill, 1979, pp. 126–227.

Perry, E. K. The cholinergic system in old age and Alzheimer's disease. *Age and Aging* 9:1–8, 1980.

Perry, R. H., Blused, G., Perry, E. K., and Tomlinson, B. E. Histochemical observations of cholinesterase activities in the brains of elderly normal and demented (Alzheimer-type) patients. *Age and Aging* 9:9–16, 1980.

Phillipson, R. Drugs and the aged: Policy issues and utilization of research findings. Paper presented at the American Association for the Advancement of Science, Boston, 1976.

Richey, D. P., and Bender, A. D. Pharmacokinetic consequences of aging. *Annu. Rev. Pharmacol. Toxicol.* 1977, pp. 45–65.

Riley, M. W. Age strata in social systems. IN: *Handbook of Aging and the Social Sciences* (Binstock, R. H., and Shanas, E., eds.) New York: Van Nostrand Reinhold, 1976, pp. 189–206.

Riley, M. W. Aging, social change, and the power of ideas. *Daedalus* Fall, 1978, pp. 39–52.

Riley, M. W. Health behavior of older people: Toward a new paradigm. IN: *Health, Aging, and Behavior* (Parron, D. L., Solomon, F., and Rodin, J., eds.) Washington, D.C.: National Academy Press, 1981.

Rodin, J., and Langer, E. Long-term effects of a control-relevant intervention with the institutionalized aged. *J. Pers. Soc. Psychol.* 35:897–902, 1977.

Ryder, N. B. The cohort as a concept in the study of social change. *Am. Sociol. Rev.* 30:843–861, 1965.

Samarajski, T. Age-related changes in brain biogenic amines. IN: *Aging Volume. Clinical, Morphologic, and Neurochemical Aspects in the Aging Central Nervous System* (Brody, H., Harman, D., and Ordy, J. M., eds.) New York: Raven Press, 1975.

Schaie, K. W. (Ed.) *Longitudinal Studies of Adult Psychological Development* New York: Guilford Press, 1981.

Schleifer, S. J., Keller, S. E., McKegney, F. P., and Stein, M. Bereavement and lymphocyte function. Paper presented at the American Psychiatric Association Meeting, 1980 (Abstract, New Research Reports).

Schuckit, M. A. Geriatric alcoholism and drug abuse. *Gerontologist* 17:168–174, 1977.

Seidl, I. G., Thornton, G. F., Smith J. W., and Cluff, L. E. Studies on the epidemiology of adverse drug reactions. III Reactions in patients on a general medical service. *Bull. Johns Hopkins Hosp.* 119:299, 1966.

Shock, N. W. Systems integration. IN: *Handbook of the Biology of Aging* (Finch, C. E., and Hayflick, L., eds.), New York: Van Nostrand Reinhold, 1977, pp. 639–655.

Siassi, I., Crocetti, G. and Spiro, H. R. Drinking patterns and alcoholism in a blue collar population. *Q. J. Stud. Alcohol* 34:917–926, 1973.

Simon, A., Epstein, L. J., and Reynolds, L. Alcoholism in the geriatric mentally ill. *Geriatrics* 23:125–131, 1968.

Solomon, G. F., Amkraut, A. A., and Kasper, P. Immunity, emotions and stress with special reference to the mechanisms of stress effects on the immune system. *Psychother. Psychosom.* 23:209–217, 1974.

Uhlenberg, P. Demographic change and problems of the aged. IN: *Aging from Birth to Death: Interdisciplinary Perspectives, Vol. 1* (Riley, M. W., ed.) Boulder, Colo.: Westview Press, 1979, pp. 153–166.

Vestal, R. E. Drug use in the elderly: A review of problems and special considerations. *Drugs* 16:358–382, 1978.

Wack, J., and Rodin, J. Nursing homes for the aged: The human consequences of legislation-shaped environments. *J. Soc. Issues* 34:6–21, 1978.

Walford, R. L. *The Immunologic Theory of Aging* Copenhagen: Munksgaard, 1969.

Walford, R. L. Immunology and aging. *Am. J. Clin. Pathol.* 74:247–253, 1980.

Walford, R. L., Liv, R. K., Gerbase-Delima, M., Mathies, M., and Smith, G. S. Long term dietary restriction and immune function in mice: Response to sheep red blood cells and to mitogenic agents. *Mechan. Aging Devel.* 2:447–454, 1973.

Wetle, T., and Whitelaw, N. Person centered service delivery. IN: *Justice and Older Americans* (Rafai, M., ed.) Lexington, Mass.: Heath, 1977.

Williamson, J., Stokoe, I. H., Gray, S., Fisher, M., Smith, A., McGhee, A., and Stephenson, E. Old people at home: Their unreported needs. *Lancet 1*:1117–1120, 1964.

Zimberg, S. The elderly alcoholic. *Gerontologist 14*:221–224, 1974.

12
Social Disadvantage and Health

The burden of illness rests disproportionately on the socially disadvantaged. Social disadvantage includes any attribution of social position or role carrying with it the likelihood of reduced resources, opportunity, or social power. Empirical data comparing physical and mental health of the poor with the rest of the U.S. population provide consistent evidence that socioeconomic status is associated with higher rates of death and disability (Brenner, 1973, 1982; Kosa, and Zola, 1975; National Center for Health Statistics, 1980).

History has shown that, even when causative factors of a disease are unknown and treatments are unavailable, changes in socioeconomic conditions and literacy rates can reduce mortality. One example of this phenomenon is the decline in mortality from tuberculosis before the availability of chemotherapy. Still, even when treatments are available, technology cannot always overcome social, economic, and behavioral factors (Eisenberg, 1982). Improvements in U.S. literacy rates and in general socioeconomic conditions over the past 20 years have been linked with rapid declines in health differentials between the poor and those who are better off. Still, substantial discrepancies remain (Feldman, 1982), most noticeably in the poorer health of people in the areas of greatest poverty—the rural South, Appalachia, urban ghettos—and particularly among the very young who live in disadvantaged environments.

Biobehavioral and psychosocial research has begun to disentangle the complexities of the role social factors play in the ecology of disease. A growing body of research goes beyond documenting the inequities in the health of the poor to examining such issues as the effects of differential exposure to and treatment by health care professionals (Howard, 1982). Theories about the cumulative effects of psychosocial and economic stress have been examined (Harburg et al., 1973; Jenkins et al., 1979; Brenner, 1982) and show promise of uncovering some mechanisms by which the environment can influence the health of the disadvantaged. Thus, even though physiological mechanisms that translate environmental factors into illness are not well understood, the influence of social disadvantage on the development of disease, on recovery opportunities, and on survival changes is becoming increasingly clear (Parron et al., 1982).

Social Disadvantage and the Burden of Illness

Most available data on the health of the nation's poor were collected on the basis of minority-white differentials, rather than on the basis of other markers of social disadvantage such as income or education. Despite the scientific fallacy of equating race or ethnicity with social or personal characteristics, these data provide usable estimates, because the proportion of black families with incomes below the poverty line is three times that of white families (National Center for Health Statistics, 1980). Still, the few studies that have examined the relationship between socioeconomic status and mortality found that differentials in minority-white health status now are negligible when controlled for social class. Direct measures of socioeconomic status and social disadvantage should be gathered in addition to, or instead of, ethnicity in ongoing and future studies of health in the population.

Evidence of the significant role that psychosocial and economic factors play in health and disease has been demonstrated directly (Jenkins et al., 1977) and also can be inferred from comparisons of major health indices for whites and minorities. Despite greater overall declines in mortality and morbidity rates for minorities over the past two decades, minority-white differentials persist in all indices (Figure 12.1). Minority death rates exceed white death rates in all age groups up to age 80. Similar differentials between social classes continue in Great Britain, despite major efforts to improve health service availability to the poor (Morris, 1979).

Large differentials in neonatal and early childhood minority and white death rates indicate a special vulnerability of infants and children and suggest that social disadvantage has a strong role in shaping and modifying their environmental risks. The disparities are greatest in neonatal and infancy periods, when minority death rates are double those for white children. Figure 12.2 disaggregates the overall mortality indices into specific causes of infant mortality. Low birth weights, deaths associated with the birth

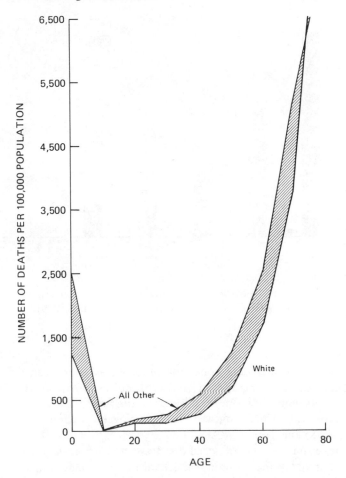

FIGURE 12.1   Deaths and death rates by age and color in the
United States in 1977. For minority children under age one, the
number of deaths is nearly double that of whites; the death rate
among minorities exceeds that among whites at all levels until
age 80. SOURCE: Health Resources Administration (1980).

process, and congenital disorders are the principal causes of minority neonatal deaths (cf. Chapter 13). Sudden infant death syndrome is the leading
cause of death in minority children over the age of one month. Death rates
for minority infants are double those for white infants in all categories
except congenital defects.

Differentials continue into the adolescent period (Figure 12.3). Minority

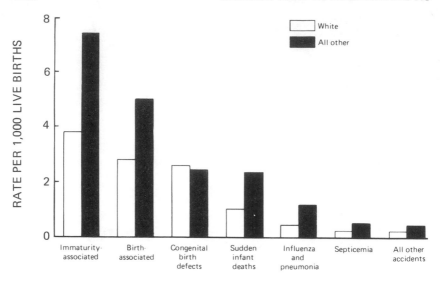

FIGURE 12.2   Major causes of infant mortality in the United States in 1976. SOURCE: U.S. Department of Health, Education, and Welfare (1979).

children have higher mortality rates for all causes except cancer, influenza, and pneumonia. Accidents, cancer, and birth defects dominate as principal causes of death among minority children, and the figures also suggest underlying differentials in maiming and handicapping of children who survive accidents and violence.

The longer-term effects of social disadvantage such as its impact on the environment and human response mechanisms are apparent in the consistently documented excesses of mortality and morbidity among adult minorities (National Center for Health Statistics, 1980; U.S. Department of Health, Education, and Welfare, 1979).

Relative narrowing of the gaps between minorities and whites has been attributed to increased availability of health care services, e.g., prenatal care, improved socioeconomic conditions, changes in nutrition, housing, and sanitary practices, and dissemination of advanced diagnostic and treatment technologies. Persistent differences in health have been attributed to the failure of minorities and other disadvantaged groups to benefit equally in these changes (National Center for Health Statistics, 1980).

The Institute of Medicine conference *Behavior, Health Risks, and Social Disadvantage* (Parron et al., 1982) emphasized the similar role social dis-

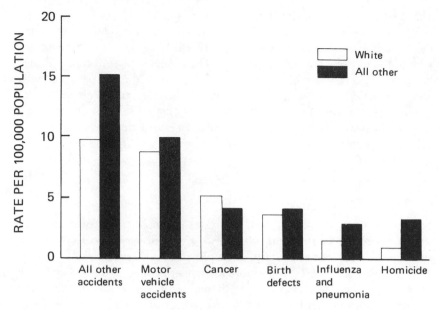

FIGURE 12.3   Major causes of death for ages 1–14 years in the United States in 1976. SOURCE: U.S. Department of Health, Education, and Welfare (1979).

advantage plays in the etiology and pathogenesis of two families of major diseases—cancers and schizophrenias. Conference participants emphasized these similarities between the two diseases:

- both are diseases of multiple etiologies;
- both affect persons who are socially disadvantaged much more often and more severely than they do people with greater resources and higher education;
- both are thought to have pathogenic outcomes that depend on a complex synergism of predisposing and precipitating factors or combinations of risk-enhancing effects (constitutional, socioeconomic, behavioral, and environmental factors and psychosocial stress); and
- both have similar methodological problems related to the time sequence of impact and to the need for integrative, collaborative, interdisciplinary research.

Comparisons of cancer death rates provide evidence of the extra burden of illness experienced by blacks (National Center for Health Statistics, 1980;

U.S. Department of Health, Education, and Welfare, 1979). Studies by the American Cancer Society (1979) indicate that reported cancer mortality rates for blacks have increased by 26 percent over the past 25 years; for whites, the increase has been 5 percent. The excess in rates of cancer deaths has been especially notable in cancers of the stomach, esophagus, prostate, and uterus (U.S. Department of Health, Education, and Welfare, 1979). Some increases are the result of increased use of specific diagnostic methods and are in part reflected in reduced rates of death that are attributed in disadvantaged groups to "other and ill-defined causes" and "other malignant neoplasms, site not specified."

Interactions Between Ethnic and Socioeconomic Factors

Studies of social differentials in death rates for most causes of death have shown relative consistency that suggests a significant etiological role for such social conditions as poverty, unemployment, and substandard housing. Yeracaris and Kim (1978) found that malignant neoplasms and other causes of death are inversely associated with socioeconomic status in urban and suburban cohorts. Lerner (1980) found higher mortality rates for lower socioeconomic groups in nearly all major causes of death and for all age groups. Jenkins et al. (1979) found that death rates attributable to hypertensive diseases are significantly higher in areas with low median education, poverty, low occupational status, and substandard housing. The most potent geographic indicators of risk of death from hypertensive disease are low education and low occupational status.

Research on hypertension provides an example of the importance of distinguishing factors of socioeconomic status from those of race. Hypertension-related disease is the leading cause of death among blacks, who have triple the rates experienced by whites (Krantz et al., 1981). Differences in the prevalence among socioeconomic groups cannot be accounted for by genetic factors alone. Hypertension rates in middle-class blacks more closely resemble rates among middle-class whites than among lower-class blacks (Krantz et al., 1981). Hypotheses to explain these differences include the suggestion that persons in lower social strata experience more negative life changes (Dohrenwend, 1973). Harburg et al. (1973), who found that blood pressure levels are higher in areas of high social stress, supports this hypothesis with some physiological evidence.

Contributions of Environmental Exposure

Even under conditions of equal employment, minorities have been found to experience differential exposure to pathogenic agents. For example, Michaels (1982) found that discriminatory practices in the steel industry significantly elevate cancer incidence and death rates among minority workers. These effects depend not on race but on job assignment. The coke ovens produce the most hazardous carcinogenic substances of the steel-making process. Of coke plant workers, 80 percent of blacks are employed at jobs near the coke ovens, compared with 32 percent of whites. Blacks are not only overrepresented in the most risky jobs but also tend to remain in those jobs longer. Coke oven workers with 15 or more years of full-time exposure have 10 times the lung cancer rate, 7 times the rate of kidney cancer, and elevated rates of skin cancer compared with other steel workers (Lloyd, 1971; Redmond et al., 1972). Studies of the rubber industry reveal similar findings: discriminatory job assignments correlate with elevated rates of stomach, lung, blood, bladder, lymphatic, and prostate cancers in black workers (McMichael et al., 1976).

Contributions of Health Care Delivery

Evidence of differential exposure to pathogens on the job is mirrored by that of differential treatment within the health care system. Blacks and other disadvantaged persons have cancers diagnosed at later stages of the disease process (Howard, 1982). Tumor registry data show that the metastatic rate of black breast cancer patients is higher than that of whites, and that the proportion of metastatic breast cancer rates is inversely correlated with the socioeconomic status of patients (Howard et al., 1980). Some explanation for delayed diagnosis and treatment can be found in data from the National Ambulatory Medical Care Survey, which indicate that the disadvantaged and minorities are less likely to receive such preventive services as blood pressure checks, Pap smears, and breast exams (Cypress, 1979). Generally, preventive care relates directly to socioeconomic status; however, blacks have been found to receive services of less quality and comprehensiveness than do whites of equal socioeconomic status (Howard et al., 1980).

There is a strong interdependence between poverty and illness. Lack of resources and discrimination reduce chances of early diagnosis and treatment and increase chances of poor-quality care. The same factors that modify chances of developing and surviving cancer also alter chances of recovering from serious mental illness. Jenkins (1982) has emphasized that inadequate resources, low-status jobs, social stigma, and inadequate education interact with changes in immunity, nutrition, environmental risks, and coping styles to create a "circle of disadvantage."

Almost without exception, studies show a higher incidence and prevalence of schizophrenia and other psychoses among the socially disadvantaged (Kohn, 1972; McCabe, 1975). Best estimates indicate that the average lifetime prevalence of schizophrenia is one percent; prevalence rates rise to 6 percent in urban ghettos (Pardes, 1982). However, as in the case of physical illness, most national data on prevalence of mental illness are not by socioeconomic status but by minority status. Most of these data are based on populations in public hospitals (Health Resources Administration, 1980).

There is considerable evidence in the research literature for the role of social disadvantage in mental illness. Fried (1975) reviewed 34 studies that examined the relationship between social class and severe psychiatric disorders; he concluded that rates of severe mental illness are highest among lower social classes.

Two broad hypotheses are offered about increased prevalence of mental illness in lower socioeconomic groups. One is that people in poor mental health become members of lower socioeconomic classes—the social drift hypothesis (Kosa and Zola, 1975). A second is that being in a lower class puts one at increased risk of becoming and remaining ill—the social etiology hypothesis (Fried, 1975, 1982; Kohn, 1976; Lerner, 1976). Within the second hypothesis, four explanations of increased prevalence of mental illness among the socially disadvantaged have been posited: (1) increased chances of receiving a more severe diagnosis (Adebimpe, 1981; Williams, 1982), (2) greater frequency and duration of stress among the socially disadvantaged (Kohn, 1976; Dohrenwend and Egri, 1981; Strauss, 1982), (3) more restricted options for dealing with stresses (Fried, 1975, 1982; Kohn, 1976), and (4) fewer and less equal treatment resources available to the socially disadvantaged (Flaherty and Meagher, 1980; Mollica et al., 1980).

Williams (1982) has suggested that disadvantaged minorities are more likely to receive severe diagnoses. Discrimination may affect the way health professionals perceive, diagnose, and treat severe mental illness in the black population. Adebimpe (1981) has found evidence for this hypothesis in national data. The relationship between race and mental illness seems to be largely explained by socioeconomic status (Warheit et al., 1975).

Dohrenwend (1973), Kohn (1976), Lerner (1975), Strauss (1982), and others have reported that lower social class groups have more negative life changes and that social deprivations result in more unstable and unsafe environments and more stressful family and social conditions. Brenner (1982) found evidence to support the concept that incipient tendencies toward illness are exacerbated by increased vulnerability to socioeconomic changes. Kohn (1973) has suggested that part of the explanation for these differences is that the problems faced by the poor are less alterable by individual action than are those faced by people in higher socioeconomic classes. Those who are better off can use financial and social resources to compensate for or diminish the effects of disabilities.

Social disadvantage also increases the likelihood of receiving inferior treatment. A classic study by Hollingshead and Redlich (1958) found that minorities and the poor received psychiatric care almost entirely in large state hospitals with low staff-to-patient ratios and few outpatient services. Follow-up studies by Mollica and Redlich (1980) showed that 90 percent of minorities receive inpatient psychiatric care in state hospitals; even when they receive outpatient services in community mental health centers, they are more likely to be treated in chronic care, alcohol, and drug treatment units with lower professional staff-to-patient ratios. Flaherty and Meagher (1980) found similar utilization characteristics among blacks in a Veterans Administration hospital: black psychiatric patients were discharged more quickly and were given fewer outpatient and rehabilitation services than were white veterans.

Once again, it is difficult to distinguish effects of social disadvantage on choice of treatment from those of race-related discrimination. Patients with lower education levels—white or black—are less likely to receive psychotherapy and other supportive services. Despite apparent changes in access to expanded community mental health centers and Veterans Administration psychiatric services over the past two decades, it appears that discriminatory practices toward the poor, especially blacks, result in differential management by health care providers. This may lessen chances of early detection and appropriate treatment interventions.

Opportunities for Successful Interventions

Including psychosocial factors in the analysis of the etiology and pathogenesis of major diseases increases chances to improve the health of the country's socially disadvantaged. Access to economic resources and the ability to mobilize personal, family, and community resources—especially those of the health care system—have the most dramatic modifying effects on pathogenic outcomes (Parron et al., 1982). Feldman (1982) noted that the greatest differential in mortality rates is associated with the attainment of higher levels of education. For example, in 1970, 40 percent of mothers of black newborns completed high school and 44 percent received prenatal care; in 1978, 61 percent completed high school and 60 percent received prenatal care (Feldman, 1982).

Hypertension Detection and Treatment

An example of a highly successful experimental intervention is the Hypertension Detection and Follow-Up Program (1979). It used a randomized controlled design to compare five-year mortality effects of "stepped care" antihypertensive treatment with more traditional forms of care involving referral to community medical services (cf. Chapter 15). Blood pressure levels of experimental patients were consistently lower than those of control patients. The five-year mortality rate from all causes was 17 percent lower for experimental patients than for controls; even those in the former group with only mild hypertension showed a 20 percent reduction in mortality rates, compared with mild hypertensives in the control group. Of interest, black patients in stepped care achieved more than twice the reduction in five-year mortality rates as whites receiving the same care.

The above study has significant policy and research implications for improving the health of the socially disadvantaged. Of special interest are characteristics of the program that may overcome the psychosocial forces that often interfere with the disadvantaged receiving equitable health care services: vigorous and systematic early detection; treatment and follow-up of patients by health professionals; patient education, group counseling, and, in some sites, social functions; child care services during treatment; transportation to the clinic; and clinic hours compatible with work schedules. The study also demonstrates that adherence can be achieved and dropout rates reduced to negligible levels when high-quality services are provided at equal cost to all patients.

Other Successful Programs

Williams (1982) has described another example of successful intervention for the socially disadvantaged, in this case for chronic psychiatric patients following long-term hospitalization. This group therapy program was located in a community church in a poor urban black community. Sessions were conducted by a community mental health worker who was also head of the neighborhood's union of welfare recipients. Welfare agencies both feared and respected her political power. When patients discussed their problems with welfare agencies, the community mental health worker would intervene on their behalf as the welfare union representative, usually with positive results. The worker encouraged patients to join the welfare union. Over a two-year period, more than half of this group of chronically disabled persons found jobs and got off welfare.

Other highly successful intervention programs share similar characteristics. A hospital-based program in Cleveland achieved a 60 percent reduction in perinatal mortality with patient education, nutrition counseling, social service intervention, special services for adolescents, and delinquent appointment follow-up (Sokol, 1982). Adolescent peer counseling programs conducted in high schools result in reductions in smoking, alcoholism, and drug use (cf. Chapter 14). Teenage pregnancy intervention programs have experienced success in getting teenagers into immediate prenatal care; counseling and follow-up have ensured continued participation (Welcher, 1982).

Differences between the health of the poor and the nonpoor have not been reconciled by physical and mental health services, which have not been geared to broader needs of the patients and their social group. The results of successful intervention programs suggest that improvement in the health care of the socially disadvantaged may require more active involvement in the total social milieu on the part of health care workers and more creative use of natural support systems. The ability to mobilize personal, family, and community resources—especially those of the health care system—can substantially affect illness outcomes (cf. Chapter 18). Programs may be needed that are especially designed for particular high-risk groups and not modeled after typical private medical practice.

Research Opportunities

Studies of the effects of social disadvantage and of intervention programs present important opportunities for research. Biobehavioral research in this area should focus on identifying preventable causal factors and successful interventions, even when the physiological mechanisms of disease still are not well understood. Present socioeconomic realities make it crucial to use existing health care resources to the best advantage. Evidence from intervention studies suggests that there are excellent primary and secondary prevention opportunities within the existing health care system for meeting many of the health care needs of the socially disadvantaged.

In basic research, promising areas include the fields of immunology, endocrinology, and toxicology. Many research opportunities and priorities cut across all social classes and ethnic groups. Research that traces an association between illness and social isolation, bereavement, and measures of cumulative life change and stress is especially required to understand why social disadvantage alters disease ecology and to identify preventive measures (cf. Chapter 3). Psychoneuroimmunological research may yield specific evidence about the relationship between social disadvantage and increased burden of illness.

A better understanding of the origins, prevalence, and effects of institutional discrimination may shed light on the causes of higher morbidity and mortality among blacks and other minorities. Such discrimination is a major source of psychological stress, unemployment, lack of resources, and lack of power to improve matters. Knowledge of how racial and social factors influence clinical judgment, diagnosis, and treatment is necessary to ensure equitable as well as more effective delivery of health care services (Institute of Medicine, 1981).

Controlled studies of specially tailored interventions should include measures of the type, features, and mixture of various types of health care personnel, their attitudes toward patients, and the relationship of staff social class to differential management of minorities and the poor. Staff education aimed at producing more concerned and sensitive approaches to the socially disadvantaged should be evaluated. Knowledge of and adaptation to patient attitudes and motivation may be central to more effective use of diagnostic and treatment technologies among the disadvantaged.

Cost-efficacy studies are needed to determine which intervention strategies are best for specific ethnic and socioeconomic groups. Specially targeted interventions for specific problems in designated subpopulations can be highly effective, as in the instance of hypertension (Urban Health, 1981).

Past federal initiatives have supported the development of research, service, and professional training programs to improve physical and mental health care programs to the disadvantaged. It is likely that federal support will be reduced substantially in the next few years, and it is unclear how states will cope with the major transition of shifting to block grant mechanisms. Health services research can be helpful in guiding this transition.

Lack of appropriately directed funds may seriously impair prevention and treatment programs for disadvantaged minorities. In this context, maternal and infant care projects are of special interest. Outcome studies of these prenatal and perinatal care programs suggest that social factors that depress the prenatal and perinatal environment can be neutralized and interventions can have substantial influence both on the survival of the infant and on its growth and development. Changes in infant health created through effects on the health and behavior of mothers have been shown to have important long-term effects on the intellectual and physical development of the child. Improvement in the intellectual and physical conditions of socially disadvantaged children can have long-term effects on their chances to break the "circle of disadvantage" (Jenkins, 1982). Thus, if funds were to be saved by terminating maternal and infant care projects, they might well be lost many times over each year by the costs of institutional care and special education for retarded and handicapped children whose disabilities could have been prevented inexpensively.

Conclusions

Emergent priority research questions related to the burden of illness and social disadvantage are:

- Will health gains made by the socially disadvantaged in the past two decades be maintained in times of relative scarcity?

- Will gaps between minorities and whites widen and will children show particular sensitivity to changes in health resources such as elimination or reduction of child nutrition programs and prenatal care services?
- What will be the costs of missed opportunities in disease prevention, especially early in life?
- What mechanisms translate environmental stresses into disease?
- What kinds of interventions are most likely to minimize the consequences of social disadvantage?
- What aspects of economic condition are particularly harmful to the health of the disadvantaged?

Continued scientific progress requires that researchers be trained to integrate behavioral and biomedical functions and that they be sensitive to and aware of sociocultural and ethnic issues. To be fully successful, epidemiological and intervention studies of socially disadvantaged populations should have minority community leaders involved in their formulation, execution, and interpretation.

The current body of biobehavioral research confirms that some forms of health care delivery can bring about more equitable chances for survival and recovery from disease. Opportunities for disease prevention by changing behavior and the immediate environment are especially significant for disadvantaged segments of the population.

References

Adebimpe, V. R. Overview: White norms and psychiatric diagnosis of Black patients. *Am. J. Psychiatry 138*:279–285, 1981.

American Cancer Society *The Challenge of Cancer Among Black Americans.* Proceedings of the National Conference, Washington, D.C., February 1979.

Brenner, M. H. *Mental Illness and the Economy* Cambridge, Mass.: Harvard University Press, 1973.

Brenner, M. H. Mental illness and the economy. IN: *Behavior, Health Risks, and Social Disadvantage* (Parron, D. L., Solomon, F., and Jenkins,C.D., eds.) Washington, D.C.: National Academy Press, 1982, pp. 75–92.

Cypress, B. K. The role of ambulatory medical care in hypertension screening. *Am. J. Publ. Health 69*:19–24, 1979.

Dohrenwend, B. S. Social status and stressful life events. *J. Pers. Soc. Psychol. 28*:225–235, 1973.

Dohrenwend, B. P., and Egri, G. Recent stressful life events and episodes of schizophrenia. *Schiz. Bull. 7*:12–23, 1981.

Eisenberg, L. Overview. IN: *Infants at Risk of Developmental Dysfunction. Interim Report No. 4, Health and Behavior: A Research Agenda* (Parron, D. L., and Eisenberg, L., eds.) Washington, D.C.: National Academy Press, 1982. pp. 3–12.

Feldman, J. J. Health of the disadvantaged: An epidemiological overview. IN: *Behavior, Health Risks, and Social Disadvantage* (Parron, D. L., Solomon, F., and

Jenkins, C. D., eds.) Washington, D.C.: National Academy Press, 1982, pp. 13–18.

Flaherty, J. A., and Meagher, R. Measuring racial bias in inpatient treatment. *Am. J. Psychiatry* 137:679–682, 1980.

Fried, M. Social differences in mental health. IN: *Poverty and Health: A Sociological Analysis* (Kosa, J., and Zola, I. K., eds.) Cambridge, Mass.: Harvard University Press, 1975.

Fried, M. Disadvantage, vulnerability, and mental illness. IN: *Behavior, Health Risks, and Social Disadvantage* (Parron, D. L., Solomon, F., and Jenkins, C. D., eds.) Washington, D.C.: National Academy Press, 1982, pp. 113–124.

Harburg, E., Erfurt, I., Hauenstein, L., Chape, C., Schull, W. J., and Shork, M. A. Socioecological stress, suppressed hostility, skin color and Black-White male blood pressure. *Psychosom. Med.* 35:276–296, 1973.

Health Resources Administration *Health of the Disadvantaged. II: Chart Book* Washington, D.C.: U.S. Government Printing Office, 1980, DHHS Publ. No. (HRA) 80–663.

Hollingshead, A. B., and Redlich, F. C. *Social Class and Mental Illness* New York: Wiley, 1958.

Howard, J., Lund, P., and Bell, G. Hospital variations in metastatic breast cancer. *Med. Care* 18:442–455, 1980.

Howard, J. In-reach: An approach to the secondary prevention of cancer. IN: *Behavior, Health Risks, and Social Disadvantage* (Parron, D. L., Solomon, F., and Jenkins, C. D., eds.) Washington, D.C.: National Academy Press, 1982, pp. 51–61.

Hypertension Detection and Follow-Up Program Cooperative Group. Five-year findings of the hypertension detection and follow-up program. I. Reduction in mortality of persons with high blood pressue, including mild hypertension. *J. Am. Med. Assoc.* 242:2562–2577, 1979.

Institute of Medicine *Health Care in the Context of Civil Rights* Washington, D.C.: National Academy Press, 1981.

Jenkins, C. D. Overview: Behavioral perspectives on health risks among the disadvantaged. IN: *Behavior, Health Risks, and Social Disadvantage* (Parron, D. L., Solomon, F., and Jenkins,C. D., eds.) Washington, D.C.: National Academy Press, 1982, pp. 3–12.

Jenkins, C. D., Tuthill, R. W. , Tannenbaum, S. I., and Kirby, C. R. Zones of excess mortality in Massachusetts. *N. Engl. J. Med.* 296:1354–1356, 1977.

Jenkins, C. D., Tuthill, R., Tannenbaum, S., and Kirby, C. Social stressors and excess mortality from hypertensive disease. *J. Hum. Stress* 5:29–40, 1979.

Kohn, M. L. Class, family and schizophrenia: A reformulation. *Soc. Forces* 50:295–313, 1972.

Kohn, M. Social class and schizophrenia: A critical review and reformulation. *Schiz. Bull.* 7:60–79, 1973.

Kohn, M. L. The interaction of social class and other factors in the etiology of schizophrenia. *Am. J. Psychiatry* 133:1778–1800, 1976.

Kosa, J., and Zola, I. K. (Eds.) *Poverty and Health: A Sociological Analysis* Cambridge, Mass.: Harvard University Press, 1975.

Krantz, D., Glass, D., Contrada, R., and Miller, N. Behavior and health. Paper commissioned by NRC/ABASS Committee on Basic Research in Behavioral and Social Sciences and Social Sciences Research Council, 1981.

Lerner, M. The social differences in physical health. IN: *Poverty and Health: A*

Sociological Analysis (Kosa, J., and Zola, I. K., eds.) Cambridge, Mass.: Harvard University Press, 1975.

Lerner, M. Socioeconomic differentials in mortality in Baltimore, 1959–61 and 1969–71. *Proc. Am. Stat. Assoc.* 1980.

Lloyd, J. W. Long term mortality study of steelworkers. V: Respiratory cancer in coke plant workers. *J. Occup. Med. 13:*53–68, 1971.

McCabe, M. Demographic differences in functional psychoses. *Br. J. Psych. 127:*320–323, 1975.

McMichael, A. J., et al. Mortality among rubber workers: Relationship to specific jobs. *J. Occup. Med. 18:*176–185, 1976.

Michaels, D. Minority workers and occupational cancer: The hidden costs of job discrimination. IN: *Behavior, Health Risks, and Social Disadvantage* (Parron, D. L., Solomon, F., and Jenkins, C.D., eds.) Washington, D.C.: National Academy Press, 1982, pp. 43–50.

Mollica, R. F., and Redlich, F. Equity and changing patient characteristics, 1950–1975. *Arch. Gen. Psychiatry* 37:1257–1265, 1980.

Mollica, R. F., Blum, J. D., and Redlich, F. Equity and the psychiatric care of Black patients 1950 to 1975. *J. Nerv. Ment. Dis. 168:*279–286, 1980.

Morris, J. N. Social inequalities undiminished. *Lancet* 1:87–90, 1979.

National Center for Health Statistics *Health United States, 1979* Washington, D.C.: U.S. Government Printing Office, 1980, DHEW Publ. No. (PHS) 80–1232.

Pardes, H. Behavioral perspectives on health risk among the disadvantaged. IN: *Behavior, Health Risks, and Social Disadvantage.* (Parron, D. L., Solomon, F., and Jenkins, C. D., eds.) Washington, D.C.: National Academy Press, 1982, pp. 159–174.

Parron, D. L., Solomon, F., and Jenkins, C. D. (Eds.) *Behavior, Health Risks, and Social Disadvantage. Interim Report No. 6, Health and Behavior: A Research Agenda* Washington, D.C.: National Academy Press, 1982.

Redmond, C. K., Ciocco, A., Lloyd, J. W., and Rush, H. W. Long-term mortality study of steelworkers. VI. Mortality from malignant neoplasms among coke plant workers. *J. Occup. Med. 14:*621–629, 1972.

Sokol, R. A biological perspective on substance use in pregnancy: Alcohol as a paradigm for possible effects of drugs on the offspring. IN: *Infants at Risk for Developmental Dysfunction. Interim Report No. 4, Health and Behavior: A Research Agenda* (Parron, D. L., and Eisenberg, L., eds.) Washington, D.C.: National Academy Press, 1982, pp. 93–104.

Strauss, J. S. Behavioral aspects of being disadvantaged and risk for schizophrenia. IN: *Behavior, Health Risks, and Social Disadvantage.* (Parron, D. L., Solomon, F., and Jenkins, C. D., eds.) Washington, D.C.: National Academy Press, 1982, pp. 63–73.

United States Department of Health, Education, and Welfare *Healthy People* Washington, D.C.: U.S. Government Printing Office, 1979, DHEW Publ. No. (PHS) 79–55071.

Urban Health. State of the art in community programs for hypertension outreach. *Urban Health* 10:61–72, 1981.

Warheit, G. J., Holzer, C. E., III, and Arey, S. A. Race and mental illness: An epidemiologic update. *J. Health Soc. Behav.* 16:243–255, 1975.

Welcher, D. The effect of early childbearing on the psychosocial development of adolescent parents. IN: *Infants at Risk for Developmental Dysfunction. Interim Report*

No. 4, Health and Behavior: A Research Agenda (Parron, D. L., and Eisenberg, L., eds.) Washington, D.C.: National Academy Press, 1982, pp. 115–123.

Williams, D. American racism and the study and treatment of severe mental illness in Afro-Americans. IN: *Behavior, Health Risks, and Social Disadvantage* (Parron, D. L., Solomon, F., and Jenkins, C. D., eds.) Washington, D.C.: National Academy Press, 1982, pp. 125–131.

Yeracaris, C. A., and Kim, J. H. Socioeconomic differentials in selected causes of death. *Am. J. Publ. Health* 68:342–351, 1978.

IV
CROSS-CUTTING THEMES: PREVENTION AND TREATMENT

13
Prevention Efforts
in Early Life

Low birth weight, birth-associated conditions, congenital defects, accidents, influenza and pneumonia, cancer, and violence are leading contributors to mortality early in life (U.S. Department of Health and Human Services, 1980). That portion of morbidity readily quantified by such measures as physician visits, hospitalizations, or school days lost is caused to a great extent by acute conditions such as respiratory infections and injuries (U.S. Department of Health, Education, and Welfare, 1978a; U.S. Department of Health and Human Services, 1980). About 10 percent of school days are lost because of chronic conditions. The prevalence of and the degree of disability associated with mental disorders and learning disorders are less easily measured, because the symptoms cover a wide range of behaviors and often do not entail contacts with the health care system that would be monitored by statistical surveys. It has been estimated that 5 to 15 percent of children age 3–15 years suffer from chronic mental health problems. These conditions include the so-called conduct disorders, emotional disorders, and impairments or delays in psychological development (President's Commission on Mental Health, 1978).

With the control of infectious disease, childhood morbidity in which behavior plays a prominent role has come to the fore: school and learning problems, chronic illness, emotional disorders, and special adolescent health concerns (Haggerty et al., 1975). A recognition of this shift in the burden of illness has provided impetus to a number of reassessments of child health care needs that serve as a valuable resource for focusing attention on research that might help reduce the new morbidity.

Among the Institute of Medicine activities related to health needs of infants and children have been the Health and Behavior conference *Infants at Risk for Developmental Dysfunction* (Parron and Eisenberg, 1982) and the paper by Richmond and Filner (1979) on infants and children for *Healthy People, The Surgeon General's Report on Health Promotion and Disease Prevention*. In addition, *Better Health for Our Children: A National Strategy*, the report of the Select Panel for the Promotion of Child Health, is a comprehensive review (U.S. Department of Health and Human Services, 1981a,b).

Parental Influence on Prevention in Early Life

Physical and mental well-being in infancy, childhood, and adult life is greatly influenced by parental behavior in early life, which suggests the potential value of further analysis of opportunities for prevention during this period. During infancy, children are totally dependent on their parents for pre- and perinatal care; good nutrition and a supportive emotional environment; and appropriate preventive and therapeutic interventions, including immunizations and antibiotics. In addition, parents explicitly and implicitly teach their children health-relevant behaviors and attitudes in such matters as dental care, diet, exercise, and risk taking. These can continue to affect health status over the course of a lifetime.

Parental influence does not occur in isolation. The schools, mass media, peer pressures, and other community considerations such as the organization of health care services also shape the behavior of children and their parents. Even the police and the courts have a role, for example, in prevention of child abuse and neglect.

Although the goal of prevention is to stop a problem before it starts, successful treatment or amelioration of an existing condition also is of value. Again, behavioral approaches show great promise for helping children deal with such limitations as physical handicaps, learning disabilites, and emotional problems.

Several issues emerge repeatedly in an analysis of the role of behavior in the etiology, prevention, or treatment of disorders of concern in infancy and childhood: how to prevent accidents, how to stop substance abuse, how to organize health care services to enhance their utility and accessibility, and how to structure school-based health education. This chapter highlights a few specific health concerns, including low birth weight, mental retardation, learning disability, and emotional disorders.

Low Birth Weight

A low birth weight infant is defined as weighing less than 2,500 grams (about 5.5 pounds); a preterm infant is one born before 38 weeks of gestation. Any infant, term or preterm, may be small, average, or large for gestational age. A preterm infant need not be a low birth weight infant, and a low birth weight infant is not necessarily preterm. Being preterm and being of low birth weight contribute independently to risk of mortality and morbidity.

Mortality and Morbidity

Low birth weight infants have a higher infant mortality rate than do other infants. Only about 7 percent of infants in the United States are low birth weight, but they account for about two thirds of deaths in the first year of life (Shapiro et al., 1968; Rosen, 1982). The smaller the infant, the greater the risk of death. Breech or transverse fetal positions, which increase risk of perinatal mortality, are found in about one third of deliveries of infants who weigh less than 1,500 grams (3.3 pounds), in contrast to only 5 percent such positions for all deliveries (Rosen, 1982).

Low birth weight infants who survive, especially those weighing less than 1,500 grams at birth, are at increased risk for developmental difficulties (Fitzhardinge, 1976). For example, term low birth weight infants appear later to have increased rates of learning disability and school problems; preterm low birth weight infants have elevated risk of neurological damage (Rosen, 1982). Prematurity and low birth weight are associated with increased risk of cerebral palsy, epilepsy, mental retardation, autism, and blindness (Solnit and Provence, 1978).

Risk Factors for Low Birth Weight

Maternal behaviors during pregnancy that increase risk of having a low birth weight infant include cigarette smoking, abuse of alcohol and other drugs, poor nutrition, and delay in seeking prenatal care. Young teenage women also are at greater risk (U.S. Department of Health, Education, and Welfare, 1978b). The low birth weight rate for teens is 1.5 to 2 times that for older women, and the rate of preterm deliveries for teens is almost 3 times the average for older women (U.S. Department of Health, Education, and Welfare, 1979). Many promising avenues for research have been identified (Institute of Medicine, 1979, 1980, 1982; Parron and Eisenberg, 1982).

Addictions With regard to cigarette smoking and substance abuse, including excessive alcohol use, further understanding is needed of influences that lead to initiation of these behaviors. Research on effective drinking and smoking cessation programs also is vital, not only to prevent low birth weight but also to promote health in general. Promising avenues of inquiry are enumerated in Chapters 4 and 5.

Age   Risk for the infant born to a teenage mother may be associated either with her biological or her socioeconomic status. More information about the contributions of each is clearly needed. In terms of prevention, reducing the frequency of pregnancy among teens would reduce the incidence of low birth weight and associated mortality and morbidity, regardless of the underlying cause. This is especially important because 40 percent of teenage mothers have a second child within one year of the first, in contrast to only 22 percent of older women (Welcher, 1982).

One third of sexually active respondents in a national survey of 15- to 19-year-old women did not use any contraceptive method the last time they had sexual intercourse, and over 70 percent of the conceptions tallied in this survey were unintended (Zelnick and Kanter, 1978). Risk-taking behavior among adolescents includes not only unprotected sexual intercourse but also such behaviors as drinking and reckless driving. As discussed in Chapters 3 and 14, there is a need to understand how influences such as peer pressure and level of cognitive development influence such behaviors. With regard to teen pregnancy, there is a need for psychosocial research on decisions to use contraceptives and on specific decisions to become pregnant, including such factors as design and ready availability of contraceptives, personnel and structure of the health care system, sex education programs in the schools, and family and social environment (Klerman, 1982).

Prenatal Care   Variables independently identified as having potential for placing the developing fetus at risk—youth, low socioeconomic status, few years of education, high number of prior pregnancies, smoking, and drinking—often coexist in a particular family and may coincide with delay in seeking prenatal care. Little is known of interactions among these factors, and this further confounds studies of cause-effect relationships. But several indicators suggest the effectiveness of contact with the health care system during pregnancy (Richmond and Filner, 1979; Parron and Eisenberg, 1982). Research on the precise role of such care in reducing risk, the relative effectiveness of different types of services (private physicians, clinics, home visits), and research on characteristics of the health care system that facilitate or deter decisions to seek care are relevant. In addition, improved techniques for estimating fetal weight might be of great value. Mortality of low birth weight infants appears to be much lower when the obstetrician has correctly assessed fetal weight before birth. When predictions are correct, the mortality rate is 20 percent, compared with 50 percent mortality among very low birth weight infants for whom weight estimates did not agree with actual birth weights (Rosen, 1982).

Prevention of Developmental Difficulties

Research to prevent developmental difficulties focuses on medical procedures during birth and the neonatal period, as well as on parental practices and other environmental influences once the infant is home. It is the interaction of the developmental potential of the infant with the characteristics of the care-taking environment that leads to greater or lesser intellectual competence at a later age (Eisenberg, 1977).

Neurobehavioral Tests Adequate predictive neurobehavioral tests of infants are not available. Until such tests are developed and shown to correlate with infant outcome, long-term follow-up studies of infants will be needed to assess new interventions for premature labor or care of low birth weight or preterm infants. Childhood differs from later developmental stages in that rapid changes are taking place in physical and mental processes. Interventions determined to be effective by early measures, for instance, in the first year of life, often correlate poorly with assessments later in childhood. It may be more realistic to target assessment to the next developmental stage, rather than to a more long-term outcome.

Parent-Child Interactions A supportive environment can protect low birth weight and preterm infants from further developmental difficulties (Eisenberg, 1982). Recent studies indicate that premature infants exhibit interactional difficulties during the first year. For example, they may be difficult to arouse and keep alert. In addition, mothers of ill neonates touch, vocalize to, smile at, and look at their child less often than do mothers of healthy infants. These differences usually disappear gradually as the infant recovers, but mothers' behaviors seem to correlate more highly with their perception of the infants' health than with the actual state of health (Minde, 1982). Adolescent mothers also differ from older ones in appearing less responsive and exhibiting less attachment behavior (Klerman, 1982). "Successful" adolescent mothers usually have supportive families who help in baby care; these young mothers also usually have effective short-term goals and realistic plans for their futures (Welcher, 1982).

Interactions between low birth weight infants and caretakers (physicians, nurses, parents) are complex, depending on a number of biological, psychological, and social variables. Relationships depend on long-term factors and cumulative interpersonal experiences. These processes must be understood more thoroughly before developmental problems of low birth weight infants can be fully elucidated. Psychosocial studies of parental perceptions are needed to help health professionals learn how best to communicate a child's health status and needs. Knowledge about family interactions and supports also is needed for designing effective treatment and prevention programs. Related research would identify environments and arrangements in families, schools, work places, and communities that are supportive of breastfeeding. Breastfeeding promotes attachment, provides some protection against infection by transmission of maternal antibodies, and helps ensure adequate nutrition (MacFarlane, 1977; Jelliffe and Jelliffe, 1981).

Clinical Research

During the last 20 years, researchers and clinicians have learned a great deal about physical and neurological maturation, about the unfolding subtleties of interpersonal patterns between infants and caretakers, and about affective and cognitive development and related coping strategies. Even so, a comprehensive assessment that simultaneously attends to the multiple clinically relevant areas of human functioning remains a challenge both to professionals in the clinic and to researchers in the laboratory (Greenspan, 1981, 1982).

Sound intervention programs have shown the interdependence of research and practice, of evaluation and treatment, and of assessment and counseling in the service of children in the first months of life. In the first 18 months, indicators of healthy and deviant development are always expressed and observed in the context of the infant's care by an adult, usually a parent.

Keeping in mind some of the unique characteristics of infants is of particular importance, because failure to do so results in a lack of understanding. The following principles have emerged from clinically oriented infant research (Parron and Eisenberg, 1982):

1. Young children are likely to react to adversity with global responses and symptoms rather than with differentiated ones. This is a reflection of the closeness of the psychic and somatic systems in infancy.

2. A situation of adversity of the young child's experience such as maternal depression or a chaotic environment with few positive experiences but numerous negative ones is highly likely to disturb more than one area of development. It also causes trouble in the organization and integration of those functions. Older children who have had reasonably good care and developed well up to the point of a traumatic event or difficult situation will react, of course; but, because of greater maturation, differentiation, and integration of functions, they will have more differentiated or structured reactions, including a more extensive repertoire of defenses and coping abilities.

3. Some infants are more vulnerable than others to psychosocial stress;

some not so vulnerable biologically may, nonetheless, be at risk for disorders of development because of adverse experiences. When there is both biological vulnerability and an adverse psychosocial environment, conditions that produce disturbance in the child are maximized. Prematurity, traumatic birth, primary mental subnormality, and sensory defects such as blindness or deafness are a few of the sources of biological vulnerability. When combined with problems in the nurturing environment, they present especially difficult problems for the developmental process, often leading to disruptions.

Additional research on infants and families with multiple sources of high risk for developmental dysfunction is likely to enhance both basic understanding and provision of care.

Mental Retardation

Over six million persons in the United States are mentally retarded. Underlying causes are diverse and include genetic defects, abnormalities in fetal development, birth injuries, infections, and early environmental experiences. The degree of mental handicap can vary considerably, from profound to mild mental impairment; mild forms may not be apparent until school age (Goldstein et al., 1980).

Genetic Influences

Chromosomal abnormalities such as the extra chromosome of Down's syndrome, and metabolic defects caused by genetic variants of essential enzymes, as in the case of phenylketonuria, may occur as a new event or may be inherited from earlier generations. The overall incidence of single-gene disorders is about 10 per 1,000 births, and the incidence of chromosomal aberrations is about 6 to 7 per 1,000 births. However, not all such disorders lead to mental retardation (Ash et al., 1977).

Genetic counseling and testing for carriers can identify high-risk couples who may then be provided with the maximum available information on which to base reproductive decisions. The current prevention arsenal consists mainly of prevention of conception or testing of the fetus by procedures such as amniocentesis or serial sonography in high-risk pregnancies, with selective termination of pregnancy if serious genetic or other birth defects are found. Faster and less invasive procedures that may be applied after only a short gestation period have been developed for some hemoglobin abnormalities (Kan and Dozy, 1978; Orkin et al., 1978; Williamson et al.,

1981), but much research still is needed to apply such tests to the genetic causes of mental retardation.

Until recently, most Down's syndrome infants were born to women over the age of 35, who are at greater risk of having such an infant than are younger women, but now at least two thirds of Down's syndrome infants are born to younger women (Richmond and Filner, 1979). Furthermore, in about one quarter of the cases, the extra chromosome in Down's syndrome was contributed by the father, not by the mother (Magenis et al., 1977).

Much research is needed to understand the role of hereditary factors and their interaction with other influences, such as alcohol and drug abuse, smoking, medications, radiation, and exposure to other chemical and physical agents in the environment, in the etiology of birth defects. Questions of dose and susceptible periods are of special importance (Richmond and Filner, 1979). Research toward more effective education of health professionals about genetic services also is needed (National Academy of Sciences, 1975).

Environmental Influences

Maternal malnutrition and substances ingested during pregnancy are examples of environmental factors identified as significant to the etiology of mental retardation, as are radiation and maternal infections during pregnancy (Goldstein et al., 1980). Areas alluded to earlier, including motivation to use the health care system, as for rubella vaccination, and substance use and abuse, also are pertinent to preventing mental retardation.

After birth, the environment, especially the social environment, can profoundly affect the degree of disability of a retarded child. Expectancy of failure, reduced motivation and aspirations, lack of stimulation, and ineffectiveness in controlling experiences may lead children to appear more retarded than their "biological" potential would suggest (Goldstein et al., 1980).

The Carolina Abecedarian Project provides medical and nutritional aid to families, promotes educational efforts in schools, and provides early intensive day-care experience (as early as six weeks of age for high-risk children). Developmental lags, especially in language, appear to be reduced by such programs (Heber and Garber, 1975; Ramey and Campbell, 1977). In a fashion yet to be understood, appropriate stimulation appears to protect against the deleterious effects of undernutrition on mental development (Eisenberg, 1982). The possibilities and constraints imposed by developmental stages on biobehavioral interactions merit considerable further study.

Learning Disorders and Behavior Disorders

A child's behavior varies in different situations, which means that parents and teachers may experience different problems with the same child. Also, parents vary in their tolerance of particular behaviors. As children mature, behavior patterns change rapidly, and such variation poses additional difficulties in interpreting surveys of childhood problems (Goldstein et al., 1980).

As many as 3 percent of American school children may be hampered academically and interpersonally by a syndrome known as attention deficit disorder with hyperactivity (American Psychiatric Association, 1980). These children show a short attention span, distractability, impulsiveness, and erratic behavior and performance in tasks. A wide range of behaviors is covered, and many different etiologies have been reported, such as brain damage (in about 10 percent of cases) (Stewart and Olds, 1973), genetic influences (Safer, 1973), environmental lead (Baloh et al., 1975), and food additives (Feingold, 1975). Further multidisciplinary study is needed to confirm and explore the role of each of these possible etiological agents and how they may interact with psychosocial influences in family and school environments.

In addition, long-term study of the natural history of this disorder might suggest new and more effective forms of intervention. There is a decrease in gross motor hyperactivity in adolescence, but academic problems and impairment in concentration often persist (Kinsbourne and Caplan, 1979). Furthermore, hyperactive children who were judged to have made favorable progress were later found to be lonely and unpopular (Minde et al., 1971). Study of the determinants of full or partial remission may eventually lead to the ability to prevent or ameliorate hyperactivity in its earliest stages.

Therapy typically involves stimulant medication and some form of behavior management or psychotherapy (Allyon et al., 1975; Baker, 1976; Granbard et al., 1977). Studies of the best application of these therapies, either separately or in combination, are needed.

Behaviors are classified as disorders when they persist beyond a certain age or beyond a certain intensity. Many cases of tics, bed wetting, sleep disorders, and stuttering remit spontaneously. For example, about 80 percent of children who stutter attain normal speech by their teens (Goldstein et al., 1980). Some children are extremely fearful, and objects of fear may change as the child matures (Jersild, 1968). School phobia may relate to separation anxiety, academic failure, and peer relationships (Eisenberg, 1958; Goldstein et al., 1980). Childhood depression may result from death of a parent, failure at school, physical abuse, parental divorce, or lengthy illness;

but there is considerable variation in individual susceptibility among children.

Fewer than one child in a thousand exhibits psychotic behavior (Goldstein et al., 1980). Infantile autism, usually starting before age two and one-half, and childhood schizophrenia, with an onset from age 5 to 12, are two major disorders (Kolvin, 1971; Werry, 1979). Autism is thought to derive from a combination of biological influences and parental responses to these effects in the child (Goldstein et al., 1980). There is partial abatement of symptoms by age 5 to 6, but the prognosis is favorable only in cases in which effective speech ability is developed by age 5 (Eisenberg, 1956).

Research to understand further the etiology, determinants of prognosis, and response to various interventions for the wide range of learning and behavior disorders is needed. High priority should be given to studies of family dynamics. Developmental studies of children should reveal functional and causal aspects of behavior, as well as elucidating maturational processes. Animal models also can provide insights into cognitive and social development that relate to childhood stages of development. Current research into computer programs that mimic cognitive processes in problem-solving behaviors offers considerable promise for teaching children with learning and language difficulties (Estes et al., 1981). Finally, development of measures to assess the integration of an individual in a social milieu and the variation of a total environment over time—such as the Family Functioning Indices and Social Network Indices—holds great promise (Haggerty et al., 1975; Falkner, 1980; Berkman, 1981).

Conclusions

Early life provides a wealth of opportunities to make useful preventive interventions, many of which may have lifelong benefits. Such interventions can take several forms. Some, such as neonatal metabolic screens, are designed to identify problems before they do permanent damage. Others, including immunizations, help to forestall some future risk. Still others, for example, good dental hygiene, can provide the child with a more general orientation toward prevention. All are important and require active collaboration between parents and the health professions.

Research efforts are needed in all of these types of prevention. They range from the development of new techniques for earlier, safer, and more reliable methods of detecting abnormalities to exploration of ways to encourage people to seek preventive interventions for their children and to help them teach their children to engage in health-promoting activities. Also needed is research into specific behavioral and mental problems of childhood, including mental retardation and clinically apparent behavior disorders. Progress in this area holds promise of yielding substantial gains, both in decreasing the burden of illness and in increasing the quality of life.

References

Allyon, T., Layman, D., and Kandel, H. J. A behavioral-educational alternative to drug control of hyperactive children. *J. Appl. Behav. Anal.* 8:137–146, 1975.

American Psychiatric Association *Diagnostic and Statistical Manual of Mental Disorders, 3rd Ed.* Washington, D.C.: American Psychiatric Association, 1980.

Ash, P., Vannart, J., and Carter, C. O. The incidence of hereditary disease in man. *Lancet* 1:849–850, 1977.

Baker, B. L. Parent involvement in programming for developmentally disabled children. IN: *Communication Assessment and Intervention Strategies* (Lloyd, L. L., ed.) Baltimore: University Park Press, 1976, pp. 691–773.

Baloh, R., Sturm, R., Green, B., and Gleser, G. Neuropsychological effects of asymptomatic increased lead absorption: A controlled study. *Arch. Neuro.* 32:326–330, 1975.

Berkman, L. F. Physical health and the social environment: A social epidemiological perspective. IN: *The Relevance of Social Science for Medicine* (Eisenberg, L., and Kleinman, A., eds.) Boston: D. Reidel, 1981, pp. 51–76.

Eisenberg, L. The autistic child in adolescence. *Am. J. Psych.* 112:607–612, 1956.

Eisenberg, L. School phobia: A study in the communication of anxiety. *Am. J. Psychiatry* 114:712–718, 1958.

Eisenberg, L. Development as a unifying concept in psychiatry *Brit. J. Psychiatry* 131:225–237, 1977.

Eisenberg, L. Overview. IN: *Infants at Risk for Developmental Dysfunction* (Parron, D. L., and Eisenberg, L., eds.) Washington, D.C.: National Academy Press, 1982, pp. 3–12.

Estes, W. K., Shiffrin, R. M., Simon, H. A., and Smith, E. E. The science of cognition. IN: *Outlook for Science and Technology: The Next Five Years* San Francisco: Freeman, 1981, pp. 165–200.

Falkner, F. Introduction. IN: *Prevention in Childhood of Health Problems in Adult Life* (Falkner, F., ed.) Geneva: World Health Organization, 1980, pp. 1–7.

Feingold, B. *Why Your Child is Hyperactive* New York: Random House, 1975.

Fitzhardinge, P. Follow-up studies on the low birth weight infant *Clin. Perinat.* 3:503–516, 1976.

Goldstein, M. J., Baker, B. L., and Jamison, K. R. *Abnormal Psychology: Experiences, Origins and Interventions* Boston: Little, Brown, 1980.

Granbard, P. S., Rosenberg, H., and Miller, M. B. Student applications of behavior modification to teachers and environment or ecological approaches to social deviancy. IN: *Classroom Management: The Successful Use of Behavior Modification, 2nd Ed.* (O'Leary, K. D., and O'Leary, S. G., eds.) New York: Pergamon Press, 1977, pp. 235–249.

Greenspan, S. I. *Psychopathology and Adaptation in Infancy and Early Childhood: Principles of Clinical Diagnosis and Preventive Intervention. Clinical Infant Reports, Number 1* New York: International Universities Press, 1981.

Greenspan, S. I. Infant morbidity in multi-risk factor families. *Publ. Health Reports* 97:16–23, 1982.

Haggerty, R. J., Roghmann, K. J., and Pless, I. B. *Child Health and the Community* New York: John Wiley and Sons, 1975.

Heber, R., and Garber, H. The Milwaukee project: A study of the use of family intervention to prevent cultural-familial mental retardation. IN: *Exceptional Infant, Vol. 3: Assessment and Intervention* New York: Brunner/Mazel, 1975.

Institute of Medicine *Alcoholism, Alcohol Abuse, and Related Problems: Opportunities for Research* Washington, D.C.: National Academy Press, 1979.

Institute of Medicine *Smoking and Behavior. Interim Report No. 1, Health and Behavior: A Research Agenda* Washington, D.C.: National Academy of Sciences, 1980.

Institute of Medicine *Marijuana and Health* Washington, D.C.: National Academy Press, 1982.

Jelliffe, D. B., and Jelliffe, E. F. P. Recent trends in infant feeding (in the U.S.A.) *Annu. Rev. Publ. Health* 2:145–158, 1981.

Jersild, A. T. *Child Psychology, 6th Ed.* Englewood Cliffs, N.J.: Prentice-Hall, 1968.

Kan, Y. W., and Dozy, A. M. Antenatal diagnosis of sickle-cell anemia by DNA analysis of amniotic fluid cells. *Lancet* 2:910–911, 1978.

Kinsbourne, M., and Caplan, P. J. *Children's Learning and Attention Problems* Boston: Little, Brown, 1979.

Klerman, L. Teenage parents: A brief review of research. IN: *Infants at Risk for Developmental Dysfunction* (Parron, D. L., and Eisenberg, L., eds.) Washington, D.C.: National Academy Press, 1982, pp. 125–132.

Kolvin, I. Psychosis in childhood—A comparative study. IN: *Infantile Autism: Concepts, Characteristics and Treatment* (Rutter, M., ed.) Edinburgh: Churchill and Livingstone, 1971.

MacFarlane, A. The psychology of childbirth. IN: *The Developing Child Series* (Bruner, J., Cole, M., and Lloyd, B., eds.) Cambridge, Mass.: Harvard University Press, 1977.

Magenis, R. E., Overton, K. M., Chamberlin, J., Brady, T., and Lovrien, E. Parental origin of the extra chromosome in Down's syndrome. *Hum. Genet.* 37:7–16, 1977.

Minde, K. Lowbirth weight infants: A psychosocial perspective. IN: *Infants at Risk for Developmental Dysfunction* (Parron, D. L., and Eisenberg, L., eds.) Washington, D.C.: National Academy Press, 1982, pp. 85–92.

Minde, K., Lewin, D., Weiss, G., Laviqueur, H., Douglas, V., and Sykes, E. The hyperactive child in elementary school: A five-year controlled follow-up. *Except. Child.* 38:215–221, 1971.

National Academy of Sciences, National Research Council, Assembly of Life Sciences *Genetic Screening: A Study of the Knowledge and Attitudes of Physicians* Washington, D.C.: National Academy of Sciences, 1975.

Orkin, S. H., Alter, B. P., Altay, C., Mahoney, N. J., Lazarus, H., Hobbins, J. C., and Nathan, D. G. Application of endonuclease mapping to the analysis and prenatal diagnosis of thalassemias caused by globin-gene deletion *N. Engl. J. Med.* 299:166–172, 1978.

Parron, D. L., and Eisenberg, L. (Eds.) *Infants at Risk for Developmental Dysfunction. Interim Report No. 4, Health and Behavior: A Research Agenda* Washington, D.C.: National Academy Press, 1982.

President's Commission on Mental Health *Report to the President, Vol. 1* Washington, D.C.: U.S. Government Printing Office, 1978.

Ramey, C. T., and Campbell, F. A. Prevention of developmental retardation in high risk children. IN: *Research to Practice in Mental Retardation, Vol. 1* (Mittler, P., ed.) Baltimore: University Park Press, 1977, pp. 157–164.

Richmond, J., and Filner, B. Infant and child health: Needs and strategies. IN: *Healthy People. The Surgeon General's Report on Health Promotion and Disease Prevention: Background Papers* (U.S. Department of Health, Education, and Welfare, Public Health Service) Washington, D.C.: U.S. Government Printing Office, 1979, DHEW Publ. No. 79–55071A, pp. 305–332.

Rosen, M. G. Low birth weight infants: A biological perspective. IN: *Infants at Risk for Developmental Dysfunction* (Parron, D. L., and Eisenberg, L., eds.) Washington, D.C.: National Academy Press, 1982, pp. 69–83.

Safer, D. J. Drugs for problem school children. *J. Sch. Health* 41:491–495, 1971.

Shapiro, S., Schlesinger, E. R., and Nesbitt, R. E. L. *Infant, Perinatal, Maternal, and Childhood Mortality in the United States* Cambridge, Mass.: Harvard University Press, 1968.

Solnit, A. J., and Provence, S. Vulnerability and risk in early childhood. IN: *The Handbook of Infant Development* (Osofsky, J., ed.) New York: Wiley Interscience, 1978.

Stewart, M. A., and Olds, S. W. *Raising a Hyperactive Child* New York: Harper and Row, 1973.

United States Department of Health, Education, and Welfare, Public Health Service, National Center for Health Statistics *Current Estimates from the Health Interview Survey: United States-1977. Vital and Health Statistics* Series 10, No. 126. Washington, D.C.: U.S. Government Printing Office, 1978a, DHEW Publ. No. (PHS) 78–1554.

United States Department of Health, Education, and Welfare, Public Health Service, National Center for Health Statistics *Characteristics of Births, United States, 1973–1975. Vital and Health Statistics* Series 21, No. 30. Washington, D.C.: U.S. Government Printing Office, 1978b, DHEW Publ. No. (PHS) 78–1908.

United States Department of Health, Education, and Welfare, Public Health Service, National Center for Health Statistics *Vital Statistics of the United States, 1977. Vol. 1* Washington, D.C.: U.S. Government Printing Office, 1979.

United States Department of Health and Human Services, Public Health Service *Health United States, 1980, with Prevention Profile* Washington, D.C.: U.S. Government Printing Office, 1980, DHHS Publ. No. (PHS) 81–1232.

United States Department of Health and Human Services, Public Health Service, Office of the Assistant Secretary for Health and the Surgeon General *Better Health for Our Children: A National Strategy. The Report of the Select Panel for the Promotion of Child Health. Vol. 1. Major Findings and Recommendations* Washington, D.C.: U.S. Government Printing Office, 1981a, DHHS (PHS) Publ. No. 79–55071.

United States Department of Health and Human Services, Public Health Service, Office of the Assistant Secretary for Health and Surgeon General *Better Health for Our Children: A National Strategy. The Report of the Select Panel for the Promotion of Child Health. Vol. 3. A Statistical Profile* Washington, D.C.: U.S. Government Printing Office, 1981b.

Welcher, D. W. Teenage parents: A psychosocial perspective. IN: *Infants at Risk for Developmental Dysfunction* (Parron, D. L., and Eisenberg, L., eds.) Washington, D.C.: National Academy Press, 1982, pp. 115–123.

Werry, J. S. Psychosomatic disorders, psychogenic symptoms and hospitalization. IN: *Psychopathological Disorders of Children, 2nd Ed.* (Quay, H. C., and Werry, J. S., eds.) New York: John Wiley and Sons, 1979, pp. 134–184.

Williamson, R., Eskdale, J., Coleman, D. V., et al. Direct gene analysis of chorionic villi: A possible technique for first-trimester antenatal diagnosis of haemoglobinopathies *Lancet* 2:1125–1127, 1981.

Zelnik, M., and Kantner, J. F. Contraceptive patterns and premarital pregnancy among women age 15–19 in 1976. *Fam. Plann. Perspect. 10*:135, 1978.

14

Prevention Efforts
in Adolescence

In recent years, increasing attention has been given to adolescence as a crucially important, developmentally complex, and lengthy period of life. Early adolescence, which can be roughly equated with ages 10 to 14, is a time of much physical, cognitive, and emotional change, accompanied by the often stressful shift from elementary school to junior high or middle school and concomitant entry into "teen culture." Later adolescence is a period of transition to adult autonomy and responsibilities. Young people move into the wider social and occupational world and gradually adopt fully adult behaviors in personal, family, and work roles.

Although adolescence is a life stage in which experimentation is developmentally appropriate and socially adaptive, it is also a time when young people typically try out types of behavior that are risky or may otherwise lead to unfortunate consequences. Some behaviors affect health immediately, as in contracting venereal disease, or in suffering severe accidents related to alcohol use. Others produce deleterious effects only later in life, for example, cancer and cardiovascular disease stemming from health-damaging habits such as high-calorie, high-fat dietary patterns, inadequate exercise, heavy smoking, or alcohol abuse (Brook and Ball, 1977; Neill et al., 1977). Long-term effects also include effects on life options such as the restrictions placed on a teenage mother who fails to finish high school and whose lifetime employment prospects are significantly diminished by early childbearing.

The adolescent period is the only one for which mortality rates are rising. The fact that the three leading causes of death among adolescents—accidents, suicide, and homicide—are behavior-related suggests that in this age group especially, the interaction of health and behavior is paramount (Kovar, 1978; U.S. Department of Health, Education, and Welfare, 1979a). It is essential to consider measures of behavior in adolescence that add to the more traditional indices of health status to provide a better picture of the health problems and needs of this population. This chapter presents data on selected behaviors that carry a high risk of adverse health effects in both the short and long term.

Cigarette Smoking

Cigarette smoking is the number one national target for disease prevention efforts (cf. Chapter 5). Unfortunately, it is still quite prevalent in the youth culture, although recent trends indicate that there is a tapering off in the proportion of adolescents smoking (U.S. Department of Health, Education, and Welfare, 1979b). In 1974, among 12- to 14-year-olds, 5 percent of females and 4 percent of males smoked, compared with 4 and 3 percent, respectively, in 1979. Figures for 15- to 16-year-olds were 20 percent of females and 18 percent of males in 1974 and 12 and 14 percent in 1979. For 17- to 18-year-olds, comparable figures were 26 and 31 percent in 1974 and 26 and 19 percent in 1979. Such statistics confirm the importance of adolescence—particularly early adolescence—in the formation of health-related behavior. Of special concern is the fact that, although adolescent females used to smoke less than their male counterparts, they are now as likely to be smokers as adolescent males. When the high prevalence of smoking in older teenage girls is considered along with the rates of pregnancy in this population, even greater concern may be raised because of the known risk of fetal harm due to maternal smoking (U.S. Department of Health and Human Services, 1980; also cf. Chapter 2).

Alcohol Use

Recent surveys report that young people of junior high school age drink alcohol to a far greater extent than was true a generation ago: a larger proportion of them drink, they begin to drink earlier, they drink larger quantities, and they report more frequent intoxication (Rachal et al., 1975; San Mateo County, 1975; Weschler and McFadden, 1976). The generational shift has been greater for adolescent girls than for adolescent boys. Although girls still drink less than boys, the percentage who drink and who report intoxication experiences has increased more rapidly for girls than for boys. Estimates for 1977 from the National Institute on Drug Abuse are that 31 percent of adolescents age 12–17 had had a drink within the past month. For those 16–17, the rate is 52 percent (Abelson et al., 1977). In the *Third Special Report to the U.S. Congress on Alcohol and Health*, the National Institute on Alcohol Abuse and Alcoholism (1978, pp. 23–24) stated:

Recently, a national survey of students grades 7 through 12 examined teenage drinking and problem drinking. Seventy-four percent of the teenagers were drinkers—79 percent of the boys and 70 percent of the girls. . . . [N]early 19 percent of the students were problem drinkers—23 percent of the boys and 15 percent of the girls. Drinking among college students has been rising steadily since 1936. Today's collegians drink more frequently and become intoxicated more often than today's high school students. Young people drink less regularly than older people, but tend to consume a larger amount on a drinking occasion. The risk of incurring negative consequences associated with the acute effects of alcohol are higher in late adolescence and early adulthood than at any other point in the lifespan.

Alcohol use, like tobacco consumption, has both short- and long-range effects on health. Alcohol initially may appear to be a stimulant, but it is actually a central nervous system depressant and anesthetic. The immediate consequences of use vary among individuals, but the consensus is strong that there are positive relationships between, for example, alcohol use and poor school performance and excessive driving accidents. Chronic use can produce a moderate degree of tolerance, so that larger doses must be taken to achieve the desired psychological effects. A comparable tolerance does not develop to psychomotor effects on coordination and reaction time that predispose to accidents. Deleterious pathological consequences of chronic alcohol use are diverse and affect the central nervous system, gastrointestinal tract (stomach, liver, and pancreas), heart, and skeletal muscles. In addition, secondary malnutrition or vitamin deficiency disease frequently develops (Institute of Medicine, 1980). The influences of alcohol consumption on health are further reviewed in Chapter 4.

Marijuana Use

The National Household Survey found that marijuana is the most commonly used psychoactive drug (Fishburne et. al., 1980). In 1979, 50 million people had tried marijuana at least once in their life: 7 million (31 percent) fell within the 12–17 age group; 21 million (68 percent) in the 18–25 age group, and 25 million (20 percent) in the 26 and over age group. Male users outnumbered females in all age groups.

The marked increase in marijuana use began in 1967 (Miller and Cisin, 1980), but recent trends may indicate a slowing. The proportion of high school seniors who had ever used marijuana leveled off at 60 percent for the years 1979 and 1980. This figure may, however, be an underestimate of actual use, because the survey only included high school seniors in school, thereby excluding dropouts and those showing high rates of absenteeism (Johnston et al., 1980). In 1980, marijuana was used daily by 9 percent of high school seniors, alcohol by 6 percent, and tobacco by 21 percent (Johnston et al., 1980). Although those figures indicate that daily use of marijuana exceeds daily use of alcohol, they also mark the first time since the late 1960s that the percentage of daily users of marijuana among high school seniors seems to have decreased—from 10 percent in 1979. Here again, however, studies of patterns of marijuana use in school dropouts and chronic absentees are much needed. They are a population in which drug use is extremely prevalent. Kandel (1975) found that 56 percent of absentees report using marijuana, compared with 38 percent of students attending class. Dropping out of school and chronic absenteeism have been shown to impair later chances of steady employment and to reduce markedly potential earning capacity.

Early experimentation with marijuana is correlated with the higher likelihood of using more serious drugs later (Johnston et al., 1980; Miller and Cisin, 1980; Kandel et al., 1981). Between 1975 and 1980, there was a significant increase in first use of marijuana at very early ages. Among high school seniors surveyed in 1980, 25 percent reported first use of marijuana in the eighth grade, 14 years or younger. The comparable figures for 1975 were 15 percent reporting first use in eighth grade (Johnston et al., 1980). Rittenhouse (1980) found that of the 18- to 25-year-olds surveyed in 1979–80 who used illicit drugs, 87 percent first tried marijuana or alcohol at age 13–14. There were 65 percent of marijuana users among high school seniors in 1980 who also used other illicit drugs, compared with 61 percent in 1979 (Johnston et al., 1980).

Drugs that are manufactured or sold illicitly often are contaminated, of uncertain potency, or misrepresented, leading to greater chances of medical emergencies (Nightingale et al., 1978). Dangerous as any illicit drugs may be of themselves, polydrug use (including use with alcohol) increases the physical hazard markedly.

It was formerly believed that marijuana users tapered off the habit in their mid-20s, but current prevalence rates indicate persistence into later adult life, as indicated by the increasing use of marijuana by people in their mid-30s (Cisin et al., 1978). Use by men 26 years and over has increased from 4 percent in 1977 to 9 percent in 1979. Especially noteworthy is the evidence that daily use persists longer into adult life than had been anticipated. In 1979, four years after graduation from high school, 51 percent of daily marijuana users from the senior class of 1975 were still smoking marijuana on a daily basis (Johnston, 1981). It is important to survey these older age groups and to monitor these trends, because of the possibility of cumulative long-term effects (Institute of Medicine, 1982).

Public concern over the acute and chronic effects on young persons of the use of marijuana has increased substantially now that usage is so entrenched and pervasive in the youth culture. Current evidence indicates that there are well-established acute effects on psychomotor function. Marijuana at concentrations corresponding to those attained in social use of the drug impairs responses to complex, integrated visual-motor tasks. These findings cause concern about driving and marijuana as well as performance of other complex man-machine tasks. Marijuana also impairs short-term memory. There is good evidence for bronchial irritation and lung pathology associated with marijuana smoking. Effects on other bodily systems have been suggested but not confirmed (Institute of Medicine, 1982).

Sexual Activity

In 1976, there were 12,000 births and 13,000 abortions to girls under 15 years of age. Among older teenage girls, there were 560,000 births and 3,000,000 abortions. In a national survey of 15- to 19-year-olds, one third of sexually active respondents had not used contraceptives the last time they engaged in sexual intercourse and 70 percent of conceptions were not intended. In 1977, 17 percent of births were to teenage girls, whose incidence of low birth weight infants was half again more than the national average (Richmond and Filner, 1979).

Adolescent Pregnancy and Childbirth

Especially at younger ages, adolescent pregnancy and childbirth pose physical, psychological, and socioeconomic risks to both the mother and baby. Physical risks to the mother include such complications as toxemia, premature birth, and problems during labor and delivery (Chez et al., 1976). Socioeconomic risks include interruption of the mother's education, lowered prospects for income and vocational attainment, and an increased probability of lifetime poverty and welfare dependence (Card and Wise, 1978; Moore et al., 1978). Infants of young adolescent mothers also are at medical risk, especially if mothers are regular smokers or users of alcohol or other drugs (Clarren and Smith, 1978).

Cognitive development in children of adolescent mothers may suffer. In addition to possible biological factors, inadequacies of caretaking by very young mothers may be important. Mothers in their 20s are more likely than adolescent mothers to be married and maintain more stable early environments for their infants. Adolescent mothers have been reported to differ from older ones in tending to be less responsive and sensitive to the needs of the child. They also tend to have more infants in quick succession than do older mothers, which may also place infants at risk for biological and behavioral difficulties (Welcher, 1982).

Children of adolescent mothers typically have more emotional and behavioral problems at all stages of development than do children of older mothers (cf. Chapter 13). Follow-up studies on adolescent mothers, however, reveal some promising responses to intervention efforts. At the conclusion of a demonstration project conducted by a team from Johns Hopkins, 80 percent of young mothers had returned to school or had become employed and also ranked average or above average in self-esteem. Successful mothers usually came from supportive families who helped in baby care, and these young mothers also had more realistic plans for their futures and had formulated effective short-term goals (Welcher, 1982).

Sexually Transmitted Diseases

Gonorrhea and other sexually transmitted diseases are another adverse consequence of sexual activity. By the mid-1970s, gonorrhea had reached epidemic proportions in the United States (Brown, 1979). However, recent data suggest that the rate has stabilized. Although reports of gonorrhea are relatively rare among young adolescents, adolescent males are more likely to report the disease than are females. Gonorrhea is difficult to diagnose and treat in women; as a result, it progresses to pelvic inflammatory disease in 17 percent of all women who contract it; pelvic inflammatory disease may result in sterility in 15 to 40 percent of women having a single episode, even if they obtain adequate treatment (Rendtorff and Curran, 1979).

Diet and Exercise

Fad diets and "fast foods" are popular with adolescents and may result in reduced caloric and nutrient intakes that are damaging to health. Data from the Health and Nutrition Examination Survey suggest that adolescents both below and above the poverty level had a mean dietary intake of calories and iron below the recommended daily allowance (U.S. Department of Health, Education, and Welfare, 1977). However, some adolescents consume too many calories, and approximately 10 percent of all adolescents are obese. An underweight adolescent also can be of concern, particularly if the food avoidance takes the form of anorexia nervosa; although relatively rare, this disorder can be potentially life threatening.

Data on adolescent exercise and physical fitness are of special concern.

One of six young people in the United States age 10–17 is weak or uncoordinated enough to be classified as physically underdeveloped by the standards of the President's Council on Physical Fitness and Sports (1977). A life pattern of inadequate exercise promises poor cardiopulmonary fitness and its consequences. Patterns of passive television viewing and shifts from active exercise to spectator sports activities are possible explanations. Also, many schools have reduced sports and physical education programs for budgetary reasons.

Schooling

Adolescence is a time for academic pursuits and challenges. School can be either a major resource or a problem area and is a source of stress and low self-esteem for many adolescents. Academic success is related in part to ability to concentrate and read. Rutter and Yule (1973) found that attributes strongly associated with very low reading attainment are poor concentration, restlessness, and impulsivity. Origins of these attributes are not well understood. Chronic physical illnesses not involving brain disorders are associated with an increased rate of reading difficulty (Rutter et al., 1970). Biological hazards related to childbirth and the tendency for these to be associated with socially disadvantaged rearing environments may also contribute to learning difficulties. Language stimulation and other experiences during early development contribute to communication skills. Parental attitude to learning and school also will influence the child's motivation to succeed in these areas (Rutter and Madge, 1976). Family size and birth order may also influence intellectual attainment, particularly those skills related to reading and verbal reasoning. In general, such abilities are best developed in first-born children rather than in those born later. These birth order effects are most marked for boys (Rutter et al., 1970).

Delinquency

Delinquency and antisocial behaviors often are associated with reading difficulties and educational failure (Rutter and Yule, 1973). Learning failure, regardless of cause, can lead to discouragement and loss of self-esteem, which in turn can contribute to delinquent behavior (Rutter and Madge, 1976).

Delinquency is more frequent in adolescents from homes where there is poor parental supervision, lax or overly stringent discipline, very little involvement by fathers in family activities, and little leisure time spent by the boys at home (West and Farrington, 1973). Boys whose mothers have low maternal aspirations for their sons' careers, especially if these boys have above-average scholastic achievements, appear to be delinquency prone. About 24 percent of such boys show delinquent behavior, compared with a rate of 5 percent in sons of mothers with high aspirations (West and Farrington, 1973).

Delinquents constitute a heterogeneous group in which multiple influences seem to be operating (Rutter and Madge, 1976; Jessor and Jessor, 1977). Some factors include genetic predisposition, chromosomal abnormalities, and early rearing in family environments characterized by high marital discord. Power et al. (1974) showed that even during adolescence, family discord predisposed to recidivism among delinquents; and Rutter (1971) found that deviant behaviors were much less frequent in children who moved to more harmonious family situations after a stormy early childhood. Unfortunately, children who start off in disadvantaged situations usually remain in these same poor circumstances throughout development (Rutter, 1974).

A Research Agenda

The need for more adolescent-oriented research on prevention and on behavioral issues pertinent to health and disease is now widely recognized. Examples of especially promising lines of research are:

• Identifying pediatric antecedents of adult disease, particularly chronic diseases such as cancer and cardiovascular disease. Although the link between numerous pediatric problems, conditions, and behaviors and ill health in later life is increasingly appreciated, its full dimensions and details remain to be defined.

• Designing better health education and strategies to promote health-enchancing behaviors in adolescents, and thereby lessen or prevent adult illnesses that may have their antecedents in habits begun in youth.

• Increasing the awareness of pregnant women, particularly pregnant teenagers, of the hazards posed to the developing fetus by various drugs, chemicals, radiation, and other environmental assaults, particularly in the first trimester of pregnancy.

• Finding ways to intervene in certain identifiable patterns of drug use and in movement from use of some illicit drugs to others.

The workshop on teenage pregnancy included in the Health and Behavior conference *Infants at Risk for Developmental Dysfunction* (Parron and Eisenberg, 1982) enumerated a large number of areas requiring sustained research. The group concluded:

Teenage pregnancy affects many parts of our society. . . . Seeking the right methods of prevention and intervention requires data on all aspects of adolescent pregnancy and its consequences. . . . These include the need for new data on unresearched topics such as middle-class adolescent mothers, the application of existing knowledge from other disciplines to specific problems arising from teenage pregnancy and motherhood, the evaluation of institutions such as schools and hospitals that play a strategic role in adolescent pregnancy, and the creation of new programs that will help lower the incidence of adolescent pregnancies or will provide ways of improving the lives of teenage mothers and their infants.

A number of recent reports have highlighted the urgent need for multidisciplinary research of great breadth in the behavioral areas outlined in this chapter (U.S. Department of Health, Education, and Welfare, 1979a; U.S. Department of Health and Human Services, 1981; Parron and Eisenberg, 1982). The perspective emerges that an appreciation of the significance of short-term and long-term links between health and behavior in adolescence is growing, but our need for additional information and insights remains substantial.

Conclusions

Adolescents constitute a group for which the death and physical illness rates are lower than for either infants or adults; the illnesses and life-threatening conditions of infancy and young childhood are largely past, and the chronic, disabling conditions of adulthood are not yet manifest. Nonetheless, adolescents experience their own unique burdens of anxiety, illness, and premature death, often from causes that are closely associated with development and maturation—both physical and psychosocial. Prominent adolescent health problems with a behavioral component include accidents, suicide, homicide, mental illness, and abuse of alcohol and other drugs. Other problems such as adolescent pregnancy—though not typically life threatening—are burdensome as much for their psychosocial impact as for their threat to physical health. Still other problems are of concern because of long-term risks; an example is tobacco use as a risk factor of cancer and cardiovascular disease in adulthood. The special nature of adolescent health issues makes the conjunction of health and behavior of the highest significance in this population.

Much remains to be learned about how best to foster behavior and attitudes in adolescents that will be associated with health and well-being in both their present life and more distant future. Much of the behavior that threatens adolescent health and life reflects major social change and is a central part of contemporary American culture: alcohol and other drug use, risky driving, interpersonal violence, smoking, and a new sexual code. Moreover, some of the health-damaging behaviors of adolescents serve developmental functions of exploratory and identity-seeking activities. It has also been suggested that specific health-compromising behaviors such as smoking and drug use may help some adolescents to cope with feelings of boredom, isolation, purposelessness, and poor self-image (Institute of Medicine, 1978).

The challenge of maintaining and improving adolescent health is especially complex. The task of health promotion and disease prevention for adolescents requires the contributions of a wide range of health professionals, educators, researchers, and, perhaps even more important, community, family, and peer groups. Particularly for this period of life, health concerns are enmeshed with the total environment of a young person and are not the exclusive concern or responsibility of any single profession or social sector.

In recent years, some promising programs have been organized based on community systems rather than on the health sector. These are efforts to meet the goals both of short-term and long-term disease prevention and health promotion (Institute of Medicine, 1978). Such community institutions and programs—none of them traditionally health-oriented—have a great potential for working creatively with adolescents to encourage enhanced self-esteem and positive health practices. However, in isolation, they are each able to accomplish only a limited amount. It is important that community-based prevention and treatment programs be closely linked with complementary school-based programs and with more traditional health care systems.

References

Abelson, H. I., Fishburne, P. M., and Cisin, I. *National Survey on Drug Abuse: 1977.* Washington, D.C.: National Institute on Drug Abuse, 1977.

Brook, C. G. D., and Ball, K. P. Prevention of coronary heart disease starts in childhood. Report of a symposium. *Arch. Dis. Child.* 52:904–906, 1977.

Brown, S. S. The health needs of adolescents. IN: *Healthy People. The Surgeon General's Report on Health Promotion and Disease Prevention: Background Papers* (U.S. Department of Health, Education, and Welfare, Public Health Service) Washington, D.C.: U.S. Government Printing Office, 1979, pp. 333–364.

Card, J. J., and Wise, L. L. Teenage mothers and teenage fathers: The impact of early childbearing on the parents' personal and professional lives. *Fam. Plann. Perspect.* 10:199–205, 1978.

Chez, R. A., Haire, D., Quilligan, E. J., and Wingate, M. G. High risk pregnancies: Obstetrical and perinatal factors. IN: *Prevention of Embryonic, Fetal and Perinatal Disease* (Brent, R. L., and Harris, M. I., eds.) Bethesda, Md.: National Institutes of Health, 1976, DHEW Publ. No. (NIH) 76–853.

Cisin, I., Miller, J. D., and Harrell, A. *Highlights from the National Survey on Drug Abuse, 1977* Washington, D.C.: U.S. Government Printing Office, 1978.

Clarren, S. K., and Smith, D. W. The fetal alcohol syndrome. *N. Engl. J. Med.* 298:1063–1067, 1978.

Fishburne, P. M., Abelson, H. I., and Cisin, I. *National Survey on Drug Abuse: Main Findings, 1979.* Washington, D.C.: U.S. Government Printing Office, 1980, DHHS Publ. No. (ADM) 80–976.

Institute of Medicine *Adolescent Behavior and Health: A Conference Summary* Washington, D.C.: National Academy of Sciences, 1978.

Institute of Medicine *Marijuana and Health* Washington, D.C.: National Academy Press, 1982.

Jessor, R., and Jessor, S. L. *Problem Behavior and Psychosocial Development* New York: Academic Press, 1977.

Johnston, L. D. Frequent marijuana use. Paper presented at conference on Treating the Marijuana Dependent Person, sponsored by American Council on Marijuana and Other Psychoactive Drugs, Bethesda, Md., May 4, 1981.

Johnston, L. D., Bachman, J. G., and O'Malley, P. M. *Highlights from Student Drug Use in America, 1975–1980* Washington, D.C.: U.S. Government Printing Office, 1980, DHHS Publ. No. (ADM) 81–1066.

Kandel, D. B. Reaching the hard-to-reach: Illicit drug use among high school absentees. *Addict. Dis.* 1:465–480, 1975.

Kandel, D. B., Adler, I., and Sudit, M. The epidemiology of adolescent drug use in France and Israel. *Am. J. Publ. Health* 71:256–265, 1981.

Kovar, M. G. Adolescent health status and health-related behavior. IN: *Adolescent Behavior and Health: A Conference Summary* Washington, D.C.: National Academy of Sciences, 1978.

Miller, J. D., and Cisin, I. H. *Highlights from the National Survey on Drug Abuse: 1979* Washington, D.C.: U.S. Government Printing Office, 1980, DHHS Publ. No. (ADM) 80–1032.

Moore, K., Waite, L. J., Caldwell, S. B., and Hofferth, S. *The Consequences of Age at First Childbirth: Educational Attainment* Washington, D.C.: The Urban Institute, 1978.

National Institute on Alcohol Abuse and Alcoholism *Third Special Report to the U.S. Congress on Alcohol and Health* Washington, D.C.: U.S. Government Printing Office, 1978.

Neill, C. A., Ose, I., and Kwiterovich, P. O., Jr. Hyperlipidemia: Clinical clues in the first two decades of life. *Johns Hopkins Med. J.* 140:171–176, 1977.

Nightingale, E. O., Cureton, M., Kalmar, V., Trudeau, M. *Perspectives on Health Promotion and Disease Prevention in the United States* Washington, D.C.: National Academy of Sciences, 1978.

Parron, D. L., and Eisenberg, L. (Eds.) *Infants at Risk for Developmental Dysfunction. Interim Report No. 4, Health and Behavior: A Research Agenda* Washington, D.C.: National Academy Press, 1982.

Power, M. J., Ash, P. M., Schoenberg, E., and Sorey, E. C. Delinquency and the family. *Brit. J. Soc. Work* 4:13–38, 1974.

President's Council on Physical Fitness and Sports *The Physically Underdeveloped Child* Washington, D.C.: U.S. Government Printing Office, 1977, p. 1.

Rachal, J. V., Williams, J. R., Brehm, M. L., et al. *A National Study of Adolescent Drinking Behavior, Attitudes and Correlates.* Springfield, Va.: National Technical Information Service, 1975, National Institute on Alcoholism and Alcohol Abuse Publ. No. PB–246–002.

Rendtorff, R. C., and Curran, J. W. Memphis gonorrhea complication study—A progress report. *J. AVDA* 2, 1979.

Richmond, J., and Filner, B. Infant and child health: Needs and strategies. IN:

Healthy People. The Surgeon General's Report on Health Promotion and Disease Prevention: Background Papers (U.S. Department of Health, Education, and Welfare, Public Health Service) Washington, D.C.: U.S. Government Printing Office, 1979, pp. 305–332.

Rittenhouse, J. D. Learning drug use: From "legal" substance to marijuana and beyond. Paper presented at the American Psychological Association Annual Convention, Montreal, Canada, September 1980.

Rutter, M. Parent-child separation: Psychological effects on children. *J. Child. Psychol. Psychiatry* 12:233–260, 1971.

Rutter, M. Epidemiological strategies and psychiatric concepts in research on the vulnerable child. IN: *The Child in His Family: Children at Psychiatric Risk* (Anthony, E. J., and Koupernik, C., eds.) New York: John Wiley and Sons, 1974.

Rutter, M., and Madge, N. *Cycles of Disadvantage* London: Heinemann, 1976.

Rutter, M., and Yule, W. Specific reading retardation. IN: *The First Review of Special Education* (Mann, L., and Sabatino, D., eds.) Philadelphia: Butterwood Farms, 1973.

Rutter, H., Tizard, J., and Whitmore, K. (Eds.) *Education, Health and Behavior* London: Longmans, 1970.

San Mateo County, California Department of Public Health and Welfare *Student Drug Use Surveys, 1968–1975* San Mateo, Calif., 1975.

United States Department of Health, Education, and Welfare, Public Health Service, Health Resources Administration, National Center for Health Statistics *Advance Data*, No. 6. Hyattsville, Md., 1977.

United States Department of Health, Education, and Welfare, Public Health Service *Healthy People. The Surgeon General's Report on Health Promotion and Disease* Washington, D.C.: U.S. Government Printing Office, 1979a, DHEW (PHS) Publ. No. 79–55071, pp. 43–52.

United States Department of Health, Education, and Welfare, Public Health Service, Office of the Assistant Secretary for Health, Office on Smoking and Health *Patterns and Prevalence of Teenage Cigarette Smoking* Washington, D.C.: U.S. Government Printing Office, 1979b.

United States Department of Health and Human Services, Office of the Assistant Secretary for Health and the Surgeon General, Office on Smoking and Health *Health Consequences of Smoking for Women* Washington, D.C.: U.S. Government Printing Office, 1980, pp. 235–239.

United States Department of Health and Human Services, Office of the Assistant Secretary for Health and the Surgeon General *Better Health for Our Children: A National Strategy. The Report of the Select Panel for the Promotion of Child Health*, *Vol. I* Washington, D.C.: U.S. Government Printing Office, 1981, DHHS (PHS) Publ. No. 79–55071, pp. 116–127.

Wechsler, H., and McFadden, M. Sex differences in adolescent alcohol and drug use: A disappearing phenomenon. *J. Stud. Alcohol* 37:1291–1301, 1976.

Welcher, D. W. The effect of early childbearing on the psychosocial development of adolescent parents. IN: *Infants at Risk for Developmental Dysfunction* (Parron, D. L., and Eisenberg, L., eds.) Washington, D.C.: National Academy Press, 1982.

West, D. J., and Farrington, D. P. *Who Becomes Delinquent?* London: Heinemann, 1973.

15

Prevention Efforts in Adult Life: Cardiovascular Risk Factors

For most of the diseases considered in this volume, optimal interventions involve preventing or altering certain behaviors such as smoking or dietary habits. Common experience has taught that many of these behaviors are not readily changed. Thus, some physicians, scientists, and public administrators are justified in asking if there is any evidence that it is possible to change widespread behavioral patterns in ways that affect the public health. While a brief survey of such evidence has been presented in Chapter 2, "The Contribution of Behavior to the Burden of Illness," it may be useful to review one particular set of programs in more detail, because they reflect both the ingenuity required to do good research in large-scale prevention efforts and because they provide some of the strongest evidence that such interventions can produce meaningful, long-lasting changes in behavior.

During the past 30 years, epidemiological studies have shown that certain objective measures are useful indicators of people likely to develop coronary heart disease (Levy, 1981; Winkelstein and Marmot, 1981). These measures are called "risk factors," because people who have them are at greater risk of getting heart disease. Major known risk factors for coronary heart disease include high blood pressure (hypertension), cigarette smoking, obesity, high blood levels of cholesterol (hypercholesterolemia), and lack of exercise. As discussed in Chapter 7, "Cardiovascular Disease and Behavior," certain psychosocial factors also are risk factors. Probably the best known of these is "Type A behavior," which refers to a cluster of behavioral responses, including an unusually forceful and constant sense of time urgency, strong competitiveness, and intense work orientation.

Identification of risk factors for coronary heart disease was a major advance in understanding cardiovascular disease. However, the epidemiological studies that identified risk factors could not indicate their role in the process. For example, does smoking somehow damage the heart or blood vessels and thereby promote cardiovascular disease? Or do people who are prone to develop heart disease also have a tendency to be smokers? Similarly, is hypertension a cause of heart disease, or does it reflect an early stage of the disease process? The answers to such questions are crucial. If risk factors are involved in causing the disease, then it should be possible to reduce the chances of getting it by removing the risk factors; if they are the result of the disease, then prevention efforts would have to be directed elsewhere.

This chapter discusses some of the research that examines the effects on cardiovascular disease rates of altering known risk factors. Two types of evidence are considered. First, over the past 20 years, there have been major changes in public attitudes about eating habits, cigarette smoking, and exercise. How has the incidence of coronary heart disease changed over this same period? Such correlational data cannot prove that there is a causal association between the changes in habits and changes in disease rates. Unknown factors that affect both may be involved. However, it can suggest linkages between certain behaviors and disease. Second, several large-scale projects examined large groups of people over time to determine what health effects result from changing risk factors in a particular population. Both suggest that people can stop unhealthy behaviors and that, by doing so, they can decrease their likelihood of developing cardiovascular disease.

Effects of Lifestyle Changes That Reduce Risk Factors

Since the early 1960s, people in the United States have been hearing about dangers of hypertension, hypercholesterolemia, obesity, and cigarette smoking. The connection of these factors with heart disease has been taught in schools and publicized widely by such organizations as the American Heart Association. The 1964 statement of the Surgeon General on smoking and health (U.S. Department of Health, Education, and Welfare, 1964) signaled the beginning of a long and continuing effort by many organizations to discourage smoking. The federal government also has taken a strong role in supporting efforts to identify and treat individuals who have hypertension (National Heart, Lung, and Blood Institute, 1973). This government interest in promoting health has continued, as reflected in the recent publication *Healthy People: A Report on Health Promotion and Disease Prevention*, which provided a comprehensive survey of existing challenges to the health of people in the United States at each stage of life (U.S. Department of Health, Education, and Welfare, 1979b). Thus, information on risk factors has been available to the public from a variety of sources. It seems reasonable to ask whether any changes in lifestyle have occurred over this time and, if so, whether there has been any accompanying change in rates of cardiovascular disease. From a recent review by Stamler (1981), the answer to both of those questions appears to be yes.

Dietary Habits

Since 1950, there have been major changes in the kinds of foods that people routinely eat, much of it in keeping with recommendations to decrease cholesterol and fat intake. Egg yolks are the single largest source of dietary cholesterol; egg consumption has dropped 30 percent (Stamler, 1978). A 30 percent drop also has occurred in consumption of milk fats, with much less of a decline in nonfat and low-fat dairy products. During that same period, per capita consumption of lard has decreased by 80 percent and of butter by 55 percent (Page and Friend, 1978). In contrast, use of margarines and vegetable oils that are low in saturated fats and high in unsaturated fats has increased markedly. These trends have been offset somewhat by increased consumption of meat, especially beef, which is high in saturated fat and cholesterol. However, the overall trend has been a substantial decrease in the proportion of caloric intake that is consumed as fat (Rizek and Jackson, 1980).

These trends have been accompanied by declines in average serum cholesterol levels in the population. Current cholesterol concentrations average about 7 percent lower than those measured in the 1950s (Levy, 1979). The decrease is more marked among the more educated than among the less educated.

Cigarette Smoking

Smoking continues to be a major public health problem (cf. Chapter 5). Most of the public is now aware of the dangers of cigarette smoking; attitudes toward smokers have changed greatly since the first Surgeon General's report was published in 1964. Public efforts to discourage smoking have included warning labels on all cigarette packages and advertisements and a ban on television advertising. The exact impact of these interventions is not completely clear. For example, the ban of television advertising also resulted in loss of free public service advertisements against smoking.

Although the exact causes remain to be determined, the prevalence of smoking in the general population peaked in the early 1950s and has continued to decline since then. Between 1965 and 1978, the percentage of smokers dropped from 42 percent to 33 percent (U.S. Department of Health, Education, and Welfare, 1979a). The decline was greater for men than for women. Smoking among adolescents has declined much less than has adult smoking. Again, more educated segments of the population have lower rates of this health-damaging behavior than do less educated ones; the greatest decline occurred among physicians.

High Blood Pressure Control

In the 1960s and 1970s, it became clear that millions of people in the United States had undetected hypertension. The Veterans Administration helped lead the way in providing careful large-scale studies that demonstrated that control of hypertension with appropriate medications could reduce morbidity and mortality (Veterans Administration Cooperative Study Group, 1972). This led to a federal initiative in 1973 called the National High Blood Pressure Education Program. In the intervening years, hypertension detection and treatment have improved steadily, and more than 50 percent of hypertensives now have their blood pressure under adequate control (Stamler et al., 1976). That means that many more remain to be identified and treated appropriately, but clear progress has been made from the 12 percent of hypertensives estimated to have been adequately treated in 1972 (Stamler, 1981).

Effects of Changing Lifestyles on Coronary Heart Disease

Deaths from coronary heart disease rose steadily through the 1950s and 1960s, particularly for men, both black and white (Stamler, 1981). This trend stopped in 1968, and there has been a steady and substantial decline in mortality since then. Between 1968 and 1978, there was a 27 percent decrease in deaths from coronary heart disease for individuals age 35–74. Mortality rates from stroke declined even more markedly (40 percent). This results in a calculated savings of more than 800,000 lives during that decade (Stamler, 1981).

Large-Scale Prevention Programs

Evidence of changes in lifestyle in the United States is encouraging. It suggests both that change is possible and that those changes are paralleled in decreased mortality and probably in decreased illness. Still, about one million individuals die from cardiovascular diseases each year, emphasizing that there still is much to do. Given the large numbers of people at risk for developing cardiovascular disease, there have been strong pressures to seek ways in which to introduce interventions on a large scale, both for economic reasons and to ensure that as many people as possible benefit from the program. This has resulted in programs that focus on a specific setting such as a community or work place. The results of such projects have been encouraging.

Hypertension Detection and Control

One of the best-known success stories in preventing cardiovascular disease is the increased detection and treatment of hypertension. In the past few decades, public awareness of the dangers of high blood pressure has increased substantially; many more people are having their blood pressure checked regularly and many more hypertensives are receiving appropriate and adequate therapy. Large-scale studies of the long-term effects of treating hypertension played a critical role in these developments, because they provided the first convincing evidence of the value of such interventions. Probably the best known of these efforts was the Hypertension Detection and Follow-Up Program (1979), which was supported by the National Heart, Lung, and Blood Institute. More than 150,000 people in 14 communities across the United States were screened for hypertension, and nearly 11,000 participated in the study. Some components of the program focused on identifiable subpopulations, such as a work group; others covered entire communities.

Those who had repeated diastolic blood pressures above 90 mm Hg either were randomly assigned to a standard medical program that escalated treatment until the blood pressure declined sufficiently (stepped care) or were referred for treatment in the community (regular care). After five years, the stepped-care group had a 20 percent reduction in mortality from cardiovascular disease, compared with the regular-care group; they also had a 17 percent reduction in mortality from all causes. Stepped-care treatment was especially effective in reducing mortality of people who had relatively mild hypertension and no evidence of damage to the heart or other major organs; for this group, mortality was reduced by 28 to 36 percent (Hypertension Detection and Follow-Up Program, 1979).

Multifactorial Intervention Strategies

One implication of the epidemiological studies cited earlier is that risk factors can act in concert to increase an individual's risk of cardiovascular disease. Thus, individuals who have several risk factors are more likely to develop coronary heart disease than are those with only a single risk factor.

For that reason, some programs have sought to address several risk factors simultaneously. Theoretically, this has the advantage of approaching a disease with multiple causes from a variety of directions, with the possibility that even small reductions in several risk factors could have additive effects that would decrease disease rates. Practically, it usually is easier to help people modify a constellation of activities than it is to focus on a single behavior, suggesting that the multifactorial approach also may improve short- and long-term success rates. Three projects have been especially influential as prototypes of this type of multifactorial approach. Several additional projects are under way, extending on the successes and failures of these original studies.

North Karelia Project   In 1971, people in North Karelia, Finland, asked their government for help in reducing the community's rate of cardiovascular disease morbidity and mortality, among the highest in the world. The North Karelia project was initiated with specific objectives of improving hypertension detection and treatment; reducing the incidence of smoking; and changing dietary habits to lower intake of saturated fat and increase use of vegetables and low-fat products (Puska, 1973).

The program was integrated into existing health and social services. Screening for hypertension became part of routine contacts, and a countywide hypertension register was established to facilitate follow-up. A broad spectrum of activities was fostered, including an extensive education program for reducing risk factors. For example, special courses were offered on smoking cessation. The program used all of the media, public campaigns at school and work, and health education meetings. Community leaders and groups were recruited to influence the change process further (Puska et al., 1981).

Effects of these multiple interventions were assessed by surveys in 1972 and 1977 of random samples of community members and of a neighboring province, Kuopio, that had similar cardiovascular disease rates and in which no interventions were made (Puska et al., 1980). The number of smokers decreased over the five-year interval in both areas to about an equal extent, probably as a result of a highly successful, nationwide antismoking campaign; however, the total amount of smoking decreased nearly 10 percent more in North Karelia than in Kuopio. In 1972, average serum cholesterol was higher in North Karelia than in Kuopio; by 1977, the values no longer differed from those for Kuopio. Blood pressure, higher for North Karelia men and women than for controls in 1972, decreased relative to Kuopio by 4 percent for men and 5 percent for women; prevalence of uncontrolled hypertension decreased by about 45 percent for both men and women, compared with Kuopio controls.

Mortality rates also decreased in North Karelia from 1972 to 1977 (Puska et al., 1980). For example, comparing two-year means of 1972–73 with 1976–77, death from cardiovascular disease fell by 13 percent for men and 36 percent for women; incidence of stroke declined by 28 and 63 percent, respectively, and all-cause mortality decreased by 6 and 10 percent. Although these changes are impressive, comparable reductions occurred in Kuopio as well. No statistically significant differences were found between group changes in mortality rates for the two communities. Reasons for the parallel declines in mortality between North Karelia and Kuopio are still being considered. The communities may have been too close together; information and enthusiasm about the North Karelia project may have spread to Kuopio, so that it no longer was a true control. Careful analysis of similarities and differences between the two communities may provide valuable new insights into important influences on changing community-wide habits and customs.

Stanford Heart Disease Prevention Project In 1972, a group at Stanford University began a systematic investigation of factors that might influence the effectiveness of a community-based, multifactorial, risk factor reduction campaign (Farquhar, 1978). The group selected three communities in northern California that were of similar size and socioeconomic composition and sufficiently separated geographically to have few interactions. One community served as a control. The other two received interventions directed against the risk factors of cigarette smoking, hypercholesterolemia, and hypertension. Both of those communities were exposed to an intensive and extensive media campaign, including advertisements, television and radio commercials and specials, newspaper columns, billboards, and direct mailings. In one community, media campaigns were supplemented with educational interventions for identified high-risk individuals. A random sample within each community was surveyed at the beginning and end of the study.

In designing the project, the Stanford group drew on members of a variety of disciplines in the behavioral sciences, including psychologists, physicians, sociologists, and media specialists. Deficits in public knowledge about cardiovascular risk factors were identified, so that the media campaign could focus on them; and patterns of media usage were assessed, so that messages would be most likely to reach the intended audiences. Approaches to the media campaign and to the face-to-face interventions were based on the best available principles of learning and were designed both to convey information and to teach skills such as how to prepare an attractive low-fat diet. The research design also enabled the researchers to draw conclusions about the relative merits of the different approaches, because appropriate control conditions were selected and followed from the beginning.

The study results strongly suggest that community interventions can reduce risk factors (Maccoby et al., 1977). Public awareness of the importance of risk factors increased by 41 and 26 percent in the two communities that received the media campaign; it increased by 54 percent for people who also received individualized counseling. In both communities, consumption of saturated fat decreased by 25 percent and cigarette smoking declined by 5 to 20 percent, compared with the control community. Serum cholesterol and blood pressure also declined, although somewhat more modestly. Calculations of the additive effects of reductions in all these risk factors suggest overall reduction in risk of 16 percent for the media-only community and 20 percent for the media-plus-counseling community, each as compared with the control community.

Multiple Risk Factor Intervention Trial (MRFIT)   A major medical model of multiple risk factor interventions is currently under way. In 1971, the National Heart, Lung, and Blood Institute invited proposals for a special intervention program against cigarette smoking, hypertension, and hypercholesterolemia in men free of cardiovascular disease but at high risk for it. The purpose of the project was to determine, over a six-year period, if such interventions could significantly reduce cardiovascular mortality, nonfatal myocardial infarctions, and mortality of all causes (Zukel et al., 1981).

The approved study involves 22 clinical centers. Between 1974 and 1976, more than 360,000 men were screened. Nearly 13,000 of those judged to be at high risk on the basis of smoking habits, blood pressure, and serum cholesterol were randomly assigned to a Special Intervention program designed to alter those risk factors or to a Usual Care group. Men in the Usual Care control group were evaluated once each year, with no direct efforts to change risk factors. The Special Intervention program consisted of an initial series of small-group sessions intended to help participants modify behaviors affecting the three identified risk factors. Didactic techniques were used to convey information about the three risk factors, the expected benefits of reducing them, and ways in which they could be reduced. Wives were also invited to attend, to provide support for their husbands. Important principles of behavior modification were applied to dietary change, adherence to antihypertensive medication, and quitting smoking. Those in the Special Intervention group were invited to the clinic at least three times each year to help them maintain and improve changes that reduced risk factors (Sherwin et al., 1981).

Goals of the Special Intervention program were complete cessation of cigarette smoking, maintenance of diastolic blood pressure below 89 mm Hg, and adoption of a cholesterol-lowering diet (Sherwin et al., 1981). Those unable to stop smoking immediately were encouraged to reduce their amount of smoking or to switch to low-tar, low-nicotine brands as a transitional step; alternative forms of tobacco use such as cigars or pipe smoking were not encouraged. Standard stepped-care drug therapy was used to control hypertension. Diets were designed to reduce intake of saturated fat and of cholesterol and to increase intake of polyunsaturated fat.

Risk factor reduction in the Special Intervention group has been marked in the first four years of the program. Among more than 4,000 smokers, 47 percent had quit four months after the program and 46 percent were not smoking at four years (Hughes et al., 1981). Quit rates were strongly associated with the initial level of smoking; light smokers had higher initial quit rates and lower rates of recidivism than did heavy smokers throughout the study (cf. Chapter 5). Compared to the Usual Care group at four years, the Special Intervention group had fewer smokers, and those who smoked smoked fewer cigarettes (Neaton et al., 1981). The latter group also showed substantial control of blood pressure. At four years, 87 percent of those diagnosed as hypertensive were on medications, and 65 percent were at or below the goal pressure (Cohen et al., 1981). Blood pressure for the Usual Care group also dropped during this period, although not as much; the decrease in the control group is attributed to treatment received as part of their usual care (Neaton et al., 1981). Finally, the Special Intervention program helped to reduce serum cholesterol by 7 percent more over the four years than occurred in the Usual Care group. Most of this occurred during the first year of intervention (Caggiula et al., 1981).

Mortality and morbidity data for this important study will not become available until late in 1982. However, the study already has demonstrated that medical interventions can substantially reduce risk factors. Relative merits of medical models and community-based programs such as that at Stanford remain to be assessed.

Conclusions

Over the past decade, an impressive change has occurred in the lifestyle of many people in the United States, belying the pessimism that often clouds prevention efforts. The evidence clearly demonstrates that, at least for cardiovascular disease, large-scale interventions are feasible and effective. The success of smoking prevention and cessation programs has positive implications for prevention of the most prevalent types of cancer and for chronic pulmonary disease. Much remains to be learned about the most cost-effective methods of conducting such prevention efforts. For example, more studies are needed of how to select the optimal medium for specific kinds of messages. Although knowledge about the learning process already is substantial, it needs to be applied more systematically in prevention programs. Some types of prevention efforts—particularly those that can be expressed in simple, short, and clear messages—may be especially suitable for the mass media. Others, such as helping people to stop smoking, will also require more individualized and group attention.

References

Caggiula, A. W., Christakis, G., Farrand, M., Hulley, S. B., Johnson, R., Lasser, N. L., Stamler, J., and Widdowson, G. The Multiple Risk Factor Intervention Trial (MRFIT). IV: Intervention on blood lipids. *Prevent. Med.* 10:443–475, 1981.

Cohen, J. D., Grimm, R. H., Jr., and Smith, W. M. The Multiple Risk Factor Intervention Trial (MRFIT). VI: Intervention on blood pressure. *Prevent. Med.* 10:501–518, 1981.

Farquhar, J. W. The community-based model of life style intervention trials. *Am. J. Epidemiol.* 108:103–111, 1978.

Hughes, G. H., Hymowitz, N., Ockene, J. K., Simon, N., and Vogt, T. M. The Multiple Risk Factor Intervention Trial (MRFIT). V: Intervention on smoking. *Prevent. Med.* 10:476–500, 1981.

Hypertension Detection and Follow-Up Program Cooperative Group. Five-year findings of the Hypertension Detection and Follow-Up Program. I. Reduction in mortality of persons with high blood pressure, including mild hypertension. *J. Am. Med. Assoc.* 242:2562–2571, 1979.

Levy, R. I. Testimony before the Subcommittee on Nutrition of the Committee on Agriculture, Nutrition, and Forestry, United States Senate, 96th Congress, May 22, 1979. Washington, D.C.: U.S. Government Printing Office, 1979, pp. 30–59.

Levy, R. I. The decline in cardiovascular disease mortality. *Annu. Rev. Publ. Health* 2:49–70, 1981.

Maccoby, N., Farquhar, J. W., Wood, P. D., and Alexander, J. Reducing the risk of cardiovascular disease: Effects of a community-based campaign on knowledge and behavior. *J. Community Health* 3:100–114, 1977.

National Heart, Lung, and Blood Institute *National Conference on High Blood Pressure Education* Washington, D.C.: U.S. Government Printing Office, 1973. DHEW Publ. No. (NIH) 72–137.

Neaton, J. D., Broste, S., Cohen, L., Fishman, E. L., Kjelsberg, M. O., and Schoenberger, J. The Multiple Risk Factor Intervention Trial (MRFIT). VII: A comparison of risk factor changes between the two study groups. *Prevent. Med.* 10:519–543, 1981.

Page, L., and Friend, B. The changing United States diet. *BioScience* 28:192–197, 1978.

Puska, P. The North Karelia project: An attempt at community prevention of cardiovascular disease. *WHO Chron.* 27:55–58, 1973.

Puska, P., Tuomilehto, J., Nissinen, A., Salonen, J., Maki, J., and Pallonen, U. Changing the cardiovascular risk in an entire community: The North Karelia project. IN: *Childhood Prevention of Atherosclerosis and Hypertension* (Lauer, R. M., and Shekelle, R. B., eds.) New York: Raven Press, 1980, pp. 441–451.

Puska, P., Neittaanmaki, L., and Tuomilehto, J. A survey of local health personnel and decision makers concerning the North Karelia project: A community program for control of cardiovascular disease. *Prevent. Med. 10*:564–576, 1981.

Rizek, R. L., and Jackson, E. M. Current food consumption practices and nutrient sources in the American diet. Hyattsville, Md.: Consumer Nutrition Center—Human Nutrition Science and Education Administration, U.S. Department of Agriculture, 1980.

Sherwin, R., Kaelber, C. T., Kezdi, P., Kjelsberg, M. O., and Thomas, H. E., Jr. The Multiple Risk Factor Intervention Trial (MRFIT). II: The development of the protocol. *Prevent. Med. 10*:402–425, 1981.

Stamler, J. Introduction to risk factors in coronary artery disease. IN: *Baylor College of Medicine Cardiology Series, Vol. 1, Part 3* (McIntosh, H. D., ed.) Northfield, Tex.: Medical Communications, 1978.

Stamler, J. The primary prevention of coronary heart disease. *Amer. J. Cardiol. 47*:722–735, 1981.

Stamler, J., Stamler, R., Riedlinger, W. F., Algera, G., and Roberts, R. H. Hypertension screening of 1 million Americans—Community Hypertension Evaluation Clinic (CHEC) Program, 1973 through 1975. *J. Am. Med. Assoc. 235*:2299–2306, 1976.

United States Department of Health, Education, and Welfare *Smoking and Health* Washington, D.C.: U.S. Government Printing Office, 1964, DHEW Publ. No. 1103.

United States Department of Health, Education, and Welfare *Smoking and Health* Washington, D.C.: U.S. Government Printing Office, 1979a, DHEW Publ. No. (PHS) 79–50066.

United States Department of Health, Education, and Welfare *Healthy People* Washington, D.C.: U.S. Government Printing Office, 1979b, DHEW Publ. No. (PHS) 79–55071.

Veterans Administration Cooperative Study Group on Antihypertensive Agents. Effects of treatment on morbidity in hypertension. III. Influence of age, diastolic pressure, and prior cardiovascular disease. Further analysis of side effects. *Circulation 45*:991–1004, 1972.

Winkelstein, W., Jr., and Marmot, M. Primary prevention of ischemic heart disease: Evaluation of community interventions. *Annu. Rev. Pub. Health 2*:253–276, 1981.

Zukel, W. J., Paul, O., and Schnaper, H. W. The Multiple Risk Factor Intervention Trial (MRFIT). I: Historical perspectives. *Prevent. Med. 10*:387–401, 1981.

16

The Interface of Drug and Psychosocial Treatments

Many people equate the medical model of treating diseases with using pharmacological agents, largely because biomedical research during the past several decades has provided a large armamentarium of drugs to treat a variety of diseases, including infections, diabetes, hypertension, cancer, and depression. Ready availability of reasonably safe and effective drugs has fostered among many physicians and patients an orientation toward illness as an outcome of specific agents or bodily malfunctions, unrelated to someone's lifestyle or psychosocial environment.

Drug treatments have improved the health of people throughout the world. However, as documented in Chapter 2, their effectiveness has produced a shift in the major kinds of disorders from which people suffer. Much of the present burden of illness in the United States and other developed nations results from chronic diseases. For many of these, drugs do not cure in the way that penicillin treats pneumonia; rather, they may arrest the disease progress or ameliorate the worst symptoms, as insulin works to control blood sugar in diabetics.

Nonpharmacological aspects of treatment are important even when the primary focus is on drugs. At the simplest level, the most powerful drugs are useless if patients carry them home but never take them. An understanding of the psychological and social factors that influence attitudes toward illness and help seeking may be of great value in determining how best to design a treatment regimen for a particular individual. In addition, evidence suggests that some forms of psychosocial interventions may be therapeutic, either in their own right or as adjuncts to drugs. Some contributions of and opportunities for future research in the biobehavioral sciences at this junction of drug and psychosocial treatments were the subjects of the Health and Behavior conference *Combining Psychosocial and Drug Therapy: Hypertension, Depression, and Diabetes* (Parron et al., 1981).

Types of Psychosocial Interventions

Broadly speaking, psychosocial interventions are of two types—management and specific therapies. Management refers to issues that arise during the course of treatment of any type. It includes many aspects of patient care such as explaining diagnosis and treatment plans, warning about possible drug side effects, and helping the patient in other ways to maintain some perception of control over what is happening. The principles are applicable across many treatment settings and for many different kinds of disorders. For someone with hypertension, management might include sessions about ways to reduce dietary salt; for a depressed patient, it might entail discussions of sleep disturbances and how to minimize them.

In contrast to management, specific psychotherapies are designed to relieve the symptoms of a disease state. For example, relaxation techniques might be used as an alternative to drugs for reducing mild hypertension; or cognitive therapy might be used to treat depression. Sometimes, psychotherapy is regarded as a competitor of drug treatments. This need not be so. In some instances, psychotherapy may be more effective than drugs. In others, it may be useful as an adjunct, so that patients receiving both types of therapy do much better than those who receive only one of them. At times, specific psychotherapy may not be needed, because drugs are sufficient.

Adherence

For several years, patient adherence to treatment regimens has been of great interest to health care providers. Even clearly effective treatments fail to work if they are not followed. For example, Heinzelman (1962) studied penicillin prophylaxis among college students with a history of rheumatic fever or rheumatic heart disease. Of these well-educated patients, all of whom knew about the need for prophylaxis, only 19 percent were taking penicillin. Extent of adherence was influenced markedly by beliefs and attitudes about three factors: personal susceptibility to disease, severity of previous attacks, and benefits of prophylaxis. Half of the subjects scoring high on all three dimensions were taking penicillin, compared with only 4 percent for those scoring low on all three.

Recognition of the importance of patient attitudes and beliefs has led to suggestions that it is inappropriate to focus attention on patient adherence, with implications that failure to comply is a deviant behavior. Becker (1979) has argued that lack of adherence may make good sense from the patient's point of view. For example, everyone is aware of cases in which faithful adherence to a treatment does not lead to getting better or in which failure to follow instructions nonetheless was followed by a good outcome. It seems more useful to view the problem as one of needing to know the psychosocial factors that influence an individual's adherence to a treatment regimen (Stimson, 1974; Dunbar and Stunkard, 1979).

The health belief model is one promising theoretical framework for studying adherence. Developed initially by Rosenstock (1966), it has recently been elaborated by Becker (1979). The model first was used to account for variations in adherence to prevention efforts such as regular check-ups, immunizations, and screening tests. It has subsequently been applied to a broad range of illness-related behaviors. The health belief model postulates that people are likely to adhere to health-improving behavior only if they perceive themselves as potentially at risk for an undesirable outcome such as severe illness, believe that the required behavior is effective in decreasing or removing that risk, and anticipate few difficulties in undertaking the recommended action. These attitudes can be modified by an array of demographic, sociocultural, and personal factors.

The model has been useful both for predicting adherence and in seeking ways to improve adherence. In a prospective study of patients on antihypertensive drugs, Taylor et al. (1978) found that patient health beliefs measured during screening did not correlate with subsequent adherence to therapy. But an assessment of beliefs after six months of therapy correlated strongly with adherence during the next six months. This suggests that actual experience can affect beliefs in ways that alter subsequent behavior.

The health belief model predicts that it should be possible to modify adherence at a number of points. Haefner and Kirscht (1970) have shown that messages about selected health problems can alter willingness to follow recommendations for preventing the development of those problems. Janis (in press) points out that the model, like other models of rational choice, fails to specify the conditions under which people will give priority, at the cost of endangering their lives, to avoiding the subjective discomfort of being authoritatively informed that they have a life-threatening disease. This model also does not specify under what conditions they will make a more adaptive decision by seeking for and taking into account the available medical information about the real consequences of alternative courses of action so as to maximize their chances of survival.

Treatment of hypertension is a clear example of the importance of better understanding adherence. A study of the costs and benefits of investing in various aspects of hypertension treatment concluded that efforts to increase adherence would produce greater benefits than would a comparable expenditure for detecting new cases of hypertension (Weinstein and Stason, 1976). It seems reasonable that additional benefits would be gained by investigating ways in which to modify behaviors that contribute to the incidence of hypertension, including overeating, high sodium intake, and smoking. All of these types of behavior are resistent to change. However, as discussed in Chapter 15, they can be modified on a community-wide basis. The health belief model suggests that such efforts would be improved by gaining more precise information about specific beliefs of particular groups at special risk for hypertension and about the most influential psychosocial factors that might be applied to modifying those beliefs in healthful ways.

Issues of adherence also are of central importance in insulin-deficiency diabetes mellitus, which demands the intimate involvement of the patient and family in management activity and decision making throughout the patient's life (Chapter 8). Problems are especially acute during adolescence. Diabetic children are expected to become experts on nutrition, learn to monitor glucose concentrations and adjust insulin doses, develop an appropriate program of physical exercise, and meet other demands that are far from typical of that age group (Drash, 1980). As discussed in a recent conference, *Behavioral and Psychosocial Issues in Diabetes*, much remains to be learned about how best to help diabetics meet these rigorous and life-long challenges (Hamburg et al., 1980).

Some nonadherence may be advantageous for the patient (Janis, in press). For example, medical errors such as those identified by Sackett (1976)—wrong diagnosis, wrong treatment, inadequate dosages of correct drugs, and overprescribing—can complicate issues of adherence. By not adhering to treatment recommendations, patients may be spared possible adverse effects of ineffective treatment. However, patients must make difficult discriminations in order to engage in advantageous nonadherence for unsound recommendations and advantageous adherence for sound ones. Most research on the issue of adherence has been geared to increasing compliance with physician recommendations. A largely neglected area of research pertains to determining how people can be motivated and educated to improve their discrimination, so that they will not adhere to medical advice that is likely to be wrong. Wheeler and Janis (1980) have presented some preliminary hypotheses about cues that people can use to discriminate competent and incompetent medical advisers. The numerous suggestive leads described by Wheeler and Janis need more intensive study.

Specific Psychotherapies

For some disorders, specific nonpharmacological treatments have been developed. Such therapies have been studied most thoroughly with respect to major mental disorders, particularly depression. Typically, these approaches have been developed independently of or as alternatives for pharmacological treatments. A considerable shift in emphasis has occurred over the past few decades (Pfefferbaum, 1977). In the early 1950s, the introduction of drugs was resisted because of fears that they would interfere with psychotherapies. Now, the efficacy of drugs for treating such major disorders as schizophrenia and depression has been thoroughly documented, and it is the psychotherapies whose efficacy is being questioned.

The difficulties of rigorously testing the efficacy of psychotherapies are beyond the scope of this project, but thorough analyses have been undertaken (Parloff et al., 1978; Smith et al., 1980). More relevant to this chapter are studies of the effects of combining drug and nonpharmacological treatment approaches. Theoretically, combinations of treatments could result in one of five possible outcomes (Table 16.1).

The most favorable result from such a combination would be a synergistic interaction, because one then is getting otherwise unobtainable effects for the patient. However, augmented or additive interactions also may be of use, particularly if they involve different aspects of the disease process. No interactions or inhibitory effects also may occur. This possibility makes it particularly important to study combined treatments carefully before adopting them on a large scale.

Combined approaches in treating depression were reviewed at one of the Health and Behavior conferences (Weissman, 1981). Relatively few studies are available, but substantial improvements have been made in

TABLE 16.1   Possible Outcomes from Treatment Combinations

Inhibitory Interaction   The combined treatments produce less of a response than either treatment alone.

No Interaction   The combination equals that of the most effective treatment alone.

Augmented Interaction   The combined effect is somewhat greater than either treatment alone.

Additive Interaction   The total effect is the sum of individual treatments added together.

Synergistic Interaction   The combined treatments produce an effect that is greater than the effects of the individual treatments added together.

SOURCE: Klerman (1981).

methodologies in recent years, and a reasonably consistent picture is emerging. In general, the combination of drug and psychosocial treatments appears to be superior to either one alone in relieving the major symptoms of depression. There is no evidence that the two treatment modalities interact; rather, they appear to affect different aspects of depression syndrome, thus producing a simple additive effect. Drugs seem to work primarily on physical and psychological symptoms; psychotherapy improves primarily such areas as work performance, submissive dependence, family attachments, and other aspects of social adjustment. Similarly, studies of schizophrenics provide evidence of long-term benefits from supplementing antipsychotic drug therapy with psychosocial treatment aimed at providing job advice, helping to fill out forms and manage finances, and intervening in family crises (Hogarty et al., 1974).

Nonpharmacological treatments also have been suggested for other major disorders, including hypertension. With the accumulation of information about the effects of high blood pressure on mortality and morbidity, it has become evident that even mild hypertension carries some risk (Hypertension Detection and Follow-Up Program, 1979). As many as 25 million people in the United States have mild hypertension, making them candidates for treatment. Although antihypertensive drugs are effective and relatively safe, they do have side effects and are expensive, particularly if they have to be taken for life. Thus, development of an effective and easily used nonpharmacological intervention would be of considerable interest.

A number of behavioral approaches have been applied to blood pressure reduction (Seer, 1979). Relaxation techniques involve relaxing all of the voluntary muscles in the body and encouraging feelings of calmness. Biofeedback focuses more specifically on physiological variables such as heart rate, blood pressure, or muscle tone; subjects are trained to control such variables under laboratory conditions. In general, studies suggest that people can learn to increase blood pressure more easily than they can learn to lower it. In part, this may be an artifact of the typical laboratory setting, where subjects first sit quietly at rest and then attempt to change their blood pressure. Under such conditions, it might be very difficult to decrease blood pressure further. It might be better to train subjects to maintain a lower blood pressure under physical or emotional conditions that usually are accompanied by increases in blood pressure. The clinical significance of such an approach remains to be studied.

Luborsky et al. (1980) conducted one of the few studies in which antihypertensive therapy has been compared directly with nonpharmacological treatments—one study group using relaxation and another using biofeedback. Subjects were only borderline to mild hypertensives. Comparisons among the groups showed that drugs were superior to both controls and nonpharmacological treatments. However, for both the biofeedback and the drug groups, about half of the subjects had blood pressures in the normal range by the end of the study. A potentially important difficulty with the study was that 40 percent of the subjects had to drop out of the study during the baseline period, because their blood pressures returned to normal. It would be of tremendous interest to know why those subjects became normotensive and whether they remained so over time.

Finally, it is important to note that many other types of nondrug interventions might be useful in hypertension treatment programs and deserve further study, particularly for the mild hypertensives. These include dietary changes to reduce weight and decrease salt intake, exercise programs, and possibly stress reduction or relaxation techniques. The effect of such psychosocial interventions, either singly or in combination, remains to be assessed. They are of such small cost and are so benign that they deserve careful study.

Conclusion

For many of the most serious remaining public health problems, drugs alone simply are not enough. Psychological and social variables also have important effects on the course and progress of the disease process. Needed studies are beginning to emerge; already they suggest better ways to approach treatment of these disorders. In some cases, psychosocial interventions require skills for which many health practitioners lack training, time, or interest. For that reason, their incorporation into health care may require innovations in the delivery system. Some of the issues around that possibility are discussed in the next chapter.

References

Becker, M. H. Understanding patient compliance: The contributions of attitudes and other psychosocial factors. IN: *New Directions in Patient Compliance* (Cohen, S. J., ed.) Lexington, Mass.: Heath, 1979, pp. 1–31.

Drash, A. L. The child with diabetes mellitus. IN: *Behavioral and Psychosocial Issues in Diabetes* (Hamburg, B. A., Lipsett, L. F., Inoff, G. E., and Drash, A. L., eds.) Washington, D.C.: U.S. Government Printing Office, 1980, NIH Publ. No. 80–1993, pp. 33–42.

Dunbar, J. M., and Stunkard, A. J. Adherence to diet and drug regimen. IN: *Nutrition, Lipids, and Coronary Heart Disease* (Levy, R., Rifkind, B., Dennis, B., and Ernst, N., eds.) New York: Raven Press, 1979, pp. 391–423.

Haefner, D. P., and Kirscht, J. P. Motivational and behavioral effects of modifying health beliefs. *Publ. Health Rep.* 85:478–484, 1970.

Hamburg, B. A., Lipsett, L. F., Inoff, G. E., and Drash, A. L. (Eds.) *Behavioral and Psychosocial Issues in Diabetes* Washington, D.C.: U.S. Government Printing Office, NIH Publ. No. 80–1993, 1980.

Heinzelman, F. Factors in prophylaxis behavior in treating rheumatic fever: An exploratory study. *J. Health Soc. Behav.* 3:73–81, 1962.

Hogarty, G. E., Goldberg, S. C., and Schooler, N. Drug and sociotherapy in the aftercare of schizophrenic patients. III. Adjustment of nonrelapsed patients. *Arch. Gen. Psychiatry* 31:609–618, 1974.

Hypertension Detection and Follow-Up Program Cooperative Group. Five-year findings of the Hypertension Detection and Follow-Up Program. I. Reduction in mortality of persons with high blood pressure, including mild hypertension. *J. Am. Med. Assoc.* 242:2562–2571, 1979.

Janis, I. L. Improving adherence to medical recommendations: Descriptive hypotheses derived from recent research in social psychology. IN: *Handbook of Medical Psychology, Vol. 4* (Baum, A., Singer, J. E., and Taylor, S. E., eds.) Hillsdale, N.J.: Lawrence Erlbaum, in press.

Klerman, G. L. Conceptual issues in combined psychosocial and pharmacological treatments. IN: *Combining Psychosocial and Drug Therapy: Hypertension, Depression, and Diabetes* (Parron, D. L., Solomon, F., and Haggerty, R. J., eds.) Washington, D.C.: National Academy Press, 1981.

Luborsky, L., Ancona, L., Masoni, A., Scolari, G., and Longoni, A. Behavioral versus pharmacological treatments for essential hypertension: A pilot study. *Int. J. Psychiatry Med.* 10:33–40, 1980.

Parloff, M. B., Wolfe, B., Hadley, S., and Waskow, I. E. Assessment of psychosocial treatment of mental disorders: Current status and prospects. An invited paper of the Advisory Committee on Mental Health of the Institute of Medicine, 1978.

Parron, D. L., Solomon, F., and Haggerty, R. J. (Eds.) *Combining Psychosocial and Drug Therapy: Hypertension, Depression, and Diabetes. Interim Report No. 2, Health and Behavior: A Research Agenda* Washington, D.C.: National Academy Press, 1981.

Pfefferbaum, A. Psychotherapy and psychopharmacology. IN: *Psychopharmacology: From Theory to Practice* (Barchas, J. D., Berger, P. A., Ciaranello, R. D., and Elliott, G. R., eds.) New York: Oxford University Press, 1977, pp. 481–492.

Rosenstock, I. M. Why people use health services. *Milbank Mem. Fund Q.* 44:94–124, 1966.

Sackett, D. L. The magnitude of compliance and non-compliance. IN: *Compliance with Therapeutic Regimens* (Sackett, D. L., and Haynes, R. B., eds.) Baltimore, Md.: Johns Hopkins University Press, 1976.

Seer, P. Psychological control of essential hypertension: Review of the literature and methodological critique. *Psychol. Bull.* 86:1015–1043, 1979.

Smith, M. L., Glass, G. V., and Miller, T. I. *The Benefits of Psychotherapy* Baltimore, Md.: Johns Hopkins University Press, 1980.

Stimson, G. V. Obeying doctor's orders: A view from the other side. *Soc. Sci. Med.* 8:97–104, 1974.

Taylor, D. W., Sackett, D. L., Haynes, R. B., Johnson, A. L., Gibson, E. S., and Roberts, R. S. Compliance with antihypertensive drug therapy. *Ann. N.Y. Acad. Sci.* 304:390–403, 1978.

Weinstein, M. C., and Stason, W. B. *Hypertension: A Policy Perspective* Cambridge, Mass.: Harvard University Press, 1976.

Weissman, M. M. Psychosocial and pharmacological treatments for depression: Evidence for efficacy and research directions. IN: *Combining Psychosocial and Drug Therapy: Hypertension, Depression, and Diabetes* (Parron, D. L., Solomon, F., and Haggerty, R. J., eds.) Washington, D.C.: National Academy Press, 1981.

Wheeler, D., and Janis, I. L. *A Practical Guide for Making Decisions* New York: Free Press, 1980.

17
Mental Health Care in General Health Care Systems

The primary care sector is the sole source of mental health care for most people with discernible mental disorders. Regier et al. (1978) estimated that 15 percent of the general population could be diagnosed as having a mental disorder in a given year. In its study of mental health needs, the President's Commission on Mental Health (1978) found that 5 to 15 percent of children 3 to 15 years old suffer from persistent, handicapping mental health problems.

The potential benefit of the general health care system to the delivery of mental health care is illustrated by recent epidemiological findings: 21 percent of identifiably disordered individuals receive specialty mental health services; 54 percent are seen in the outpatient primary care sector, with a 6 percent overlap with the specialty mental health sector; 3 percent are found in the general hospital/nursing home sector; and 22 percent may be receiving no treatment (Regier et al., 1978). The pediatrician and general and family practitioners serve as the main source of contact with the health care system for most of the nation's children, including those who are emotionally disturbed.

Mental health aspects of primary care practice involve more than treating patients with diagnosable mental disorders. A large portion of primary care practice is devoted to caring for patients with a host of psychosocial problems such as marital difficulties, significant loss, aging, and illness. The portion of primary care resources devoted to patients with vague symptoms thought to have underlying emotional causes may be as high as 40 percent in the typical primary care practice. Scheslinger and Mumford (1980) noted

279

that 40 percent of all health insurance claims are for nonspecific, symptomatic diagnoses. These encounters—the "worried well" visits described by Mechanic (1975) and Tessler et al. (1976)—often mask unidentified and vaguely perceived mental health problems.

As in the case of adults, a major contributor to pediatric medical utilization is unrecognized emotional stress (Haggerty et al., 1975; Diehr et al., 1979). Difficulties previously considered to be outside the purview of pediatric medical practice are gaining greater attention. Social and psychological deviance, including behavior problems in preschool children, poor school performance in older youngsters, and adolescent adjustment issues, often are brought to the pediatrician and family practitioner (Haggerty et al., 1975). The younger the children, the more global their maladaptation to stressful events. Psychosomatic illnesses such as vomiting, diarrhea, and skin rashes may be responses to upsetting life experiences (Cohen et al., 1975).

The primary care sector is likely to retain a major role in delivering mental health care for the following reasons: better insurance coverage for treatment of physical illnesses than for care of mental disorders; reluctance of many persons to seek care from officially labeled mental health providers; and current and likely future inability of mental health practitioners to accommodate all the patients who are in need of services. In addition, the primary care sector undoubtedly will continue to play a role in treating chronic psychiatric patients who have been released from state mental hospitals with inadequate community health alternatives. The 1960s and 1970s saw a growing awareness of the need for mental health care, and a network of services was developed with various levels and types integrated at the community level. Although much has been accomplished in developing this network, there are too few ambulatory mental health programs, and this lack is compounded by the lack of well-developed linkages to general health care providers. Deinstitutionalization of state mental hospital patients is forcing more involvement of general hospitals in community mental health problems, as the mentally ill come to them for care that previously had been provided in mental hospitals.

In the primary care sector, the need for integrated mental health services is becoming increasingly clear. The process of change will be complex. Linking community mental health programs to general hospitals for acute interventions requires coordination with relatively few providers for the most obvious psychiatric disabilities such as acute psychotic episodes. Integrating more basic mental health services into the array of primary care practice models (solo practitioners, clinics, group practices, health maintenance organizations) will require many changes for a large number of virtually autonomous medical practitioners.

Interest in strengthening links between physical and mental health care has been stimulated by evidence of the health benefits that accrue to patients. For example, better integration of mental health and general medical and surgical services produces such benefits as less need for anesthetics and analgesics, faster recovery, and shorter lengths of stay (Scheslinger et al., 1980a,b). Greater incorporation of mental health services into primary care settings may similarly improve quality and cost-effectiveness of these health services. In accord with this expectation, illness months and periods of drug therapy decline for selected problems when primary care is supplemented with psychologically attuned interventions (Shephard et al., 1966; Johnstone and Goldberg, 1976).

The interplay of physical and emotional needs in disease processes is increasingly recognized, and hypotheses about it can be separated into three basic approaches: (1) emotional factors "mark" or precede the onset of physical health problems; (2) emotional stresses are aggravated by physical health problems; or (3) emotional factors influence the course of and recovery from physical disease (Scheslinger et al., 1980a). Each of these hypotheses has specific implications for primary care practice (Houpt et al., 1979). A substantial body of evidence shows that early identification of emotional problems and associated risk factors can aid in prevention and treatment of mental and physical disorders and can increase the rapidity and extent of patient recovery. The fact that children with emotional problems usually are seen relatively early in life in the general health care setting puts the primary care physician in a particularly strategic position to identify potential and developing problems (cf. Chapter 13). Studies strongly suggest that the primary care sector has yet unrealized potential to increase substantially the quality of its health care delivery by paying more explicit attention to pertinent emotional problems presented by patients.

Optimization of mental health services will require careful assessment of many aspects of primary care: the types of mental health problems presented; the kinds and relative effectiveness of available therapies; the competence, training needs, and differential cost-effectiveness of various practitioners confronted with particular disorders; the effects and special constraints on care provided in various delivery settings; and the incentives, cost offset, and total resource implications inherent in alternative mental health funding options. The task for health services research posed by these questions is formidable and largely unattempted to date.

Delivery Settings

As noted previously, far more mental health encounters occur in a primary care setting than in specialty mental health care settings. This makes moot some of the debates about the theoretical superiority of a specialized versus integrated mental health system. With shrinking public resources for human services, it is unlikely that the mental health system will receive another large injection of funds in the near future. In fact, problems encountered in setting up adequate community programs to meet the needs of deinstitutionalized patients probably are harbingers of more serious shortfalls. Therefore, it is both fiscally and clinically incumbent on mental and general health professionals to study ways of improving the delivery of mental health care in the general health sector.

Unfortunately, there are many difficulties involved in upgrading programs of mental health care in the general health care setting. Some researchers and clinicians have questioned the compatibility of effective psychotherapy sessions within the relatively hectic and unpredictable nature of health care delivery in the primary care setting (Hankin, 1979). A similar concern has been raised about primary care mental health services for children (Haggerty et al., 1975). This criticism is especially cogent to solo practitioners, because, unlike group practices, such settings offer no opportunity to dedicate specific staff to carry out mental health counseling without interruption. One perceived advantage of integrating physical and mental health care in one setting is the holistic treatment of patients by broadly trained individuals; yet much of the benefit may be lost if the practitioners truncate psychotherapy to respond to more immediate medical crises. In group practices, mental health services can be provided by all adequately trained practitioners, with coverage arrangement to ensure no disruption of sessions, or by nonmedical mental health personnel (Pakula, 1980). The relative effectiveness of these latter approaches has received little assessment, but the value of making some arrangement for mental health care seems apparent.

Training Primary Care Providers

Beyond the sheer organizational problems of delivering mental health care in general health settings is the difficult task of ensuring appropriate training of primary care practitioners and other medical personnel in mental health matters. Many primary care physicians are empathic and supportive to patients through their normal life crises, but their interviewing skills and abilities to develop therapeutic relationships may be inadequate for mental disorders most commonly seen in the primary care setting, including psychosomatic disorders, behavioral disturbances of childhood, major depression, and schizophrenia (Lawrence, 1980). Primary care practitioners often make inappropriate responses to primary care patients with mental disorders, possibly because these problems provoke anxiety in the physician (Lazarson, 1972). Their ability to assess emotional disorders accurately is closely related to personality variables and interviewing styles (Johnstone and Goldberg, 1976); their detection of psychiatric disorders is haphazard (Goldberg, 1980); their prescription of psychotropic drugs frequently is inappropriate (Hankin and Oktay, 1979); and their counseling skills are frequently insufficient (Lawrence, 1980).

The training of primary care practitioners must emphasize the development of certain skills that appear to be generically relevant to effective mental health practice. According to Goldberg (1980), these skills include interviewing, detecting, assessing, managing, and referring. Practitioners should be adept at spotting certain important disorders that are well defined and require specific management, for example, depressive states that are especially responsive to some drug regimen.

Murphy (1975) examined one type of adverse effect of poor management of psychiatric problems in the primary care sector. He found that primary care physicians did not do well in monitoring the condition of patients who later committed suicide. About two thirds of the patients had histories of suicide attempts, yet only half of the physicians knew of the past gestures. Most of the patients had clinically evident signs of depression, and the majority killed themselves by overdosing with medications prescribed by their primary care physicians.

Goldberg (1980) has suggested that the first task in mental health training is to train the teachers. Some aspects of psychiatry need to be redefined to put more emphasis on liaison, consultation, and more strictly defined therapeutic interventions and outcome measures. In the primary care setting, practitioners who are called upon for case identification and treatment must receive training in the areas of interviewing, diagnostic sensitivity, psychotherapy, and ability to make an appropriate referral (Lawrence, 1980). In addition, psychoactive drug therapy is a special skill that should receive major emphasis. Similarly, primary providers of children's health care either need appropriate training in behavioral pediatrics or professional mental health partners to deliver appropriate care (Haggerty et al., 1975).

Case Identification

Only 3 out of 100 primary care users with discernible mental disorders are identified and specifically treated (Hoeper, 1980). Researchers using independent patient assessments estimate that about one quarter of all adults seeking primary care have dysfunctional and diagnosable mental disorders (Hoeper, 1980). Another 25 percent may suffer stressful and debilitating emotional problems that cannot be diagnosed as a specific disorder. From 50 to 90 percent of the children who need mental health services do not receive help, largely because their problems are not identified in the primary care setting (Irigon et al., 1981).

Poor case identification of mental disorders in the primary care setting has been attributed to a variety of factors, including lack of mental health training; unclear diagnostic criteria; weak referral chains that reduce the perceived payoff from better case identification; and feelings of helplessness, especially in view of the time pressures of the practice setting. Resource waste from poor case identification appears to be substantial; for example, Goldberg (1980) found that illness months were reduced by 50 percent in a controlled trial in which primary care physicians were informed of their patients' self-perceived emotional problems. Adults with mental illness and emotional stress exhibit higher rates of organic illness and utilization of health services (Densen et al., 1959; Fink et al., 1969; Cooper et al., 1975; Hoeper, 1980). Haggerty et al. (1975) and Diehr et al. (1979) found a similar pattern for children. Evidence suggests strongly that some problems could be substantially diminished if physical and mental health services were better integrated.

A substantial portion of inappropriate, potentially dangerous medical treatments could be avoided with improved mental health case identification. Lawrence (1980) found that primary care providers typically respond to mental health problems with extensive diagnostic workups and inadequate drug therapies. Cooper et al. (1975) noted major differences in the use of psychotropic drugs and their effects on illness in various experimental situations. There seem to be substantial cost offsets associated with fortifying mental health services in a primary care setting (Jones and Vischi, 1979).

Good referral systems and adequate treatments are needed to translate better case identification into improved patient outcomes. Just as diagnostic criteria are not sufficiently clear for optimal use by the primary care provider, referral guidelines are not adequate to ensure the most appropriate disposition of identified mentally ill patients. Referrals are difficult for general health practitioners, in part because of the diversity of mental health providers and uncertainty about the appropriate role of each type.

Mental Health Therapies and Primary Care Settings

The Institute of Medicine conference *Mental Health Services in a General Health Care Setting* (Parron and Solomon, 1980) devoted considerable attention to the two key types of mental health therapy, psychotherapy and drug therapy (cf. Chapter 16). Schlesinger et al. (1980b) pointed out that psychotherapy is a complex process subject to multiple influences. Assessments of psychotherapy must consider type of therapy (individual, couples, family, or group); time (frequency and duration of visits); psychotherapeutic "purity"; and psychotherapeutic quality. In a review of 400 studies of psychotherapeutic intervention, Smith and Glass (1977) concluded that psychodynamic, behavioral, and cognitive approaches are all effective with some kinds of problems. Disorders that were most responsive were nonpsychotic depressions; mild to moderate anxieties and phobias; and reactions to the stresses of adolescence, marital difficulties, vocational problems, aging, and loss. Psychotherapy appeared to be beneficial in most cases, and improvements were achieved using a wide variety of therapies, including some short-term group therapies and therapies conducted by relatively inexperienced therapists. The latter are of interest because of their low cost.

Parloff (1981) has expressed reservations about the generalizability of some of the conclusions of the above review. The collection of studies included in the analysis is not representative of therapy modes most commonly used, typical kinds of patients seen, and average level of experience of the therapist. Acknowledging that these atypicalities would tend to mask positive results of psychotherapy, it is possible to accept Parloff's criticisms of the study and still be optimistic about the potential of cost-effective mental health intervention in the primary care sector.

The other major form of mental health intervention—drug therapy—recently has drawn an increasing amount of attention. Competency in using drugs is a particularly controversial aspect of the debate regarding the suitability of primary care practitioners for delivering mental health services. Published studies suggest that primary health care practitioners prefer to prescribe psychotropic drugs to manage recognized mental disorders (Hankin, 1980). Nonpsychiatric physicians use drug therapy in almost 70 percent of visits by patients with diagnosed mental health disorders; psychotherapy in some form is used in about 20 percent of those visits (Brown et al., 1979). Fink et al. (1969) found that, in the Health Insurance Plan of Greater New York, 57 percent of patients with identified mental disorders were treated solely with drugs. Little is known about the extent to which psychotropic drugs are used in combination with psychotherapy in primary care settings.

In a review of the literature, Hankin (1980) found few studies that addressed the question of appropriateness of psychotropic drug prescribing by primary care physicians. It is difficult to identify effects of artifacts such as reluctance to assign and to record a diagnosis of mental disorder, but not every patient given a psychoactive drug appears to have a mental disorder. Primary care practitioners use psychoactive drugs in ways other than those well established by scientific criteria. For example, such drugs are widely used in treating obesity, insomnia, cardiovascular disease, and gastrointestinal problems. An underlying consideration is the emotional distress associated with these conditions (cf. Chapter 3).

Sleeping pills are among the most frequently prescribed psychoactive drugs. The Institute of Medicine (1979) recently examined the appropriateness of prescribing practices for hypnotics. The report describes the nature and extent of drug prescriptions for insomnia complaints and the major role of the primary care practitioner in prescribing hypnotics. The findings suggest that doctors often prescribe for insomnia before making an adequate diagnosis; the complaint of insomnia is too readily treated with drugs as a disease rather than as a manifestation of some other disorder, for example, masked depression. The elderly may be at particular risk for adverse effects of sleep-inducing drugs (cf. Chapter 11). In all age groups, sleep and energy disturbances have been found to mimic or mask depression, increasing the risk of misdiagnosis and inappropriate treatment (cf. Chapter 6).

The many manifestations of childhood stress and depression place children at greater risk of being treated for the symptoms rather than for the underlying emotional problems. Children are the passive recipients of what adult authority figures consider appropriate for them. Inappropriate prescribing of drugs to keep a child tractable at the request of the parent, teacher, or other caretaker may expose the child to health risks while the underlying problems go untreated. Conversely, not using appropriate drugs when there is a specific need causes unnecessary hardships for the child, parents, siblings, and classmates. As with psychopharmacology for adults, there is strong evidence that maximum effectiveness is obtained only when drugs are prescribed as part of a comprehensive psychosocial and pharamacological treatment program (Halpern and Kissel, 1976).

Service Delivery Alternatives

Specific issues of competence raised earlier merge into broader debates about the relative effectiveness of physician and nonphysician mental health personnel. It is not possible to analyze these issues here, but a few points merit attention. Discussions of mental health manpower needs are inherently affected by views of the nature, scope, and distribution of mental health disorders and services. Thus, those who employ relatively broad definitions, including many problems of living as psychiatric disorders, typically see a need for a diversified stock of providers of mental health services. The health practitioner in a primary care setting is exposed to a range of psychosocial problems: marital difficulties; sexual dysfunction; school phobias and learning problems; and adjustment problems related to old age, dependency, loss, and illness. Various types of skills may be needed to deal successfully with these problems.

A common assumption is that manpower substitutions inevitably entail a trade-off between cost and quality in choosing physician and nonphysician personnel. In fact, many physicians receive only brief exposure to psychiatric diagnosis and therapy during their training, and this limitation is not necessarily compensated for by their competence in physical diseases. Thus, the choice of manpower deserves a knowledgeable assessment of the relative ability of practitioners with varying education and experience to achieve good results in carefully distinguished clinical situations.

Richman (1980) and Greenblatt (1975) have observed that personnel who vary widely in discipline, training, and outlook may be able to perform counseling and psychotherapy with roughly equivalent results. An important area of research is to delineate criteria for appropriate levels of care by discipline, training, and experience of provider and to define criteria for deciding which types of therapies for which kinds of patients should be provided by psychiatrists and nonpsychiatrists. It still is unclear what kinds of personnel can most effectively provide different types of mental health services, but there are clear indications that the well-informed primary care practitioner can be very effective within limited periods of time if patients are given the opportunity to address emotional problems explicitly (Lawrence, 1980).

Costs, Reimbursement, and Resource Allocation

In recent years, mental health funding has received a relatively large amount of attention. This attention has been generated by a number of developments: exposure of deplorable conditions in some state hospitals, court mandates for state hospital improvements, scandals associated with homeless and poorly tended deinstitutionalized patients, controversies about health insurance benefits for treatment of mental disorders and substance abuse, and the growing participation of general hospitals in delivery of acute psychiatric services. Each of these developments implies resource commitments, but tax pressure and other political limitations will probably constrain growth of funds for mental health care. This is one stimulus for the investigation of possible cost offsets.

In analyzing cost efficiency, Reinhardt (1980) distinguished between micro- and macro-efficiencies. Micro-efficiency refers to achieving maximal levels of output from particular personnel or service settings, and macro-efficiency refers to the larger issue of whether the community is getting the largest total benefit from its investment. For example, a clinic might get maximum performance from a psychiatrist on its staff, thus achieving micro-efficiency; however, if equal patient outcomes can be obtained from a less expensive staff person, then the community's resources are being inefficiently used because they are supporting a higher cost without achieving added benefits. Another type of inefficiency is that of suboptimal delivery of mental health services by poorly trained general health personnel. Inappropriate drug therapies, for example, are not efficient. The problem is compounded if manpower that could be effective in delivering physical health services is employed in providing low-quality mental health care.

Improved mental health services probably can produce offsetting decreases in general health care service utilization and expenditures. Scheslinger and Mumford (1980) found that even relatively minor psychologically informed interventions can substantially benefit a patient's physical health. Other controlled studies have shown that both brief counseling and psychotherapies conducted by nonmedical mental health personnel can improve a variety of outcomes related to physical illness. Goldberg (1980) found that illness months and use of psychotropic medications were reduced by one half in a controlled trial in which primary care physicians were informed of their patients' self-reported emotional problems and invited to discuss them with their patients. Shephard (1980) noted remarkable differences in patients' drug use and need for health services under experimental conditions in which a social worker was incorporated into primary care practice. In this study, patients had less need for medical treatment and an increased sense of self-esteem and coping ability. These studies usually have not specifically addressed mental health interventions in primary care settings. More research is needed to quantify potential offsets in particular categories. Especially useful would be studies of fixed and marginal costs, so that reasonable judgments can be made regarding short- and long-term fiscal offsets.

Third-party reimbursement policies can act as major incentives or disincentives to the integration of mental health and general health care. In the future, reimbursement mechanisms are needed that will encourage collaboration, cooperation, and appropriate referral. Methods are needed to link reimbursement to appropriate levels of care by specific mental health disciplines and by training and experience for various types of mental health problems. Such reimbursement policies can ensure that provider coverage is tied to specific, relevant mental health training and experience. Thus, the primary care practitioner who has sought mental health training to augment skills in the diagnosis and treatment of physical illnesses could qualify for reimbursement for mental health services. Research can help in the formulation of appropriate guidelines for reimbursement for this service.

Conclusions

With the primary care sector playing a major role in caring for much of the adult and child population with discernible mental illness, a concerted effort must be made to improve communication between mental health and general health services. Resolution of problems calls for sensitivity about the needs of practitioners and patients within the context of the primary care delivery setting. The beneficial health results that can be achieved from relatively minimal integration of services bolster arguments for increased primary care commitment to case identification, better referral mechanisms, more effective counseling, and improved drug therapy. The ability of primary care practitioners to convey their interest in pertinent behavioral and psychosocial issues to patients may be important in the prevention and recovery process.

Based on conceptual issues raised by the Institute of Medicine conference *Mental Health Services in General Health Care* (Parron and Solomon, 1980), a research agenda that especially emphasizes improved collaboration and cooperation includes:

- development of more precise mental health criteria for use by primary care practitioners;
- development of more clearly outlined treatment patterns for particular mental health disorders;
- development of clear-cut referral criteria for use by primary care practitioners;
- development of guidelines for appropriate drug intervention across the gamut of mental health disorders;
- rigorous tests of efficacy aimed at identifying which therapies work best, for what kinds of patients, and under what conditions;
- tests of alternative strategies for providing integrated mental health care in primary health care settings; and
- investigations of the relative effectiveness of various manpower categories in dealing with differentiated problems in various treatment settings.

References

Brown, B. S., Regier, D. A., and Balter, M. B. Key interactions among psychiatric disorders, primary care, and the use of psychotropic drugs. IN: *Clinical Anxiety/Tension in Primary Medicine* (Brown, B. S., ed.) Princeton, N.J.: Excerpta Medica, 1979.

Cohen, D., Granger, R. H., Provence, S. A., and Solnit, A. J. Mental health services. IN: *Issues in the Classification of Children* (Hobbs, N., ed.) San Francisco: Jossey-Bass, 1975.

Cooper, B., Harwin, B. G., Depla, C., and Shephard, M. Mental health care in the community: An evaluative study. *Psychol. Med.* 5:372–380, 1975.

Densen, P. M., Shapiro, S., and Einhorn, M. Concerning high and low utilizers of service in a medical care plan, and the persistence of utilization levels over a three year period. *Milbank Mem. Fund Q.* 37:217–250, 1959.

Diehr, P., Williams, S. J., Shortell, S. M., Richardson, W. C., and Drucker, W. The relationship between utilization of mental health and somatic health services among low income enrollees in two provider plans. *Med. Care* 17:937–952, 1979.

Fink, R., Goldensohn, S., Shapiro, S., and Davy, E. Changes in family doctor's services for emotional disorders after addition of psychiatric treatment to a prepaid group practice program. *Med. Care* 7:209–224, 1969.

Goldberg, D. Training family physicians in mental health skills: Implications of recent research findings. IN: *Mental Health Services in Primary Care Settings: Report of a Conference, April 2–3, 1979* (Parron, D. L., and Solomon, F., eds.) Washington, D.C.: U.S. Government Printing Office, 1980, DHHS Publ. No. (ADM) 80–995, pp. 70–87.

Greenblatt, M. Psychiatry: The battered child of medicine. *N. Engl. J. Med.* 292:246–250, 1975.

Haggerty, R. J., Roghmann, K. J., and Pless, I. B. *Child Health and the Community* New York: Wiley, 1975.

Halpern, W. I., and Kissel, S. *Human Resources for Troubled Children* New York: Wiley, 1976.

Hankin, J. Management of emotionally disturbed patients in primary care settings: A review of the North American literature. IN: *Mental Health Services in Primary Care Settings: Report of a Conference, April 2–3, 1979* (Parron, D. L., and Solomon, F., eds.) Washington, D.C.: U.S. Government Printing Office, 1980, DHHS Publ. No. (ADM) 80–995, pp. 235–246.

Hankin, J., and Oktay, J. S. *Mental Disorder and Primary Medical Care: An Analytical Review of the Literature* Washington, D.C.: U.S. Government Printing Office, 1979, DHEW Publ. No. (ADM) 78–661.

Hoeper, E. Observations on the impact of psychiatric disorder upon primary medical care. IN: *Mental Health Services in Primary Care Settings: Report of a Conference, April 2–3, 1979* (Parron, D. L., and Solomon, F., eds.) Washington, D.C.: U.S. Government Printing Office, 1980, DHHS Publ. No. (ADM) 80–995, pp. 88–96.

Houpt, J. L., Orleans, C. S., George, L. K., and Brodie, H. K. H. *The Importance of Mental Health Services to General Health Care* Cambridge, Mass.: Ballinger, 1979.

Institute of Medicine *Sleeping Pills, Insomnia, and Medical Practice* Washington, D.C.: National Academy of Sciences, 1979.

Irigon, F. F., Sarno, M., Sera, J., and Westgard, R. Child development centers program: An effective school based mental health service. *Child Welf.* 60:569–577, 1981.

Johnstone, A., and Goldberg, D. Psychiatric screening in general practice: A controlled study. *Lancet* 1:605–608, 1976.

Jones, K. R., and Vischi, T. R. Impact of alcohol, drug abuse, and mental health treatment on medical care utilization: A review of the literature. *Med. Care* 17(Suppl.), 1979.

Lawrence, R. The primary care physician: Mental health issues. IN: *Mental Health Services in Primary Care Settings: Report of a Conference, April 2–3, 1979* (Parron,

D. L., and Solomon, F., eds.) Washington, D.C.: U.S. Government Printing Office, 1980, DHHS Publ. No. (ADM) 80–995, pp. 109–118.

Lazarson, A. M. The learning alliance and its relation to psychiatric teaching. *Psychiatry Med.* 3:81–91, 1972.

Mechanic, D. Sociocultural and sociopsychological factors affecting personal responses to psychological disorder. *J. Health Soc. Behav.* 16:393–404, 1975.

Murphy, G. E. The physician's responsibility for suicide. I: An error of commission. *Ann. Intern. Med.* 82:301–304, 1975.

Pakula, L. Delivery of mental health services in a fee-for-service pediatric practice. IN: *Mental Health Services in Primary Care Settings: Report of a Conference, April 2–3, 1979* (Parron, D. L., and Solomon, F., eds.) Washington, D.C.: U.S. Government Printing Office, 1980, DHHS Publ. No. (ADM) 80–995, pp. 57–61.

Parloff, M. Psychotherapy evidence and reimbursement decisions: Bambi meets Godzilla. Paper presented at the 112th annual meeting of the Society for Psychotherapy Research, Aspen, Colo. June 1981.

Parron, D. L., and Solomon, F. (Eds.) *Mental Health Services in Primary Care Settings: Report of a Conference, April 2–3, 1979* Washington, D.C.: U.S. Government Printing Office, 1980, DHHS Publ. No. (ADM) 80–995.

President's Commission on Mental Health *Report to the President, Vol. I.* Washington, D.C.: U.S. Government Printing Office, 1978.

Regier, D. A., Goldberg, I. D., and Taube, C. A. The defacto U.S. mental health services system: A public health perspective. *Arch. Gen. Psychiatry* 35: 685–698, 1978.

Reinhardt, U. E. Additional comments on the final report of the committee on the study of dental alternatives. Memorandum to members of the committee and of the Institute of Medicine, 1980.

Richman, A. Reimbursement by Medicare for mental health services by general practitioners: Clinical, epidemiologic and cost containment implications of the Canadian experience. IN: *Mental Health Services in Primary Care Settings: Report of a Conference, April 2–3, 1979* (Parron, D. L., and Solomon, F., eds.) Washington, D.C.: U.S. Government Printing Office, 1980, DHHS Publ. No. (ADM) 80–995, pp. 122–150.

Schlesinger, H. J., and Mumford, E. The patient variable in "offset studies." Background paper prepared for the conference Impact of Alcohol, Drug Abuse, and Mental Health Treatment on Medical Care Utilization, Bethesda, Md., October 16–17, 1980.

Schlesinger, H. J., Mumford, E., and Glass, G. The effects of psychological intervention on recovery from surgery. IN: *Emotional and Psychological Response to Anesthesia in Surgery* (Guerra, F., and Aldete, A., eds.) New York: Grune-Stratton, 1980a.

Schlesinger, H. J., Mumford, E., Glass, G. Problems analyzing the cost offset of including a mental health component of primary care. IN: *Mental Health Services in Primary Care Settings: Report of a Conference, April 2–3, 1979* (Parron, D. L., and Solomon, F., eds.) Washington, D.C.: U.S. Government Printing Office, 1980b, DHHS Publ. No. (ADM) 80–995, pp. 151–167.

Shepherd, M. Mental health as an integrant of primary care. IN: *Mental Health Services in Primary Care Settings: Report of a Conference, April 2–3, 1979* (Parron, D. L., and Solomon, F., eds.) Washington, D.C.: U.S. Government Printing Office, 1980, DHHS Publ. No. (ADM) 80–995, pp. 168–186.

Shephard, M., Cooper, A. B., Brown, A. C., and Kalton, G. W. *Psychiatric Illness in General Practice* London: Oxford University Press, 1966.

Smith, M. L., and Glass, G. V. Meta-analysis of psychotherapy outcome studies. *Am. Psychol.* 32:752–760, 1977.

Tessler, R., Mechanic, D., and Diamond, M. The effect of psychological distress on physician utilization: A prospective study. *J. Health Soc. Behav.* 17:353–364, 1976.

18

Changes in Human Societies, Families, Social Supports, and Health

The human species is intensely social. This fact is so much a part of daily life that it is easy to overlook its significance in human adaptation. People everywhere are organized in societies. They repeatedly must choose between serving individual interests and those of the group. Basic characteristics of human societies are highly pertinent to health and disease.

Social existence requires orderly procedures to make the environment predictable and to channel adaptive behavior through group as well as individual means. This rule of social organization must become reasonably clear to each individual in the course of growth and development. People can draw on the strength of membership in a valued group; but to do so, they must mold personal inclinations into socially acceptable modes of behavior, subordinating personal ends to community requirements when serious conflicts arise. Behavior is shaped by learning processes (cf. Chapter 3). Typically, rewards and punishments are mixed in ways that link individual needs with social values. Social organizations must allow for change to survive, but they historically have emphasized continuity, transmitting shared experience from one generation to another (Goldschmidt, 1959).

New technology such as navigation, warfare, and printing often has been a powerful stimulus for social change. The technological changes of the industrial revolution exceeded anything that had gone before and fueled institutional changes necessary to take advantage of the new opportunities. Modern industrial production, rapid transportation, and advanced communication systems have required the creation of large-scale enterprises that far transcend older modes of production based on family and neigh-

293

borhood groups. In this century, there has been a rapid emergence of large social units engaged in a common enterprise, with established lines of authority and decision making oriented to efficiency. In such settings— drastically different from the small, face-to-face groups that characterized most of human experience over many centuries—it is difficult to sustain unity of purpose and a sense of community. The stressful aspects of such large organizations as industry, government, and schools are related to this problem (cf. Chapter 10).

It is useful to view the drastic technological and social changes of this century in historical perspective (Lenski, 1978). In the simplest societies, life was largely centered on the family. For many centuries, kinship groups served a variety of purposes in daily living: biological, psychological, political, educational, economic, and religious. As technology opened new opportunities, societies grew in size and complexity. So too did human relations. For thousands of years, kin relations changed only slowly, and they remained the predictable core of human experience. Modern industrial societies have made far more rapid and drastic changes in such relations than ever happened before. Mankind is still learning to cope with these dislocations, especially because the pace of change has accelerated in the twentieth century. Social complexity is now at an all-time high.

Attachment

There is no reason to suppose that human attachment is less significant now than in the past. The tendency to form interpersonal attachments is a fundamental characteristic of human biology (Bowlby, 1969). The process of attachment seems to be involved in significant human relationships at all life stages, although the reasons for attachment and the way in which it is expressed vary with different ages and contexts. Studies of attachment behavior have focused mostly on early mother-infant interactions. Attachment between mother and infant may help both of them adapt to each other and also provide a suitable environment in which infants can gain knowledge about their surroundings (Ainsworth, 1967; Bowlby, 1969; Schaffer, 1977). These early experiences in attachment processes are also interesting because they represent precursors for social attachment processes later in life (Bowlby, 1969; Dunn, 1976; MacFarlane, 1977; Schaffer, 1977).

In their first years of life, human infants instigate care from available and interested adults by a very effective, if somewhat limited, repertoire of behaviors (Schaffer, 1977). The effectiveness of their actions is increased profoundly if the available adults are biologically equipped to respond to the cues and meet demands. The infant's biological mother typically is so equipped, and the two of them are a dynamic, interactional system in which needs and behaviors are intermeshed and adjusted over time (Schaffer, 1977).

The human infant is fundamentally predisposed to be social. The environment to which infants have had to adapt has been primarily social for millennia. The more complex nonhuman primates also are highly social and manifest a strong bond between mother and infant. The infant comes equipped with behavior patterns to begin social learning. How caretakers respond to and guide these social propensities affects immediate and long-term social adjustment processes (Richards, 1974).

Roles of the Family

In modern times, the fundamental human propensity for attachment is expressed in a largely unprecedented sociotechnical context. In advanced industrial societies, especially those characterized by high geographic mobility, the family is often so scattered that relations among its members are changed and attenuated. The nuclear family is no longer the basic unit of production. Family control of government is minimized. The mass media enter intimately into family life. Schools have taken over some family responsibilities for preparing the young for future adaptation. Moreover, such preparation is less predictable than it was in traditional societies.

Yet the family survives. It retains responsibility for some of its traditional functions: reproduction, much of childrearing, maintenance of lifelong ties, and mediation of stressful experiences. In some ways, these tasks are made easier by modern science and technology; in other ways, they are more difficult, as seen in the ambiguity fostered by rapid change and the separation induced by geographic mobility (Bane, 1976). In much of the United States, people move frequently, are involved in many organizations, and live in large population centers. This provides ample opportunity for superficial contact but often makes it harder to establish a deep relationship that involves all aspects of the person over time, including, for instance, the memories of long-shared experiences or a sense of loyalty to an institution.

Since the industrial revolution, there has been a drastic reduction in the number of children per family, as well as in the number of extended family members per household. The small, mobile nuclear family with ties to absent relatives has come to be the dominant mode, and even this now is changing further with growing divorce rates and single-parent households.

Almost every month brings new statistics on changing patterns of family life in America (Levitan and Belous, 1981). Divorce rates continue to climb. Marriage is postponed, if not rejected. Fertility rates continue to decline. More children are raised only by their mothers, who are either divorced or never were married. Women are entering the labor force at a high rate. Religious authority is changing for many and overall probably diminishing, although there are impressive exceptions to the trend. Norms for sexual behavior have changed markedly. Family members still share much, yet they often live in distinct worlds, differing in peer relations, interests, and values.

To what extent can other institutions such as schools or media substitute for traditional family functions? How severe is the stress placed on families by these very recent and rapid changes? In what ways is health most likely to be affected? These are questions of much practical significance that call for cooperative research between behavioral and biomedical scientists. They also have considerable bearing on the practice of medicine.

There are two main kinds of change in household structure. Within living memory, there was one predominant household, which consisted of a husband in the labor market, a full-time housewife, and several children. Today, this predominant mode has been replaced by a number of more fragmented family structures. A majority of wives have entered the labor market. With wives contributing part of the family income, women tend to expect not only a more equal division of household tasks but also of family decision making on all consequential matters.

These rapid changes generate tension. How can a stable, dependable, supportive environment for the rearing of children be provided while attempting to achieve acceptable and personally satisfying lives for all family members? There is no reason to suppose that the problems are insuperable, but they require a high quality of objective scrutiny and analysis by scientific methods to determine more adequately what is happening and to consider ways to cope.

The recent work of Masnick and Bane (1980) is helpful in clarifying trends and making reasonable projections for the next few decades. The population trends that produced the "baby boom" of the late 1950s and early 1960s were a potent stimulus for many recent socioeconomic changes. In the post-World War II era, many people married early, started relatively large families, and moved to the suburbs. They stimulated the huge market for single-family suburban homes and concomitant goods and services. They largely abandoned the cities to the poor. They moved freely around the country in keeping with opportunities and preferred lifestyles.

Now, the children of the baby boom are becoming young adults. There is evidence that they tend to establish different lifestyles from their parents: they marry later and have fewer children, more divorces, and more working wives. Instead of following their parents' footsteps into a renewed suburban expansion and a large demand for additional single-family houses, they may move more toward the cities, toward apartments and condominiums, and toward kinds of goods and services that fit with life in smaller, transient household units.

The remainder of this century is likely to be characterized by new stresses and new opportunities, including the growing emphasis on nonparental care of children. Young women are marrying late, postponing childbearing, and planning to have small families. They are in the labor force in much larger numbers, and they show a greater commitment to their work careers. They tend to seek a new combination of work and family life, using nursery schools, day-care centers, and paid child-care help more extensively than did earlier generations. Today, most such child care is provided informally. But there may be increasing demands on the public schools to provide preschool care for 3- to 5-year-olds and afterschool care for older children. If so, how can it be done in health-promoting ways?

Importance of Social Supports

Many of the changes that have occurred in society are positively valued by the participants. People move in search of economic, social, and environmental opportunities. Modern communities provide many facilities and choices for those whose health and economic circumstances permit. Privacy and independence are valued along with attachment and a sense of belonging. Family ties are built more on common interests and mutual attraction than in earlier times, when social and economic circumstances offered people few choices. Though nonfamily relations have become exceedingly important in recent times, family relations are still a significant element of the social support networks that are conducive to good health.

The role of social support networks in mediating the effects of stress is currently a matter of growing interest, both in promoting health and in responding to illness (Hamburg and Killilea, 1979). Disruption of social ties and community contexts is a highly stressful experience for many people. Such disruption can occur for both positive and negative reasons. These include moves to a new job, community, or school; loss of spouse; impaired health; and loss of income or employment. Such experiences often trigger intense emotional reactions (cf. Chapter 3). Availability of support, help, and guidance can crucially affect efforts in coping with such changes.

Support systems are attachments among individuals that tend to promote mastery of difficult experiences by offering guidance about tasks and strategies, identifying personal and social resources, and providing feedback about behavior that fosters improved competence. The cumulative findings from studies in this area are highly suggestive that social support can:

• reduce the number of complications of pregnancy for women under high life stress (Nuckolls et al., 1972);

• aid recovery from surgery (Egbert et al., 1964);

• aid recovery from myocardial infarctions (Mather et al., 1971; Mather, 1974);

• reduce the dosage of steroid therapy needed in adult asthmatics during periods of life stress (de Araujo et al., 1973);

• protect against clinical depression in the face of adverse events (Brown et al., 1975);

• reduce psychological distress and physiological abnormalities following job loss (Gore, 1973; Cobb, 1974) and bereavement (Maddison and Walker, 1967; Parkes et al., 1969; Burch, 1972; Parkes, 1972);

• protect against emotional problems associated with aging (Lowenthal and Haven, 1968; Blau, 1973); and

• promote adherence to therapeutic regimens (Haynes and Sackett, 1974; Baekeland and Lundwall, 1975; Caplan et al., 1976).

Social support networks provide a buffer against the effects of stress (Cassel, 1974a,b; Kaplan et al., 1977). They have mediating effects that stimulate development of effective coping strategies (Hamburg et al., 1953; Hamburg and Adams, 1967; Dimsdale, 1974; Hamburg, 1974). Future research is likely to identify further the health consequences of different degrees and kinds of social support.

Emotional support from family and friends typically has been of great importance in difficult circumstances. In high anxiety, most people actively seek comfort. Isolated persons and those who tend to withdraw under stress lack this valuable resource and are especially vulnerable. An ethnographic survey of help-seeking behavior in a minority community identified existing functional networks employed in times of emotional distress (Martinez, 1977). Informal helping systems provided twice as much help as did formal systems. Relatives, friends, and spouses were the principal informal helpers. The informal helping network also operated as a screening and referral mechanism for medical care.

Coping with stressful experiences often requires that tangible services be mobilized. A valuable skill in this context is the ability to signal one's need for help and to elicit constructive responses from family and friends. These responses include concrete aid in day-to-day needs such as introduction to new employment contacts, baby sitting, extended child care, help with household chores, sharing of food, and assistance with transportation needs. Beyond family and friends, there often is an indigenous network pertinent to health care. Community networks provide emergency services and everyday support; they involve neighborhood-based helping networks, self-help groups, and community gatekeepers such as clergy, teachers, and police (Gottlieb, 1976). Community studies have shown that socioeconomic instability and disintegration are associated with greatly increased mortality and morbidity from hypertension, strokes, and myocardial infarctions (Stout et al., 1964; James and Kleinbaum, 1976).

Formal care-giving institutions are studying the function of natural helpers in neighborhoods and collaborating with them (Collins and Pancoast, 1976). A number of descriptive studies suggest ways of enlisting natural caregivers, including working with neighbors who provide neighborhood day-care services for children (Collins, 1973); identifying central figures who provide needed services within their neighborhood to the elderly (Smith, 1975); working with quasi-matriarchal families in single-room occupancy hotels of a large city (Shapiro, 1971); working with a natural network of managers of boarding homes for discharged mental patients in an urban poverty area (Pancoast, 1970); developing an outreach program to the newly bereaved (Silverman, 1970); and developing mental health services in a rural area using natural helpers and local counselors such as ministers, lawyers, bankers, and county extension agents (Patterson and Twente, 1971).

One special attribute of social support networks is that people often become involved in them for reasons unrelated to problem behaviors or health concerns. An example is the Boys' Club of America, whose purpose is to promote educational, vocational, and character development of boys. Many of its members live in urban areas with single-parent low-income families (Fried, 1978). Religious leaders are in personal contact with large numbers of people in stressful circumstances such as illness, accidents, moving, divorce, natural disasters, unemployment, loss, and grief. Such contacts continue to be a major source of emotional support and personal facilitation.

Conclusions

Many research opportunities exist for further understanding of the relations among stress, illness, social support, and the utilization of medical services. High-priority needs include the following lines of inquiry:

1. Development of methodological tools. Is it possible to create more precise measures that would facilitate studies of effects of social support on health?

2. Examination of possible mechanisms by which support systems act. In what ways do such systems provide buffering or mediating effects on health, e.g., neuroendocrine mechanisms or alterations in risk factor behavior such as smoking?

3. Differentiated assessments of social supports. Do specific types of social support networks have identifiable advantages with certain kinds of stressful situations?

4. Testing of different models of intervention. What are the relative merits and appropriate uses of interventions to remove a stressor, moderate its effects, teach individual coping skills, or strengthen social supports?

5. Examination of different ways to foster attachment behavior. What are the best methods for creating or enhancing attachment?

6. Clinical and field experiments of ways to strengthen social networks. Is it possible to stimulate development of social support networks where they are weak or to mobilize social supports for those with inadequate support systems?

7. Comparison of experimentally created networks with naturally occurring ones. Are there meaningful differences between natural and constructed social networks; if so, what are their respective effects on health?

References

Ainsworth, M. D. S. *Infancy in Uganda: Infant Care and the Growth of Love* Baltimore, Md.: Johns Hopkins University Press, 1967.

Baekeland, F., and Lundwall, L. Dropping out of treatment: A critical review. *Psychol. Bull.* 82:738–783, 1975.

Bane, M. J. *Here to Stay: American Family in the Twentieth Century* New York: Basic Books, 1976.

Blau, Z. S. *Old Age in a Changing Society* New York: New Viewpoints, 1973.

Bowlby, J. *Attachment and Loss. Vol. I: Attachment* New York: Basic Books, 1969.

Brown, G. W., Bhrolchain, M. N., and Harris, T. O. Social class and psychiatric disturbance among women in an urban population. *Sociology* 9:225–231, 1975.

Burch, J. Recent bereavement in relation to suicide. *J. Psychosom. Med.* 16:361–366, 1972.

Caplan, R. D., Robinson, E. A. R., French, J. R. P., Caldwell, J. R., and Shinn, M. *Adhering to Medical Regimens: Pilot Experiments in Patient Education and Social Support* Ann Arbor, Mich.: University of Michigan, 1976.

Cassel, J. C. Psychosocial processes and "stress": Theoretical formulation. *Int. J. Health Ser.* 4:471–482, 1974a.

Cassel, J. C. Psychiatric epidemiology. IN: *American Handbook of Psychiatry, Vol. 2* (Caplan, G., ed.) New York: Basic Books, 1974b, pp. 401–410.

Cobb, S. Psychophysiological changes in men whose jobs were abolished. *J. Psychosom. Res.* 18:245–258, 1974.

Collins, A. H. Natural delivery systems: Accessible sources of power for mental health. *Amer. J. Orthopsychiatry* 43:46–52, 1973.

Collins, A. H., and Pancoast, D. L. *Natural Helping Networks: A Strategy for Prevention* New York: National Association of Social Workers, 1976.

de Araujo, G., Van Arsdel, P. P., Holmes, T. H., and Dudley, D. L. Life change, coping ability and chronic intrinsic asthma. *J. Psychosom. Res.* 17:359–363, 1973.

Dimsdale, J. E. The coping behavior of Nazi concentration camp survivors. *Am. J. Psychiatry* 131:792–797, 1974.

Dunn, J. How far do early differences in mother-child relations affect later development? IN: *Growing Points in Ethology* (Bateson, P. P. G. B., and Hinde, R. A., eds.) Cambridge: Cambridge University Press, 1976, pp. 481–496.

Egbert, L. D., Battit, G. E., Welch, C. E., and Bartlett, M. K. Reduction of postoperative pain by encouragement and instruction of patients: A study of doctor-patient rapport. *N. Engl. J. Med.* 270:825–827, 1964.

Fried, J. Boys' clubs embark on special health project. *Community Focus*, United Way of America, March 1978.

Goldschmidt, W. *Man's Way a Preface to the Understanding of Human Society* Cleveland: World Publishing, 1959.

Gore, S. *The influence of social support and related variables in ameliorating the consequence of job loss.* Unpublished doctoral dissertation, University of Pennsylvania, 1973.

Gottlieb, B. H. Lay influences on the utilization and provision of health services: A review. *Can. Psychol. Rev.* 17:126–136, 1976.

Hamburg, B. Early adolescence: A specific and stressful stage of the life cycle. IN: *Coping and Adaptation* (Coelho, G. V., Hamburg, D. A., and Adams, J. E., eds.) New York: Basic Books, 1974.

Hamburg, B. A., and Killilea, M. Relation of social support, stress, illness, and use of health services. IN: *Healthy People. Background Papers* (U.S. Department of Health, Education, and Welfare) Washington, D.C.: U.S. Government Printing Office, 1979, DHEW Publ. No. 79–55071A.

Hamburg, D. A., and Adams, J. E. A perspective on coping behavior: Seeking and utilizing information in major transitions. *Arch. Gen. Psychiatry* 17:277–284, 1967.

Hamburg, D. A., Hamburg, B., and deGoza, S. Adaptive problems and mechanisms in severely burned patients. *Psychiatry* 16:1–20, 1953.

Haynes, R. B., and Sackett, D. L. *A Working Symposium: Compliance with Therapeutic Regimens: Annotated Bibliography* Hamilton, Ontario: McMaster University Medical Center, Department of Epidemiology and Biostatistics, 1974.

James, S., and Kleinbaum, D. G. Socioecologic stress and hypertension: Related mortality rates in North Carolina. *Am. J. Publ. Health* 66:354–358, 1976.

Kaplan, B. H., Cassel, J. C., and Gore, S. Social support and health. *Med. Care 15 (Suppl.)*:47–58, 1977.

Lenski, G., and Lenski, J. *Human Societies, An Introduction to Macrosociology, 3rd Ed.* New York: McGraw-Hill, 1978.

Levitan, S. A., and Belous, R. S. *What's Happening to the American Family?* Baltimore, Md.: Johns Hopkins University Press, 1981.

Lowenthal, M. F., and Haven, C. Interaction and adaption, intimacy: A critical variable. *Am. Sociol. Rev.* 33:20, 1968.

MacFarlane, A. The psychology of childbirth. IN: *The Developing Child* (Bruner, J., Cole, M., and Lloyd, B., eds.) Cambridge, Mass.: Harvard University Press, 1977.

Maddison, D., and Walker, W. L. Factors affecting the outcome of conjugal bereavement. *Br. J. Psychiatry* 113:1057–1067, 1967.

Martinez, T. Alternative mental health resources for the Spanish-speaking: Latino helping networks. Paper presented at a meeting of the American Psychological Association, San Francisco, August 1977.

Masnick, G., and Bane, M. J. *The Nation's Families 1960–1980* Boston: Auburn House, 1980.

Mather, H. G. Intensive care. *Br. Med. J.* 2:322, 1974.

Mather, H. G., Pearson, N. G., Read, K. L. A., Steed, G. R., Thorne, M. G., Jones, S., Guerrier, C. J., Eraub, C. D., McHugh, P. M., Chowdhury, N. R., Jafary, M. H., and Wallace, T. J. Acute myocardial infarction: Home and hospital treatment. *Br. Med. J.* 3:334–338, 1971.

Nuckolls, K. B., Cassel, J. C., and Kaplan, B. H. Psychosocial assets, life crisis and prognosis of pregnancy. *Am. J. Epidemiol.* 95:431–441, 1972.

Pancoast, D. L. Boarding home providers for released mental hospital patients. Unpublished manuscript, 1970.

Parkes, C. M. *Bereavement: Studies of Grief in Adult Life* New York: International Universities Press, 1972.

Parkes, C. M., Benjamin, M. B., and Fizgerald, R. E. Broken heart: A study of increased mortality among widowers. *Br. Med. J.* 1:740, 1969.

Patterson, S. L, and Twente, E. Older natural helpers: Their characteristics and patterns of helping. *Publ. Welf.*, 400–403, Fall 1971.

Richards, M. P. M. (Ed.) *The Integration of a Child into a Social World* Cambridge: Cambridge University Press, 1974.

Schaffer, R. Mothering. IN: *The Developing Child* (Bruner, J., Cole, M., and Lloyd, B., eds.) Cambridge, Mass.: Harvard University Press, 1977.

Shapiro, J. *Communities of the Alone* New York: Association Press, 1971.

Silverman, P. R. The widow as a caregiver in a program of preventive intervention with other widows. *Ment. Hygiene* 54:540–545, 1970.

Smith, S. A. *Natural Systems and the Elderly: An Unrecognized Resource* Unpublished report, Oregon State Programs in Aging and Portland State University School of Social Work, 1975.

Stout, C., Morrow, J., Brandt, N., and Wolfe, S. Unusually low incidence of death from myocardial infarction. *J. Am. Med. Assoc.* 188:845–855, 1964.

V
HEALTH SCIENCE
POLICY CONSIDERATIONS

19
Health Science Policy Considerations

The Broad Context of Health Science Policy

In recent years, several Institute of Medicine study groups have examined the entire gamut of science policy pertinent to health. Of particular relevance in this regard was an analysis of the U.S. Department of Health, Education, and Welfare's research planning effort (Institute of Medicine, 1979, 1980). Basic points germane to the present report emerged with a high degree of consensus from a broad range of biomedical scientists and other scientists participating in that analysis (Table 19.1). The following quotations from that study affirm the importance of the biobehavioral sciences in efforts to decrease the current burden of illness (Institute of Medicine, 1979):

A key feature [is] a concept of the health sciences that is much broader than was the view as recently as ten years ago. Rather than equating health research with biomedical research only, the principles recognize the importance of such areas as epidemiology and biostatistics, . . . and the behavioral and social sciences for disease prevention and health maintenance. . . . The committee regards this broadened concept as a desirable advance in policy formulation, and supports efforts to translate this perspective into tangible and adequate support for the full complement of the health sciences (p. 25).

Individual behavior . . . is now recognized more widely than ever as an important determinant of health. . . . Even the nature of stress in our society and our personal relationships at work and at home have changed. The effects of these many factors are profound . . . and most of the long-term consequences are poorly understood (p. 12).

Each component of these health sciences has special contributions to make to . . . improved health and disease prevention. An overriding emphasis on any one part of the spectrum, or the exclusion or neglect of individual fields, would limit the benefits to be derived from scientific research (p. 15).

We endorse a major theme, . . . that fundamental research is a component . . . of the behavioral and social sciences, and population sciences such as biostatistics and epidemiology. We also suggest that fundamental research in these areas has not been adequately developed (p. 28).

We strongly endorse . . . multidisciplinary, collaborative research programs, particularly in applied research. Health problems, by their very nature, are often complex and are not readily resolved by unidisciplinary research. There is need to facilitate the multidisciplinary collaboration . . . so that the scientists may join in generating research programs that are of a scale suited to the dimensions of many of our health problems (p. 53).

This chapter suggests a framework in which health and behavior research can usefully be considered by policy makers. The report is replete with specific suggestions about scientific and insititutional opportunities, but the steering committee explicitly decided not to undertake detailed prescriptions. Rather, policy makers in different settings can consider how progress can best be made in light of the framework and suggestions provided in this report.

TABLE 19.1   Basic Concepts of Research in Health and Behavior

---

The burden of illness has shifted from acute infectious diseases to chronic diseases with multiple interacting risk factors, which prominently include such behavioral elements as smoking, alcohol, exercise, diet, and response to stress.

The definition of health sciences must be expanded beyond biomedical fields to include the biobehavioral sciences.

The biobehavioral sciences have a major role to play in elucidating and alleviating many components of the current burden of illness.

Biobehavioral sciences already have made significant contributions to improved health and hold great promise for further progress.

The science base in the biobehavioral sciences should be strengthened, and adequate support should be provided for such research.

Multidisciplinary, collaborative programs are a valuable and needed component of some types of health research.

SOURCES: Brown (1977); Institute of Medicine (1979, 1980).

Role of Basic Research Relating to Health and Behavior

The health sciences are a series of related disciplines, linked together and contributing to each other. Links between and among the disciplines must be strong if developing knowledge is to move smoothly and efficiently from basic research into useful applications. Because various research efforts often operate in isolation from one another, and especially from clinical practice, feedback from practitioners to clinical investigators and to basic scientists must be forged and maintained. Improved mechanisms are also needed for systematic surveys of basic and clinical science advances for their potential application to prevention and treatment of disease, particularly for very burdensome problems.

In efforts to achieve comprehensiveness in health research, there currently is interest in revitalizing such disciplines as epidemiology and biostatistics, in strengthening such disciplines as biomedical engineering and behavioral sciences, and in forming novel conjunctions of disciplines in health services research and prevention research. Such developments are in accord with a traditional appreciation in the United States of the importance of strong basic sciences such as biochemistry, genetics, physiology, pharmacology, and related fields in better understanding the human body.

Basic research has great merit in its own right and is also relevant to preventing and treating disease. However, the time interval to "payoff" in terms of effective diagnosis, treatment, or prevention is hard to predict. Sometimes movement from basic science to clinical application is dramatic and rapid. For example, less than 20 years elapsed after the discovery of brain amines before their distinctive distribution within the brain had been mapped, hypotheses about their role in Parkinson's disease were proposed, and the first reasonable treatment of this serious disease emerged. Other times, applications of basic knowledge to clinical problems can take much longer. Can wise policy foster rapid advances that benefit health?

The remarkable progress in neurosciences toward a better understanding of the physiological and chemical properties of neural systems is of considerable importance. Recently acquired insights into such neuroregulators as catecholamines, hypothalamic hormones, and endorphins offer great promise for clinical medicine. Contributions in the neurosciences can be expected to accelerate and have attracted several Nobel prizes in recent years.* These advances are pertinent to such diverse conditions as hypertension, stroke, stress resistance, blindness, fertility and its regulation, Par-

---

*Among Nobel prizes awarded for work in the biobehavioral sciences were those going to Julius Axelrod, Ulf Von Euler, Niko Tinbergen, Konrad Lorenz, Roger Guillemin, Andrew Schally, David Hubel, Torsten Wiesel, and Roger Sperry.

kinson's disease, schizophrenia, depression, and the many manifestations of pain. Implications of neurobiology for health constitute an exciting research frontier for the remainder of this century. Such research, together with newer methods and concepts in behavioral sciences, are being pursued with vigor and interdisciplinary cooperation. The potentiality exists for detailed understanding of behavior and its biological foundations for health. Such understanding would offer unprecedented opportunities in prevention and therapy.

In principle, all basic research in the life sciences has long-run implications for disease prevention. But there still is much to learn about most of the mechanisms of disease before it will be possible to offer prevention at a fundamental level. As a practical matter, prevention today typically relies on modification of specific behaviors or conditions, often in the absence of any firm understanding of their role in producing disease. Knowledge about the best ways of altering the occurrence of such behaviors may be extremely useful in devising near-term strategies for prevention of disease. Such attempts to change behavior for health can be greatly facilitated by advances in the biobehavioral sciences.

Careful examination of the burden of illness in the nation helps to point up the importance of behavioral factors for health. As noted throughout this report, cardiovascular disease, cancer, lung disease, accidents, and homicides and other violence constitute major drains on life and health. Such disorders have substantial behavioral components, so approaches to preventing or managing them must include a strong biobehavioral perspective. As the burden of illlness changes, the sciences needed to lessen it also must change.

One useful perspective for research on health and behavior is the influence of the life course. Some of these issues are illustrated in the three chapters on prevention efforts (Chapters 13, 14, and 15) and in Chapter 11, "Aging and Health." Available research suggests that certain times of life such as early life, adolescence, and old age are associated with particular kinds of vulnerability, as reflected in unique patterns in the burden of illness. More precise assessment of such life-course differences may help to pinpoint groups in special need of preventive interventions for certain types of behavior-related illnesses. Because evidence indicates that age groups differ markedly in the interventions that have the greatest and most long-lasting impact, a developmental perspective would appear crucial for designing effective approaches.

Increasingly, it will be in the public's interest to foster progress in the full range of health sciences. Discovering how best to achieve this goal will require cooperation and innovation within and among the scientific community; the health professions; and policy makers in government, philanthropies, industry, and academic institutions.

Problems Shared by Biobehavioral and Other Health-Related Sciences

The Institute of Medicine (1981a,b,c,d) recently organized and conducted four invitational conferences sponsored by the Charles H. Revson Foundation. They were designed to examine diverse areas of biomedical research policy that have particular significance to health and medicine today. Each conference brought together a multidisciplinary array of participants from academic institutions, government, industry, labor, clinical medicine, public health, and private foundations. The four conferences dealt with widely divergent issues, but certain common themes emerged, including the following needs (Institute of Medicine, 1981e):

* *greater interdisciplinary collaboration* within the scientific community and more communication between it and clinical practitioners, medical educators, public and private policy makers, and the general public;
* *productive allocation of resources* in an era of economic constraints;
* *better understanding of the impact of research discoveries and science policy decisions* on individuals and society, and concomitant ethical dilemmas;
* *strengthened data collection, epidemiology, and other supporting sciences* to improve disease prevention and health promotion efforts; and
* *improved research methods.*

The remainder of this chapter focuses mainly on the first two themes. The others are implicit in the earlier chapters.

Interdisciplinary Cooperation and Collaboration

Dual Needs for Subspecialty and Interdisciplinary Research

This report focuses attention on the need for joint efforts among the sciences, especially between biomedical and behavioral sciences. As knowledge in the life sciences has accumulated during the past few decades, a remarkable transformation has occurred. The amount of information and its complexity has overwhelmed anything imagined when the great expansion of research began shortly after World War II. To gain technical depth, research workers have had to specialize and master the complexities of a narrow area.

One field in which specialization has occurred with great success is neuro- and behavioral biology. Illumination is emerging on anatomy, physiology, biochemistry, pharmacology, pathology, and behavioral aspects of the nervous system. Each discipline was subdivided in order to untangle the complexity of the brain and its functions. Yet, as pieces of knowledge were gained, their relation to other pieces became a matter of great interest. Subspecialty barriers have begun to diminish in the face of needs to combine perspectives and pool technical strengths—to bring order out of complexity. An integrative trend has become apparent in recent years, along with continuing and essential specialized research. The joint ventures contribute greatly to the picture of a functioning nervous system in a living organism and of ways in which it can malfunction.

The biobehavioral sciences need to be strengthened, and deliberate efforts should be made to bring them into closer contact with pressing problems in health. However, meeting such goals inevitably will require considerable interdisciplinary interactions. Mutual benefits of interdisciplinary collaboration are the key to its success. A policy opportunity is to create conditions that favor mutual benefit in joint efforts. Some conditions can draw disciplines together in ways that promote multidisciplinary collaborations, for instance, geographic proximity of investigators and communication devices such as regular seminars or special retreats that encourage exploration across disciplinary barriers. Where disciplines with very different traditions are involved, time is needed for each to learn the essential language, style, and substance of the other, so that communication about a shared interest can be based on understanding and respect for the value of the contributions each can make to the other in solving a complex problem. Examples set by a few outstanding scientists can have widely ramifying effects, but recognition of the inherent difficulties by research administrators and by funding agencies is essential.

Encouraging Interdisciplinary Research on Health and Behavior

Typically, interdisciplinary and interdepartmental teams arise because investigators have identified a scientific problem that is inherently multifaceted. Interdisciplinary collaboration is not an end in itself; rather, it is a means to a higher goal—solving a problem. Such collaboration is achieved only when the task actually demands it. Still, there are several key determinants to how easily and productively cooperation among disciplines occurs.

Communication   Specialties within the biomedical and behavioral sciences each have developed highly technical and often idiosyncratic vocabularies that facilitate communication within the field. Increased communication across specialties can help to identify similarities and differences in the approaches of different fields to a common problem. Such shared perspectives are especially vital to the success of cross-disciplinary research efforts, in which investigators must develop mutually satisfactory solutions to problems of design. For example, how should a research psychologist who typically relies on verbal information from test subjects go about incorporating into a research design some biochemical measures that require collecting and processing of blood or urine samples? Which experimental features are crucial to the success of each type of discipline? Which can be discarded or modified? Only a few forums presently exist where researchers can become acquainted with investigators in other disciplines who may be interested in examining questions of mutual interest. Scientific publications, conferences, and institutions typically focus either on a particular discipline or a specific health problem viewed from a single biomedical or behavioral perspective. It is important to encourage opportunities to forge a meaningful conjunction of biomedical and behavioral perspectives. The conferences held as part of the *Health and Behavior* study serve as examples for this type of activity.

Institutional Structure Most academic institutions form departments along disciplinary lines. Existing divisions of science fields are often arbitrary, and some have become outmoded as a result of advancing knowledge. New forms of organization may be needed to permit researchers to cross into new, substantive areas. Some institutions are successfully supporting interdisciplinary research, and such models merit further analysis and encouragement. Structures should be designed to simplify administrative arrangements for research that draws on resources from more than one department. They also must ensure that investigators whose interests cross disciplinary or departmental lines have adequate chances for rewards and prestige, including academic tenure. Such issues are exacerbated by economic stringency, with attendant pressures on department funds.

Study Review Committees Many of the investigators who participated in the conferences held as part of this study emphasized the need for better funding mechanisms for interdisciplinary research. Within the federal funding structure, most grant proposals are considered by peer review committees set up along traditional, unidisciplinary lines. It is not clear that this parallel to the academic structure is optimal for evaluating and supporting research. Study review committees for multidisciplinary research proposals should have members from a range of relevant disciplines who are aware of and sensitive to both the complexities of interdisciplinary research and the trade-offs in methodological rigor that sometimes are necessary when developing an interdisciplinary technology. Narrowly composed study sections are vulnerable to lacunae in knowledge that undermine informed judgments about appropriateness and scientific caliber within the context of a proposed study. As with other parts of the research community, productive consideration of multidisciplinary research is most likely to occur when members of the review committee have developed a common basis for communicating to each other. Also of importance is the need to balance basic biochemical and animal studies with applied and clinical research, so that both receive the support needed to advance the field. With current reductions in research budgets, researchers are concerned that funding agencies now tend to retreat into familiar patterns of within-discipline support.

Mechanisms for Linking Biomedical and Biobehavioral Sciences

Opportunities inherent in linking biomedical and biobehavioral sciences currently are being pursued in a variety of contexts (National Heart, Lung, and Blood Institute, 1981). Policy makers interested in research on health and behavior are seeking to foster collaboration of biomedical and biobehavioral scientists through a variety of devices. Where possible, they are building on existing grant, contract, fellowship, and research training mechanisms. Some research support should be constructed so that it can be obtained *only* by such collaboration.

In a substantial number of major research awards, funding agencies should give explicit recognition to the importance of biobehavioral factors in disease. In the areas considered in this report, agencies should systematically review the nature and extent of support for research on biobehavioral factors in pathogenesis, clinical care and rehabilitation, and primary or secondary prevention. Consideration should include ways to foster interdisciplinary activities between the neural and behavioral sciences and the biomedical disciplines.

Universities or medical centers with appropriate capabilities may find it useful to establish centers in which the goals of funded research will require sustained collaboration across disciplines. A potential focus for such a center could be the study of biobehavioral factors in disease or in specific diseases. Such centers should reflect this orientation in their names and in the range of disciplines represented. To be effective, they will require long-term commitment of funds, personnel, space, and other resources.

In academic medical centers, interdisciplinary research would benefit from active involvement of departments of medicine, family medicine, geriatrics, pediatrics, and psychiatry. Similar links to basic science departments of genetics, biochemistry, pharmacology, and neurobiology also can be helpful. Such cooperative ventures could be fostered by joint grants, given only for research clearly built on a cooperative effort to link biobehavioral and biomedical disciplines. Specific arrangements would have to be individually tailored. In some places, collaboration might involve several departments; in others, one department or even a major laboratory might have the necessary breadth of interests and skills.

The Interplay of Basic and Clinical Research

With respect to disease and disability, progress depends on a balance between attention to the problems of contemporary patients and patients of future generations. This requires policy judgments about which efforts are likely to yield prompt benefit for current patients and which offer great promise that can be fulfilled only with long-range effort. These judgments affect resource allocations for research and institutional arrangements that foster or hinder interplay between basic science and clinical research. In recent years, there has been growing concern in the biomedical research community that ties between basic and clinical investigation are weakening (Brown, 1977; Institute of Medicine, 1979, 1980). It is a matter of special interest for research on health and behavior, where some past successes give reason to believe that such linkages are of great importance.

As an example of important interactions of basic and clinical research, studies of brain function have been powerfully stimulated by drug treatment for mental disorders. These investigations began as an attempt to learn the mechanisms of action of drugs used to treat major mental disorders such as depression and schizophrenia (cf. Chapter 9). Such research brought a generation of young scientists into contact with the emerging field of neurobiology. Details of the hypotheses of major mental disorders that have arisen are not important in this context, but their impact on the field is. They have aroused interest, stimulated basic and clinical research, and led to insights about neuroregulation, endocrine function, and behavioral biology. Also, this research has contributed to improving the quality of treatment not only of mental disorders but also of cardiovascular disorders that are influenced by the nervous system.

Thus, the dynamic interplay of clinical and basic research can be profoundly beneficial over time—in this field as in others. Fruits of basic research can grow into valuable applications, and the stimulus of clinical observations can lead to new basic discoveries. This poses important questions for agencies that sponsor research and for research-conducting institutions. How can programs be devised, applications reviewed, grants made, and research organized in ways that foster the interplay of basic and clinical research? What institutional arrangements are conducive to such linkage? These fundamental science-policy questions merit sustained attention from government, industry, philanthropies, and universities.

Strengthening Research Capabilities in Health and Behavior

Essential to the success of the mission delineated in this report is attraction of talented and dedicated young people to the health and behavior research arena. The first step is wider recognition of the importance of these problems, the burden of illness they impose, their human impact, and the urgency of progress. The second is awareness that scientific opportunities exist for grappling with the problems. Progress so far has been achieved by a relatively small number of scientists and clinicians in a few fields working for a rather short time. There were earlier pioneering contributions, but scientific study of human behavior on a substantial scale is largely a product of the mid-twentieth century; the focus of this approach on major health problems has been modest indeed. An infusion of young scientists, clinical and basic, offers great promise for future advancement of knowledge.

Training Programs for Biobehavioral Scientists

Interdisciplinary research depends first on training young investigators to expand the scope of inquiry beyond their primary discipline. The need for researchers with experience in biobehavioral research has led to the introduction of training programs in psychological and behavioral aspects of arteriosclerosis (National Heart, Lung, and Blood Institute, 1981). This development is a direct recognition that biobehavioral factors are involved in several major aspects of arteriosclerotic diseases. By the same token, training programs in cardiology should be strongly encouraged to develop a biobehavioral component. The same is true in other fields of medicine in which biobehavioral factors are important, such as pediatrics, family medicine, and geriatrics.

Professional development and training can also be enhanced by interdisciplinary workshops, conferences, and symposia. The National Heart, Lung, and Blood Institute and the National Institute of Mental Health have provided leadership in promoting such training. An extension of this approach would help to strengthen research capability, especially when biomedical and biobehavioral sciences are closely juxtaposed, as occurred in the conferences held as part of the Health and Behavior project (Appendix A).

A vigorous, systematic interdisciplinary research training effort in this area is essential to bring young investigators into the field and provide settings in which they can make significant contributions. Among requirements for such research training are:

- *M.D.-Ph.D. training programs in biobehavioral sciences* This approach has been highly successful in biological sciences and urgently needs to be broadened now to include such fields as psychology and sociology.
- *Realistic research training stipends* It must be feasible for young scientists to learn their craft well, and this takes considerable time.
- *Targeted funding to institutions supporting postdoctoral training programs on the design and conduct of biobehavioral research* Such training should be available both to physicians and nonphysicians. Programs for the former could emphasize basic science; those for the latter, pathology and aspects of clinical medicine, helping to build bridges between the laboratory and clinic.
- *Stipends for students to do biobehavioral research* Such projects could spark interest at a crucially formative stage of career development; stipends for appropriate graduate and medical students in biological and biobehavioral sciences could be valuable in developing the essential scientific cadre.

Career Pathways for Biobehavioral Scientists

When young people have completed research training in health and behavioral sciences, there must be appropriate career pathways if these precious skills are not to be wasted. Relevant agencies and institutions must consider long term career pathways through which the problems delineated in this report can be addressed effectively.

In the decade ahead, the time will be ripe for appointing more behavioral scientists to medical school faculties. It is already apparent that behavioral scientists from several disciplines have important roles in departments of psychiatry and family medicine. They now are beginning to appear in other medical school departments, including pediatrics, internal medicine, preventive medicine, and some basic science departments. Behavioral scientists have been appointed in schools of public health, but the numbers so far are small. Some of the most productive research on problems of behavior has been carried out at medically oriented research institutes such as the intramural program of the National Institute of Mental Health, the Walter Reed Army Institute of Research, and a number of medical schools. With growing interest in and recognition of neurobiology and behavioral biology, it is appropriate to consider appointments in these specialties in basic science departments, not only in medical schools but also in faculties of arts and sciences. This is one way to ensure full participation of behaviorally oriented research in the broad front of profound advances sweeping the life sciences.

One encouraging development is the emergence of departments of behavior in research-oriented schools of medicine. At least four models of orientation can be discerned from the few schools that have created such departments: behavioral biology, human development, behavioral medicine, and social medicine. The intellectual focus of the first type is biological; of the second, psychological; of the third, psychophysiological; and of the fourth, social factors that influence health. Regardless of the perspective chosen, such departments will be most effective if they are thoroughly interdisciplinary and emphasize research methods. Such departments can provide a basic resource for many fields of medicine and a powerful stimulus for research advances in health and behavior.

The importance of creating career pathways is nowhere clearer than in the domain of this report. For example, the dramatic advances in the neurosciences are only beginning to be related to behavior. Every new neuroregulator is a potential index of brain disease. Physiologically oriented scientists are in short supply to undertake the effort of learning how these substances produce their molecular and cellular effects and how the effects influence bodily functions and behavior. The human organism will, in a sense, be constructed scientifically in light of the new molecular and cellular biology. This can be done if there is an ample supply of well-trained, broad-minded neuroscientists interacting effectively with well-trained clinical investigators across the breadth of the biobehavioral sciences. At the other end of the spectrum in the social sciences, there is a need also for a cadre of well-grounded scholars who can pursue implications of various social contexts as these influence health (National Research Council, 1980).

Allocation of Resources for Research on Health and Behavior

The many manifestations of the large burden of illness described in Chapter 2, including the economic costs to society, indicate a great need for research programs to identify behaviors that have adverse health consequences. It is vital to determine what factors contribute to these behaviors and how to prevent or modify behavior in ways that promote health. However, research of any type consumes scarce resources that have alternative uses. Allocation of research dollars necessitates explicit and implicit choices about priorities, costs, and potential benefits of various alternatives.

Comprehensive and accurate data are seldom available on direct and indirect costs of illnesses and the investment in related research (Institute of Medicine, 1981f). Some analysis has been carried out on relative investments and costs of alcohol-related problems, cancer, heart and vascular disease, and respiratory disease (Table 19.2).

Just as it is difficult to establish with certainty the economic costs of a given disorder, so it is difficult to calculate research expenditures for it. Typically, relevant research is supported by a variety of agencies that may or may not have disease-specific missions. Also, disease-specific research ultimately may be relevant to a number of other disorders. Furthermore, research costs may be hidden in other funding categories, such as training. Still, available figures indicate quite clearly that research on many illnesses with substantial behavioral components is not funded at a level commensurate with the costs they impose on society. For example, in a paper prepared at the request of the Institute of Medicine for the President's Commission on Mental Health, Barchas et al. (1978) compared the per patient commitment of federal research dollars in the mid 1970s for mental illness and alcoholism on the one hand with that for cancer and heart disease on the other (Table 19.3). Expenditures pertinent to alcoholism and mental illness are very modest compared with research funding for cancer and heart disease. Yet the burden of illness in terms of human suffering and economic costs is comparably heavy in all these cases.

Federal funding for the biobehavioral sciences now comes mainly from three sources. In 1981, the National Science Foundation spent $10 million in its Behavioral and Neurological Section and $0.4 million in its Social and Economic Section for biobehavioral science. For example, among its important contributions has been an extension of knowledge about basic processes of learning, including the neural substrates of learning. Since 1976, the National Institutes of Health has more than doubled support for health-related social and behavioral science research, to a current annual level estimated to exceed $100 million. Especially impressive has been the

TABLE 19.2 Health Research Dollars in Relation to Economic Cost

Disorder	NIH/ADAMHA Lead Institute Research Effort, 1978 (million dollars)	Economic Cost to Nation, 1975 (million dollars)	Ratio of Research Effort to Economic Cost (percent)
Alcoholism/drug abuse	16[a]	43,000[c]	0.04
Cancer	627[b]	19,000[d]	3.3
Cardiovascular disease	284[b]	46,000[d]	0.6
Respiratory disease	69[b]	19,000[d]	0.4

SOURCES: [a] U.S. Department of Health, Education, and Welfare (1979); [b] Carrigan et al. (1979); [c] Berry et al. (1977); [d] U.S. Department of Health, Education, and Welfare (1978).

TABLE 19.3   Research Expenditures Per Patient for
Several Diseases in Mid-1970s

Disease	Research Dollars Per Patient
Cancer	203
Cardiovascular disease	88
Schizophrenia	7
Depression	5
Drug Abuse	6
Alcoholism	2

SOURCE: Barchas et al. (1978).

growth of the Behavioral Medicine Branch of the National Heart, Lung, and Blood Institute. Since 1979, cardiovascular biobehavioral research has had a threefold increase, to a current annual level of $25 million. A major current expenditure is the Multiple Risk Factor Intervention Trial (MRFIT), a multicenter effort to change certain risk factors related to cardiovascular disease; interventions include smoking cessation, diet, and adherence to antihypertensive regimens (cf. Chapter 15). Finally, it seems reasonable to classify all of the expenditures of the Alcohol, Drug Abuse, and Mental Health Administration as biobehavioral research, which in fiscal year 1981 amounted to just over $250 million.

Most health problems considered in this report fall in the domain of the scientific missions of the National Institutes of Health. We have noted with approval their recent progress in addressing problems of health and behavior; yet $100 million is still a small part of their total budget, which exceeds $3.5 billion. The National Science Foundation also has devoted a small, though valuable, fraction of its approximately $1 billion budget for support of research pertinent to health and behavior. We recognize the importance of contributions that have been made, but we doubt seriously whether the current level of effort is commensurate with the burden of illness and the scientific opportunities described in this report. The National Institutes of Health and the National Science Foundation will be crucial in the remainder of this century as sources of support for research aimed at alleviating this burden of illness.

The fostering of the biobehavioral sciences in relation to mental illness, alcohol-related problems, and drug abuse has been an outstanding achievement of the constituent institutes of the Alcohol, Drug Abuse, and Mental Health Administration. However, two of these institutes are small, and budgets for all three are decreasing. In any event, this agency is much smaller and less influential than either the National Institutes of Health or the National Science Foundation. Altogether, there is at present a remarkable discrepancy between unprecedented scientific opportunities on the one hand and diminishing support for such research on the other.

A few private foundations have recently taken a creative and valuable interest in this field.* But such efforts are necessarily small in relation to governmental research support capability. In 1981, the total expenditures of all philanthropies for all purposes came to about $2.6 billion. The amount allocated to research on health and behavior is no more than several million dollars annually. Thus, foundations can play a vital, path-breaking role, but they cannot take primary responsibility for progress in this sphere. Similarly, contributions from industry, except for drug development, are modest indeed and are unlikely to increase greatly in the foreseeable future.

Although it is encouraging to see that some areas of support have been expanding in the past few years, the overall trend has been, at best, no increase in funding. In light of the enormous burden of illness, resource commitments to research on behavioral factors and their biological substrates still are very small. Interest even in such a crucial behavior as heavy cigarette smoking was slight for a long time. Recently, there has been an upsurge of awareness of the importance of such behavioral factors as smoking, not only in the scientific and health professional communities, but also, and perhaps especially, in the public at large. Now as never before, there are manifestations in the media and elsewhere of general public interest in health and behavior problems.

Given the deep national concern and strong data on the contribution of behavioral factors to the national burden of illness, do scientific opportunities exist that could provide a logical response to this great challenge? The bulk of this report has examined various lines of potential scientific inquiry. Many substantial opportunities for research do in fact exist. They offer the promise of clarifying linkages of health and behavior and the potential of suggesting more effective therapeutic and preventive interventions in the future. This being the case, the present low level of funding of research deserves serious reexamination. It would be tragic to allow a prolonged decline in support at a time of expanding scientific opportunity. A major opportunity for health science policy today is to find ways to bring support of the promising lines of research described in this report into more rational alignment with the costs to society of the heavy burden of behavior-related illnesses.

---

*Especially noteworthy are efforts of the MacArthur Foundation (biobehavioral sciences and mental health) and the W. T. Grant Foundation (behavioral pediatrics; stress and coping in child development).

Concluding Perspective

The scientific work considered in this report is largely a product of the past three decades. Thirty years ago, biobehavioral sciences lacked the fundamental knowledge, well-designed clinical research, abundant clinical experience, and interdisciplinary cooperation to make possible a useful contribution to the large clinical and public health problems of behavior-related disease and disability. Now the situation is very different.

A new generation of investigators possessing first-rate scientific training, abundant research accomplishment, and extensive clinical experience has constructed a valuable guide to the mysterious territory of human behavioral biology. The field is growing markedly in quality. There is intense intellectual stimulation and a sense of the moving frontiers of research. This work increasingly highlights an area of immense human suffering that is beginning to be lifted. But areas of ignorance are still large, and many opportunities remain to be grasped.

We have emphasized repeatedly both the enormous contribution of behavioral factors to the current burden of illness in this country and the critical need for scientific exploration of that contribution. But the point is more general. When the burden of illness changes, the sciences needed to lessen it also change. As new opportunities for scientific advances arise, their relevance to disease must be assessed. Outmoded conventions must be set aside in the face of new observations, fresh ideas, and neglected responsibilities. Not so long ago, the emerging field of biochemistry was viewed suspiciously by chemists as weak chemistry and by biologists as weak biology; today this hybrid discipline is central to all biomedical research. Similarly, conventional wisdom of three decades ago discounted the potential importance of research on neurochemistry and neuroendocrinology. That misguided wisdom also discouraged—and still does to some extent—the study of behavior in its own right. Prejudices and inherent complexities have presented formidable obstacles to efforts to link biological and behavioral phenomena. The tasks are surely complex but also fascinating. Above all, the practical problems of clinical medicine and public health demand novel conjunctions and open-minded, cooperative explorations.

In the foreseeable future, it should be possible to construct a reasonably unified biobehavioral science pertinent to health and disease, with major applications in all the health professions and by the public at large. Such applications require deeper understanding of human adaptation. This would produce large strides both in disease prevention and in diagnosis and treatment. Research on health and behavior promises no quick fix. It can offer long-term dedication to a fundamentally humanitarian goal of bringing the strengths of science to bear on a major component of the national burden of illness. If the nation is able to grasp this opportunity, the United States can provide world leadership in attacking problems of pervasive importance that have long been neglected.

References

Barchas, J. D., Berger, P. A., and Elliott, G. R. *Scientific Advances in Psychobiological Treatment of Severe Mental Disorders* Invited paper for the President's Commission on Mental Health, Institute of Medicine, National Academy of Sciences, 1978.

Berry, R. E., Boland, J. P., Smart, C. N., and Kanak, J. R. *The Economic Cost of Alcohol Abuse—1975* Final Report, Contract No. ADM 281–76–0016. Prepared for the National Institute on Alcohol Abuse and Alcoholism, August 1977.

Brown, S. S. *Policy Issues in the Health Sciences* A staff paper for the Institute of Medicine. Washington, D.C.: National Academy of Sciences, 1977.

Carrigan, W. T., Armstrong, A. B., and Moehring, J. T. (Eds.) *Basic Data Relating to the National Institutes of Health* Washington, D.C.: U.S. Government Printing Office, 1979, NIH Publ. No. 79–1261.

Institute of Medicine *DHEW's Research Planning Principles: A Review* Washington, D.C.: National Academy of Sciences, 1979.

Institute of Medicine *DHEW Health Research Planning, Phase II* Washington, D.C.: National Academy of Sciences, 1980.

Institute of Medicine *Genetic Influences on Responses to the Environment* Washington, D.C.: National Academy Press, 1981a.

Institute of Medicine *Evaluating Medical Technologies in Clinical Use* Washington, D.C.: National Academy Press, 1981b.

Institute of Medicine *Evaluating Health Promotion in the Workplace* Washington, D.C.: National Academy Press, 1981c.

Institute of Medicine *International Policies for Cancer Research* Washington, D.C.: National Academy Press, 1981d.

Institute of Medicine *The Revson Conferences: Critical Issues in Health Sciences* Washington, D.C.: National Academy Press, 1981e.

Institute of Medicine *Costs of Environment-Related Health Effects: A Plan for Continuing Study* Washington, D.C.: National Academy Press, 1981f.

National Heart, Lung, and Blood Institute *Arteriosclerosis, 1981. Report of the Working Group. Summary, Conclusions and Recommendations* Washington, D.C.: U.S. Government Printing Office, 1981, NIH Publ. No. 81–2034.

National Research Council *Personnel Needs for Training for Biomedical and Behavioral Research* Washington, D.C.: National Academy of Sciences, 1980.

United States Department of Health, Education, and Welfare *Health, United States, 1978* Washington, D.C.: U.S. Government Printing Office, 1978, DHEW Publ. No. (DHS) 78–1232.

United States Department of Health, Education, and Welfare *ADAMHA Data Book, Fiscal Year 1978* Washington, D.C.: U.S. Government Printing Office, 1979, DHEW Publ. No. (ADM) 79–662.

VI
APPENDIXES

A
Conferences Comprising
the Study Health and Behavior:
A Research Agenda

Biobehavioral Issues in the Assessment, Continuing Care, and Rehabilitation of
Patients at Risk for Life-Threatening Arrhythmias
Biobehavioral Elements in the Pathophysiology of Sudden Cardiac Death

Infants at Risk for Developmental Dysfunction
LEON EISENBERG, M.D., *Chair*
Low Birth Weight Infants
Substance Use in Pregnancy
Teenage Parents

Health, Behavior, and Aging
JUDITH RODIN, Ph.D., *Chair*
Health Behavior of the Elderly
Immunology and Behavior in Aging
Alcohol Use as a Health Problem in Aging

Behavior, Health Risks, and Social Disadvantage
C. DAVID JENKINS, Ph.D., *Chair*
Mechanisms for the Unequal Burden of Malignancies Among the Disadvantaged
Mechanisms for the Unequal Burden of Schizophrenic Disorders Among the
Disadvantaged
The Future of Collaborative Biomedical, Social, and Behavioral Research

Summaries of each of these conferences have been published and are available
from:

NATIONAL ACADEMY PRESS
2101 Constitution Avenue, N.W.
Washington, D.C. 20418

B

Participants in the Health and Behavior Conferences

Smoking and Behavior

Josephine D. Arasteh, Ph.D.
Health Scientist Administrator
National Institute of Child Health and
Human Development
Bethesda, Maryland

Joseph H. Autry, M.D.
Coordinator
Clinical Research Center Program
National Institute of Mental Health
Rockville, Maryland

Albert Bandura, Ph.D.
Professor of Psychology
Department of Psychology
Stanford University
Stanford, California

Diana Baumrind, Ph.D.
Family Socialization Project
Institute of Human Development
University of California
Berkeley, California

Anne Brunswick, Ph.D.
Adolescent and Young Adult Health Unit
Columbia University
New York, New York

John J. Conger, Ph.D.
Professor of Psychology
University of Colorado Medical Center
Colorado Psychiatric Hospital
Denver, Colorado

Peter Dews, Ph.D.
Professor of Psychiatry and Psychobiology
Harvard Medical School
Boston, Massachusetts

Bernard H. Ellis, Jr., M.A.
Program Director for Smoking and
Occupational Activities
Officer of Cancer Communication
National Cancer Institute
Bethesda, Maryland

Richard I. Evans, Ph.D.
Professor of Psychology
Director, Social Psychology/Behavioral
Medicine Research and Graduate
Training Group
Department of Psychology
University of Houston
Houston, Texas

327

Diana Fink, M.D.
Associate Director for Medical Applications
  of Cancer Research
National Cancer Institute
Bethesda, Maryland

Bernard H. Fox, Ph.D.
Manager, Social Science Biometric Branch
National Cancer Institute
Bethesda, Maryland

*Ruth T. Gross, M.D.
Katherine Dexter and Stanley McCormick
  Professor of Pediatrics
Stanford University School of Medicine
Stanford, California

Ellen Gritz, Ph.D.
Department of Psychiatry and Bio-
  behavioral Sciences
University of California School of Medicine
Los Angeles, California

*Beatrix A. M. Hamburg, M.D.
Senior Research Psychiatrist
National Institute of Mental Health
Bethesda, Maryland

*David A. Hamburg, M.D.
President
Institute of Medicine
National Academy of Sciences
Washington, D.C.

Jeffrey E. Harris, M.D., Ph.D.
Assistant Professor of Economics
Department of Economics
Massachusetts Institute of Technology
Cambridge, Massachusetts

Jules Hirsch, M.D.
Professor and Senior Physician
Laboratory of Human Behavior and
  Metabolism
Rockefeller University
New York, New York

---

*Member, Institute of Medicine.

Renee Jenkins, M.D.
Assistant Professor
Department of Pediatrics
Howard University College of Medicine
Washington, D.C.

Shirley Jessor, Ph.D.
Institute of Behavioral Science
University of Colorado
Boulder, Colorado

Chris-Ellyn Johanson, Ph.D.
Research Psychologist
Division of Research
National Institute on Drug Abuse
Rockville, Maryland

Lorraine V. Klerman, Dr.P.H.
Associate Professor of Public Health
The Florence Heller Graduate School for
  Advanced Studies in Social Welfare
Brandeis University
Waltham, Massachusetts

Mary Grace Kovar
Analytical Coordinator Branch Chief
National Center for Health Statistics
Hyattsville, Maryland

Charles Krauthammer, M.D.
Director, Division of Science
Alcohol, Drug Abuse, and Mental Health
  Administration
Rockville, Maryland

Howard Leventhal, Ph.D.
Professor of Psychology
Department of Psychology
University of Wisconsin
Madison, Wisconsin

Alfred McAlister, Ph.D.
Assistant Professor
Department of Behavioral Sciences
Harvard School of Public Health
Boston, Massachusetts

Nathan Maccoby, Ph.D.
James M. Peck Professor of International
    Communications
Director, Institute for Communication
    Research
Stanford University
Stanford, California

*Gilbert S. Omenn, M.D., Ph.D.
Associate Director for Human Resources
    and Social and Economic Services
Office of Science and Technology
Executive Office of the President
Washington, D.C.

Carole S. Orleans, Ph.D.
Assistant Professor of Medical Psychology
Department of Psychiatry
Duke University Medical Center
Durham, North Carolina

Betty Pickett, Ph.D.
Deputy Director, National Institute of
    Child Health and Human Development
National Institutes of Health
Bethesda, Maryland

John Pinney
Director, Office on Smoking and Health
Rockville, Maryland

*Julius Richmond, M.D.
Assistant Secretary for Health
Department of Health, Education, and
    Welfare
Washington, D.C.

*Henry W. Riecken, Ph.D.
Professor of Behavioral Sciences
University of Pennsylvania School of
    Medicine
Philadelphia, Pennsylvania

Judith Rodin, Ph.D.
Professor, Department of Psychology
Yale University
New Haven, Connecticut

_____

*Member, Institute of Medicine.

Othoniel Rosado
Director, Career Program
United School District
Vintage High School Career Center
Napa, California

Michael A. H. Russell, B.M.,
    M.R.C.P., M.R.C. Psych.
Institute of Psychiatry
The Maudsley Hospital
Addiction Research Unit
London, England

Philip Sapir
Chief, Human Learning and Behavior
    Branch
Center for Research for Mothers and
    Children
National Institute of Child Health and
    Human Development
Bethesda, Maryland

Stanley Schacter, Ph.D.
Professor of Social Psychology
Department of Psychology
Columbia University
New York, New York

Albert J. Stunkard, M.D.
Professor of Psychiatry
University of Pennsylvania
Philadelphia, Pennsylvania

Stephen Weiss, Ph.D.
Chief, Behavioral Medicine Branch
National Heart, Lung, and Blood Institute
Bethesda, Maryland

Myrna M. Weissman, Ph.D.
Senior Scholar in Residence
Institute of Medicine
National Academy of Sciences
Washington, D.C.

Combining Psychosocial and Drug Therapy: Hypertension, Depression, and Diabetes

George N. Aagaard, M.D.
Professor of Medicine
University of Washington School of
  Medicine
Seattle, Washington

Juanita Archer, M.D.
Associate Professor of Medicine
Howard University School of Medicine
Washington, D.C.

*A. Clifford Barger, M.D.
Pfeiffer Professor of Physiology
Harvard Medical School
Boston, Massachusetts

*Mildred Mitchell-Bateman, M.D.
Professor and Chair
Department of Psychiatry
Marshall University School of Medicine
Huntington, West Virginia

Marshall Becker, Ph.D
Professor, Department of Health Behavior
  and Health Education
University of Michigan School of Public
  Health
Ann Arbor, Michigan

Frank N. Beckles, M.D.
Institute of Psychiatry and Human
  Behavior
University of Maryland School of Medicine
Baltimore, Maryland

Philip A. Berger, M.D.
Director, Psychiatric Research Center
Stanford University School of Medicine
Stanford, California

Barry M. Blackwell, M.D.
Professor of Psychiatry and Psychology
Wright State University School of Medicine
Dayton, Ohio

---

*Member, Institute of Medicine.

*H. Keith Brodie, M.D.
Professor and Chair
Department of Psychiatry
Duke University Medical Center
Durham, North Carolina

George Cahill, M.D.
Director of Research
Howard Hughes Medical Institute
Boston, Massachusetts

Caren M. Carney, M.A.
Research Associate
Institute of Medicine
Washington, D.C.

John K. Davidson, M.D., Ph.D.
Chief, Diabetes Unit
Emory University School of Medicine
Atlanta, Georgia

Allan L. Drash, M.D.
Professor of Pediatrics
Children's Hospital of Pittsburgh
Pittsburgh, Pennsylvania

*Harriet P. Dustan, M.D.
Director, Cardiovascular Research and
  Training Center
University of Alabama Medical Center
Birmingham, Alabama

*Carl Eisdorfer, M.D., Ph.D.
Senior Scholar in Residence
Institute of Medicine
Washington, D.C.

Peter L. Frommer, M.D.
Deputy Director, National Heart, Lung,
  and Blood Institute
National Institutes of Health
Bethesda, Maryland

Kenneth Gaarder, M.D.
Private Practice (Psychiatry)
Chevy Chase, Maryland

Elmer E. Green, Ph.D.
Chief, Voluntary Controls Program
Menninger Foundation
Topeka, Kansas

*Ruth T. Gross, M.D.
Katharine Dexter and Stanley McCormick
  Professor of Pediatrics
Stanford University School of Medicine
Stanford, California

*Robert J. Haggerty, M.D.
President
W. T. Grant Foundation
New York, New York

*Beatrix A. M. Hamburg, M.D.
Senior Research Psychiatrist
National Institute of Mental Health
Bethesda, Maryland

*David A. Hamburg, M.D.
President
Institute of Medicine
Washington, D.C.

R. Brian Haynes, M.D., Ph.D.
Department of Epidemiology and
  Biostatistics
McMaster University Medical Center
Hamilton, Ontario, Canada

Adrian O. Hosten, M.D.
Director, Division of Nephrology
Howard University Hospital
Washington, D.C.

Stevo Julius, M.D., Sc.D.
Professor of Internal Medicine
Director, Division of Hypertension
University of Michigan Medical Center
Ann Arbor, Michigan

Berton Kaplan, Ph.D.
Professor of Epidemiology
University of North Carolina
Durham, North Carolina

---

*Member, Institute of Medicine.

Jacob J. Katzow, M.D.
Private Practice (Psychiatry)
Washington, D.C.

*Gerald L. Klerman, M.D.
Administrator
Alcohol, Drug Abuse, and Mental Health
  Administration
Rockville, Maryland

B. Wayne Kong, Ph.D.
Research Associate in Cardiology
Provident Hospital
Baltimore, Maryland

Maria Kovacs, Ph.D.
Assistant Professor of Psychiatry
Western Psychiatric Institute and Clinic
Pittsburgh, Pennsylvania

Charles Krauthammer, M.D.
Director, Division of Science
Alcohol, Drug Abuse, and Mental Health
  Administration
Rockville, Maryland

Henry Krystal, M.D.
Professor of Psychiatry
Michigan State University
Lansing, Michigan

*Robert Lawrence, M.D.
Director, Division of Primary Care and
  Family Medicine
Harvard Medical School
Boston, Massachusetts

*Sol Levine, Ph.D.
University Professors Program
Boston University
Boston, Massachusetts

Lester Luborsky, Ph.D.
Department of Psychiatry
University of Pennsylvania
Philadelphia, Pennsylvania

Charles Mertens, M.D., Ph.D.
Visiting Professor
Harvard School of Public Health
Boston, Massachusetts
(Professor of Psychiatry,
University of Louvain, Belgium)

Leona V. Miller, M.D.
Director, Diabetes Institute of Southern
California
St. Vincent's Hospital
Los Angeles, California

Morris Parloff, Ph.D.
Chief, Psychotherapy and Behavioral
Intervention Section
National Institute of Mental Health
Rockville, Maryland

Lester V. Salans, M.D.
Associate Director for Diabetes
Endocrinology and Metabolic Diseases
National Institutes of Health
Bethesda, Maryland

Dean Schuyler, M.D.
Private Practice (Psychiatry)
Washington, D.C.

Gary Schwartz, Ph.D.
Professor of Psychiatry and Psychology
Yale University
New Haven, Connecticut

Martin E. Seligman, Ph.D.
Professor of Psychology
University of Pennsylvania
Philadelphia, Pennsylvania

Alvin P. Shapiro, M.D.
Professor of Medicine
University of Pittsburgh School of
Medicine
Pittsburgh, Pennsylvania

Peter E. Sifneous, M.D.
Associate Director, Psychiatric Service
Beth Israel Hospital
Boston, Massachusetts

Dorothea F. Sims
Diabetes Health Educator
South Burlington, Vermont

Ethan Sims, M.D.
Professor of Medicine
University of Vermont Medical School
Burlington, Vermont

Robert Spitzer, M.D.
Chief, Department of Biometric Research
New York State Psychiatric Institute
New York, New York

William A. Stason, M.D.
Associate Professor of Health Policy and
Management
Harvard School of Public Health
Boston, Massachusetts

Albert J. Stunkard, M.D.
Professor of Psychiatry
University of Pennsylvania
Philadelphia, Pennsylvania

Richard S. Surwit, Ph.D.
Associate Professor of Medical Psychology
Duke University Medical Center
Durham, North Carolina

Gerald E. Thomson, M.D.
Director of Medicine
Harlem Hospital Center
New York, New York

Donald Ware, M.D.
National Heart, Lung, and Blood Institute
Rockville, Maryland

Irene E. Waskow, Ph.D.
Clinical Research Branch
National Institute of Mental Health
Rockville, Maryland

Myrna M. Weissman, Ph.D.
Senior Scholar in Residence
Institute of Medicine
Washington, D.C.

Redford B. Williams, M.D.
Professor of Psychiatry
Duke University Medical Center
Durham, North Carolina

Steven Woods, Ph.D.
Professor of Psychology
University of Washington
Seattle, Washington

Bruce Zimmerman, M.D.
Chief, Diabetes Clinic
Mayo Clinic
Rochester, Minnesota

Andrew J. Zweifler, M.D.
Professor of Internal Medicine
University of Michigan Medical Center
Ann Arbor, Michigan

Observers

Jack Blain, M.D.
National Institute of Mental Health

Victor Cohn, Ph.D.
Domestic Policy Staff
The White House

Harold Ginzburg, Ph.D.
National Institute on Drug Abuse

Gilman Grave, M.D.
National Institute on Child
   Health and Human Development

Peter Kramer, M.D.
Alcohol, Drug Abuse, and Mental Health
   Administration

Lois Lipsett
National Diabetes Information
   Clearinghouse

Joseph Perpich, M.D., J.D.
National Institutes of Health

Carolyn Robinowitz, M.D.
American Psychiatric Association

Gail Schechter
Alcohol, Drug Abuse, and Mental Health
   Administration

Tina Vanderveen, Ph.D.
National Institute on Alcohol Abuse
   and Alcoholism

Stephen Weiss, Ph.D.
National Heart, Lung, and Blood Institute

Biobehavioral Factors in Sudden Cardiac Death

Joseph H. Autry, M.D.
Coordinator, Clinical Research Center
   Program
National Institute of Mental Health
Rockville, Maryland

*Eugene Braunwald, M.D.
Hersey Professor of the Theory and
   Practice of Physic (Medicine)
Harvard Medical School
Boston, Massachusetts

---

*Member, Institute of Medicine.

James C. Buell, M.D.
Chief of Cardiology
Omaha Veterans Administration Medical
   Center
Omaha, Nebraska

William Castelli, M.D.
Medical Director
Framingham Heart Study
Framingham, Massachusetts

Marilyn Cebelin, M.D.
Deputy Coroner and Associate Pathologist
Cuyahoga County Coroner's Office
Cleveland, Ohio

David Cohen, Ph.D.
Chair of Neurobiology and Behavior
  Department
State University of New York
Stony Brook, New York

Frances Cohen, Ph.D.
Assistant Professor of Medical Psychology
University of California School of Medicine
San Francisco, California

Louis Cohen, M.D.
Professor of Medicine (Cardiology)
University of Chicago School of Medicine
Chicago, Illinois

Theodore Dembroski, Ph.D.
Professor of Psychology
Eckerd College
St. Petersburg, Florida

Regis DeSilva, M.D.
Brigham and Women's Hospital
Harvard Medical School and Cardiovascular
  Laboratory
Harvard School of Public Health
Boston, Massachusetts

Peter Dews, M.S., Ch.B., Ph.D.
Stanley Cobb Professor of Psychiatry and
  Psychobiology
Harvard Medical School
Boston, Massachusetts

Joel Dimsdale, M.D.
Assistant Professor of Psychiatry
Harvard Medical School
Massachusetts General Hospital
Boston, Massachusetts

James Dingell, M.D.
Scientific Officer
National Heart, Lung, and Blood Institute
Bethesda, Maryland

Robert Eliot, M.D.
Chairman, Department of Preventive and
  Stress Medicine, and Director,
  Cardiovascular Center
University of Nebraska Medical Center
Omaha, Nebraska

Peter L. Frommer, M.D.
Deputy Director
National Heart, Lung, and Blood Institute
Bethesda, Maryland

William Greene, M.D.
Professor of Medicine and Psychiatry
University of Rochester School of Medicine
  and Dentistry
Rochester, New York

Thomas P. Hackett, M.D.
Chief, Psychiatry Services
Massachusetts General Hospital
Boston, Massachusetts

Jacob Haft, M.D.
Chief of Cardiology
St. Michael's Medical Center
Newark, New Jersey

James P. Henry, M.D.
Professor of Physiology and Biophysics
University of Southern California
Los Angeles, California

J. Alan Herd, M.D.
Associate Professor
New England Regional Primate Research
  Center
Harvard Medical School
Southborough, Massachusetts

Lawrence Hinkle, M.D.
Professor of Medicine
The New York Hospital—Cornell Medical
  Center
New York, New York

C. David Jenkins, Ph.D.
Director
Department of Behavioral Epidemiology
Boston University Medical Center
Boston, Massachusetts

John Lacey, Ph.D.
Senior Scientist in Psychophysiology
Fels Research Institute
Yellow Springs, Ohio

James Lawler, Ph.D.
Associate Professor of Psychology
University of Tennessee
Knoxville, Tennessee

*Robert F. Murray, Jr., M.D.
Senior Scholar in Residence
Institute of Medicine
Washington, D.C.

William Orr, Ph.D.
Director, Clinical Physiology
University of Oklahoma Health Sciences
  Center
Oklahoma City, Oklahoma

Oglesby Paul, M.D.
Professor of Medicine
Harvard Medical School
Boston, Massachusetts

Harold Pincus, M.D.
Special Assistant to the Director
National Institute of Mental Health
Rockville, Maryland

David Randall, Ph.D.
Associate Professor of Physiology and
  Biophysics
University of Kentucky College of
  Medicine
Lexington, Kentucky

Peter Reich, M.D.
Chief, Psychiatry Service
Peter Bent Brigham Hospital
Boston, Massachusetts

Donald Reis, M.D.
Director, Laboratory of Neurobiology
Cornell Medical College
New York, New York

Judith Rodin, Ph.D.
Professor of Psychology and Psychiatry
Yale University
New Haven, Connecticut

*Richard S. Ross, M.D.
Vice President and Dean
Johns Hopkins University Medical School
Baltimore, Maryland

William Ruberman, M.D.
Director for Medical Research
Health Insurance Plan
New York, New York

Daniel D. Savage, M.D., Ph.D.
Chief, Noninvasive Laboratories
Framingham Heart Study
Framingham, Massachusetts

Gary Schwartz, Ph.D.
Professor of Psychology and Psychiatry
Yale University
New Haven, Connecticut

Charles Spielberger, Ph.D.
Professor of Psychology
University of South Florida
Tampa, Florida

Richard L. Verrier, Ph.D.
Assistant Professor of Physiology
Harvard Medical School and Cardiovascular
  Laboratory
Harvard School of Public Health
Boston, Massachusetts

Stephen Weiss, Ph.D.
Chief, Behavioral Medicine Branch
National Heart, Lung, and Blood Institute
Bethesda, Maryland

Theodore Weiss, M.D.
Assistant Professor of Psychiatry
University of Pennsylvania Hospital
Philadelphia, Pennsylvania

Myrna M. Weissman, Ph.D.
Department of Psychiatry
Yale University
New Haven, Connecticut

Redford Williams, M.D.
Professor of Psychiatry
Duke University Medical Center
Durham, North Carolina

----
*Member, Institute of Medicine.

Observers

Ronald Abeles, Ph.D.
National Institute on Aging

Marsha Goldberg
Institute of Medicine

Margaret Mattson, Ph.D.
National Heart, Lung, and Blood Institute

Angela Mikalide
National Heart, Lung, and Blood Institute

Michelle Trudeau
Institute of Medicine

Stephen Weinstein, Ph.D.
National Heart, Lung, and Blood Institute

Infants at Risk for Developmental Dysfunction

Sigurd H. Ackerman, M.D.
Assistant Professor of Psychiatry
Albert Einstein College of Medicine
Montefiore Hospital and Medical Center
Bronx, New York

Gordon B. Avery, M.D., Ph.D.
Director, Division of Neonatology
Children's Hospital National Medical
   Center
Washington, D.C.

Wendy Baldwin, Ph.D.
Chief, Social and Behavioral Sciences
   Branch
Center for Population Studies
National Institute of Child Health and
   Human Development
Bethesda, Maryland

Lisa F. Berkman, Ph.D.
Assistant Professor of Epidemiology
Yale University School of Public Health
New Haven, Connecticut

Charlotte Catz, M.D.
Chief, Pregnancy and Perinatology Section
National Institute of Child Health and
   Human Development
Bethesda, Maryland

Stella Chess, M.D.
Professor of Child Psychiatry
New York University Medical Center
New York, New York

Ezra Davidson, M.D.
Professor and Chairman
Department of Obstetrics and Gynecology
Charles R. Drew Postgraduate Medical
   School
Los Angeles, California

Felton J. Earls, M.D.
Children's Hospital Medical Center
Boston, Massachusetts

Carol Eckerman, Ph.D.
Associate Professor
Department of Psychology
Duke University
Durham, North Carolina

*Leon Eisenberg, M.D.
Presley Professor of Social Medicine and
   Chairman, Department of Social
   Medicine and Health Policy
Harvard Medical School
Boston, Massachusetts

Peter Fried, Ph.D.
Professor
Department of Psychology
Carleton University
Ottawa, Ontario

Norman Garmezy, Ph.D.
Principal Investigator for Project
   Competency
Professor of Psychology
University of Minnesota
Minneapolis, Minnesota

---

*Member, Institute of Medicine.

Frederick C. Green, M.D.
Associate Director
Children's Hospital National Medical
  Center
Washington, D.C.

Stanley I. Greenspan, M.D.
Chief, Mental Health Study Center
National Institute of Mental Health
Rockville, Maryland

*Beatrix A. M. Hamburg, M.D.
Senior Research Psychiatrist
National Institute of Mental Health
Bethesda, Maryland

Sydney Hans, Ph.D.
Research Associate—Assistant Professor
Department of Psychiatry
Pritzker School of Medicine
University of Chicago
Chicago, Illinois

Myron A. Hofer, M.D.
Professor of Psychiatry
Associated Professor of Neurosciences
Albert Einstein College of Medicine
Montefiore Hospital and Medical Center
Bronx, New York

Melvin Jenkins, M.D.
Chair, Department of Pediatrics
Howard University Hospital
Washington, D.C.

John H. Kennel, M.D.
Professor of Pediatrics
Rainbow Babies and Children's Hospital
Cleveland, Ohio

Marshall Klaus, M.D.
Professor of Pediatrics
Rainbow Babies and Children's Hospital
Cleveland, Ohio

---

*Member, Institute of Medicine.

Lorraine V. Klerman, Dr.P.H.
Associate Professor of Public Health
The Florence Heller Graduate School for
  Advanced Studies in Social Welfare
Brandeis University
Waltham, Massachusetts

P. Herbert Liederman, M.D.
Professor of Psychiatry
Stanford University School of Medicine
Stanford, California

Lewis Lipsitt, Ph.D.
Professor of Psychology and Medical
  Science
Director of Child Study Center
Walter S. Hunter Laboratory of Psychology
Brown University
Providence, Rhode Island

Elizabeth McAnarney, M.D.
Associate Professor of Pediatric Medicine
  and Psychiatry
Strong Memorial Hospital
Rochester, New York

William J. McGanity, M.D.
Director, Department of Obstetrics and
  Gynecology
University of Texas Medical Branch
Galveston, Texas

Klaus Minde, M.D.
Director of Psychiatric Research
Hospital for Sick Children
Toronto, Ontario

*Robert F. Murray, Jr., M.D.
Senior Scholar in Residence
Institute of Medicine
Washington, D.C.

Elena Nightingale, M.D., Ph.D.
Senior Program Officer
National Academy of Sciences
Washington, D.C.

Arthur H. Parmelee, M.D.
Professor of Child Development
Department of Pediatrics
School of Medicine
University of California at Los Angeles
Los Angeles, California

Betty H. Pickett, Ph.D.
Deputy Director
National Institute of Child Health and
   Human Development
Bethesda, Maryland

Sally Provence, M.D.
Professor of Pediatrics
Child Study Center
Yale University
New Haven, Connecticut

Robert Resnick, M.D.
Associate Professor
Department of Reproductive Medicine
University Hospital
San Diego, California

Henry N. Ricciuti, Ph.D.
Professor of Human Development and
   Family Studies
Project Director, Infant Care and Resource
   Center
College of Human Ecology
Cornell University
New York, New York

*Henry W. Riecken, Ph.D.
Professor of Behavioral Sciences
University of Pennsylvania School of
   Medicine
Philadelphia, Pennsylvania

Mortimer G. Rosen, M.D.
Director, Department of Obstetrics and
   Gynecology
Cleveland Metropolitan General Hospital
Cleveland, Ohio

_____

*Member, Institute of Medicine.

Arnold Sameroff, Ph.D.
Illinois Institute of Developmental
   Disabilities
Chicago, Illinois

Robert Sokol, M.D.
Associate Professor of Obstetrics and
   Gynecology
Co-Program Director of Perinatal Clinical
   Research Center
Department of Obstetrics and Gynecology
Cleveland Metropolitan General Hospital
Cleveland, Ohio

*Albert J. Solnit, M.D.
Professor of Psychiatry
Director, Child Study Center
Department of Pediatrics
Yale University School of Medicine
New Haven, Connecticut

Philip Sapir
Chief, Human Learning and Behavioral
   Branch
National Institute of Child Health and
   Human Development
Bethesda, Maryland

Zena Stein, M.D.
Professor of Public Health (Epidemiology)
Sergievsky Center
Columbia University
New York, New York

Mervyn W. Susser, M.B., B.Ch.,
   D.P.H. F.R.C.P.(E)
Sergievsky Professor of Epidemiology
Director, Sergievsky Center
Columbia University
New York, New York

Joanne Weinberg, Ph.D.
Division of Human Nutrition
School of Home Economics
The University of British Columbia
Vancouver, British Columbia

Doris Welcher, Ph.D.
Assistant Professor of Pediatrics
Johns Hopkins University
Baltimore, Maryland

Lee Willerman, Ph.D.
Associate Professor of Psychology
University of Texas
Austin, Texas

Marian Yarrow, Ph.D.
Chief, Laboratory of Developmental
 Psychology
National Institute of Mental Health
Bethesda, Maryland

Edward Zigler, Ph.D.
Sterling Professor of Psychology
Department of Psychology
Yale University
New Haven, Connecticut

Observers

Phyllis Berman, Ph.D.
Human Learning and Behavior Branch
National Institute of Child Health and
 Human Development

Mary Blehar, Ph.D.
Mental Health Science Reports Branch
National Institute of Mental Health

Helen Chao, Ph.D.
National Institute on Alcohol Abuse and
 Alcoholism

Juralyn Gaiter, Ph.D.
Pediatric Research Psychologist
Department of Neonatology
Children's Hospital National Medical
 Center
Washington, D.C.

Vincent Hutchins, M.D.
Associate Bureau Director
Office for Maternal and Child Health

Samuel Kessel, M.D.
Special Assistant to the Surgeon General
U.S. Department of Health and Human
 Services

A. Hussain Tuma, Ph.D.
Chief, Clinical Research Branch
Division of Extramural Programs
National Institute of Mental Health

Health, Behavior, and Aging

Ronald Abeles, Ph.D.
Health Scientist Administrator
National Institute on Aging
Bethesda, Maryland

Willa Abelson, Ph.D.
Department of Psychology
Yale University
New Haven, Connecticut

Robert Ader, Ph.D.
Professor of Psychiatry
University of Rochester Medical School
Rochester, New York

Reubin Andres, M.D.
Medical Director
Gerontology Research Center
National Institute on Aging
Baltimore, Maryland

Joseph H. Atkinson, Jr., M.D.
Assistant Professor of Psychiatry
University of California Medical Center,
 San Diego
San Diego, California

Richard W. Besdine, M.D.
Hebrew Rehabilitation Center for the Aged
Roslindale, Massachusetts

David Blau, M.D.
Assistant Clinical Professor of Psychiatry
Harvard Medical School
Boston, Massachusetts

George W. Bohrnstedt, Ph.D.
Professor of Sociology
Indiana University
Bloomington, Indiana

C. Edward Buckley III, M.D.
Professor
Department of Medicine
Duke University Medical Center
Durham, North Carolina

Donna Cohen, Ph.D.
Associate Professor
Department of Psychiatry and Sciences
University of Washington School of
    Medicine
Seattle, Washington

Gene Cohen, M.D.
Chief, Center on Aging
National Institute of Mental Health
Rockville, Maryland

Richard Dietrich, Ph.D.
Professor and Vice-Chair
Department of Pharmacology
University of Colorado Health Sciences
    Center
Denver, Colorado

*Leon Eisenberg, M.D.
Presley Professor of Social Medicine and
    Chairman, Department of Social
    Medicine and Health Policy
Harvard Medical School
Boston, Massachusetts

Glen Elliott, Ph.D., M.D.
Division of Health Policy Research and
    Education
Harvard University
Cambridge, Massachusetts

Leon Epstein, M.D.
Assistant Director
Langley Porter Institute
San Francisco, California

Anne Foner, Ph.D.
Professor
Department of Sociology and Anthropology
Rutgers College
Rutgers University
New Brunswick, New Jersey

———————

*Member, Institute of Medicine.

Frederick B. Glaser, M.D.
Head of Psychiatry and Health Care
    Development Services
Toronto Addiction Research Foundation
Toronto, Ontario, Canada

Dr. Colin Godber
Psychogeriatric Unit
Moorgreen Hospital
Highfield, Southampton, England

Barry Gurland, M.D.
Director
Center for Geriatrics and Gerontology
Columbia University
New York, New York

*David A. Hamburg, M.D.
Director
Division of Health Policy Research and
    Education
Harvard University
Cambridge, Massachusetts

William Hazzard, M.D.
Chief, Division of Gerontology and
    Geriatrics
Harborview Medical Center
Seattle, Washington

Jules Hirsch, M.D.
Professor and Senior Physician
Laboratory of Human Behavior and
    Metabolism
The Rockefeller University
New York, New York

William E. Hurwitz, M.D.
Private Practice
Washington, D.C.

Lissy F. Jarvik, M.D., Ph.D.
Professor of Psychiatry
University of California at Los Angeles
Los Angeles, California

Shirley Jessor, Ph.D.
Institute of Behavioral Science
University of Colorado
Boulder, Colorado

Morton Kramer, Sc.D.
Professor
School of Hygiene and Public Health
Johns Hopkins University
Baltimore, Maryland

Peter D. Kramer, M.D.
Medical Officer
Division of Science
Alcohol, Drug Abuse, and Mental Health
    Administration
Rockville, Maryland

Ellen Langer, Ph.D.
Associate Professor
Department of Psychology
Harvard University
Cambridge, Massachusetts

Elaine Leventhal, M.D., Ph.D.
Geriatrics Fellow
Department of Medicine
William S. Middleton Memorial Veterans
    Medical Center
Madison, Wisconsin

Howard Leventhal, Ph.D.
Professor of Psychology
University of Wisconsin
Madison, Wisconsin

William McCready, Ph.D.
Professor
National Opinion Research Center
University of Chicago
Chicago, Illinois

*George L. Maddox, Ph.D.
Director
Center for the Study of Aging and Human
    Development
Duke Medical Center
Durham, North Carolina

Meredith A. Minkler, Dr.P.H.
Assistant Professor
School of Public Health
University of California
Berkeley, California

---

*Member, Institute of Medicine.

Elena Nightingale, M.D., Ph.D.
Senior Program Officer
Institute of Medicine
Washington, D.C.

Adrian M. Ostfeld, M.D.
Lauder Professor of Epidemiology and Public
    Health
Yale University School of Medicine
New Haven, Connecticut

Elizabeth Parker, Ph.D.
Laboratory of Clinical Studies
National Institute of Alcohol Abuse and
    Alcoholism
Bethesda, Maryland

Harold Pincus, M.D.
Special Assistant to the Director
National Institute of Mental Health
Rockville, Maryland

*Henry W. Riecken, Ph.D.
National Library of Medicine
National Institutes of Health
Bethesda, Maryland

*Matilda W. Riley, D.Sc.
Associate Director for Social and Behavioral
    Research
National Institute on Aging
Bethesda, Maryland

*Frederick Robbins, M.D.
President
Institute of Medicine
Washington, D.C.

*Judith Rodin, Ph.D.
Professor of Psychology and Psychiatry
Yale University
New Haven, Connecticut

Malcolm P. Rogers, M.D.
Assistant Director for Ambulatory Services
Brigham and Women's Hospital
Boston, Massachusetts

Jack Rowe, M.D.
Chief, Gerontology Unit
Beth Israel Hospital
Boston, Massachusetts

William Satariano, Ph.D.
Epidemiologist
Michigan Cancer Foundation
Detroit, Michigan

Martin E. Seligman, Ph.D.
Professor of Psychology
University of Pennsylvania
Philadelphia, Pennsylvania

*Ethel Shanas, Ph.D.
Professor of Sociology
University of Illinois at Chicago Circle
Chicago, Illinois

Alexander Simon, M.D.
San Francisco, California

George Solomon, M.D.
Professor in Residence and Vice Chairman
Department of Psychiatry
University of California, San Francisco School
  of Medicine
San Francisco, California

Marvin Stein, M.D.
Professor and Chair
Department of Psychiatry
Mount Sinai School of Medicine
New York, New York

Edward M. Stricker, Ph.D.
Professor of Psychology
Department of Biological Sciences
University of Pittsburgh
Pittsburgh, Pennsylvania

Robert E. Vestal, M.D.
Director, Clinical Pharmacology Department
VA Medical Center
Boise, Idaho

———————————

*Member, Institute of Medicine.

Jack Weinberg, M.D.
Director, Illinois Mental Health Institutes
Chicago, Illinois

Herbert Weiner, M.D.
Chair, Department of Psychiatry
Montefiore Hospital
Bronx, New York

Marc E. Weksler, M.D.
Wright Professor of Medicine
Cornell University Medical College
New York, New York

Observers

Thomas Crook, Ph.D.
National Institute of Mental Health
Bethesda, Maryland

Bernard H. Fox, Ph.D.
National Cancer Institute
Bethesda, Maryland

Susan Green, Ph.D.
George Washington University
Washington, D.C.

Nancy Miller, Ph.D.
National Institute on Mental Health
Rockville, Maryland

Eugenia Parron, Ph.D.
Brookdale Community College
Lincroft, New Jersey

Elizabeth Robertson-Tchabo, Ph.D.
National Institute on Aging
Baltimore, Maryland

Beatrice Rouse, Ph.D.
National Institute on Alcohol Abuse and
  Alcoholism
Rockville, Maryland

Edward Schneider, M.D.
National Institute on Aging
Bethesda, Maryland

Behavior, Health Risks, and Social Disadvantage

Juan Albino, M.D.
Staff Internist
Brookside Park Family Life Center
Jamaica Plains, Massachusetts

*Robert M. Ball, M.A.
Senior Scholar
Institute of Medicine
National Academy of Sciences
Washington, D.C.

Ruth Batson, M.S.W.
Acting Project Consultant
Project Commitment
Harriet Tubman House
Boston, Massachusetts

C. Christian Beels, Ph.D.
Director of Training
Washington Heights Community Service
    Center
New York, New York

Carolyn Bell, M.S.M.S.
Industrial Hygienist
Occupational Health Program
University of Tennessee
Center for Health Sciences
Memphis, Tennessee

M. Harvey Brenner, Ph.D.
Professor
Department of Operations Research
Johns Hopkins University
School of Hygiene and Public Health
Baltimore, Maryland

Paul B. Cornely, M.D.
Senior Medical Consultant
Systems Sciences, Inc.
Bethesda, Maryland

Joseph W. Cullen, Ph.D.
Deputy Director
Cancer Center
University of California at Los Angeles
Los Angeles, California

Thomas Drury, Ph.D.
Acting Chief
Health Statistics and Measurement Branch
Division of Environmental Epidemiology
Office of Analysis and Epidemiology
    Programs
National Center for Health Statistics
Hyattsville, Maryland

Felton J. Earls, M.D.
Children's Hospital Medical Center
Pediatric Research Building
Boston, Massachusetts

Glen Elliott, Ph.D., M.D.
Division of Health Policy Research
    and Education
Harvard University
Cambridge, Massachusetts

John P. Enterline
Bio-statistician
Howard University Cancer Center
Washington, D.C.

*Jacob J. Feldman, Ph.D.
Associate Director for Analysis and
    Epidemiology
National Center for Health Statistics
Office of Health Research, Statistics and
    Technology
Hyattsville, Maryland

Bernard H. Fox, Ph.D.
Biometry Branch
Division of Cancer Cause Prevention
National Cancer Institute
Bethesda, Maryland

Harold P. Freeman, M.D.
Director of Surgery
Harlem Hospital
New York, New York

Marc Fried, Ph.D.
Professor of Psychology and Research
    Professor of Human Science
Department of Psychology
Boston College
Chestnut Hill, Massachusetts

*Member, Institute of Medicine.

H. Jack Geiger, M.D.
Arthur C. Logan Professor of Community
   Medicine
City College of New York
New York, New York

William Gibson
Superintendent/Area Director
Solomon Carter Fuller Center
Boston, Massachusetts

Cecilia Gregory, M.D.
Indian Health Service
Portland, Oregon

*David A. Hamburg, M.D.
Director
Division of Health Policy Research and
   Education
Harvard University
Cambridge, Massachusetts

*M. Alfred Haynes, M.D., M.P.H.
President/Dean
Charles R. Drew Postgraduate Medical
   School
Los Angeles, California

Lawrence T. Hill, M.D.
Associate Director
Radiation Medicine
Georgetown University Hospital
Washington, D.C.

Jan Howard, Ph.D.
Special Assistant to the Director of
   Resources, Center and Communities
National Cancer Institute
Bethesda, Maryland

Sherman A. James, Ph.D.
Department of Epidemiology
School of Public Health
University of North Carolina
Chapel Hill, North Carolina

---

*Member, Institute of Medicine.

Roberto Jimenez, M.D.
Clinical Associate Professor of Psychiatry
Santa Rosa Medical Center
San Antonio, Texas

Samuel J. Keith, M.D.
Chief
Center for Studies of Schizophrenia
National Institute of Mental Health
Rockville, Maryland

Sheppard G. Kellam, M.D.
Professor and Director
Social Psychiatry Study Center
University of Chicago
Chicago, Illinois

*Seymour S. Kety, M.D.
Director
Laboratories for Psychiatric Research
Mailman Research Center
MacLean Hospital
Belmont, Massachusetts

L. Erlenmeyer-Kimling, Ph.D.
Director, Division of Developmental
   Behavioral Studies
Department of Medical Genetics
New York State Psychiatric Institute
New York, New York

*Gerald L. Klerman, M.D.
Professor of Psychiatry
Director of Research
Stanley Cobb Psychiatric Research
   Laboratories
Massachusetts General Hospital
Boston, Massachusetts

Melvin Kohn, Ph.D.
Chief
Laboratory of Socio and Environmental
   Studies
National Institutes of Health
Bethesda, Maryland

Morton Kramer, Sc.D.
Professor
School of Hygiene and Public Health
Johns Hopkins University
Baltimore, Maryland

Peter Kramer, M.D.
Medical Officer
Division of Science
Alcohol, Drug Abuse, and Mental Health
  Administration
Rockville, Maryland

Monroe Lerner, Ph.D.
Professor
Department of Health Services
  Administration
Johns Hopkins University School of
  Hygiene and Public Health
Baltimore, Maryland

Sandra Levy, Ph.D.
Acting Chief
Behavioral Medicine Branch
Division of Resource Centers and
  Community Activities
National Cancer Institute
Bethesda, Maryland

Elliott Liebow, Ph.D.
Chief
Center for Work and Mental Health
National Institute of Mental Health
Rockville, Maryland

David Michaels, M.P.H.
Curriculum Coordinator
Division of Occupational Health
Department of Social Medicine
Montefiore Hospital
Bronx, New York

*Robert F. Murray, Jr., M.D.
Senior Scholar in Residence
Institute of Medicine
Washington, D.C.

Herbert Pardes, M.D.
Director
National Institute of Mental Health
Rockville, Maryland

———————————
*Member, Institute of Medicine.

Leonard Pearlin, Ph.D.
Research Sociologist
University of California, San Francisco
San Francisco, California

*Matilda W. Riley, D.Sc.
Associate Director for Social and
  Behavioral Research
National Institute on Aging
Bethesda, Maryland

*Frederick C. Robbins, M.D.
President
Institute of Medicine
Washington, D.C.

Sheldon Samuels
Director
Health Safety and Environment
Industrial Union Department
AFL-CIO
Washington, D.C.

Alvin L. Schorr
Leonard W. Mayo Professor of Family
  Child Welfare
School of Applied Social Sciences
Case Western Reserve University
Cleveland, Ohio

*Lisbeth Bamberger Schorr
Visiting Professor
Department of Maternal and Child Health
School of Public Health
University of North Carolina
Chapel Hill, North Carolina

Margaret H. Sloan, M.D.
Acting Chief
Occupational Cancer Branch
Division of Resource Centers and
  Community Activities
National Cancer Institute
Bethesda, Maryland

John Strauss, M.D.
Professor of Psychiatry
Yale University
New Haven, Connecticut

Donald Ware, M.D.
Division of Health Policy Research and
   Education
Harvard University
Cambridge, Massachusetts

Richard B. Warnecke, Ph.D.
Deputy Director
Survey Research Laboratory
University of Illinois at Chicago Circle
Chicago, Illinois

Donald H. Williams, M.D.
Assistant Director of Outpatient
   Department
The Connecticut Mental Health Center
New Haven, Connecticut

Richard A. Williams, M.D.
Chief, Heart Station
Cardiology Section
VA Wadsworth Medical Center
Los Angeles, California

John L. Young, Jr., Dr.P.H.
Biometry Branch
National Cancer Institute
Bethesda, Maryland

Observers

Ronald Abeles, Ph.D.
National Institute on Aging

Catherine Bell
National Cancer Institute

Betty Houston
Health Care Financing Administration

Haitung King
National Cancer Institute

Alex Rodriguez, M.D.
U.S. Department of Health and Human
   Services

Steven Sharfstein, M.D.
National Institute of Mental Health

George Sherman, Ph.D.
National Center for Black Aged

Richard Suzman, Ph.D.
National Institute on Aging

Rosemary Yancik, Ph.D.
National Cancer Institute

Index